THE VOICE OF THE MIDDLE AGES

IN PERSONAL LETTERS 1100–1500

Edited by
CATHERINE MORIARTY

PETER BEDRICK BOOKS
NEW YORK

First American edition published by
PETER BEDRICK BOOKS
2112 Broadway
New York, NY 10023

First published in the UK by Lennard Publishing 1989.
Published by agreement with Lennard Publishing.

Library of Congress Cataloging-in-Publication Data

The Voice of the Middle Ages : in personal letters 1100–1500 / edited by Catherine Moriarty
p. cm.
"First American edition"—T.p. verso.
Includes bibliographical references.
ISBN 0-87226-343-6
1. Civilization, Medieval—History—Sources. 2. Middle Ages--History—Sources. I. Moriarty, Catherine.
CB351.V59 1990
909.07—dc20 90-39161
CIP

Printed in the United States of America

a b c d e

•••••

The publishers wish to thank the following for permission to reproduce illustrative material from their collections:–

The Royal Commision on the Historical Monuments of England:
Fountains Abbey; Mundham Church; South Bersted Church; Chester Cathedral; Norwich Castle; Hailes Abbey; Canterbury Cathedral; Winchester Castle.

The Warburg Institute:
Eleanor of Castile.

The National Portrait Gallery, London:
Henry IV; Elizabeth of York; Philippa of Hainault; Henry VII; Edward, The Black Prince; Richard II; Thomas Cromwell, Earl of Essex.

CONTENTS

ACKNOWLEDGMENTS

For their help in the preparation of this book I should like to thank James Blake, Sarah Brown, Chris Gilmore and Dr Eric Poole. I am grateful to the staff of the London Library, Sussex Archaeological Society Library and Sussex University Library for their assistance. Especial thanks to Tat Brennan and Sarah Seymour-Smith.

I would like to dedicate certain letters to the following: pages 264-5 to my mother, pages 240-4 to my father, pages 120-4 to Patrick, pages 158-9 to Sean and pages 54-5 to Lucy Noakes.

GENERAL INTRODUCTION

This book contains a collection of correspondence which covers four centuries, the writers and recipients being of varying status, occupation and nationality. The subject matter is diverse, and the style and language of the letters ranges from the very private to the highly formal. The book is an attempt to convey something of the lives and characters of medieval men and women, and to encourage an understanding of the period by the comparison of a unique form of primary source. As the historian Eileen Power observed:

'It will be admitted without difficulty, I think, that the most valuable documents for the history of the Middle Ages are letters, missive letters, both official and private correspondences.'

The letters are arranged thematically although many examples include information on numerous topics; within the thematic divisions a chronological sequence has been employed. Each letter is accompanied by an introduction, containing enough biographical information to clarify a letter's content and context. No attempt has been made to offer opinions, in the hope that the reader will develop his own, nevertheless the very process of compilation and seemingly objective comment is notoriously stamped with the author's own values; I make no claim to have avoided the major pitfalls of history-writing in general.

This collection is not comprised of a selection of the 'best' letters of the Middle Ages, whatever that may imply. Some have been used and quoted many times, others have never been published and some are translated into English for the first time. My main task and hope has been to provide a stimulating variety of material. As history education has been moving away from the use of established texts towards a greater emphasis on primary sources and empathetic interpretation of a situation, I would hope that this book might provide some suitable material for discussion. Being neither a political nor a strictly social history, it intends to encourage a more illuminating approach to the medieval period. As Eileen Power successfully revealed in her biographical study of medieval individuals, the concerns and experiences of everyday people afford a stimulating glimpse at the frequently all too anonymous participants of this time. The examination of their letters, presented here, is an attempt to contribute to this end.

'Of all the different sorts of raw material out of which the history of ordinary people in the Middle Ages has to be made, their letters are

perhaps the most enthralling, because in their letters people live and explain themselves in all their individuality.'

The study of medieval letters has mainly been the domain of Latin scholars and paleographers. Only a small selection of material has been translated for general use and this in itself has led to the overuse of particular shining examples. During the nineteenth century anthologies of letters of all ages were particularly popular, yet many of these are difficult to obtain, often dully presented and possessing few attractions to the general reader. As J.O. Halliwell aptly remarked in the introduction to his *Letters of the Kings of England* published in 1848:

'Antiquaries may talk as they will, but the public will certainly not be readily persuaded to pore over antique spelling, or wade through a variety of antique-looking papers, for the sake of the few which are really interesting and valuable, or curious, when properly read and explained.'

In trying to justify the parameters of this selection there are also those which are beyond the control of any editor. The selection could only be made from letters which have survived and therefore past recipients, biographers, and archivists have determined which examples are available to consider at the present time*. The collecting practices of individuals have meant that many more official documents from the Middle Ages exist than private letters, since the former were retained, for future reference as proof of land ownership, pardons, and testimonials. Personal letters, by way of contrast, largely containing emphemera, have a much shorter life unless treasured by hoarders or possessing particular sentimental value. The large collections of the Paston, Cely and Plumpton families were compiled by an individual member who consciously decided to act as family archivist. There were probably more instances of this than these few remaining collections which have survived through the centuries but these are either lost or destroyed.

Many of the letters in this book formed part of such letter collections. Scholarly and eminent individuals, or their secretaries, retained copies of their letters, which they accumulated and edited to form letter collections which were regarded as a literary genre in their own right. Such letters are the most personal examples in this book and a few have been selected from the most outstanding collections.

The eleventh and twelfth centuries were the high point of letter collections, including those of Bernard of Clairvaux, Heloise and Abelard, and Peter the Venerable. English examples are the collections of John of Salisbury and Gilbert Foliot. Petrarch and Marsilio Ficino's

---

*As Elton describes it, 'Letters have, no doubt, always been written by and to all literate persons, but their preservation is another matter.'

collections of the fourteenth and fifteenth centuries provide an interesting comparison. Men such as these had a wider conception of their world than most, their letters were addressed to people from all walks of life, and reveal a deep understanding of the ordering of medieval Europe.

The letter from Gervase's secretary shows how he regarded letter collecting as a form of literary endeavour separate from his ordinary commitments. He admits to inserting certain examples sent to his master purely because they were written by eminent men, and expresses the hope that the study of the collection will provide intellectual stimulation and spiritual elevation. Hugh assumed that the addressee would be eager to receive his work; collections such as this were treasured as examples of literary skill but also for the advice and wisdom the letters imparted.

• • •

From Hugh, a canon of Prémontré to Simon, a canon of St Mary of St Eloi-Fontaine.

June 1218.

Latin.

To his beloved and worthy to be loved friend and former comrade, Simon, canon of St. Mary of St. Eloi-Fontaine, * *brother Hugh, least of the brethren of Prémontré, sends his greeting, his prayers (for the little they are worth), and his love.*

When formerly you and I, as youths, passed on from the pagan tales of the secular schools to study a superior philosophy and took the habit of religion in different monasteries, it happened that after my probation was over and I had made profession and vowed stability in the monastery and become a canon, I was often summoned by my most revered and dear father Dom Gervase, who begot me through the Gospel, to write down in his presence the letters which he composed for, as you know, I was accustomed to the practice of penmanship from childhood. I relished these letters, albeit incapable of discriminating between them, and I had heard from several people that many commended my abbot for his style of speech and of writing. For these reasons I have put together some letters composed by him and written by me, and some others which were before my time and which I lately found thrown aside; so that just as he was the pious teacher and kindly instructor of my youth, so I, if God grant it, might be his humble and

* Arrouasian abbey of regular canons, canton of Chauny (Cheney), arrond. of Laon.

diligent imitator both in way of life and in art of writing.

But since I should not deem complete any pleasure of mine which you did not share, I have decided to send you the collection I have made, together with a *Summa de stylo romani dictaminis* produced, so it is said, by Pope Gregory VIII of holy memory, and another *Summa*, entitled Master Transmundus, *De arte dictandi* - books which my abbot got for me; so that, tasting, you may aprrove, if you relish what has been alrady tasted and approved by my hungry self. Admittedly, you may with the satiety which comes from the discrimination of an unusual intelligence, regard as Abellanian nuts what I, in my hunger, account as precious delicacies. You must know, however, that I have thought fit to slip into this little book some letters sent to my abbot, not so much because their style was elegant as because their senders were important. Therefore, I beg you, out of a feeling of intimate friendship and at the risk of forfeiting it, treat carefully this collection which several people have already seen (who, having read it in part, wish to read it through and perhaps transcribe it); keep it properly and return it soon: lest if it fell out otherwise, David might be obliged to care no more for Jonathan, or - to address you according to the fables of the pagans - Theseus might abjure Pirithous, Pilades ignore Orestes, Tydeus forget Polynices. Farewell, excellent brother, and may these works I send you so work on the mind of the reader that they will be found to have brought profit to his soul, since, when you are engrossed in them, you will forget the world you have forsaken.

Dated at Prémontré in the year of grace 1218, not long after the feast of St. John the Baptist.

• • • • •

As communications old letters were considered redundant, but as treatises on philosophy, theology and other matters they continued to be valued long after their primary purpose had expired. However, some letters were written largely for their value to posterity, as revealed by the collections of Petrarch and Ficino.

Petrarch published his *Letters on Familiar Matters* in 1361, dedicating the collection to his friend 'Socrates', a Belgian musician living in Avignon. The following letter, which acts as a preface to the collection, conveys Petrarch's dismay at the outbreak of the Great Plague in 1348 which caused him to reassess and reflect upon his work. We perceive Petrarch's views on the frailty and vulnerability of human life and its inevitable end.

Petrarch vividly describes the emotions he experienced whilst reviewing old letters, the impulse of destruction combined with the desire to save something as a memento for his friends. He apologises for the editing process which he knows will not hide the faults of the poorer letters from the scrutiny of his friend, who knows them so well already.

Petrarch's review forced him to reflect on his life and at one point he nearly becomes carried away with autobiography. He reveals his knowledge of the letter collections of antiquity and acknowledges their influence. His own letters to Cicero and Seneca are indicative of the force of his feelings about these men and he attached great importance to his posthumous relationships with them.

• • •

From Petrarch to 'Socrates'.

Probably January 1350.

Latin.

What are we to do, brother? Already we have tried almost everything and nowhere have we found peace. When can we expect it? Where shall we seek for it? Time has slipped through our fingers, as they say; our former hopes lie buried with our friends. The year 1348 left us solitary and destitute, for it took from us more than the Indus or the Caspian or the Carpathian Sea could ever cover. Such losses are irreparable; there is no medicine for the wounds that their death has dealt us. There is one consolation: we too shall follow those we have sent before. How brief our expectation of life may be I know not; but this I know, that it cannot be long. Short or long, it must be burdensome. But enough of complaining, at least at this outset.

I don't know, brother, what is on your mind, what you are meditating. As for me, I am tying up my bundles and casting about, like a prospective traveller, to decide what to throw away, what to give to my friends, what to throw in the fire. Nothing is for sale. I am richer than I thought, or better, more encumbered. There is a great collection of my writings, scattered and neglected, in the house. I have dug out a lot of grimy boxes and I have dustily undone old crumbling papers. The importunate mouse had assailed me, and the ravenous race of bookworms; and the spider, Pallas's enemy, had made war on me, who was doing the work of Pallas. But there is nothing that hard, persistent labour does not overcome. Walled in by piles of letters and miscellaneous papers, I was about to follow my first impulse and throw everything on the fire and avoid a tedious job. But then, as one thought leads to another, I said: "What is to keep me from looking back, like a weary traveler from a height at the end of a long journey, and reviewing the stages of my early progress?" I decided on this course. It seemed to me no lofty task, but still no disagreeable one, to recall what had been in my mind in previous days. But making a random sampling of these miscellaneous papers, I was amazed to find how altered, how blurred the face of things appeared, so that I hardly recognized some of them - not that the things themselves had changed, but my own point of view had indeed But some other papers stirred my memory of days long past, not without a certain pleasurable sensation. Some of the writings moved with the free and easy step of prose, some were held in check by the Homeric bridle of verse. (I seldom accepted the guidance of Isocrates's oratorical rules.) A part designed to tickle the ears of the vulgar, followed their own special laws. This vernacular poetry, it is held, was reborn not long ago among the Sicilians and quickly spread throughout Italy and far beyond. It was much practised among the most ancient Greeks and Latins; we learn that the common people of Athens and Rome used this rhythmical form alone.

This hodgepodge kept me busy for many days. Though naturally I was drawn by no small affection for my own inventions, I was chiefly captured by tenderness for my major works, so long interrupted, while many men awaited their completion. The remembrance of life's brevity assailed me. I feared being trapped; for what is more fleeting than life, what more relentless than death? I wondered what foundations I had laid, what would remain of all my toils and vigils. It seemed to me very rash, nay insane, to embrace the certainty of long labours in my brief, uncertain term of life, and to dissipate my powers, hardly sufficient to complete one task. Especially since, as you well know, another task awaits me, more glorious as actions are more praiseworthy than words.*

Enough of that. Here is a remarkable fact. I threw in the fire, for Vulcan to correct, a thousand or more scattered poems and familiar letters of every sort; not that I found nothing good in them, but because their editing would require more work than pleasure. I did so with a sigh, as I am not ashamed to confess. But my mind was so occupied that I had to seek heroic remedies, as an overloaded ship on the high seas must sometimes cast overboard even precious cargo.

While these papers were burning I noticed a few others lying in a corner, preserved rather by chance than design. Some of them were copies made by my assistants; all had defied the passage of time. A few, I say; I fear they will seem many to the reader, and overmany to the copyist. I let them live, without regard for their worth but with regard for my own labour, for they did not demand any revision. Weighing the characters of my two friends, I decided to divide them by dedicating

* Perhaps a reference to his campaign to return the papacy to Rome.

the prose to you and the poetry to our dear Barbato da Sulmona. I remembered that I had made some such proposal to you and that this was your choice. So while I was in the mood to toss everything on the fire together and not even spare these letters, you both appeared to me, you on the left, Barbato on the right, and you affectionately urged me not to burn up my promise and your hopes in a single fire. That was the chief reason for their escape; otherwise believe me, they would have gone up in flame with the rest.

You will read your share of what remains, such as it is, not only patiently but even eagerly. I don't dare to repeat the boastful words of Apuleius of Madaura: "Listen, reader; you are going to have a good time!" How can I have confidence enough to promise a good time to a reader? You will read them anyway, my Socrates, and as you are very devoted to your friends, perhaps you will have a good time. If you like a man, you take pleasure in his writing. What does a writer's style matter when he expects the judgement only of a dear friend? There is no use adorning what is already acceptable. If some of my words actually please you, I admit that it is not my doing, but yours; that is, the credit is due not to my wits but to your friendship. There is no great force of eloquence in the letters, for that is not natural to me, and if it were, it would be out of key with my style. Cicero himself, who possessed that faculty most eminently, did not put it into his letters or into those books characterized by, as he has it, "an equable and temperate form of speech". But in his orations he displayed an extraordinary force, pouring forth a bright and rapid flood of eloquence. Cicero used this manner very often in defence of his friends, and often against his political enemies, as did Cato often for others, and forty-four times for himself. But I am inexpert in this kind of thing, for I have avoided public responsibilites, and while no doubt I have been pricked by vague anonymous murmurings and whisperings, I have never till now suffered any legal injury that I had to counter or evade; and it is not my practice to intervene in the case of others' wrongs. For I have not learned to frequent the law courts and to lend my tongue to others. My nature is averse and reluctant to this sort of thing. It has made me a lover of silence and solitude, an enemy of the courts, a despiser of money. It is fortunate that I haven't had to practise that lawyer-craft; I might have done it very badly.

So I have rejected the oratorical style, which I don't need and which I don't do naturally. (Even if it overflowed in me I have no occasion to use it.) You will then read this middling, domestic, familiar style benevolently, as you do everything, and you will not jib at a style appropriate to the ideas we express in ordinary conversation.

But not all my judges will be like you, for not all agree, nor do all love me as you do. How can I please all? I have always striven to please only the few. There are three poisons to sound judgement - love, hate, and envy. Be careful lest, by excess of love, you make public what had better be concealed. Love may stand in your way; other passions will perhaps move other men. Compare the blindness of love and the blindness of envy; the causes are very different, but the results may be the same. Hatred, which I put second, I certainly do not deserve nor do I fear it. You may be glad to keep my scribblings for yourself and read them to yourself to recall only our own doings and those of our friends. If so you will be doing me a great favour, for thus your request will be answered and my reputation will be safe. I won't delude myself with further expectations. How can I suppose that any friend, unless he is my *alter ego*, can read through without boredom all these diverse and contradictory remarks, with no common style or purpose, since a great variety of subjects are treated in a variety of moods, usually melancholy, rarely gay?

Epicurus, a philosopher popularly scorned but highly regarded by superior judges, wrote his letters to two or three correspondents: Indomeneus, Polyaenus, and Metrodorus. Cicero's letters went to hardly more: Brutus, Atticus, and his own relatives, that is, his brother and son. Seneca wrote to very few except his friend Lucilius. It makes one's task easy, one's success likely, if one knows the character of one's correspondent, to get used to his individual mind, to know what he will gladly hear and what one may properly say to him. But my case is far different, for up to now almost all my life has been spent in travels to and fro. Compare my wanderings with those of Ulysses; if we were equal in name and fame, it would be known that he travelled no longer or further than I. He was a mature man when he left his hometown; though nothing lasts long at any age, everything runs very fast in old age. But I was conceived in exile and born in exile. I cost my mother such labour and struggle that for a long time the midwives and physicians thought her dead. Thus I began to know danger even before I was born, and I crossed the threshold of life under the loom of death. I am not forgotten in that honourable city of Arezzo where my exiled father had taken refuge with a large band of worthy men. I was removed thence in my seventh month and borne all over Tuscany by a certain sturdy youth; as Metabus did Camilla, he wrapped me in a linen cloth suspended from a knotty stick, to protect my tender body from contact. In fording the Arno, his horse fell, and in trying to save his precious burden he nearly lost his own life in the raging stream.

After the wanderings in Tuscany we went to Pisa. I was removed from there in my seventh year* and transported by sea to France. We were shipwrecked by the winter storms not far from Marseilles, and I

* In his ninth year, according to the Epistle to Posterity.

was nearly carried off again on the threshold of my young life. But I am straying from my theme. Thenceforward, certainly, I have hardly had a chance to stand still and get my breath. No one knows better than you how many perils and fears I have experienced in my wandering life. I have ventured to recall all this, that you may bear in mind that I was born amid dangers, and amid dangers I have grown old - if in fact I have grown really old, and if worse does not await me in old age. You may say that such trials are common to all who enter upon this existence, that human life is a long war, nay a pitched battle; still, every man has his own adventures, and ever battle is different. Though each of us must bear his own burdens, they aren't all equally heavy.

But to return. Since, amid life's tempests, I never cast anchor long in any harbour, I made a great many acquaintances. But true friends? They aren't plentiful, and they are hard to be sure of. Thus I have written to many, of all sorts of character and condition, so that now, reading over my letters, I seem to have said in them the most contrary things. But I was almost forced to it, as anyone who has had a similar experience will admit. The first thought of a letter writer must be the person he is writing to; then he will know what to say, how to say it, and all the rest. We should write one way to a strong man, another to a sluggard; one way to a green youth, another to an elder who has fulfilled his life; one way to a proud, successful man, another to a victim of adversity; one way to an enlightened literary scholar, another to one who can't grasp any high thoughts. The varieties of men are infinite; there is no more similitude of minds than of faces. As the palate of one man - let alone those of many men - does not always relish the same food, so one mind is not always to be fed on the same literary style. So the writer has a double task: to envisage the person he is writing to, and then the state of mind in which the recipient will read what he proposes to write. In the face of these difficulties I have been forced into many contradictions with myself. To escape the accusations of malevolent citics I had recourse in part to my bonfire; and in part you will aid me by keeping the letters to yourself and suppressing my name. If you can't keep them secret among my few remaining friends - friendship being lynx-eyed, overlooking nothing - beg them that if they possess any of the original letters they destroy them immediately, so that they won't be upset by any changes in the matter or form. For since it never occurred to me that you would ask or that I should consent to edit these letters in a single collection, it happened that, to save trouble, I would sometimes repeat in one letter what I had already said in another - using my own as my own, as Terence says. Now that letters written over the years and despatched all over the world are assembled in one time and place, blemishes in the united corpus appear which were hidden in the separate members. Expressions that were very apt once in one letter become tiresome when often repeated in the entire work; they must be left in one place, and eliminated in the rest. Also I cut out much about everyday concerns, which was worthwhile when it was written, but would now bore the most curious reader. I remembered that Seneca derided Cicero on that score; though in these letters I follow Cicero's manner much more than Seneca's. For Seneca crammed into his letters almost all the moral system of his books, while Cicero treats philosophical matters in his books and puts domestic news and timely gossip in his letters. What Seneca may think of Cicero's letters is his own affair. For me, I confess, they are delightful reading; they relax from concentration on difficult subjects, which strains the mind if prolonged, but is pleasant if discontinuous.

You will find here many letters written familiarly to friends, you among them. Some deal with public or private matters, some with our distresses - all too frequent - some with chance occurrences. That is about all, except when I wanted to tell my friends about my state of mind, or give them some information. I agreed with Cicero, who says in his first letter to his brother that "the proper aim of a letter is to tell the addressee something he doesn't know." That was the reason for my title. The mere title of *Epistles*, I reflected, fitted the case; it had been used by many ancients, and I had adopted it for various metrical epistles sent to friends, as I mentioned above. But I was reluctant to use the title twice, and I liked the idea of a new name: *A Book on Familiar Matters*. In this book little was written in laboured style but much in a familiar tone about everyday things, although occasionally, when the subject required, a simple straightforward story may be seasoned with a few moral reflections. This was Cicero's practice.

I am driven to say so much about a small matter by fear of acrimonious critics, who, themselves writing nothing that can be judged, devote themselves to judging the talents of others. Their brazen impudence rests secure in their silence. It is easy to sit with folded hands on the shore and criticize the skill of a navigator. So please balk their insolence by keeping hidden these unpolished trifles, so lightly parted with. When you receive this work, put it in some secure strongbox. It will be no Phidian Minerva, as Cicero says, but a sort of effigy of my mind, a simulacrum of my character, contrived with great labour - if I ever do put the last touches to it.

So far so good. There is something I should like to pass over, if I decently could. But a serious illness is not easily concealed; it manifests itself by its symptoms. I am ashamed of a life grown lax and soft. The very succession of these letters will indicate that my language, in earlier years, was strong and sober, a good index of my stout spirit so that I could console not myself alone but often others. The later letters are weaker, meaner, filled with unmanly whinings. Please try to keep these especially out of sight. What would others say if I myself blush to read them over? Was I indeed a man in youth, to become a boy in old age?

I was tempted by an unhappy, a blamable impulse to change the order of the letters or to conceal from you the ones that I condemn. In neither way could I have deceived you, since you have copies of these pitiable screeds and you know the dates of them all. So all I can do is resort to excuses. Fate wore me down in the long and bitter battle. While I had spirit and courage, I stood firm myself and encouraged others to do so. But when my foothold - and my mind - began to slip under the vigorous assaults of the enemy, that stouthearted note quickly failed me and I descended to those lamentations, now so unpleasant. My affection for my friends may perhaps excuse me, for while they were secure I never moaned at any of the wounds of fate. But when almost all of them were swept away in a single calamity, it seemed inhuman, rather than strong, not to be moved. Before that time who ever heard me wail about exile, illness, lawsuits, appointments, public affairs? Or about the loss of my father's home and fortune, or about my reputation diminished, money squandered, friends absent?

Cicero shows such weakness in the midst of his troubles that as much as I love his style I am offended by his sentiments. Add to that his contentious letters, his quarrelsome, fickle abuse of distinguished men whom he had just been applauding to excess. When I read these I was so shocked and upset that, anger guiding my pen, I couldn't help writing to him as to a contemporary friend, with the familiarity of long acquaintance, to reprove him for what offended me in his writings, as if forgetting the passage of time. This experience inspired me to write to Seneca, when I reread, after years, his tragedy of *Octavia*, and later I wrote, on various subjects, to Varro, Virgil, and others. Some of these letters, which I have placed in the last section of this book, might much surprise the reader, if he were not forewarned. Others I consigned to the general bonfire.

As Cicero was submerged in his troubles, so was I in mine. Today - to inform you of my present state of mind - out of despair itself I have gained tranquillity. (It would not be invidious to attribute to myself a state which, according to Seneca, falls even to the unprepared.) What can he fear who has so often striven with death itself? "One salvation to the vanquished is that they may hope for none." You will see that I shall act and speak the more boldly from day to day. If anything worthy of my pen should present itself, my style will be all the more sinewy. In fact, many subjects will present themselves, for when I stop writing, I think, I shall stop living.

But while my other works have either been finished or approach completion, this one, begun irregularly in youth, now in age assembled and edited, will never end, thanks to the affection of my friends and faithful correspondents pressing for answers. The excuse of a multiplicity of occupations never frees me from paying them the tribute of a reply. When at last you learn that I have asked release from this task and have put finis to the work, you will know that I am dead and absolved of all life's labours. Meanwhile I shall follow the path I have marked out, not abandoning my course before my extinction. Pleasant labour will be my repose. Further, in the manner of orators and generals, I shall put my weaker members in the middle and endeavour that, as the forefront of my book was steadfast, so may the rearguard be animated with a manly morale. Indeed, I seem, with life, to have been toughened against the slings and arrows of outrageous fortune. I hardly dare profess what I may become under the press of circumstance, but I am firmly resolved not to succumb to anything. "And yet the menace of the years/Finds and shall find me unafraid." You will find me well armed with the noble thoughts of Virgil and Horace, which I have so often read and applauded in the past, and which now, in my troubles, I have learned by stern necessity to make my own.

This conversation with you has been very pleasant; I have prolonged it eagerly, almost deliberately. It has brought back your face across lands and seas; it has kept you beside me since morning, when I picked up my pen, until now, when evening is falling. The day and the letter are ending together. This book which I dedicate to you my dear brother, is, if I may put it so, a web woven of particolored threads. However, if I ever obtain a fixed home and the leisure long and vainly sought - as now begins to seem likely - I plan to weave a nobler and certainly more harmonious tapestry. I should wish to be one of those who can promise and confer fame, but you will gain celebrity on the wings of your own genius, needing no aid from me. And still, if I can surmount my present difficulties, you will be my Idomeneus, my Atticus, my Lucilius. Farewell.

• • • • •

The first letter collection of Bernard of Clairvaux was compiled by his secretary Geoffrey and published in 1145, eight years before the Saint's death. A chronological sequence was disregarded and the collection consisted of between two and three hundred letters, since then researchers have increased the number of extant examples to 467.

Bernard of Clairvaux corresponded with a vast variety of people, from kings, counts and popes to novices and other humble folk. No inhibitions prevented him from speaking his mind on matters of international or local importance, he had no fear of writing frankly and many of his letters contain criticism and home truths. At the same time Bernard expresses great feelings of love for God and humanity. The collection, therefore, is one of the most important of its time in terms of revealing the character of the author and as an overall picture of his life and times. Geoffrey, a monk at Clairvaux, became Bernard's secretary in 1140. He was succeeded by Nicholas, who had recently transferred to Clairvaux from a community of Black Monks at Montier-Ramney. Morison writes of him,

*'He was young, accomplished, and endowed with peculiarly winning manners. He was justly valued for his abilities by his new friends, the Cistercians, and a large portion of their vast correspondence devolved on him.'**

Several clerks assisted him with the copying of books and the writing of letters in the scriptorium at Clairvaux. Nicholas was also an intimate friend of such distinguished men as Peter the Venerable and Peter de la Celle.

Without the Abbot's knowledge Nicholas had been writing letters to a wide variety of persons, including the pope, and expressing opinions which Bernard would never have entertained. When Nicholas's betrayal was discovered Bernard immediately changed his seal to avoid further forgery but the treachery of one of his own caused him great distress.

'Nicholas has left because he was not one of us. But he has gone leaving behind him foul traces. I knew for some time what sort of man he was, but I was waiting either for God to convert him or for him to betray himself like Judas, and this is what has happened. When he left there was found on his person, besides books, money, and much gold, three seals, one his own, the other the prior's, and the third mine, not the old one, but the new one which I was obliged to have made on account of his cunning and frauds. I remember having written to you about this without mentioning any names, saying merely that I was in danger from false brethren. Who can tell to how many people he has written to, saying anything he wanted under my seal but without my knowledge? I sincerely hope that your Curia may be cleansed of his filthy lies, and that the very innocence of those who are with me may serve to excuse them to those who have been deceived and baffled by his lying. It has been partly proved and he has partly admitted that he has written to you falsely not once but several times. His foul deeds have poisoned the very ground and are a byword with everyone, but I will not pollute my lips or your ears by mentioning them.

---

* Morison, p. 489

He boasts that he has friends in the Curia, so if he comes to you remember Arnold of Brescia because a worse than he is here. No one has better deserved life imprisonment, no one deserves more a sentence of perpetual silence.'

Nicholas fled to England but this incident added to the troubles with which Bernard had to contend during the last years of his life.

The influence of French culture and language in England increased dramatically after the Norman Conquest but had begun during the reign of Edward the Confessor who had grown up at the Norman court, acquiring French ideas and tastes as well as a knowledge of the language. Edward's maternal cousin, William, Duke of Normandy, invaded England in 1066 and from this time on Normans were placed in positions of control, ousting English lords and bishops and influencing many aspects of English society including administration and education; Old English as a written language became obsolete. French became the language of the court, the ruling élite conversed and communicated in French, read French literature and sang French lyrics. However, Latin was used for administrative purposes, the Normans considered it to be 'the indispensable language of lordship and management'. It was not until the end of the twelfth century that French was first used for business documents but this was not entirely as a result of the Norman Conquest, the development of French as the literary language of popular romances and chroniclers throughout Europe during the thirteenth century also contributed to its wider use.

Apart from the court the French language was absorbed into the English spoken by the masses and contributed to the later foundation of English as a written language in its own right.

Most of the royal letters in this book were written in French. The letters of Edward Prince of Wales, later King Edward II show that regardless of whom he was addressing he used French, the close contact across the Channel during the reigns of the Plantagenet kings not only encouraged but necessitated a fluent understanding of French in courtly circles. Edward had grown up with Piers Gaveston and other native Frenchmen, he probably found it easier to communicate in their language than the vernacular of his homeland. Similarly, Mary writes to her brother King Edward II in French because although she must have been familiar with Latin in her day-to-day life as a nun, it was the appropriate language for a royal communication.

John de Grandisson is another example of a French writer. Despite the fact that most bishops communicated in Latin, the language of the church, Grandisson was widely travelled, had studied in Paris and in a letter to his cousin, (an earl who probably knew French from the court) was most likely using the most convenient and suitable form.

The examples cited above indicate that for the educated ruling classes and administrators, a knowledge of two or even three languages was not uncommon since different forms of communication required the use of different languages.

The papers of the Stonor family provide an interesting example of this. During the early fourteenth century formal letters are written in French whilst official documents such as indentures and charters are in Latin. By the fifteenth century the growing use of English indicates that as a written language it was becoming increasingly widespread. It was a new English which had developed from Anglo-Saxon and French, its variety reveals that it was only in the elementary stages of formation and highly susceptible to regional dialects and adaptations.

Literacy, as we now understand it, as an elementary ability to read and write, cannot be applied to the medieval period for a number of reasons. Then, literacy implied a scholastic understanding of Latin and only a minority of highly educated men could be categorized as such. Knowledge and news had long been disseminated by word of mouth and it was only the proliferation of documents issued by the bureacracy and new uses and forms of writing which encouraged the ability to read. Initially the written word was used for conveying orders and information to magnates and bishops, they in turn adopted the practice and it slowly spread down the feudal hierarchy. Many became familiar with the written word even though they may not have been skilled at interpreting it or using it themselves. Most people in England by 1300 could read a few lines of Latin, due to their familiarity with church liturgy. Reading, therefore, developed as a pragmatic necessity rather than as a desire for cultural advancement.

Writing (*scriptura*) was a completely different matter. The use of quills and parchment was considered to be a craft; scribes and scriveners were professionals in this field. Most of the letters in this book were not actually written by the sender but dictated to a scribe. Dictating was an art and was taught as such at the universities and schools. The lack of ability to use a pen did not imply illiteracy. The letter from Gervase's secretary Hugh, to Simon, a canon of St Mary of St Eloi-Fontaine illustrates this process, it reveals the distinction between dictating and writing and how Hugh studied his master's skill with the aid of treatises on dictation; those mentioned were the definitive works on the subject at this time. Similar texts existed in England during the thirteenth century which were aimed at those who were unskilled at composing letters but needed to learn the basic accepted forms. Some treatises concerned themselves with the correct beginnings and endings suitable for persons of varying status whilst others included entire letters which could be copied by a scribe to suit the occasion, ranging from requests for preferment or protection to more mundane affairs.

The ancient Romans had no set rules of letter-writing, educated men with an understanding of rhetoric were felt to be quite capable of composing a letter unaided. The collapse of the empire and the consequent barbarian invasions meant that within Europe a widespread system of education had little chance of establishing itself. Most tenth and eleventh century men, therefore were ill-equipped to cope with the growing communication needs of church and state, since there were no principles or models to follow for the composition of official letters and documents.

The importance of such correspondence necessitated a more advanced knowledge of the written word, so at the end of the eleventh century Alberic, a monk at the Benedictine monastery of Monte Cassino, attempted to apply classical rhetoric to the letter-writing of his own time. Henceforth the *ars dictaminis* was linked with the art of rhetoric. This was almost inevitable since the letter collections of Pliny, Sidonius and others pioneered this trend. Later, in the fourteenth century, Petrarch reaffirms the need to follow in the path of the rhetoricians of antiquity by his discovery of, and unbounded admiration for, Cicero's *Letters to Atticus*.

Alberic wrote the *Flores rhetorici* (Flowers of Rhetoric), which discussed the application of rhetorical embellishment to letter-writing in 1087. A later work, the *Breviarium de dictamine*, actually set down rules of composition. Alberic helped establish the five-part letter as the acceptable format, and the many examples in this book which conform to this model indicate that it remained a convention for the next four centuries at least.

In 1135 a lay teacher of Bologna wrote the *Rationes dictandi* (Principles of Letter-Writing). Its purpose was to act as a guide for those interested in the *ars dictaminis* and it assumes the widespread cognizance of the five-part principle which its writer describes thus:

'There are, in fact, five parts of a letter: the Salutation, the Securing of Good-will, the Narration, the Petition, and the Conclusion.'

Like Alberic's *Flores rhetorici* the construction of the salutation is stressed, once again emphasizing the variations which should be adopted depending on the recipient's status and relationship to the writer (dictator). Generally speaking the recipient's name and qualification precedes that of the writer and it is only when the writer is of a status significantly higher than the recipient that the order is reversed. The letter from the Bishop of Liseaux to Thomas à Becket is a typical example, as is a letter from the nuns of St Mary's Chester to Queen Eleanor. A letter from Philippa of Hainault to her clerk illustrates the reverse order. Abelard's reply to a letter begins with the salutation: "To Heloise, his dearly beloved sister in Christ, Abelard her brother in Christ."

Heloise objects to this in her next letter, pointing out its implications.

'To her only one after Christ, she who is his alone in Christ.

'I am surprised, my only love, that contrary to custom in letter-writing and, indeed, to the natural order, you have thought fit to put my name before yours in the greeting which heads your letter, so that we have woman before man, wife before husband, handmaid before master, nun before monk, deaconess before priest and abbess before abbot. Surely the right and proper order is for those who write to their superiors or equals to put their names before their own but in letters to inferiors, precedence in order of address follows precedence in rank. *

When Petrarch uses a novel opening to letter he qualifies his deviation from the norm by indicating its origin.

The conveyance of letters depended on the availability of a messenger who personally collected and delivered letters between individuals. Sometimes messengers were servants or other members of a household, who carried the letter often in conjunction with other business such as the collection of goods from town. Common carriers were also employed for this purpose, they were generally entrusted with the transportation of goods but no doubt letters were also included in their load.

Due to the desire to avoid delay in finding a messenger many letters were sent by 'return of post', this need to write in haste is sometimes used as an excuse for poor handwriting. Messengers were also asked to convey personal messages orally, secrets and other information which could not afford to fall into the wrong hands were also transferred in this way. The letter between Margery Paston and Richard Calle reveals the problems caused by intercepted letters and some included instructions that they be burnt immediately after reading. Seals were intended to prevent tampering and act as a sign of authenticity but the following account reveals that not all messengers were trustworthy, and that even security devices such as the cipher in this example, were not infallible.

Messengers were frequently expected to collect money or receive

* Radice, p. 127. Letter 3.

a fee for their services, usually before their departure or sometimes on delivery; that John de Strattone seems to have obtained the thirteen marks in silver quite easily indicates the considerable faith placed in those entrusted with letters.

• • •

From a letter book in the reign of Richard II.

1382.

Latin.

Punishment of the Pillory, for forgery and false pretences.

John de Strattone, of the County of Norfolk, was attached to make answer in the Chamber of the Guildhall of London, on the Monday next before the Feast of the Annunication of the Blessed Virgin Mary [25 March], as well to the Mayor and Commonalty of London, as to Thomas Potesgrave, citizen and hosteler, of London, in a plea of deceit and falsehood; for that, whereas one John Croul, of Godmechestre,* on the Monday next before the Feast of St. Peter's Chains [1 August] last past, had sent to the said Thomas, at London, in the Parish of St. Benedict Graschereche, a letter containing certain advice and divers countersigns† between them; on the same day, the said John Strattone, there seeing and reading that letter, took down in his tablets a copy thereof; and, compassing therein how to deceive the said John Croul and Thomas, he forged and fabricated another letter containing the same countersigns that were set forth in the first letter, and through the same, thus deceitfully made and fabricated, went a short time afterwards, in the name of the same Thomas, to the said John Croul, pretending that he was sent to him by the said Thomas; and then took of him 13 marks in silver, which he still detains in his hands, falsely and deceitfully.

And the same John de Strattone, in the same day, being questioned as to how he would acquit himself thereof, of his own accord acknowledged the falsehood and deceit aforesaid. It was therefore determined, that the same John Strattone should be taken back to the Prison of Neugate, and from thence on the same day should be led through Chepe with trumpets and pipes to the pillory on Cornhulle, and be put upon the same for one hour of the day; after which, he was to be taken back to the prison aforesaid, there to remain until the morrow, when he was again to be taken to the pillory, with trumpets and pipes, and be put upon the same for one hour of the day. And he

* Godmanchester, in Hunts.

† Probably, writing in cipher.

was then to be taken back to the prison aforesaid, there to remain until he should have made satisfaction to the same Thomas for the 13 marks, which by award of the Court the said Thomas recovered against him.

• • • • •

The following similar example stresses the importance placed on verbal messages which accompanied the delivery of a letter. A letter to the Prior of Christ Church reveals the elaborate nature of such messages but here we find a messenger intercepting a letter for his own ends, it also affords us with a suitably medieval instance of a punishment adapted to fit a crime.

• • •

From a letter book in the reign of Richard II.

1380.

Latin.

On the 9th day of August in the 4th year etc., William Lawtone, of Lawtone under the Lyn,* in the County of Chester, was brought here into the Guildhall of London, before John Haddele, Mayor, Adam Stable, and other Aldermen, and John Heylesdone, Sheriff, at the suit of William Savage, who prosecuted etc.; for that he came to the same William Savage on the Monday next before the Feast of Pentecost,† in the 3rd year of the King aforesaid, in Fletestret, in the Parish of St. Brigid,§ in the suburb of London, and delivered to him a certain letter, which he said had been given to himself by John Sadyngtone, of York, on the Wednesday before the Feast of Pentecost aforesaid, to carry to the said William Savage; directing such William, by virtue and authority of the letter aforesaid, to give to him, the same William Lawtone, 20 shillings sterling, for a certain bargain between the said John and William de Lawtone made; he knowing that the same letter was false and forged, there being no such bargain between the said John and himself, as before stated, and the said William Savage being in no way indebted to the said John Sadyngtone, as unto the aforesaid William Savage by him imputed.

And being asked how he would acquit himself thereof, he acknowledged the deceit and falsehood aforesaid, and that he was consenting and aiding falsely and deceitfully to forge the said letter;

---

* Now Church Lawton, on the borders of Staffordshire; whence the title "under the Lyme", or Boundary, (not "Lyn", as above) is said to be derived.

† Or Whitsuntide.

§ Or Bride

and he put himself upon the favour of the Court as to the same. And it was adjudged by the Court that the same William Lawtone should be put upon the pillory, there to remain for one hour of the day, the said letter being tied about his neck. And precept was given to the Sheriffs, to cause the reason for the same publicly to be proclaimed.

Execution whereof being so done, the Court having been given to understand that the aforesaid William Lawtone threatened the said William Savage, and other reputable men of the City, as to life and limb, the Sheriffs were instructed to take him back to the Prison of Neugate; there to remain until he should find sufficient surety for his keeping the peace towards the people of our Lord the King.

• • • • •

The time a messenger took to deliver a letter varied greatly depending on the season, climate and distance to be travelled, whether the messenger was travelling swiftly and directly or making many detours along the route. The Cely family tended to record the receipt of a letter accurately, and it must have been possible to estimate the expected day of arrival over familiar distances, in this instance across the Channel.

The absence of door numbering and the frequent moving from place to place of many medieval merchants, judges, churchmen and other itinerant workers, as well as landed families moving from manor to manor, meant that letters were frequently addressed to a likely port of call. Nevertheless delay and uncertainty of communications is a basic factor in all medieval correspondence.'*

The letters included in this book take many forms, many are personal missives, some are letters patent, letters of safe conduct or testimonials, yet all, in some way, convey something of the concerns and emotions of the author, recipient, or others referred to in the actual text.

Personal letters were meant to be read privately but some of the other forms were intended for public proclamation or for the eyes of a number of individuals. The medieval distinction between private and public influenced many other spheres in addition to the style, composition and content of a letter, such as architectural design and painting. The purpose of a letter also determined its format. A missive was usually in the form of a small folded sheet, whereas letters intended for constant reference took the form of a roll or were possessed with a tag on the bottom edge which allowed it to be opened

* Hay, *The Medieval Centuries* 1953, p. 661.

and closed over again.

The variety of letters in this book, from short notes by country vicars to lengthy essays, display a diversity of characters which it is interesting to compare. Some supposedly disparate individuals have surprising similarities whilst elsewhere the concerns of some are startlingly divergent.

In many ways the letters uphold traditional conceptions of the spirituality and piety of the medieval period as opposed to the pagan, heterodox age of the renaissance and the reformation, but they also force us to question the value of these broadly based categories and to appreciate the way individuals' behaviour and opinions verify or dispel these preconceptions. If, for instance, we compare the letters of the Cely family with those of Petrarch we can see, as Denis Hay describes, that the latter 'had a historical perspective significantly different from the traditional medieval view that saw history as a continuum from the Fall of Man to the Last Judgement' but on another level they shared similar concerns such as the difficulty of travel and fear of the plague.

Fifteen hundred AD was taken as the close of the period from which the letters were drawn, since the great activity in many fields during the early sixteenth century, including the increased use of the written and printed word, bestows the correspondence of this later period with a different, more sophisticated character. Indeed the later examples printed here indicate the increasing ease with which people were able to express themselves and the different types of people that were now able to communicate by means of letters.

Throughout this collection many themes seem to emerge which contribute to the coherence of the selection as a whole. The role of medieval men and women within the family, their neighbourhood and society as a whole; their understanding and constant reference to God, the sophistication of their desires and expressions; and the domination of emotions or predicaments which easily transcend the centuries separating our lives from the individuals voicing themselves here.

THE CHURCH

Many letters in this collection reveal the dominant influence of Christianity on the lives of medieval men and women. The organization of the church, which paralleled secular government, played a major part in the structure of medieval society and in the shaping of its beliefs. The power and will of the papacy was disseminated by regional bishops and the local clergy, ultimately to pervade the daily lives of the entire medieval population.

Medieval religion was strictly authoritarian. It complemented the paternalistic and feudal ordering of society and provided a code of beliefs which acted as a stable base amidst the erratic and often violent turmoil of medieval life, as the Bishop of London writes, 'by what heaps of miseries wretched humanity is oppressed,' Faith in a perpetual constant rationalized earthly hardships and suffering. Since life on Earth was regarded as merely a temporary state, the promise of salvation expounded by the Scriptures was a reliable source of comfort.

The organization of the Church, however powerful as a whole, was composed at all levels of individuals, be they popes, bishops, vicars, monks or nuns. From their letters emerges a lively and highly complex picture of the effects of the Church on their daily lives and understandings.

Some letters refer to the building and enhancement of cathedrals which visually dominated medieval towns and cities; others express the difficulties of maintaining parish churches which acted as a focus for rural communities. Monasteries and nunneries assisted secular society in practical as well as spiritual ways. The letters reveal some of the difficulties monks and nuns experienced in their isolation from normal secular life. They include voices upholding the precepts of the church as well as voices of dissent. Some are concerned with theological argument whilst others refer to the practical difficulties of a monastic life.

Throughout the entire medieval period, the all-pervasiveness of the church never faced major opposition to its hold on society. In spite of power struggles between secular and papal authority, both had to depend, to a large extent, on the support of each other. Although bishops were sometimes inclined to favour local interests and personal obligations to kings and princes, rather than the word of Rome, many fundamental factors united churchmen with the papacy including their holy orders, their acceptance of canon law, their education and the dominance of Latin as the language of the church.

The actual practices of medieval devotion were often attempts to humanize religion. Many men and women found it difficult to conceive the 'abstract' nature of God; the cult of the Virgin, the veneration of saints, relics and pilgrimages were an expression of the need to make Christianity more comprehensible and less remote; they also enabled the medieval man or women to have some degree of participation and choice. A church or cathedral containing a shrine or relic of a saint could become extremely wealthy due to the lavish gifts bestowed upon it by pilgrims and others wishing to display the extent of their devotion. Wealthy churches were sought-after and a lucrative benefice was hotly contested, as Elizabeth of York's letter to the prior of Christ Church will indicate.

The church played an important part in education. The scriptures were the major source for instruction and the many biblical references in the letters of this book reveal the extent to which the church not only shaped people's beliefs but also their manner of expression.

• • • • •

The collected correspondence of St. Bernard has been discussed in the Introduction: the next example is one of his earliest letters.

A young man named Fulk had recently taken the vows as a regular canon, but due to the influence of his wealthy uncle had forsaken the monastic life. Bernard of Clairvaux expresses his anger and paints a vivid portrait of the evil uncle and the futility of secular life. Characteristically his wrath is interspersed with expressions of affection and concern, yet Bernard's fervent belief in the reforming principles of the Cistercian order is elaborated over and over again, especially the need for holy poverty, seclusion and discipline.

As Bernard's fame spread his advice became widely sought after. Letter-writing was an important public activity enabling him to participate in national and international affairs. It allowed him to stay with his fellow monks at Clairvaux much of the time, but when he could not avoid a summons from a superior, letters then enabled him to keep in touch with events at home during his absences.

• • •

From St Bernard of Clairvaux to Fulk, a young man who later became Archdeacon of Langres.

c. 1120.

Latin.

To the youth of great promise, Fulk, from Brother Bernard, a sinner, that he may so rejoice in his youth as to have no regrets in his old age.

I do not wonder if you are surprised that I, a rustic and a monk, should address myself to you, a citizen of towns and a student, with no excuse or clear reason that can occur to you. I should wonder if you were not surprised. But you will perhaps understand how better motives than presumption dictate my letter to you if you consider those words of Scripture, 'I have the same duty to all, learned and simple', and 'Charity does not seek its own'. I am indeed bound in charity to exhort you who are in charity to be grieved for, although you do not grieve; to be sorrowed for, although you are not sorrowful. And all the more so for the very reason that, an object of grief, yet you do not grieve; of sorrow, yet you are not sorrowful. But perhaps my pity for you will not be wasted if you will only listen while I tell you why you are to be pitied. Charity would have you feel sorrow that then you may begin to have less cause to be sorry; she would have you know yourself to be shameful so you may then have less cause for shame. Our good mother Charity loves us all and shows herself differently to each one of us, cherishing the weak, scolding the restive, exhorting the advanced. But when she scolds she is meek, when she consoles she is sincere. She rages lovingly, her caresses are without guile. She knows how to be angry without losing patience, how to be indignant without being proud. It is she, the mother of angels and men, who brings peace not only on earth, but even in heaven. It is she who brings God to men and reconciles men with God. It is she, my dear Fulk, who makes those brethren with whom you once 'broke sweet bread' to live together in concert. And it is this mother whom you have wounded, whom you have affronted. Yet although you have affronted her, she does not contend with you. Spurned by you she calls you back, showing by this how truly it has been written of her 'Charity is patient; charity is kind'. Although wounded and affronted by you yet, should you return to her she will meet you as an honoured mother. She will forget how you repudiated her and throw herself into your arms, rejoicing that her son who was lost is found; who was dead has come to life again.

But, you will ask, how have I wounded and affronted Charity? Listen. You have done so by tearing yourself from her when she was feeding you with the milk of her breasts; when suddenly and frivolously you spewed her sweet nourishment from your mouth, the sweet milk of Charity on which you might have grown strong in virtue. Foolish child! A child more by reason of your folly than your years. Who has bewitched you that you should have left the good work you had begun? You say it was your uncle. Thus Adam blamed Eve and Eve blamed the serpent, making excuses in sin. Yet their excuses did not save either of them from a punishment they deserved. I would not have you accuse the Dean; I would not have you blame him for your folly. His sin does not excuse yours. There is no excuse for you. What has he done? Has he carried you off by force? He asked you, but he did not compel you. He enticed by flattery, but he did not drag you with violence. Was there any obligation to believe his flattery, to give in to his enticements? He was not bound by any vow of poverty, so that what wonder if he should want you with him whom he regards as his own? If a man loses a sheep or a calf he may seek it and no one complains. Why then should not your uncle seek you who are more precious to him than many sheep and calves? He is not obliged to that state of perfection for which it has been laid down that 'If any man take what is thine, do not ask him to restore it'. He was only seeking his own when he was entitled to do so. But were you obliged to follow a career in the world when you had renounced the world? The trembling sheep flies when the wolf comes, the timid dove hides when it sees the hawk, the hungry mouse dare not leave its hole when the cat is about, and yet you when you see the thief must you run with him? What else but a thief is he who would steal your soul, the precious pearl of Christ?

I was hoping, had it been possible, to draw a veil over the fault of your uncle for fear that I should receive no thanks but hatred for telling the truth. But I confess that I cannot let his conduct pass without mention. For he who does not what he may to restrain his hand from evil, even though that evil may sometimes be frustrated, the purpose is not less blameworthy. He certainly tried to damp my novice's ardour but, thanks to God, he was not able. He also resisted strongly the good intentions of Guarike, his other nephew and your kinsman. But he did no harm, in fact he rendered a service, for at length the old man grudgingly gave way and Guarike came through all the more glorious for having surmounted the trial. How then was he able to win you over, who could not win Guarike? How did it happen that he was able to overcome you who was overcome by him? Is Guarike stronger or more prudent than you? Certainly anyone who had formerly known you both would have put Fulk first. But when it came to the fight the result proved the judgement of men wrong. He who had been thought the stronger flies – for shame! and he who had been considered the weaker conquers.

But what shall I say of the malice of this uncle of yours who draws his nephews from the army of Christ that he may drag them with him to hell? Is this the way he rewards those he loves? Whom Christ calls to share with him his heavenly kingdom, this uncle invites to burn forever with him in hell. I should not wonder if Christ were not already angry and saying to him, 'How often have I not been ready to gather thy nephews together, and thou didst refuse it. Behold your house is left desolate to you'. Christ says, 'Let little children be, do not keep them back from me, the kingdom of heaven belongs to such as these.' But your uncle says, 'Leave my nephews to me that they may burn with me.' 'They are mine,' says Christ, 'and must serve me.' 'They shall perish with me,' replies your uncle. 'I redeemed them they are mine,' says Christ. 'But I fed them,' says your uncle. 'The bread you fed them with was mine not yours, but my blood not yours redeemed them,' says Christ. Thus their uncle after the flesh fights with their heavenly father for his nephews in order to disinherit them of heavenly joys and burden them with earthly gifts. Yet Christ thinks it no robbery to gather together his elect, who were created by him, and whom he redeemed with his blood, according to his promise, 'Him who comes to me I will never cast out.' He opened the door gladly to Fulk as soon as he knocked and with joy he embraced him. What more? He put off the old man and was clothed in the new and the ideals of a Canon, which had existed only in name, he professed in his life and conduct. The fame of it took wings, a sweet savour before Christ: the novelty of the thing was noised abroad and came to the ears of his uncle.

What would his guardian in the flesh do about this? He had lost the comfort of his nephew's presence whom he had loved too much according to the flesh. Although for others this event had been as a sweet savour of life eternal, it was not so to him. Why? 'Because the sensual man perceiveth not the things that are of God for it is foolishness to him.' Had the spirit of Christ been in him he would not have grieved so much in the flesh as he would have rejoiced in the spirit. Because he was wise rather according to the world than according to heaven, disturbed and put out he mused with himself something like this: What is this I hear? I am undone! I have been deprived of my great hope. But come! this thing cannot be done without me, without my consent. What right, what justice, what reason is there in it? My hair is already white and shall I spend the rest of my days in grief because I have lost the staff of my old age? Were my soul to be required of me this night, who would have what I have put by? 'My store-houses are full, overflowing on this side and that, my sheep are bearing fruitfully and throng the pastureland' and to whom will all this belong? Farms, meadows, houses, gold and silver vessels, for whose benefit have I amassed them all? I had acquired for myself certain richer and more sought-after honours in my Church: the rest, although it was not lawful for me to have them, yet I held on to them for the sake of Fulk. What can I do now? Must I lose all these things just because of him? For whatever I have without him to inherit, I might as well not have at all. It were better to keep everything and recall him if I could. But how can this be done? Fulk is a professed Canon Regular. This is an accomplished fact. It is known by everyone. What has been done cannot be undone. What is known cannot be hushed up. If he returns to the world now it will be known and ill spoken of. But it were better to hear this of him than to live without him. On this occasion what is right must give place to what is useful; propriety to what is necessary. I would rather sacrifice the good name of the boy than subject myself to misery.

And so consenting unto these counsels of the flesh the uncle forgot all law and reason. Fearing nothing sacred he raged and roared like a lion prepared for its prey or a lioness robbed of its cub. He burst into the dwelling of these holy men where Christ had hidden his raw recruit to protect him from the strife of tongues that he might afterwards consort with angels. He begged and implored that his nephew be given back to him. He shouted and cried that he had been unjustly left. Christ called back: 'Unhappy man, what are you doing? Why are you raving like this? Why are you persecuting me? Is it not enough for you that you should have robbed me of your own soul and, by your example, the souls of many others, so that you must also lay sacrilegious hands on this one? Have you no fear of the judgement? Do you care nothing for my anger? To whom are you doing this thing, against whom have you declared war? "Against him who is terrible, even him who taketh away the spirit of princes." Madman! put your own house in order. Remember your last hour and tremble. And you, boy,' he says, 'if you give way and consent to your uncle, you shall die the death. Think of Lot's wife. She was saved from Sodom because she believed in God. But she was turned to a pillar of salt on the way because she looked back. Learn from the Gospels that no one who has put his hand to the plough may look back. Your uncle has lost his own soul and wants yours; "The words of his mouth are iniquity and guile". Do not be one of those who will not understand lest they do well. Pay no attention to vanity and deceitful folly. Lo! On the path you tread the fowler has laid his snare and spread his nets. His words are as smooth as oil but they are very darts. Take care, my son, that you are not deceived by the lips that speak guile and the deceitful tongue. Let the love of God quicken your heart lest carnal affection deceive you. He flatters you but under his tongue lurks labour and tears, and he lieth in ambush that he may catch the innocent. I tell you, my son, take heed lest you consent to flesh and blood for my sword is sharp and shall devour all flesh. Despise his flattery, spurn his promises. He promises great things, I promise greater. He offers many things, I offer more. Will you throw away heaven for earth, eternity for time? If not you must keep the vows that have adorned your lips. You are justly bound to honour your vows since you were not bound to vow. Although I opened to you when you knocked, yet I did not force you to come in. It is therefore not permitted you to cast aside what you have promised; it is not lawful for you to seek again what you have freely put away. I warn both you and your uncle. I have salutary advice to offer you. To you, the uncle, I say do not take back to the world one who is bound to a rule or you will take him with you to hell. And to you, my son, I say do not follow after your uncle; if you do so you follow against me whom you injure. To you, the uncle, I say if you lead astray a soul for whom I have died you set yourself up as an enemy of the cross. "He that gathereth not with me, scatters," and how much more so if he scatters what has been already gathered! And you, my son, if you consent unto your uncle you dissent from me, because he who is not with me is against me. And how much more will you be against me if you desert me after having once been with me. But you, the uncle, if you offend one of these little ones who come to me, you shall be judged a seducer and a sacrilegist. Whereas you, the nephew, if you pull down again what you have built up, you will make yourself an apostate. Both of you must appear before my judgement seat, both must appear before my tribunal, the nephew to be judged for his own apostasy, the uncle for the apostasy of his nephew. And if one die in his iniquity his blood shall be required at the hands of the other.' These and the like, thou, O Christ, didst thunder unseen to the consciences of both the nephew and the uncle, with these warnings thou didst lovingly besiege the hearts of both. Who would not tremble at these words of thine and look to it with fear lest he become like unto the deaf asp who stoppeth her ears that she hear not the voice of the charmer charming wisely, and either not hear or feign not to have heard.

But I have already written enough, even perhaps too much, of what it were better to keep silent. But why, fearful of revealing the whole shameful affair, have I approached the truth by ways so round about? I will explain, although I do so with shame. I would rather say nothing but what is already known I could not hide even if I would. And indeed why should I be ashamed? Why should I be ashamed to write of what they were not ashamed to do? If it should shame them to hear what they have shamelessly done; at least let them not be ashamed to correct what they do not willingly hear. Ah the pity of it! Neither of them could be kept from his evil ways; not the one from seducing by fear or reason nor the other from apostasy by shame or his vow. What more? The crafty tongue devises words of guile: it has brought forth grief and persuaded iniquity. It perverted the converted, and the dog returned to its vomit. Their Church has taken back its alumnate whom it were better for it to have lost. It was the same thing at Lyons. By a like zeal and industry of their Dean, they disgracefully took back his nephew, one of their Canons, whom they had lost to a good purpose. Just as the one filched Fulk from St. Augustine, so the other filched Osbert from St. Benedict. How much better would it have been for these young men to have become saintly under the rule of a saint rather than to have been perverted by a pervert! How much more beautiful if the religious boy had persuaded the worldly man so that both should conquer, than that the worldly man should have led astray the religious boy so that both were overcome! Unhappy old man! Cruel uncle! Already you are infirm, soon to die, but first you must kill the soul of your nephew! You have deprived your nephew of the heritage of Christ so that you may have an heir to your sins! But 'whose friend is he that is his own enemy?' So he preferred to have an heir to his goods than an intercessor for his sins.

But what have I to do with deans? They are our instructors and they hold a high place in the Church. They hold the key of knowledge and take the first seat in the synagogues. Let them see to it how they judge their subordinates; how they call back their fugitives, and pack them off again if they so wish; how they gather together whom they have scattered and scatter again whom they have gathered together. I must confess that it was on account of my affection for you, my dear Fulk, that I have rather overstepped the bounds of my humble state. I tried at their expense to spare your own shame and to mitigate your fault. I will now pass them over in case they become more angry with me than with their fault and think more of abusing me than of correcting themselves. I am not concerned with those in high places but with an ingenuous youth who does not know how to be indignant and angry! Unless indeed a child more in good sense than in malice you should throw this very thing in my teeth and say: What have you to do with me? What concern of yours are my sins? Am I a monk? And to this, I confess, I have no answer except that I believed in the gentleness of your nature and trusted in the love of God to which, you may remember, I appealed at the beginning of this letter. It was my zeal for the love of God that moved me to pity for your error, to compassion for your unhappy state, so that I interfered beyond my accustomed measure and manner in order to save you, although you are not a monk of mine. Your sad lapse and miserable fall spurred me on to presume this thing. For whom else of your contemporaries have you seen me rebuke or write even the shortest letter? Not that I think they are saints or can find nothing to blame in their lives!

Then why, you will say, do you single me out for rebuke? I reply that I do so on account of the singular gravity of your fault, on account of the enormity of your sin. Although many of your contemporaries may lead bad lives, although they may be irregular and undisciplined, yet they have not been professed in any Order nor have they vowed to keep any rule. They may indeed be sinners, but they are not apostates.

Your case is different. No matter how quietly and honourably you may live, no matter how chastely, soberly, and even piously you may conduct yourself, yet would God be less pleased with this than he would be angered at your breaking your vows. Therefore, beloved, you must not compare yourself with these men of the world for you are separated from them by your religious profession. They are not, as you are, bound by vows. Nor must you flatter yourself on account of your, perhaps, stricter self-control, for the Lord says to you, 'Would that I had found you either hot or cold.' By this he clearly means that you please him less being lukewarm than you would if you were stone cold even as these are. God waits for these that they may at last turn from coldness to the heat of fervour, but he sees with anger that you have become lukewarm after being fervently hot. 'And because I have found you,' he says, 'neither hot nor cold, I will spew you out of my mouth,' and deservedly, because you have rejected his grace and returned to your vomit.

Alas! How soon you tired of Christ, of whom it is written, 'Honey and milk are under thy tongue.' I wonder that you should have turned against the taste of this sweet nourishment unless perhaps you have never tasted and seen how sweet is the Lord. Either you have never tasted the sweetness of Christ and so do not miss what you have never known or else, if you have tasted and yet not found sweet, your palate is sick. Wisdom itself says, 'They that eat me shall yet hunger; and they that drink me shall thirst again.' But how can anyone hunger and thirst for Christ who is filled every day with the husks of swine? You cannot drink from both the cup of Christ and the cup of devils. The cup of devils is pride; the cup of devils is slander and envy; the cup of devils is debauchery and drunkenness; and when these fill the mind and body there is no room for Christ. You must not wonder at what I am going to say. In the house of your uncle you cannot taste the plenty of the house of God. You ask why? I answer because the house of your uncle is a house of delicate living and as water cannot mix with fire, so the delights of the flesh and the joys of the spirit cannot go together. Christ does not deign to pour out his wine, sweeter than honey and the honeycomb, for one whom he sees debauched in his cups. The bread of heaven is not tasted amid a delicate variety of foods and napery of every colour, so that both eyes and belly are filled. 'Rejoice, therefore, O young man in your youth'. When the joy of life fades endless remorse will devour you. Far be this from our Fulk; may God forefend his child from such a fate! Let him rather scatter those who with lips of guile give you such counsels, who say to you, 'Well done! Well done!!' but who seek your soul that they may devour it. These are they whose evil counsels corrupt good manners.

But how long is it already, and you are still among them. What business have you in towns who have chosen the cloister? What do you in the world who have renounced the world? 'The Lord is your portion in pleasant places' and yet you still gape after worldly riches. If you wish to have both you will receive the short answer, 'Son, thou didst receive thy good fortune in thy lifetime.' It says 'received' not 'robbed', so you cannot flatter yourself even on the grounds that you are content with what you have and do not rob other people. What, in fact, are the things you have? Benefices of the Church? Quite right, they are. And if you rise from your bed for the Vigils, if you attend Masses, if you frequent choir for the day and night offices, you do well. In this case you have not received your prebend from the Church for nothing. It is fitting that he who serves the altar should live by the altar. And I grant you that if you serve the altar well, you can live by the altar, but not in luxury, not in pride. You cannot provide yourself from the altar with golden trappings for your horse, inlaid chairs, silvered spurs, and every sort of multicoloured furs for your gloves and collars. In fact what you take from the altar in excess of your bare needs is not yours, and it is sacrilege and robbery. Wisdom prays to be given only what is necessary for life, not what is superfluous, and the Apostle says that he is content with food and clothing, not with food and ornaments. And another saint has said, 'If God shall give me bread to eat and raiment wherewith to be covered.' Note you, he says 'raiment wherewith to be covered' not 'wherewith to be adorned'. So let us then be content just with clothes for covering ourselves, not for wantonness, not for effeminacy, not for pleasing lewd women. But, you say, those with whom I live do this, and if I should behave otherwise I would make myself singular. Just so, and it is for this reason that I say to you, Come out from their midst, so that you need not live in a manner to cause remark in towns or lose your soul by following the example of others.

What business have you in towns, fancy soldier? Your brother soldiers, whom you have deserted by running away, are fighting and conquering, they are knocking on the gates of heaven and it is being opened unto them, they take the kingdom of heaven by force and are kings, while you trot around the streets and market places on your horse, clothed in scarlet and fine linen. But these are not the accoutrements of war! Or are you one of those who say, 'Peace, peace and there is no peace'? Sumptuous clothes are no protection against lust and pride, they do not keep avarice at bay, nor quench any other fiery darts of the enemy. Nor do they help against the fever you fear even more and they cannot keep death away. Where, then, are your arms of war? Where is your shield of faith, your helmet of salvation, your corselet of patience? What do you fear? There are more with us than against us. Take up arms and act the man while the fight is still in progress. We have angels for witnesses and allies. The Lord himself is at hand to sustain us, to teach our hands to make war and the fingers of our hands to fight. Let us set out to help our brothers, lest they should fight and conquer, and enter the kingdom without us. It will be too late to knock when the doors are closed, we would then receive the answer, 'Verily I know you not'. Make yourself known, I pray you, first in the battle, show yourself in the fight, lest on that last day you be known only to the devils in hell and not to Christ in glory. If Christ recognizes you in battle, he will recognize you then, and as he promised, reveal himself to you. But only if you recover your senses and repent so that you may be able to say with confidence, 'Then I shall know even as I am known.' And now I have besieged enough for the present the heart of a shy youth with my invectives, it remains to besiege the ears of devine mercy on his behalf so that if the Lord should find it to have softened but a little under my blows I shall, without doubt, be able to rejoice in him with great joy.

• • • • •

In 1132 thirteen monks from the wealthy Benedictine Abbey of St Mary's at York expressed their desire to be placed under a stricter rule. Like the Cistercians in France they were distressed by the increasing laxity of monastic life and eager to return to the original edicts of St Benedict, who considered simplicity and austerity an essential vehicle for truly religious contemplation.

The elderly and weak-willed Abbot Geoffrey, refused the monks' request. So they appealed to Thurstan, Archbishop of York. After considerable disagreement and violence the monks escaped from St Mary's and the Archbishop placed them under his protection, granting them some desolate land near Ripon where Fountains Abbey was eventually built. Whilst the monks were residing with the Archbishop two of them, Gervase and Ralph, returned to St Mary's. Abbot Geoffrey wrote to St Bernard and received the following reply. Bernard shows his characteristic tact and modesty, realizing that to anger the Abbot would not ease the delicate situation. He wrote many similar letters trying to pacify abbots whose monks had defected in order to lead a more austere life. At the same time, however, he speaks from his heart, explaining his sympathies with the reformers and never fearful of expressing his true beliefs.

• • •

St Bernard of Clairvaux to Geoffrey, the Abbot of St Mary's Abbey York.

May or June 1133.

Latin.

You write from across the sea to ask my advice, and I could wish you had gone to someone else. You have put me into a dilemma, for if I do not answer you my silence will appear rude; if on the other hand I do answer you it is difficult to know what I can say without offending anyone or without seeming to favour anyone unduly or to countenance anything unwisely. I can say that it was not with the knowledge, advice, or encouragement of myself or of any of the brethren here that your monks have left you. But I believe it to have been by the inspiration of God because, in spite of all your efforts, they remain firm in their purpose. And I believe that those very brothers feel the same who implore me for my advice about themselves, I suppose because their conscience gnaws at them for going back, otherwise, according to the words of the Apostle, if they are not troubled in their conscience for what they have done, 'they are fortunate'.

And now what shall I do so as not to give offence either by not answering your letter or by what I answer? Perhaps it would be best for me to send you to one more learned than myself, one whose prestige and holiness entitle him to speak with greater authority than I. In his book on Pastoral Care [Chapter 28]. St Gregory says: 'The second best is unlawful for one who has chosen the best'. And to confirm this he quotes the words of the Evangelist: 'No man who puts his hand to the plough and then looks back is fit for the kingdom of heaven'. From this he concludes that anyone is guilty of looking back who, having once undertaken great things, leaves them for something less perfect. And likewise in his third homily on Ezechiel he says: 'There are some who while leading as good a life as they know, decide while leading it, on something more perfect, but afterwards change their minds and retract the good intentions they had. They continue in the good way they had begun, but fall away from the better one they had intended. Such persons appear to do well before the eyes of men, but before God they have fallen away.'

Behold a mirror! May they consider in it not only their bodily features, but the facts of their turning back. Herein let them examine and judge themselves, their thoughts answering for and against them, according to what that spiritual man has said who judges all things, but is himself judged by no man. It is not for me rashly to decide, but for them to make up their minds whether what they have left or what they have returned to is greater or less, higher or lower, harder or easier. St. Gregory has spoken to them. But to you, reverend father, I can say with the assurance of complete certainty and the naked truth that it would not be well for you to try to extinguish the spirit: 'Suffer him to do good who may, and thou thyself, when thou mayest, do good'. Rather should you take a pride in the progress of your sons, because it is written that a wise son is the pride of his father. For the rest let no one be offended with me because I have not hidden the righteousness of God in my heart, unless it should seem to anyone that in order to avoid giving offence I have said less than I should.

• • • • •

John of Salisbury was born between 1115 and 1120. He was a student for many years; in Paris he attended the lectures of Peter Abelard and at Chartres developed his reputation as a great classical scholar. He later studied theology and became Bishop of Poitiers in 1142. It was whilst attending a council at Rheims held by Pope Eugenius III that John of Salisbury met St. Bernard who introduced him to Theobald, Archbishop of Canterbury. He was employed for some time by the papal court but later decided to return to England. It was whilst he was travelling through France that St. Bernard wrote him the following letter of recommendation to present to Theobald.

John of Salisbury immediately joined the clerical staff at Canterbury. About five years later he returned to Rome but was soon back in England as Theobald's private secretary. The Archbishop depended greatly on his services and it was at this time that John wrote his two major works – Policraticus and the Metalogican. He had developed a friendship with the chancellor Thomas à Becket and became his secretary when Theobald died and Becket succeeded him. In 1164 he went into exile, the reasons for which are discussed in a later letter. He returned in 1170 and was present at the murder of Thomas à Becket. He spent the next few years writing a biography of Becket and in 1176 was elected as Bishop of Chartres. This post he held until his death in 1180.

• • •

From Bernard of Clairvaux to Theobald, Archbishop of Canterbury, on behalf of John of Salisbury.

c. 1148.

Latin.

You do me a signal favour and honour me very much when you favour my friends for my sake. Yet I seek not honour from any man, but the kingdom of God and the justice thereof. I am sending your Highness John, the bearer of this letter. He is a friend of mine and of my friends, and I beg that he may benefit from the friendship for which I count on you. He has a good reputation amongst good men, not less for his life than for his learning. I have not learned this from those who exaggerate and use words lightly, but from my own sons whose words I believe as my own eyes. I had already commended him to you in person, but now that I am absent I do so much more and with all the more confidence for having learned from reliable witnesses about his life and habits. If I have any influence with you, and I know that I have much, provide for him that he may have the means to live decently and honourably, and I beg you to do this without delay for he has nowhere to turn. In the meantime provide for his needs, I beg you, and let me thus experience, most loving father, those depths of affection which you retain in your heart for me.

• • • • •

Thomas à Becket was appointed chancellor in 1154 due to the recommendations of Archbishop Theobald. Becket had acted as his agent and Theobald appointed him archdeacon of Canterbury for his good services. It was during his time as chancellor that Becket became King Henry II's most trusted and intimate companion. Becket was highly capable and royal favour knew no bounds.

In the following letter Arnulf, Bishop of Lisieux, warns Becket of the unhappy consequences of the 'fickleness of Kings' and his words 'popularity departs from a man more rapidly than it came' provide an eerie portent of Becket's fate. Arnulf himself was to suffer due to a sudden decline of royal approval.

• • •

From Arnulf, Bishop of Lisieux to Thomas à Becket, Chancellor of England.

c. 1154.

Latin.

To his respected and dear friend Thomas, illustrious chancellor to the King of the English, Arnulf, humble Minister of the Church of Lisieux, health and his best love.

I have received your highness's letters, every word of which seemed to me to drop honey, and to be redolent with the sweetness of affection.

I was delighted to find that I had not lost the privilege of our early intimacy, either by the wide distance which separates us, or by the multitude of affairs in which you are involved. I was delighted, I say, because the matter is put beyond all doubt, by the receipt of your letter, which it would be unworthy of me to suspect either of flattery or of falsehood. The same interest in you exists also in my bosom, which though it has seldom an opportunity of exemplifying itself by deed, yet still lives in the devoted yearnings of the will. For in friendship, it is the will alone which is concerned, and there is no room for questions of bartering, lest our affection be thought to be prostituted or mercenary. Friendship is complete in the purity of its own existence, and gains but slight addition from being demonstrated in deed; it is but little exposed to the caprices of fortune, and derives its own dignity from itself. So true is this, that it is seldom found among the rich, for it hates riches, and seems to attach itself to the single-minded, and to the poor. It is, indeed, a rare virtue, and therefore the more precious; but nowhere is it more rarely found than between those who are invited to administer counsel to kings, and to transact the business of kingdoms. For, to say nothing of other points, ambition sits with anxious weight upon their minds, and whilst each fears to be outstripped by the vigilance of the other, envy springs up between them, which, ere long, fails not to become open hatred. For it is an old feature in the character of the envious, that they look upon others' success as their own ruin, and whatever other gain, they think has been subtracted from themselves.

Envy ever suffers torment, and dissembles its hidden pains under a smiling look, and thus a deceitful exterior cloaks secret treachery. Moreover, if the favour of the prince is changed, and he begins to look on a man with a clouded brow, all the support of his companions fails him, the applause and obsequiousness with which they crowded round him die away; those from whom he expected consolation, insult him; and when occasion offers, remind him of the wrongs he had once done them: nay, his very benefits are designated as acts of injury.

Such is the sea on which you are sailing; such the turmoil amid which your life is cast, wherein you will have to guard against the siren smiles of those who applaud you, and the venomed strains of flatterers. From all these you have but one way to escape - sincere faith accompanied with uprightness in well-doing; seek rather, with the Apostle, to obtain glory to yourself from the testimony of a good conscience, than the uncertain honours of public report, and of slippery and popular applause. Popularity departs from a man more rapidly than it came; whereas those other virtues, though they may be unpalatable in acquiring, yet lead to a happy sequel. I write to you thus plainly, not because I would, according to the proverb, teach Minerva letters: but in speaking to a friend, I could not restrain the current of my thoughts, particularly when urged by the impulse of my mind to offer you my congratulations.

I beg to commend to your care my lord Serlo, a faithful friend of mine, together with the little matters of business which he has in hand. I will only further add my request, that you use all diligence in preserving for me the favour of our prince, which I formerly earned by my services, but which may flag during my absence; for the favour of princes, particularly the young, often fails and dies outright for want of someone to remind them of it. Fare you well for ever!

• • • • •

In 1148 Gilbert Foliot became Bishop of Hereford. He had been a monk at the monastery of Cluny and was noted for his religious wisdom and eloquence. As a trusted chancellor he grew in royal favour and when the Bishop of London died in 1162, King Henry II declared his intention to appoint Foliot in his place. Foliot had been one of the English bishops who had objected to Becket's election as archbishop; Becket was known to be a devoted servant of the King and it was felt that he would only help to assert the sovereign's power over the church. Foliot also disapproved of Becket's wordly ways and humble birth but through fear of unpleasant repercussions, he withdrew his objections.

In April 1163 Foliot's bishopric was transferred from Hereford to London with the pope's approval. It was at this time that Becket wrote him the following letter. It is certainly complimentary and therefore quite surprising considering the antagonism Foliot had shown towards him. If Becket truly felt 'sincere affection' towards the Bishop of London it was not to last long. Foliot refused to make an oath of obedience to the archbishop and from henceforth there was only bitterness between them. During Becket's exile, Foliot encouraged those against him and Becket later twice excommunicated the Bishop. After Becket's death, Foliot continued to enjoy royal approval.

• • •

From Thomas à Becket, Archbishop of Canterbury to Gilbert Foliot, Bishop of Hereford.

March or April 1163.

Latin.

That the city of London surpasses in grandeur all the other cities of this kingdom, is well known to all of us, my brother: for the business of the whole realm is therein transacted; it is the residence of the king, and frequented more than any other by his nobles. For this reason, it is important that the Church of London, which has now lost its ruler, should receive for its new bishop a man whose personal merit, attainments in learning, and prudence in managing public business, shall not be unworthy of the dignity of that see. After much deliberation in this matter, it is the unanimous opinion of the clergy, the king, ourself, and the apostolic pontiff, that the general welfare of the kingdom, and the interests of the Church, will best be promoted, by your being translated to exercise the pastoral care over the diocese of London. To this end I have received the instructions of our lord the pope, and I enjoin you, by virtue of his authority, to give your assent without delay to the Church of London, passed in presence of our lord the king, and with the consent of the whole clergy and ourself; and to take the government of the aforesaid Church into your hands with promptitude corresponding to the necessity which exists for its interests to be committed to such an able person. And I entreat of you, my brother, that whereas you are bound to this by virtue of your obedience to ourself, so you may be led by your own inclinations to undertake the duties of this important trust. Thus, not only sincere affection, but also proximity of place will unite us both in the same good work, to give one another mutual assistance in ministering to the necessities of God's Church.

• • • • •

The Bishop of London writes to his friends the Earl and Countess of Leicester. In his letter to the Countess he regrets that he is unable to visit her due to the burden of duties which, 'the world daily brings'. To her husband he praises the Earl's virtues, especially his generosity to the poor and his love of God rather than riches.

Robert and his twin brother Waleran had been brought up in Henry I's household due to the gratitude the king felt for their father's services. Throughout the reigns of Stephen and Henry II Robert was highly trusted at court, he wholeheartedly supported the crown yet remained on exceptionally good terms with leading churchmen; in 1164 he actively tried to reconcile Becket and the king. He founded several religious houses during his lifetime including St Mary de Pré Leicester, the monastery of Nuneaton and the priory of Lusfield, as well as being, 'a liberal benefactor to many other houses'.

• • •

From Gilbert Foliot, Bishop of London to Amice, Countess of Leicester.

1163-68.

Latin.

Gilbert, by the grace of God a minister of the church in London, to Amice, the worshipful Countess of Leicester; he begs her to accept that which he strives piously to attain at last when he has finished his course.

I send this letter at your request, dear friend, for your pleasure, though I should have sent it even if not requested. If I have omitted this for some time, the reason is that I was myself daily expecting my messenger to you to go and return. As hope, with doubtful visage, ever leads us on to tomorrow, and says, if I have not done something, 'I shall get it done tomorrow,' I hoped that I should wind up the business, pút matters to rest for some time and forget my cares, travel swiftly to you and revive myself by the solace of your long-desired and joyful conversation. However, the more I seek the opportunity, the less I find it: I think I have slain the beast of this world by cutting of some of its heads, but am horrified by more and more heads sprouting in the very same place. There is indeed no end of cares, and the world daily brings them forth, whereby it may afflict our wretched souls and turn them away from what we had meant to do. Oh, why should I recall the holy soliloquies which my uplifted soul formerly mingled in the spirit with her betrothed, while the silences of the cloister protected and held them? While, unconscious of everyday matters, she ascended so to speak with Moses up the mountain, left the mist and the cloud below , and having left the world behind strove entirely toward that fire that God inhabits, desiring nothing but that? So, when her infirmity called her back, she did not retreat far, she did not go outside, but rested more attentively at the feet of God himself and, thinking bitterly over her past years, washed away her early offences by the very flow of her tears. Now the care of household matters distracts me from this, and the weight of everyday matters involves me. Now fear oppresses me, now hope draws me on, now prosperity lifts me up, now adversity depresses me, so that I may experience almost by the very arguments of things, by what heaps of miseries wretched humanity is oppressed. Therefore, what delightful things could my spirit now relate to you who dwell in purity of mind and seek and desire nothing for the refreshment of your delicate spirit but spiritual delights? That Dove has made her nest in you, that hovered over Christ in the Jordan and always dwells in him with all the fullness of grace. And indeed, you have received as much of this fullness as he himself bestowed, and the more plentifully you taste his gifts, the more plentifully you desire them to be administered to you, with a mind eager for spiritual things. It seems to me that I hear your soul in its spiritual fervour, declaiming and singing: 'Comfort me with flowers, strengthen me with apples, for I am faint with love.' Hence, dear friend, I have the flowers that I shall offer to your spirit, so that, ardent, it may be the more enflamed and, striving for higher things, it may the more eagerly be transported there. These are the flowers of Paradise, which the Saints communicate to you, and those who are ignorant of the things of the world, and reject them, inhabit as it were a paradise of the hallowed mind. I beg you to ask for these things for me in your prayers, so that when I am groaning under the weight of cares you may raise me up and sustain me before the Lord by their intervention. That little that I have; I have not ceased to communicate to you in the Lord from the beginnings of our friendship, nor do I omit to do so.

I hope in Christ, dear friend, that you are keeping well.

• • •

From Gilbert Foliot, Bishop of London to Robert II Earl of Leicester.
1163-68.
Latin.

To the worshipful lord, and his very dear friend, Robert Earl of Leicester, from Brother Gilbert, minister of the church in London, to come to a conclusion with blessed perseverance in consecrated service to the Lord.

As society gives a great welcome to vices and riches, I rejoice and altogether applaud, dearest friend, that in you riches are devoted to virtue by a certain singular grace. You have heard how that rich man, who was clothed in purple and fine linen, and dined splendidly each day, was carried off wretchedly to Hell where, when he was in misery and burned with flames, he could not even obtain a drop of water to cool his tongue. You have also heard in the Gospel of that rich man whose field bore abundant fruit, and who said within himself: 'I shall pull down my barns and make bigger ones, and there I shall gather all the good things that have come to me, and I shall say to my soul, "Soul, you have many good things put by for many years; rest, eat, drink and feast."' But to him the divine word came: 'Fool, they will demand your soul of you tonight; and then who will own the things you have prepared?'. If we turn our mind's eye to the fullness of the world all around us, with the spirit of God administering the light, we recognize that the world abounds with worldly riches, but that its riches are not to the increase of virtues but to the fostering of vices, since they may rather be possessed by these people, than by those who possess them by any nobility or holiness of soul. Such rich people, said the Lord, will not easily attain the kingdom of Heaven, and a camel can more easily enter the eye of a needle than they can enter the kingdom of heaven – a terrible saying, and much to be feared by such rich people. I rejoice and altogether applaud, dearest friend, that you abhor their ways, and have refused to follow in their footsteps; I am glad that you think upon your last days, and contemplate what the psalmist says: 'All men have slept their sleep, and found none of their riches in their hands.' These, if they faithfully ask for themselves the things they have believed, will awaken on that day from the sleep of death, and find these things in their hands. It has been said by the voice of God: 'You will not appear empty handed before the presence of the Lord your God.' All that you have asked in this world for the church of God, and for Christ's poor, you will find ready for you on that day; and what you generously distribute now, you will present on that day with confidence to the Lord. Many are blessed and wise, but I consider those only to be blessed, those only to be wise, who consider, with frequent meditation, those things that will endure for ever; occupy their minds with these things, watch for them, and strive with all their understanding to possess them. I believe, dear friend, that the Father is well pleased with you; I hope that the holy Dove which appeared above the Lord in the Jordan has already made her nest in you. Run after the spirit who draws you, who will adorn you within with his good things and will endue you with the perfect love of Christ. If his true love touches you, if it seizes you and absorbs you, it will raise you above yourself, next to the prophet; may he extol you above the heights. Having got the opportunity of writing to you, I can hardly contain myself, dear friend.

• • • • •

Once Becket was appointed Archbishop of Canterbury he became increasingly devout, dedicated to the papacy and an upholder of canon law. It was this last aspect which primarily led to the circumstances in which the following letter was written.

The King considered that he had the right to punish the clergy even though ecclesiastical courts had long been responsible for dealing with such offenders. Becket regarded it as an injustice that a guilty clergyman could be punished twice for 'the same fault' and that the king's interference was an invasion of the Church's independence. The Council of Westminster opened in October 1163 to discuss the issue, Becket refused to compromise and the Council of Clarendon, held in Wiltshire the following January, only served to intensify the disagreement. The King demanded the right to punish the clergy, forbid the excommunication of royal officials, and to influence episcopal elections: he also considered himself entitled to the revenues of vacant sees. Becket argued that such actions would be in breech of church law, and appealed to the Pope.

John of Salisbury, a great classical scholar and theologian, had been a clerk under Archbishop Theobald. He had already angered Henry II with his views on ecclesiastical authority and he was forced into exile after the Council of Westminster where he sided with Becket.

The letter describes his journey through France and his interviews with the Count of Flanders and Louis VII in order to gain their support for Becket's cause. It indicates that where major issues were at stake news could travel very swiftly, it is also a very eloquent letter. John of Salisbury, whilst under Theobald, was responsible for drafting the correspondence with the papal court, a talent which makes his letters enjoyable reading compared to some of the clumsier examples of the period.

John's advice to Becket about arranging a hasty departure from England if he was 'driven to this' was slightly premature, as the archbishop managed to keep Henry's fury at bay, but in October 1164 at the Council of Northampton it was evident that the king intended to humiliate Becket, either by forcing his resignation or imprisonment. It was then that the archbishop fled to France.

• • •

From John of Salisbury to Thomas à Becket, Archbishop of Canterbury.

October 1163.

Latin.

Ever since I have been on this side of the water, I seem to have been breathing an entirely different atmosphere: and the country round is so rich, and the inhabitants so happy, that it is quite a change to me after my late troubles. The count, at the request of Arnulf his uncle, had sent some of his men to receive me on my landing: they treated me with the greatest civility for your lordship's sake, and conducted me through the earl's territories, as far as St. Omer's, without charging me any of the usual duties. At this town I met a monk who had known me formerly at Chilham and Trulege, and now introduced me at the monastery of St. Bertin's. The ecclesiastics of this country are generally well disposed to your cause, and you must thank the earl and monks for their goodwill when you have an opportunity.

On arriving at Arras I found that Count Philip was at Castle Ecluse, before which the tyrant of Ypres was so baffled. Thus far God protected me on my journey, and now I found the very man I was seeking for almost in the very road. Count Philip was out in pursuit of wild fowl, like most men of his fortune, and was eager to learn from me the state of things in England: for my part, I was glad to have so easy an opportunity of fulfilling your commission without further loss of time or expense. He asked many questions about the king and the nobles, and I answered him without offending him, and yet without deviating from the truth. He sympathizes with your troubles, and promises his assistance. When you require ships, he will funish them: if you are driven to this, send your steward Philip to make a bargain with the count's sailors.

The next day I reached Noyon, where, to my astonishment, everybody knew what had taken place in England, and many things were talked of as having happened at the councils of London and Westminster which I did not know myself, though nothing was exaggerated or perverted. I pretended not to know all they talked about, but they would not believe me. You will be surprised when I tell you that the Count of Soissons told me all the articles of the so-called London council, as minutely as if he had been there himself: not only of what passed in the palace, but in almost every private circle. The French must have had some very active agents among us. The dean of Noyon, a most excellent man, is much concerned to hear the situation in which you are placed: he will receive you hospitably, and place his services and his property at your disposal. Before he had heard of the difficulties in which you are involved, he intended to visit the pope on your behalf, but now he will wait till he hears from you again. I was told at Noyon that the French king was at Laon, and that the archbishop of Rheims was not far off, waiting to have an interview with his majesty, but I was prevented from going to see them by the wars which the archbishop is carrying on against the Count de Ruzero and others: so I came to Paris instead. The people here seem to enjoy abundance of everything: the church ceremonies are performed with great splendour, and I thought, with Jacob, 'Surely the Lord is in this place, and I knew it not;' also in the words of the poet,

Blest is the banish'd man who liveth here.

After having settled myself in my lodgings, I went and laid your business before the king: he expresses great sympathy in your sufferings and promises you assistance. He said he had already written to the pope in your favour, and will, if necessary, write again, or see the pope in person. The French are much afraid of our King Henry, and hate him most intensely, but this between ourselves. As I could not see the

Archbishop of Rheims I sent your letters to the Abbot of St. Remy; but you had better write to him yourself by one of the monks of Boxley, or some other person, and send him a present. He may be of great use to you, for he is an important man in this country, and through this, and the favour of the king, has much influence with the court of Rome.

I did not go to court, because I would not excite suspicion, and the bishop of Poitiers tells me the pope is acquainted with my motives. On the receipt of your letter I told Lord Henry of Pisa, and William of Pavia, how detrimental it would be to the Church to concede what is demanded of you. When I hear from the bishop of Lisieux, and the Abbot of Saint Augustine's, I shall go to court. Master Henry, who is there, wil send me information of their arrival: though I hardly know what I shall do when I get there, for you have so many things against you, and so few in your favour. Great men will very soon be there, bestowing their bounty with a lavish hand; and Rome never yet was proof against bribes, and none of them would like to offend the king. Moreover, there are grants from the Church of Rome in their favour, and in a cause like this, bishops and friends are alike disregarded. The pope, indeed, has hitherto himself opposed us, and is always complaining of the privileges which his predecessor Adrian granted to the see of Canterbury. By the way, Adrian's mother is still living in penury amongst you.

Now what can we do, needy as we are, against such powerful enemies? We have only words to offer, and the Italians will not listen to them: for they have learnt from their own poet not to buy empty promises. You tell me in your last letter to offer them two hundred marks, but the others will imediately offer three or four.

'Tis vain, for if we offer all our store,

In hopes to win, Iolas offers more.

I will answer for the Italians, that their respect for the king and his messengers will lead them to take a large sum from them rather than a small sum from us. Not that they do not sympathize with your lordship, and the interests of the Church in general, but that your enemies endeavour to undermine you, and say that you are guided by obstinacy rather than a laudable perseverance; and, what is more, I have heard it whispered about, that the pope is to be invited to England to crown the young king. It is even added that his holiness will take possession of the see of Canterbury, and remove your lordship's candlestick out of it; but this I do not believe, for he is certainly grateful to you for your exertions in the Church's cause. When the bishop of Lisieux comes, he will stick at nothing, for I have already had a specimen of his tricks, and, as for the abbot, who can have any doubts about him? They tell me that the bishop of Poitiers cannot succeed in the matter of Saint Augustine's, though he had tried hard in the business: but as your lordship wishes it, I will go and see what I can do. If, however, I fail, it will not be my fault, for as the poet says,

The doctor cannot always cure
The patient's gaping wound,
Which sometimes, baffling all his art,
Inveterate is found.

• • • • •

Becket's first refuge in France was at the Abbey of Pontigny. The pope supported his stand but was wary of antagonizing Henry II, fearing that the English king might side with the Holy Roman Emperor and add considerable influence to the claims of the antipope, Paschal III.

In Becket's letter to Alexander he discusses his downfall, particularly the part played by the English bishops whose allegiance to the king, rather than the church, he finds difficult to understand since, 'if they had been wise, they would have seen that in attacking me they were attacking their own privileges.' In the last paragraph we have a glimpse of Becket's former friendship with Henry when he suggests that it is the bishops who should be blamed rather than the king.

• • •

From Thomas à Becket, Archbishop of Canterbury, to Pope Alexander III.

January 1165.

Latin.

In your presence, holy father, is my refuge; that you, who have redeemed the Church's liberties at your own peril, may give ear to me who have followed your example, and suffered equally for the same. The cause of the Church would have sunk before the rapacity of princes if I had not faced the coming evil. The more I loved the king, the more I opposed his injustice, until his highness's brow fell lowering upon me. He heaped calumny after calumny on my head, and I chose to be driven out rather than to subscribe. I was called before the king's tribunal like a layman, and was deserted in the quarter where I had looked for support. My brethren, the bishops, sided with the court, and were ready to pronounce judgement against me. Thus, almost crushed by the multitude of my foes, I have fled to your presence, which is the last refuge of the distressed. Under your protection will I prove that I was not amenable to that tribunal, nor to their judgement. Your privileges, holy father, are at stake: by this pernicious precedent the spiritual power would yield to the temporal. Thus I resisted, for fear that to yield would be a confession of weakness, and bring on me more extensive aggression. They say that those things which are Caesar's should be rendered to Caesar. Be it so; the king must indeed, be obeyed in many things, but not so that he shall cease to be a king: that would make him no longer Caesar but a tyrant, and those who resisted him would contend for themselves and not for me. The last judgement is admitted to be his who can kill both body and soul: is not then the spiritual judgement final on earth? Why have I been assailed for appealing to him, who cannot, must not judge falsely? They have assailed me unjustly, or else they doubt your impartiality. I wonder not that laics should thus attack the Church, but I wonder much that bishops should have led them on. Could I anticipate the hostility of those for whom I encountered such opposition? If they had been willing, I should have gained the victory. But the head faints when it is abandoned by the other members. If they had been wise, they would have seen that in attacking me they were attacking their own privileges, and serving princes to their own servitude. They left spiritual things for temporal, and so have been stripped of both. They judged me, their father, though I protested and appealed to your holy presence. If they had conspired in the same way with the king against the whole Church, what would your holiness then have said? They plead that they were fulfilling their duty to the king. I reply that their obligation to him is of a temporal nature, to me they are bound in spirituals. What obligation can be stronger than that which binds them to themselves, and the spiritual concerns of their souls? They say that this is not a favourable moment for provoking the king to anger. Alas! this refined sophistry leads to their perpetual servitude! they are even accelerating that catastrophe by lending the king's arrogance wings to fly! Had they paused, he would have paused also. But further, when is constancy required, except under persecution? Are not friends then proved? If they always yield, how can they ever succeed? They must one time or other make a stand.

Look down then, with condescension, holy father, on my exiled and persecuted condition: remember that I was once in a place of pride, from which I have been driven by injustice - and in your cause. Put forth your severity, and coerce those who have stirred up this persecution; but lay it not at the king's door; he is the instrument and the agent, not the author of these machinations.

• • • • •

In another letter John of Salisbury told Becket of the rumour circulating in France that the king intended to crown his eldest son Henry as co-king. Seven years later this was done by the Archbishop of York, a blatant snub to the bishopric of Canterbury which had long held the sole right to perform the ceremony. Thomas reacted by excommunicating the perpetrators of this deed, as did the Pope.

Henry, fearing even more drastic repercussions, arranged to meet Becket who had now been in exile for six years. It was agreed that Becket should return to Canterbury but the fundamental differences of opinion were never resolved, the king's anger mounted, only to be followed by the events leading to Becket's death.

Adrian IV was elected pope in 1154, the only Englishman ever to attain the title. The following year he crowned Frederick Barbarossa as Holy Roman Emperor, thus honouring the treaty of Constance. Barbarossa, 'one of the boldest of the monarchs of the time', was eager to attain German influence in western Europe and constantly challenged papal authority.

The following letters illustrate the growing tensions between church and state during the twelfth century, which had begun at the end of the eleventh century and would continue until the middle of the fourteenth.

In fact it was a conflict between two notions of world government. All turned on the answer to the question of whether Pope or Emperor was the prime representative of God on earth. Could, or should, the secular arm control the ecclesiastical arm of the Christian world?

The first letter was sent to Barbarossa at the Diet of Besançon and was taken to imply the Emperor's dependence on the papacy. This caused great conflict between the German princes and the papal delegation. In the second letter, Adrian IV explains that the word *beneficium* had been used to mean benefit rather than fief, but the basic disagreement was only partly assuaged, and fuelled far bitterer clashes when Alexander III ascended the papal throne.

The importance attached to letters during the medieval period is amply illustrated here since their diplomatic or inflamatory contents could influence the opinions of great men. Papal correspondence during the reign of Adrian IV totalled 130 letters. By John XXII's reign (1316-34), it had increased to 3,646.

• • •

From Pope Adrian IV to the Holy Roman Emperor Frederick I Barbarossa.

20th September 1157.

Latin.

Bishop Adrian, servant of the servants of God, to his beloved son Frederick, illustrious emperor of the Romans, greeting and apostolic benediction.

A few days ago we remember to have written to your imperial Majesty recalling to your Highness's memory that, as we believe that horrid and execrable crime and impious deed of evil committed in our time in Germany had remained for some time uninvestigated - and observing, not without great wonder, that you had allowed the barbarity of so pernicious a crime to pass until now without taking the severe vengeance that was fitting. For in what manner our venerable brother Eskill, archbishop of Lyon, while returning from the apostolic see, was captured in that land by certain impious and godless men - we cannot speak of it without great grief of mind - and is at present kept in custody; how, moreover, in the aforesaid capture the impious men, the seeds of evil, the sons of crime did violently and with drawn swords rise against him and his followers; and how vilely and disgracefully they treated them, taking away all that they had. Your serene Highness knows on the one hand, and, on the other, the fame of so great an outrage has already reached the most distant and most unapproachable regions. In vengeance of which most violent crime, as one to whom, as we believe, good things are pleasing and evil ones displeasing, you should have arisen with more steadfastness; and the sword, which was given you by divine concession to punish evil-doers but to exalt the good, ought to have raged above the neck of the impious and most sternly to have destroyed the presumptuous. But you are said so to have hushed this up - or rather to have neglected it - that they have no reason to repent of having committed the deed, inasmuch as they already feel that they have gained immunity for the sacrilege which they committed As to the cause of this dissimulation or negligence we are entirely ignorant, since no scruple of conscience accuses our mind of having offended your serene Highness in any respect; but we have always loved your person as that of our most dear and special son, and the most Christian prince, whose power we do not doubt to have been founded by the grace of God on the rock of the apostolic confession. And we have treated you always with the partiality of due benignity. For you should, oh most glorious son, bring before the eyes of your mind how graciously and how joyfully your mother the holy Roman church received you in a former year; with what affection of heart she treated you; what plenitude of dignity and honour she granted you; and how, most willingly conferring upon you the distinction of the imperial crown, she stove to cherish you in her most bountiful lap you at the summit of thy sublimity - doing nothing at all which she knew would even in the least be contrary to the royal will. Nor, indeed, do we repent having fulfilled in all things the desires of your heart, but would, not without right, rejoice if your excellency had received from our hand even greater benefices (beneficia), if that were possible; knowing, as we do, what great increase and advantage can come through you to the church of God and to us. But now, since you seem to neglect and gloss over so monstrous a crime - which is known, indeed, to have been committed to the shame of the universal church and of your empire - we suspect and likewise fear lest perhaps your mind has been led to this dissimulation and neglect for the reason that, at the suggestion of a perverse man sowing discord, you have conceived against your most lenient mother the most holy Roman church, and against our own person, some indignation or rancour - which God forbid! On account of this, therefore and of other matters which we know to be pressing upon us, we have seen fit at present to despatch to your serenity from our side two of the best and most beloved men whom we have about us, our dear sons, namely, Bernard, Cardinal Presbyter of St. Clement, and Roland, Cardinal Presbyter of the title of St. Mark and our own chancellor - as being men who are conspicuous for their religion and prudence and honesty. And we most urgently request your Highness to receive them honourably as well as kindly, to treat them fairly and to receive without hesitation, as though proceeding from our lips, whatever they say on our part to your imperial Majesty concerning this matter and concerning other things which pertain to the honour of God and of the holy Roman church, and also to the glory and exaltation of the empire. And do not doubt to lend faith to their words as though we ourselves had happened to utter them.

• • •

From Pope Adrian IV to the Emperor, Frederick I.

February 1158.

Latin.

From the time when, God disposing as it pleased himself, we received the charge of the universal church, we have so taken care to honour your Highness that, from day to day, your mind ought to have been inflamed more and more with love for us and with veneration for the apostolic see. Wherefore we cannot hear without great astonishment that when - having heard from the suggestions of certain men that your anger was somewhat aroused against us - in order to learn your will we sent to your presence two of our best and greatest brothers, the chancellor Roland, namely, of the title of St Mark and Bernard of the title of St Clement, Cardinal Presbyters, who had always been most concerned for the honour of your Majesty in the Roman church: they were treated otherwise than was becoming to the imperial magnificence. On account of a certain word, indeed - beneficium, namely - your mind is said to have been moved to anger; which word ought not by any means to have aroused the ire of so great a man, nor even of any lesser man. For although this word - namely, beneficium - is used by some in a sense different from that which it has by derivation, it should, nevertheless, have been accepted in that sense which we ourselves attributed to it and which it is known to retain from its origin. For this word is derived from bonus and factum, and a beneficium is called by us not 'a fief' but a bonum factum. It is found in this signification in the whole body of Holy Scripture, where it speaks of the beneficium of God not as of a fief but as a benediction and good deed of His by which we are said to be governed and nourished. And your Magnificence, indeed, clearly recognizes that we did so well and so honourably place the mark of the imperial dignity upon your head that it may be considered by all a bonum factum. Wherefore when some have tried to distort from its own to another signification this word and that other one, namely: 'We have conferred upon you the distinction of the imperial crown,' they have done this not upon the merits of the case, but of their own will and at the suggestion of those who by no means cherish the peace of the kingdom and the church. For by this word contulimus we mean nothing else than what we said above, imposuimus. But that you afterwards, as it is said, ordered - ecclesiastics to be restrained from visiting, as they ought, the holy Roman church - if this is so, your discretion, as we hope, O dearest Son in Christ, recognizes how wrongly this was done. For if you had against us anything of bitterness, you should have intimated it to us through your envoys and letters and we would have taken care to provide for your honour, as for that of our dearest son. Now, indeed, at the instigation of our beloved son, Henry Duke of Bavaria and Saxony, we send into your presence two of our brothers, Henry of the title of Sts. Nereus and Achilles, presbyter, and Jacinctus, Deacon of St. Mary in Cosmide - both cardinals, prudent and honest men, indeed. And we urge and exhort your Highness in the Lord to receive them honestly and kindly. And your Excellency may know that what shall be intimated by them on our part to your Magnificence has proceeded from the sincerity of our heart; and, on the ground of this, through the mediation of the aforesaid duke, our son, may your Highness strive to come to an agreement with them, so that between you and your mother the holy Roman church no soil for the seeds of discord may henceforth remain.

• • • • •

M.T. Clanchy has described the letters from Simon de Senlis to the Bishop of Chichester as evoking 'without effort a picture of country life which a rhetorician could not have bettered'. (M.T. Clanchy *From Memory to Written Record*, p.68.) The examples printed here provide just a taste of this. Senlis the bishop's steward concerned himself not only with everyday domestic management but also ecclesiastical and legal matters. Here he informs his master about the vicar of Mundeham who claimed to have received the pope's approval for having two wives. Marriage of the secular clergy was not uncommon at this time, but this occurence was most irregular. The buying of oats for sowing and the nuisance caused by foxes illustrate the more mundane aspects of Senlis's day-to-day occupations. It is a great pity that the manuscript has been damaged and is illegible in places.

• • •

From Simon de Senlis to the Bishop of Chichester.

1220-1230.

Latin.

To his Reverend Lord Ralph, by the grace of God Bishop of Chichester, his devoted Simon de Senlis, greeting, and both devoted and due obedience and reverence in all things.

Know, lord, that on my departure from London . . . . as in oats sufficient for sowing at Totehal, as I believed, but it was afterwards signified . . . less was sown than was expected wherefore if you count on coming to London shortly, signify . . . . I will provide, God willing, sufficiency for sowing both at Totehal and elsewhere, lest your letter, which God forbid, by default . . . . you will provide for yourself sufficiently in this matter . . . a certain chaplain, William Dens by name, vicar of the church of Mundeham, has two wives, as it is said, of whom one is resident at Chichester; which William indeed brought forward letters of licence from the high pontiff, as he said, but in these Sussex parts as well as in England (it is believed), that never did those letters emanate from the conscience of our lord the Pope, but were obtained contrary to the statutes of the general council wherefore, if it please your holiness, signify what you shall have decided to be notified to your official on this matter: above all things taking care, if you please, to send some man with dogs fit to catch foxes in your park of Aldyngeburn, who do us there much damage, and this shortly, since the star for taking them has passed away.

Deign to inform me, lord, if you please, of your condition, since I much desire to hear the certainty of your safety and prosperity; know for certain that I will show myself vigilant about your business, both in Sussex and elsewhere. May your holiness fare well in the Lord.

• • • • •

The Bishop of Chichester, Ralph de Neville, spent a great deal of money on the repair and maintenance of the Cathedral. One of the carpenters he employed wished to join a crusade, probably the Sixth Crusade (1228-9), and seems to have proposed a substitute to complete the work at hand. The lure of the crusades reached all walks of life, and it is tempting to wonder whether this carpenter saw the Holy Roman Emperor, Frederick II crown himself King of Jerusalem in 1229 and whether he ever returned to the cathedral.

• • •

From Simon de Senlis to the Bishop of Chichester.

1220-1230.

Latin.

To the venerable Lord and dearest Father in Christ, Ralph, by the grace of God Bishop of Chichester, Chancellor of the Lord King, his ever devoted S(imon), dean, and the chapter of the same church, with due obedience of devoted submission.

Your carpenter of Chichester church, approaching us under a vow signed with the cross, wishing to begin his journey, has presented to us a certain fit and competent young man, of whom we entertain sure hope that he will sufficiently supply the business, in order that he, in the absence of the aforesaid crusader, may be able to replace him in his duties in the said church, in like manner as he was bound. And since we are unwilling to meddle with this manner of business without your will and assent, we send the same crusader to you, devoutly supplicating your paternity, that if you are willing to admit the said young man, you will inform us, if you please, of your pleasure on this matter, by letter to us by means of the same crusader. May your serenity always prosper in Christ.

• • • • •

Between 1224 and 1244 Ralph de Neville was bishop of Chichester, and in 1226 he was appointed chancellor to King Henry III. Matthew Paris described him as ‘a steadfast pillar of loyalty and truth in state affairs'* and his position at court evidently occupied a great deal of the bishop's time, as this tactful letter from the precentor of Chichester makes clear. He appeals to the Bishop to reuturn to his see for Easter and the religious tone must surely have encouraged Neville to consider his spiritual responsibilities.

The qualities of great churchmen were often those required by the state, and bishops all over Europe found that secular duties thrust upon them often hindered their ecclesiastical roles.

• • •

To the Bishop of Chichester from his clerk William.

1219-1239.

Latin.

To his Reverend Lord and Father in Christ, Ralph, by Divine clemency Bishop of Chichester, his clerk W(illiam) Precentor [cantor] of Chichester, eternal greeting, and both devoted and due reverence.

Although the common advantage of the kingdom is to be preferred before the private advantages of individuals, yet since the glorious solemnity of the Passion and Resurrection is a hand, in which it is no less honourable than laudable for the cathedral church to be adorned with its own prelate and for sheep to rejoice in their own shepherd, I beseech you, with all the devotion in my power that, if it can in any way be done without offence to the Lord King, you will be pleased to visit your church, and celebrate the paschal services. Both the clergy and the people would congratulate indeed your presence, and I hope that, for the space of three days at least, it would be agreeable to your paternity to attend to the divine mysteries in your church of Chichester, laying aside in the meanwhile the anxieties and cares of the court, which, incessantly harassing you, scarcely permit the least, if any, period of tranquillity by day or night. Despising in all your business the threats of men, may you place your hope and trust in Him, who has the power to cast both body and soul into hell. And if it should perchance happen that you do not come into these parts, I implore the kindness of your paternity, that you will be pleased to make known to me, according to your opportunity, a day and place after Easter, or within it, where I may enjoy a much desired conference with you, for I have many things to consult with you upon, in my business and secrets. May your paternity prosper in the Lord.

---

* Matthew Paris, *Annales Monastici*, iii, 90, iv, 287.

•••••

The following letter, which took the form of a roll, was carried to various monasteries to request prayers for the founder and first prioress of the Priory of Henningham, Lucy Countess of Oxford. The obituary gives details of the qualities which were considered to be particularly desirable in a nun, especially the prioress's remarkable example of chastity. It was customary for monasteries to send a messenger from house to house, collecting an accumulating series of obituaries forming a roll when an abbot died. (Clanchy, p. 109.) If additional praises were added to Agnes's letter in this fashion there is no record of them, but the principle was no doubt the same, an unsealed roll, which could be read by many, was an effective means of inviting prayers.

•••

From Agnes, a nun at the Priory of Henningham Essex, requesting prayers.

After 1190.

Latin.

To all the children of our Holy Mother Church to whom the present writing shall come, Agnes, of the Church of the Holy Cross and Saint Mary of Henningham, a humble handmaiden of the convent in that place, sends eternal greeting in the Lord.

After the showers of tears, and floods of weeping, that we have shed on the decease of our dearest Mother the venerable Lucy, first Prioress and Founder of our house, who at the calling of the Lord went the way of all flesh, and paid to the earth the debt of human kind, on 13 July, we have taken pen in hand to acquaint all of you in writing of the calamity that we are suffering in the loss of such a blessed Mother in this vale of misery. It is no wonder that at the same time our heart fails us, when she was potent in so many virtues, shone with so many graces, and was fragrant with so many merits, that she was deservedly called by the name 'Lucy', which is 'the knowledge of light'. She was rightly termed 'Lucy', therefore, because the name imitates the example. She by merits and prayers terminated her mother's issue of blood. Restraining in herself all movement of carnal lust, she rooted out in others the flow of incontinence and uncleanness by the drought of holy conversation and a sober life. By divine urging she withdrew herself from carnal copulation with her spouse. She was, as we know, seven times bound by the link of matrimony, and yet remained unacquainted with the embraces of a man, and always uncontaminated and untouched, and so escaped in time from the snare of the hunters. And this she did by divine Providence, so that she might admit no lover but Him.

She was discreet in silence, profitable in speech grave in modesty, venerable in decency, unique in neighbourly compassion elevated above all in contemplation, and so studied how to be, by her humility companion of those who do well, that by her zeal for justice she might correct the errors of wrongdoers. Therefore in the desire of the flesh we have learned prudence from her, in adversity fortitude, in tribulation patience, in desperation solace, in danger refuge, in heat coolness, in harshness mildness. And by her example our reading became more frequent, prayer more abundant, and our love more fervent. Such a virtue of absticence flourished in this most kindly virgin, our pious mother, that by such strictness of fasts and vigils, and of clothing, her bones clove to her skin, her flesh being eaten away almost like the most holy Job, and this was so much taken away, and all these things alike.

She has departed to Him who wished the Tenths of the Firstfruits to be paid to Him, and who also instituted the Ten Commandments. Have pity therefore on us, at least have pity on us, O our friends, and show sympathy with us in our wretchedness by drying up our flowing tears by the suffrage of your prayers, because it is a pious and most wholesome thing to pray for the deceased that they may be released from their sins. Help us therefore, O kindly monks, help us, O venerable canons, and you holy virgins, in offering prayers and masses in the presence of the MOST HIGH, that He may take her into His holy mercy, Who wipes away every tear from the eyes of the Saints, so that those stains that have adhered to her from earthly contacts may be removed by the healing of His forgiveness. AMEN.

• • • • •

During the Middle Ages there were many orders of nuns, but in general they had far less influence than those of monks and friars. As women could not enter holy orders they had to depend on external priests to perform services and their rule and discipline generally came from their male counterparts.

Nunneries were frequently small, attracting little patronage and experiencing problems of administration and maintenance. Apart from the lack of endowments other factors sapped nunneries' resources such as fires, floods, plagues, tithes and taxes, as well as the burden of secular boarders.

In desperation many nuns resorted to begging for alms. Those in high authority disapproved of this practice because it meant the nuns had to leave the seclusion of their house and 'were more likely to be subversive of discipline'.* The appointment of a proctor to collect alms on the nuns' behalf overcame this problem although a licence which was usually in the form of a letters patent had to be obtained from a bishop.

This sorrowful letter must have succeeded in gaining the pity of the queen, who was regent at this time, as Alicia de la Haye is named as prioress of St Mary's in 1264.

• • •

The nuns of St Mary's of Chester to Eleanora, Queen of Henry III. 1253.

Latin.

To the most excellent lady Eleonora, by God's grace queen of England, Lady of Ireland, Duchess of Normandy and Aquitaine, Countess of Anjou, her humble convent of nuns of St. Mary of Chester wishes her, if she pleases, health and happy success to her utmost desires.

When our prioress of happy memory, lady Alicia of Stockport, lately went the way of all flesh, we, having quickly sent a messenger about it to our most excellent lord Henry, by God's grace the illustrious king of England, according to the tenor of his benignant reply, by a special letter of ratification sent to you on the morrow of St. Lawrence the Martyr's day, having invoked the aid of the Holy Spirit, without any condition or reclamation, unanimously and cordially elected the lady Alicia de la Haye our sub-prioress, a woman deserving commendation for her life and conduct, as our prioress, all things thereto appertaining being canonically observed. Therefore it is that, mentally throwing ourselves at the feet of your excellency, since bowels of pity and mercy grow in you, we humbly and devoutly seek that you will deign, by the instinct of Divine compassion, to confirm the said Alicia as our prioress to our miserable convent, amidst its multiplied desolations. For so greatly are we reduced that we are compelled every day to beg abroad our food, slight as it is. The very secret places of our afflicted hearts cry out therefore to you, expecting the wished-for effect of our pious petition. And we, each one of us, will, as is fitting, and as we formerly did, now in future much more devoutly, offer prayers to the Lord for you and yours. May your ladyship ever fare well in the Lord!

• • • • •

* E. Power, *Medieval English Nunneries* p. 174.

In contrast to St Mary's Chester, the Benedictine nunnery at Barking was one of the largest and wealthiest in England. It had been founded by Erkenwald, Bishop of London 675-693 and several royal and noble ladies became abbesses of Barking, including Thomas à Becket's sister, and natural daughters of both Henry II and King John.

This example is typical of many letters requesting official recognition of a new abbess, and the fact that the suggested choice usually met with approval tends to indicate that such letters were probably little more than a formality.

Apart from official communications nuns also wrote more personal missives, often without the permission of their superior. The restrictions of seclusion and curfews meant that contact with the outside world was extremely difficult, the sending of secret letters by way of secular visitors or lay sisters was a regular practice amongst nuns reluctant to sever ties with family and friends. Those in charge of the nuns' spiritual welfare were concerned about the implications of such correspondence and made attempts to restrict it. Plenty of interesting examples are to be found in E. Power, *Medieval English Nunneries*.

• • •

Matilda Prioress of the Convent of Barking to Henry III.

3 December 1258.

Latin.

Since the lady our mother, venerable for her religion, the lady Christina, late abbess of our house, did on the Monday next after the Feast of St. Andrew the Apostle, in the forty-third year of your reign,* of her own good and spontaneous will, yield up the government of the said abbey, on acount of the infirmity and debility fo her body, and was absolved from it by our venerable father Foulk,† Bishop of London, we now, being destitute of the solace of an abbess, send to you our beloved sisters and fellow-nuns, Roesia de Argentes, Joanna de Wantham, and Agnes Costentin, humbly and devoutly supplicating that the bowels of your compassion may be moved towards us, and that the condescension of your mercy will grant us permission to elect some other as our abbess, so that henceforth you may receive from the highest retributor a worthy reward, and we may be henceforth obligated more specially to offer up the merited suffrages of our prayers for you and yours.

* December 2nd 1258.
† Foulk Basset, Bishop of London, 1244-1259.

Given at Barking the Tuesday after the feast of St. Andrew the Apostle, in the forty-third year of your reign.

To her most excellent lord Henry, by God's grace illustrious king of England, lord of Ireland, duke of Normandy and Aquitaine, and earl of Anjou, Matilda, humble prioress of Barking, and of the convent of the same place, wishes health, with due reverence and honour, and the suffrages of her prayers.

• • • • •

In 1284, when she was six years old, Mary entered the nunnery of Amesbury which was a cell to the prestigious abbey of Fontevraud and popular with ladies of rank during the thirteenth and fourteenth centuries. Queen Eleanor of Provence, her grandmother, joined the convent in 1286 and acted as her guardian and supervisor. Unlike the other nuns, Mary enjoyed certain privileges: she visited the royal courts, went on pilgrimages and is known to have been present at at least two royal confinements.

Although she never became prioress, Mary played an influential role in the life of the nunnery. Here she uses her royal connections in an attempt to prevent the intrusion of an unfamiliar prioress from Fontevraud and in support of the popular choice, Lady Isabella.

• • •

From Mary daughter of Edward I, to her brother Edward II.

c. 1316.

French.

To the very high and noble prince, her very dear lord and brother, my lord Edward, by the grace of God king of England, his sister Mary sends health and all manner of honour and reverence.

Very dear sire, as a long time has passed since God did his will upon our prioress Dambert, we immediately after her death sent to our very dear cousin, the lady-abbess of Fontevraud, both on my part and on that of the convent, asking for a lady from this our convent, to wit, for the Lady Isabella, whom we understand to be well able and sufficient for the office, that she might be granted to us for our prioress. And we thought, dear sire, that she (the abbess) would have willingly granted us our request, for she is bound to do so since she was brought up and veiled amongst us, and so she should neither wish nor permit that the church should be so long without prelates; but as yet we have had no answer, only we understand from certain people that she intends to send us a prioress from beyond the sea there, and a prior by her counsel out there. And know, certainly, my very dear brother, that should she send any other than one belonging to our own convent, it would prove matter of discord in the convent, and of the destruction of the goods of the church, which I know well, sire, that you would not suffer willingly and wittingly; wherefore I pray you, dearest lord and brother, and require you, both for the love of me and of our convent, which after God trust surely in you, that you would please to send word by my said lady-abbess, that she do not undertake to burden our church with any prioress out of the convent, nor with prior other than the one we have now, but that she would grant us her whom we have requested. Do this, most dearest brother, that our convent may receive your aid and sustenance in this case as they have always done in their needs. May Jesus Christ give you a long life, my dearest brother. Written at Swainton, in the Isle of Wight, the 9th day of May.

• • • • •

John de Grandisson was a great scholar and had studied theology at the University of Paris. As a result of his academic success he was made Archdeacon of Nottingham in 1310, he also held canonries of York, Wells and Lincoln. Grandisson became chaplain and later acted as an ambassador of Pope John XXII. In 1327 he was consecrated Bishop of Exeter. He spent most of his time concerned with the affairs of his see and only left it when parliament or other important business required his presence.

Grandisson was largely responsible for the rebuilding of the nave of Exeter cathedral. His travels had given him sophisticated tastes and in December 1328, he wrote to the Pope, saying that when the cathedral was finished it would surpass in beauty every building of its own sort in England and France. The following exchange reveals Grandisson's methods of obtaining money, possibly to help finance his building schemes. The Bishop's cousin refuses his request and insinuates Grandisson's neglect of his episcopal duties.

• • •

From John de Grandisson, Bishop of Exeter to his cousin Hugh Courtenay, Earl of Devon.

24 January 1329.

French.

Greetings and dearest friendship, with the blessing of God, and ours.

Because, my Lord, we have hurriedly to make a very large payment of money to the court, on account of our church of Exeter which was so greatly burdened by our predecessor, and all the help that is given to us is not nearly enough, without the help of good friends, for the half of the sum that we owe, we therefore beg you as affectionately as we can, my Lord, that you would be so kind as to lend us £200 sterling over one year, on such security as you wish to command, so that by your help, my Lord, and that of other good friends, we can be delivered from the aforesaid debt. And if you please, my Lord, you will write by the bearer of this letter, what it pleases you to do about this our request.

My Lord, may our Lord have you in his protection.

Written at our manor of Chudleigh, the 24th day of January.

• • •

From Hugh de Courtenay, Earl of Devon to the Bishop of Exeter.

January 1329.

French.

To his most honourable Lord, and father in God, all honours and all reverences.

Because, my Lord, you ask by your letters that we should lend you a certain sum of money, please know, my Lord, that we have committed so much for the marriage of our daughter, and the performance of the will of our dear mother (whom God absolve), that we cannot do what you ask at this time, of which we are sorry. And moreover, your predecessor Bishop James* entered into an obligation with us for a sum of money, and we cannot get it unless we sue the executors.

My Lord your clerks say in your diocese that you have made a great gathering among them, which is something that was never done by any bishop up to this time, and the people believe that you have great means. And it is a good thing, my Lord, to begin to live of your own, and what you have, and to do right and grace to rich and poor. And know, my Lord, that a bishop ought never to be solitary, but ought often to show himself so as to comfort the souls of the people, and ought to listen to everything, and never believe too easily, for a good judge should think early but give judgement late if he is to have friends.

My Lord, may the Holy Spirit protect and guard you.

---

* James Berkeley, Bishop of Exeter March-June 1327.

•••••

The Augustinian priory of St James the Apostle at Thremhall in Essex was founded during the twelfth century by Gilbert de Mountfichet or his son, Richard. The de Vere family, the Earls of Oxford, inherited the manor of Stansted Mountfichet in 1320. This letter probably proved successful, the church in question was given to the priory at about this time, its first rector dying in 1368. The addressee was most likely John de Vere, Earl of Oxford 1331-1360.

•••

From the Prior and Brethren of Thremhall to the Earl of Oxford.

c. 1350.

Old French.

With all honour and respect.

Sire, the church of Stansted Mauntfichet, within the Diocese of London, is our responsibility, and is taxed at thirty-five marks per annum. Permission to buy the building and the land around it must be obtained, at no small expense, from that same Diocese, within a parish of which lies our own poor small house. And we are, Sire, in a sense, in daily danger from those same people within the Clergy, who covet the deeds of the property.

We have requested your cherished companion, our Lady, seeking charity and alms, to entreat you, in the name of her ancestors who lie buried here among us, to take our cause close to your heart, that you may secure our Lord the King and our Lady the Queen's agreement to submit an application to the Court for the purchase of the property.

Beyond our diligent efforts in this respect, we and our friends beg you to provide the forty marks necessary for the purchase if and when it is completed.

Most dear Sire, in the name of Charity, take up our cause, we beseech you, as we ourselves have little influence. You may be sure that we will be deeply indebted to you.

It is written that if God wills it, then it will come to pass; with this in mind, Sire, one may quickly overcome all manner of difficulties.

The church will benefit as, in our little house, we will have a vicarage of our own. As previously stated, the church lies within the Diocese of London and is taxed at thirty-five marks per annum; please inform the Court of our problem.

We are fourteen in number, twelve ordained and two laymen; at present we are overburdened with travellers seeking shelter, as we are situated close to the highway, and we have neither a church nor any other form of stipend upon which we may rely to bring in more than forty marks at best, beyond which we depend upon the benevolence of others who wish to help us.

In the name of Charity, Sire, for the love of God we beg you to take our cause closely to your heart, and to send us word by return messenger that we can rely on your goodwill. Regardless of the reply you send, dear Sire and Lady, accept our prayers for you.

The prior and Brethren of Thremhall.

• • • • •

The vicar of Bersted may have found it 'against his conscience' to sing Mass twice daily in a chantry for souls, but others were less nice in this regard. The practice of endowing a perpetual chantry, so as to mitigate the pangs of Purgatory, was the rich man's equivalent of the indulgences that so incensed Luther. Archbishop Islip, fixing the stipends of chantry priests at a mere five Marks per annum, had this to say to the Bishop of London.

• • •

Archbishop Islip of Canterbury to the Bishop of London.

1362.

Latin.

We are informed that modern priests, through covetousness and love of ease, not content with reasonable salaries, demand excessive pay for their labours and receive it; and do so despise labour and study that they wholly refuse as parish priests to serve in churches and chapels or to attend the cure of souls, though fitting salaries are offered them; and prefer to live in a leisurely manner by celebrating annuals for the quick and dead; and so parish churches and chapels remain unofficiated . . . whereupon all unbeneficed chaplains, fitted for the cure of souls shall be required to put aside any private obsequies and officiate wherever the ordinary shall appoint them, at six marks of annual stipend, while priests without cure of souls shall be content with five marks.

• • • • •

He was not the only one - the practice was seen not merely as favouring the rich above the perhaps equally sinful poor, but mechanistic - a betrayal of faith. It also diverted religious men equally from pastoral work in the community and the service of learning and the arts in the monasteries and universities. Chaucer specifically praises his 'Poure Persoun of a Toun' for sticking to his parish and not taking up chanting as a softer option.

Royalty tended to have another view of the matter. Richard III had most elaborate plans in hand for his when he died, a fact which contemporary apologists attribute to piety rather than a bad conscience. The endowment of Henry VII for his own soul was uncharacteristically generous, but Henry VIII showed his filial piety by suppressing it with the rest. In the next letter the Lord Mayor of London gives his blessing to the Pulteney Chantry, which was in his gift.

• • •

Andrew Aubrey, Lord Mayor of London, to the Dean and Chapter of St Paul's.

29 June 1352.

Probably French.

To the venerable and discreet men, the Dean and chapter of the church of S. Paul in London, Andrew Aubrey, mayor of the same city, greeting in the Lord.

We do present unto you, by these presents, our dearly beloved in Christ, Sir William Mason, priest, to fill the perpetual chantry now vacant, with all the rights thereof, which has been founded for a fitting priest, in the church of S. Paul aforesaid, to celebrate Divine service for the soul of John de Pulteneye, knight, and the souls of other persons in the will of him . . . and to our presentation, by reason of our holding the office of mayor of the city aforesaid, in virtue of the will of the said John . . . we do beg of you that you will admit the said William to the chantry aforesaid and as the usage is, will canonically institute him in the same, and will deign to do, in favour of us, the other things which in this behalf, unto your office pertain. In witness whereof we have caused these our letters patent, sealed with the seal of the mayoralty of the city to be made. Given at London, on the Thursday next after the feast of the apostles, Peter and Paul [29 June] in the twenty-sixth year of the reign of King Edward after the Conquest the Third.

• • • • •

Thomas à Becket is the most notorious of all 'turbulent priests', and his subsequent canonization, by grace first of Pope Alexander III and later Messrs T.S. Eliot and Jean Anoulih, certainly has much more to do with the manner of his death than the conduct of his life. A less ambiguous figure is Richard de Seynesbury, Prior of Chester, whose tenure was a prolonged catalogue of dissipation, dilapidation and violence. Eventually the Black Prince, no less, found it necessary to order his confinement at Conway.

• • •

Edward, Prince of Wales, to the Lieutenant of Chester.

17 May 1363.

Probably French.

Commitment to John de Delves, lieutenant of the justice of Cestre and Don Thomas de Okley, monk of the house of St. Werburgh, Cestre

In consideration of the damage and loss which has befallen the said house by the bad government of Richard de Seynesbury, last abbot there, and which will continue to befall it unless the prince puts forth his hand to save and maintain the possessions and rights pertaining thereto – of the keeping of the said house and the administration of the goods and possessions thereof, with full powers, together or separately, to remove the household servants and ministers of the house if they be found guilty of any negligence or fault, and replace them by others, and to take any other measures necessary for the good government of the house and the affairs thereof.

• • •

Edward Prince of Wales to the Constable of Conway Castle.

4 February 1364.

Probably French.

Order to the constable of the castle of Conwei

Inasmuch as the prince, in view of the manifold perils and mischiefs which might arise in the event of the escape of Richard Seynesbury, monk of the house of St. Werburgh, Cestre, who is in the keeping of the constable on account of notorious faults, destructions and damages done by him to the said house, has ordained that he be delivered to the abbot of the house to sojourn there as a monk – to deliver the said Richard by indenture to the abbot or his attorneys.

• • • • •

But it was impossible to keep the ex-Abbot away from Chester. He was sent back as a plain monk in 1364, to the embarrassment of all concerned. He was finally despatched to Avignon, and a sinecure at the Papal Court. De Seynesbury was succeeded by Thomas de Newport through a bull of Pope Urban V.

• • •

Urban V to the Bishop of Lichfield.

7 March 1363.

Latin.

Urban etc. to the Bishop of Lichfield.

The monastery of St. Werburga of Chester being vacant by the resignation of Richard, the last abbot, made at the Apostolic See into the hands of Guillermus, Cardinal priest of S. Laurence in Lucina, by Hugh Arian, clerk of Durham diocese, substitute of Willermus de Merston, monk of the said monastery and proxy of the said abbot; and no one except us being able to do anything in the matter, because long before this vacancy we reserved to our provision all monasteries then vacant at the Apostolic See and all that should be vacated there; we have provided Thomas de Newport, priest, monk of the said monastery, and committed to him the cure and administration of the said House. We ask and exhort you as Ordinary to give your favour and help to the said Abbot and monastery. Dated Avignon, ii Non. Mart. the first year of our pontificate.

• • • • •

John Wyclyf (1330-84) was an academic who inspired heresy through his many writings, but he never actually broke with Rome and escaped persecution by way of royal influence due to his friendship with John of Gaunt, the Duke of Lancaster. This letter, which is a reply to a summons by Pope Urban VI, was written in the year of Wyclyf's death. Its authenticity and dating have been debated at great length.* It is

* Dahmus, Chapter 6.

useful in that it sums up several of his beliefs; the importance of the Bible as the law of God and the value of spiritual purity as well as his distaste for many practices of the church and his opinion that the Pope should only be obeyed if he in turn obeyed God's law.

When Pope Urban VI was elected in 1378 Wyclyf had been optimistic that he would initiate reform. He failed to do this and Wyclyf blames the corrupting influence of the Pope's household. The letter shows how Wyclyf considered himself a reformer rather than a revolutionary. He was only pronounced a heretic after his death.

• • •

From John Wyclyf to Pope Urban VI.

1384.

Latin.

I am happy to reveal fully to anyone and especially to the Roman pontiff the faith I hold, for I suppose that if it is orthodox, he will graciously confirm this faith and if it be erroneous he will correct it. But I submit that the gospel of Christ is the body of the law of God, that Christ, indeed, who directly gave this gospel, I believe to be true God and true man, and in this the law of the gospel excels all other parts of scripture. Again I submit that the Roman pontiff, inasmuch as he is Christ's highest vicar on earth, is among pilgrims most bound to this law of the gospel. For the majority of Christ's disciples are not judged according to wordly greatness, but according to the imitation of Christ in their moral life. Again, from out this heart of the Lord's law I plainly conclude that Christ was the poorest of men during the time of his pilgrimage and that he eschewed all worldly dominion. This is clear from the faith of the gospel, Matthew VIII and 2 Corinthians VIII. From all this I deduce that never should any of the faithful imitate the pope himself nor any of the saints except insofar as he may have imitated the Lord Jesus Christ. For Peter, Paul, and the sons of Zebedee, by seeking worldly dignity, brought that sort of imitation into disrepute, so that they are not to be imitated in those errors. From this I infer, as a counsel, that the pope should leave temporal dominion to the secular arm, and to this he should effectually exhort his clergy. For in such wise did Christ have signified through his apostles.

If in the above I have erred, I am willing humbly to be corrected even through death if necessary. And if I were able to travel at will in person, I should like humbly to visit the Roman pontiff. But God has obliged me to the contrary, and he has always taught me to obey God rather than men. But since God has given our pope true and evangelical instincts, we should pray that those instincts are not extinguished through deceitful counsel, nor that the pope or cardinals be moved to do anything contrary to the law of the Lord. Therefore, let us ask God, the lord of everything created, that he so inspire our pope, Urban VI, as he began, so that he and his clergy may imitate the Lord Jesus Christ in their moral lives, so that they may effectually teach the people to faithfully imitate them in this. And let us pray spiritually that our pope be preserved from malicious counsel, for we also know that a man's enemies are of his household, and God does not suffer us to be tempted above that which we are able, much less does he require of any creature that he do that which he can not, for such is the manifest condition of Antichrist.

• • • • •

The Benedictine nunnery of Rowney in Hertfordshire was founded in 1164 by Conan Duke of Bretagne. Since none of the names of the prioresses at Rowney are known before 1449 it is not possible to say more about the writer of this letter. Requests for secular assistance of this kind are unusual but the fears and scandal this defecting nun might generate are similar to those expressed by St. Bernard in his efforts to recall recalcitrant monks and nuns,.

Troubles within monasteries and nunneries, which were by no means infrequent, could be solved by internal discipline, but once the offending party had penetrated the outside world, religious superiors seem to have experienced real panic. It would be interesting to know what penalty Joanna had to pay for gadding about Hertfordshire without her habit, if indeed she ever returned to the angry prioress.

• • •

From the Prioress of Rowney to King Henry IV.

12 November 1400.

Latin.

To the most excellent prince and lord in Christ, lord Henry, by God's grace illustrious king of England and France, and lord of Ireland, his humble and devoted oratrice the prioress of Rowney sends the divine suffrages of prayers, with all sorts of reverence and honour.

By the tenor of these presents I certify to your royal highness that the sister Joanna Adeleshey, a nun of the order of St. Benedict, and notoriously professed in the same house, wanders and roams abroad from country to country, in a secular habit, despising her vow of obedience, to the grievous danger of her soul, and manifest scandal of her order, and pernicious example of others. May it therefore please your royal excellency of your royal clemency; hitherto ever gracious to extend the secular arm for the capture of the said Joanna, to be chastised according to the rule of her order in a case of this kind, lest for want of due chastisement a plant given up to divine culture may thus perish. And may He who gives to all kings to reign preserve your royal majesty in prosperity. Given at Rowney, the 12th day of November, A.D. 1400.

• • • • •

Wyclyf's unorthodox ideas were vigorously upheld by his followers, derisively called Lollards after the Dutch 'mumbler'. At first the Lollards were based at Oxford but the movement began to gain supporters from farther afield and from all walks of life.

More and more emphasis was placed on Wyclyf's disapproval of the church's wealth and abuse of privileges and the consequent political implications rather than on his theological arguments. Lollardy 'moved farther and farther away from Wyclyf's outlook so that he would have certainly disowned it by the time of Oldcastle's rising in 1414.'

John Oldcastle who was a staunch Lollard who had been imprisoned for possessing heretical writings and opinions had been made Lord Cobham in 1408. He escaped from the Tower in October 1413 and spent the winter planning to kill the King, overthrow the government and to demolish all cathedrals and churches. The resultant rising in January 1414 was quickly defeated and it brought severe reprisals. The following letter concerns the conviction of John Claydon who was burned at Smithfield shortly after it was written, for his involvement with Oldcastle.

• • •

From the Mayor and Aldermen of London to King Henry V.

22 August 1415.

Latin.

To the most victorious and most excellent Prince, and their most gracious Lord Henry, by the grace of God, King of England and France, and Lord of

Ireland, the Mayor and Aldermen of his City of London, his unworthy servants, with willing obeisance, wishing him boundless might, wisdom ineffable, and, after he shall have finished the good fight, a reception in the realms of bliss.

Forasmuch as the King of all might and the Lord of Heaven, who of late graciously taught your hands to fight, and has guided your feet to the battle, has now, during your absence, placed in our hands certain persons who not only were enemies of Him and of your dignity, but also, in so far as they might be were subverters of the whole of your realm; men commonly known as 'Lollards,' who for long time have laboured for the subversion of the whole Catholic faith and of Holy Church, the lessening of public worship, and the destruction of your realm, as also, the perpetration of very many other enormities horrible to hear; the same persons, in accordance with the requirements of law, we have unto the Reverend Commissaries of the Reverend Father in Christ, and Lord,* Richard, by Divine permission, the Lord Bishop of London, by indenture caused to be delivered. Whereupon, one John Cleydone by name, the arch-parent of this heretical depravity, was by the most Reverend Father in Christ, and Lord,† Henry, by Divine permission, the Lord Archbishop of Canterbury, Primate of all your realm, and other Bishops, his brethren, as well as very many§ Professors of Holy Scripture and Doctors of Laws, in accordance with the canonical sanctions, by sentence in this behalf lawfully pronounced, as being a person relapsed into heresy, which before had been by him abjured, left in the hands of the secular Court; for the execution of whose body, and the entire destruction of all such enemies, with all diligence, to the utmost of our power we shall be assisting.

[The rest of the letter has been omitted, it is of little interest and its meaning doubtful.]

• • • • •

The next curious letter, in the form of a petition, illustrates that although the rising of 1414 had been a fiasco, Lollard opinions continued to be held, and severe punishments inflicted on those who were discovered. The author, J.B., was accused, amongst other things, of possessing a Lollard book called *The Lantern of Light* which attacked the Pope and bishops. It is known that John Claydon was also found with a copy.

In the letter J.B. expresses his desire to scourge heretics and to

* Richard Clifford, Bishop of London 1407-21.
† Henry Chichele 1414-43.
§ Otherwise *Doctors of Divinity.*

unify the church under the Pope. Other seemingly contradictory statements to his actions indicate that he was either renouncing Lollard beliefs in an attempt to save his skin or was possessed of a peculiarly individual form of heresy.

Another Lollard rising occurred in 1431 but by this time both its popularity and influence had rapidly dwindled.

• • •

From J.B. (a suspected Lollard) to King Henry V.
Spring of 1421.
English.

J.B., your true subject and always your devout beadsman,* sorrowfully, humbly and sincerely beseeches you, since by false lies he has found it necessary to take to God's Sanctuary and yours at Westminster, through fear of false imprisonment and greater wrongs, that you would give him permission and fortitude to petition you, in your own majestic person, with no other spiritual or temporal judge being assigned to the case, to hear him, as far as it lies in your jurisdiction; and to hear whoever makes objections or allegations against him, and judge them; and then finally, when you have heard everything, and understood it all, give your own definitive judgement.

And in particular pass judgement on a Service of Our Lady (in Latin), containing all the Bible and much of *Catholic Doctrine,* for the better understanding of that same Bible. And this service should be used for devotional purposes, whoever likes it or not, and should be used four times a year, or at least twice; *and that should take just under three hours on each occasion;* which form of service he asks to be ratified, so that whoever uses it may do so openly, without fear of slander or defamation in respect of any manner of illegality; and he asks the same for a private office, called *Knights of Christ.* And also licence to attack the heathen, and other heretics, both spiritually and physically, by all lawful means, so as to make one fold and one flock for our Lord Jesus Christ, and his chief vicar on Earth, our holy father the pope of Rome.

* Bead(s)man. Literally, a pensioner who, as a condition of his sustenance, prayed for the soul of his benefactor. Here it is used in the more general sense of beneficiary. It appears in this sense in many of the letters, and carries the implication that the writer will continue to pray for the soul of the addressee if he gets what he is asking for, otherwise not.

With regard to these matters, the same John took three books to his Ordinary, the Bishop of London, shortly after last Easter, for examination, and asked him for his judgement. But he has been unable to obtain any, nor the return of his books, nor reply to various letters that he has sent since. In respect of which, he asks of you, his liege lord, both compensation and restitution; and also that you should judge and declare him to be innocent of the false lies told about him, he knows not by whom, for God knows, so he is. Of these lies, the first is that he wrote a letter which was placed on the door of Mr Falconer, who was then Mayor of London, for which he was imprisoned in St Paul's penitentiary;* the third, that he came out in favour of Sir John Oldcastle; the fourth concerns a book called *The Lantern of Light;* the fifth, that on the third Sunday before Lammas last, he stirred up an uprising of Lollards in Coventry; the sixth, that he made 600 tabbards† in the same cause. And by God, my liege lord, all this is falsely invented. And he is always ready to declare himself in your own noble presence, as you yourself and your own righteous law will stipulate. And yet every day they coin new lies, so that he may not seek for judgement on his aforesaid service and office.

And therefore, my liege lord, until all these matters shall be disposed of, he asks as a free man your unequivocal, faithful, highest and unencumbered protection, in all sorts of cases, and against all sorts and conditions of men, that he should not be molested in any way, but should go about in safety, to attend to his interests in this matter; and that you may defend him so that he can seek advice without being imprisoned in any way, or any other hindrance. And further, always to have free and open access to your royal presence, at proper times and places, on request; for he finds you gracious, and easy to approach.

He will never fly from your presence, but appear willingly, and abide by your judgement according to law, and accept it with good will. And on this condition, but not otherwise, he forgoes all the privileges and liberties of Sanctuary, and will always be bound by yourself and your righteous laws; for God knows, he never took Sanctuary except for fear of false imprisonment, and therefore he beseeches that you should not believe liars against him, for by God, he speaks and means nothing but the truth.

And all this, my liege lord, as far as it may please God and not displease you, he requests you, before God in his infinite wisdom, that you examine and judge a memorandum in Latin concerning the same

* Either J.B. left out the second accusation, or he absent-mindedly called the second the third.

† Tabards would in this case be special ones carrying a blazon or device, so that the rebels/rioters would recognise each other in the melée. To be worn over armour.

office, which he took to my excellent and worthy lord your brother, at that time your lieutenant, and the noble Duke of Bedford. And moreover, all that he asks you concerning this matter is proper, and all that is irrelevant or harmful may be removed. And he asks discretion to add and subtract from it, to change and improve, as may best bring it forward; and for no delay or hindrance, for any reason, even one he knows nothing about. Therefore he will always ask you for all sorts of honest and faithful advice in this matter, for he is quite straightforward, and has no greater trust than in God and yourself. Therefore let him not be betrayed, for the love of God Almighty. And therefore, if any objection should be raised against this petition before any spiritual or temporal judge, and if the case should go against this same John, then he hereby appeals against it directly to the righteousness of God and his liege lord, for he has the greatest suspicions of other judges in this matter, on account of the great wrongs he has suffered, fearing to suffer further. He therefore utterly rejects them, and submits entirely to yourself.

He pleads each and every part of this before you, and seeks only justice, for the love of God.

• • •

From Cardinal Beaufort to E.L.B. and his reply.

July 1433.

English.

My most high, noble and mighty Lord, I seek your gracious lordship's favour, as humbly as I know how; wishing (for which I will be most grateful) to hear confirmation of your continuing good fortune and material prosperity, both of which I pray that God will always manage and preserve according to his own will and pleasure, as you yourself would wish.

I acknowledge to your lordship that I have been honoured to receive your letters, in which you command that I look into certain shops which your squire, Thomas Christopher, manages in Calais, and ensure that they are being rented out as profitably as possible. I shall execute this order, as all others within the limits of what is possible, with the utmost diligence by God's Grace, so that I hope your lordship will be pleased with the result; and if there is any other matter that you can think of, there or elsewhere, to command, your servant will always be ready to obey your noble orders, to the limit of my power.

It is my intention, by the Grace of God, to go from here to Calais next Friday, and as soon as I have got there, either to ride out myself or send an agent to my lord the Regent of France, to sue for restitution of my ship, that was recently captured while leased to the king; and I beseech your good and gracious lordship that you write to the said Regent in support of my case, to bring it forward.

Furthermore, my Lord, a good friend of mine, Richard Chichester, a clerk in orders with my Lord the Bishop of Exeter, has recently received the living of a church in the diocese of Exeter, called Littletory, where he has been inducted, and has taken possession. This church is in your giving, as the Clerk of the Rolls has certified to you, by a warrant under seal. I beseech you therefore, that your lordship will grant a ratification to the said Richard, to confirm his title to that church.

My most high, mighty and noble lord, I pray to the Blessed Trinity to retain you in His holy keeping, and to grant you a very long and good life.

H. Wre

• • •

Most dear and well-beloved Cousin, we send best greetings.

This is to let you know that we have sent you a letter to present to my Lord of Bedford; which please take to him, or arrange to have taken to him, at your own discretion. We have also sent you an ampoule (sacramental flask) which we ask you to recommend personally to my lord, and bring to him in our name.

Nothing else now; but may Almighty God look after you, and bring you yet greater honour.

E.L.B.

• • • • •

The following plea from the elderly and impoverished vicar of Bersted, Sussex, illustrates that although many of the larger churches were extremely well endowed there were a great number of smaller ones desperately trying to make ends meet. The decay he speaks of presumably meant he was unable to procure an adequate income from his tenants, at least not one which could meet his expenses or provide him with a living, the church's value as a benefice was consequently reduced. He asks that his income be suitably increased no doubt so that he could end his days at Bersted free from financial burdens. The church had been erected in 1400 and the tomb of Sir John Hotham,

Knight, who founded the town of Bognor, can still be found in the churchyard.

• • •

From the Vicar of Bersted to the Prior of Christ Church Canterbury.

1465.

English.

To the Right Reverend and Worshipful father in God, the Prior of Christchurch in Canterbury.

Your poor chaplain and orator [offerer of prayers], Thomas Walton, Vicar of the parish church of Bersted, humbly petitions you, because the parish has over a long period sunk into decay, and is for various reasons greatly impoverished, to such an extent that two or three properties in various parts of the parish, that used to be worth twenty shillings a year to the vicar, are standing empty and are not worth three and fourpence to him now.

What with the costs of repair and other charges to the vicarage, costs and wages in food, drink and clothing for his servant, coming to forty shillings a year, and then the costs levied by the Dean at the time of the annual visitation, and when all the other charges on this church are clearly accounted for and added on, what remains from the value of the living amounts to barely five marks a year. When he used to have the Chapel in Bognor as well, undivided, and served there by himself, he had enough to live on, but then he had to sing Mass twice daily, which was against his conscience; but since it has been divided between himself and the Chantry Priest from Pagham, by the activity and great influence of Master John, Dean of Pagham, your said poor chaplain and orator has been plunged into poverty and great distress.

Could your most gracious lordship therefore provide me a sufficient living for the church at Bersted, so that I may cease to work at Bognor, and remain in my great age and debility at Bersted, from charity, and for the love of God.

• • • • •

This letter provides an interesting mixture of information and illustrates the diverse concerns of the Prior of Christ Church at this time.

• • •

From the Prior of St Mary's Coventry to the Prior of Christ Church. c. 1474. English.

To the right worshipful and reverend Father in God the Prior of Christchurch in Canterbury.

Most honourable and reverend father in God, I seek your favour, and confirm that I have examined the miracle that was proclaimed in this district, and which you sent me to enquire into on behalf of Sir William Catesby. And to certify that I have examined it, I send it to you under the seal of a notary as well as my own. And to verify it yet further, the same person whom you saw at Canterbury about the same miracle intends, by the Grace of God, to be there again with you by next Michaelmas, to verify and testify to it.

Moreover, father, the said Sir William Catesby has informed me that you expressed great surprise, sometime of Oxford, I understand, at the dismissal of a brother of mine [i.e., a monk]. This is the truth of the matter: Mr Richard Blake, being at that time at Oxford, and whom I suppose you knew, having made his home at our monastery, applied for an appointment without my knowing of it, though his conversation was neither virtuous nor good, and he encouraged the same in others. And when I became aware of this, I urged him in the other direction, but he wanted to place conditions on his compliance, with which I was not prepared to agree. I knew what his condition was, now that he had obtained an appointment so without hurt to my conscience and by advice, seeing that he was assured of an annual stipend, I dismissed him from my congregation.

If he has given you any other discreditable account, I ask you urgently to let me have it in writing, so that I can answer it; and once the truth is out, I trust that no fault will be found with me.

May the Grace of Jesus always have you in his most blessed keeping.

Written at Coventry, the last day of June.

Thomas, Prior of the Cathedral Church of Our Lady of Coventry.

• • • • •

The use of a letter as a substitute for a personal appearance is demonstrated by the case of the French bishop. The fact that messengers were employed to convey information by word of mouth as well as letters is amply illustrated by Louis XI's request for a token of St Thomas à Becket which he could wear in his hat whilst praying, this was passed from Louis XI to the Prior's messenger, who in turn told the London correspondent who then wrote to the Prior. Apparently the French King wore a badge of the virgin whilst performing his devotions to her, but the London correspondent's tone suggests that he found the request a little peculiar.

The Prior is told that Doctor Langton was 'not verry merry in his sperytts' even though he had recently been granted the treasurership of the Cathedral Church at Exeter. Maybe he would have been more cheerful if he could have known how swiftly he was to rise in influence – four years later he gained the coveted benefice of All Hallows, Lombard Street (mentioned later), next year the Bishopric of St David's, in another two years he was promoted to that of Salisbury and finally in 1493, became Bishop of Winchester.

The wine mentioned is a reference to the annual gift of sixteen thousand gallons to the monks of Christ Church. This gesture had originated with King Louis VII who had visited the tomb of St Thomas; it had been continued by successive kings of France until the time of Phillipe of Valois when England and France were at war. Louis XI not only reintroduced the gift but ordered that it should be of a superior quality, probably due to the influence of Langton, who is described here supervising its arrival.

• • •

From a London Correspondent to Prior Sellyng at Canterbury.

1478.

English.

Be these letters delivered to my sole and special good Lord of Christ's Church of Canterbury.

With all proper respects, may it please your Lordship to know that I have spoken with the French bishop at Westminster, who cannot be with you this Easter, but will send you a letter by his own man; and he will be with you before he goes over the sea; and intends to join your chapter as a brother; but as for a pipe of wine, he would not take one from you for his bishoprick. Also, sir, there is a man of his, the same who took your letters and the copy of your letters patent to the King of France, who said to me that the King of France had asked if he could have a token [badge] of St Thomas sent to him from your lordship's generosity, that he could wear in his hat while worshipping St Thomas, which would please him greatly. What should be done about this I leave to your lordship.

As for Master Salinger, he had gone from London before I came; also, when I learned that Dr Langton had left the King, I made haste to speak to him, and found with the Master of the Rolls. I completed my errand with the Master of the Rolls, incidentally, it seemed to me that Dr Langton was not in very good spirits, When I asked him various questions about what I should do next, he said that he was sorry that you had lost so much of your wine, and he neither could nor would want any from you; notwithstanding that, I heard him say that the Bishop of Exeter, to whom he is much in debt because he gave him a benefice of a hundred Marks, wanted Master Langton to buy him two hogsheads of claret, to which I heard Master Langton say that he wished he knew where he might obtain good claret for him, as long as he was paid for it. What is to be done about this I leave to your lordship.

Also, as I understood that he was without a horse, I have made so bold with your lordship as to lend my own horse to him to bring him to Canterbury, instead of the horse that he intended to borrow in London, and I promised that he would be brought home again at your lordship's charge, and he was very pleased with that. Also, sir, I have word from your man Kyngg that the King will pay only £6 for a tun. I have not yet spoken to my lord of Norwich, nor with any of the other lords, as I was staying with Dr Langton to attend to the delivery of the wine. Also my Lord Howard set sail before Dr Langton, as he can tell you.

May Blessed God keep your lordship.

Written in haste without a secretary.

• • • • •

Canterbury College, Oxford, later part of Christ Church College, was founded by Archbishop Simon Islip in 1362 with the aim of encouraging scholarship among the clergy. The undergraduates consisted of Benedictine monks and secular clerks.

Richard Sellyng the writer of the next letter seems to have been aware, or maybe he was told by his friends at All Souls (founded in 1434) that 'training in law, generally common or civil law or both, was the golden road to the rich cathedral'. Once the cleric had obtained his degree in law, service in diocesan administration, if possible that of Canterbury, was the most obvious road to profit, and, for the more able or the more fortunate few, to bishoprics. On his return to Canterbury, Richard was appointed Chancellor of the monastery and as 'this office demanded some little proficiency in legal knowledge', we may infer that the Prior granted the request so passionately urged in the letter.

• • •

From Richard Sellyng of Canterbury College Oxford to the Prior of Christ Church Canterbury.

c. 1480.

English.

Be this delivered to his most reverend in Christ and the Father, the Prior of Christ Church Canterbury.

Most reverend father in Christ, I seek your favour with all due obedience. And since I understand that you have been informed that I have made application in writing to my Lord the Bishop of Norwich, he having made representations to you that I should go into Law, I certify to your Fatherhood that I never sent any letter to him, on that account or any other. Moreover, I never applied to him on any account, except by this means: I opened my heart to a certain kinsman of his, named Master John Playforde, Fellow of All Souls College, who often visits me, showing him the loss and small profit that I had in (the Liberal) Arts; showing him also what an urgent desire I had to go into Law, for the salvation of my own honour; and it may be because of this he has solicited my Lord of Norwich to help me achieve my heart's desire. I used no other means.

Nevertheless, though it be the case that I never applied, nor dared to apply, to him, to use such means on my behalf, yet my heart's desire for this Faculty is never reduced, and only because I can see that I gain little or no profit from the Arts course, which, if I continue with it, will bring about my great dishonour, and I am in utter despair over it. Therefore I beseech your good Fatherhood, in whom under God and the Holy Saints is my whole and only trust, that it may please your Fatherhood to transfer me to Law as soon as your Fatherhood pleases.

I have had, for which I thank your Fatherhood, a long trial in Arts, and the time has been wasted, which it saddens may heart to think of, and my only comfort is to reflect, that if it pleases you to let me go into Law, that such small crumbs as I have gathered in Arts will feed me a little in Law. And if it shall please your fatherhood to transfer me into Law I shall by God's help apply such labour and diligence to get it, that people will have no reason to say that I wanted to go into Law to conceal my truancy from my Fellowship. I shall, as near as I can, recover in Law such time as I have lost in Arts, by the Grace of God; may He ever preserve and keep you. Amen.

At Oxford the fourteenth day of July.

Your child of obedience and novice,

R. Sellyng.

• • • • •

In 1473 Marsilio Ficino became a priest and this letter illustrates his belief that a priest was God's representative on Earth and had to live a life worthy of this honour. Ficino later became a Canon of Florence Cathedral and his sermons were extremely popular. He strove to show how the dignity of the priest was reflected by his outward behaviour in the same way that an individual's conduct should be a credit to the inherent dignity of man.

• • •

From Marsilio Ficino to the Priest Pace, Professor of Canonical Law.

Before 1499.

Latin.

The dignity of the priest

Marsilio Ficino to the Prest Pace, Professor of Canonical Law: greetings.

Riccardo Angiolieri, the distinguished theologian, and I often discussed together the dignity of the priest. We concluded at last that, just as after God nothing is more virtuous than a good angel, and nothing more pernicious than an evil one, so nothing on earth is fairer than an honourable priest, and nothing more disgraceful than a base one. The former is the salvation of religion and mankind, the latter their destruction. What is a real priest, but a soul dedicated to God? An angel of God standing in God's place, performing His work amongst men; His living temple. One who has rightly considered the dignity of the priesthood will not abuse it Let us, therefore, consider what it is to be a real priest. It is surely almost to be God. A priest is a king of temporal God, but God is priest eternal.

• • • • •

The following document concerns the procurement of a benefice and an extremely valuable one at that.

A Church was a benefice (or a great church a collection of benefices) which its holder regarded as a freehold to be financially exploited as well as spiritually served - a legal independence and an attitude of mind which made it extremely difficult for ecclesiastical superiors to maintain a salutary discipline. (Lander p.64).

All Hallows, Lombard Street was situated in a very wealthy area of the city, devoted to commerce and inhabited by merchants and bankers which would make the real value of the benefice something more to be coveted than the bare sum to which the tithes amounted (Sheppard, p.36). The benefice had become vacant upon the death of the Rector Marcus Husee, and the Queen asks the Prior to send her 'the presentation under your convente seale of the said benefice, with a blanke space in the same'.

Richard Southayke became the next Rector of All Hallows and it was most likely his name which was inserted in the presentation. However, benefices were commonly held by secular persons and even those held by priests meant that the parish in question often experienced a great deal of absenteeism and neglect. Important benefices were given as favours or payment by the state or papacy, and the letter concerning the Bishop of Chichester reveals his dual role of senior civil servant. Men of his standing were almost permanently absent from their sees and their responsibilities placed in the hands of deputies.

• • •

From Elizabeth, Queen of Henry VII, to the Prior of Christ Church Canterbury.

6 June 1499.

English.

To our Right trusty and well beloved in God the Prior of the monastery of Christ's Church at Canterbury.

Right trusty and well beloved in God, we greet you well, and as we recently in other letters desired you to grant unto us the living of the parish church of All Saints in Lombard Street in my Lord's city of London, whenever it should fall vacant through the death of Sir Marques Husy, the late incumbent; whereupon it pleased you, out of your living and kindly heart, to grant us freedom of the said benefice in writing, to nominate for it whichever of our chaplains we should choose at its next vacancy, for which we heartily thank you: we have been informed that it is now the case, the said Sir Marques being recently departed out of this transitory life into the mercy of God, so that the said benefice is now vacant.

We therefore request and require you, that in honouring the said promise, you shall send us under your usual seal the giving of the said benefice, with a blank space on it, with the intention that we shall enter the name of whichever of our chaplains we will think able and suitable to have charge of the curacy there. We sincerely trust that you will effect this desire of ours, whereby you will greatly deserve our special thanks, to be recalled in connection with any reasonable desires of your own concerning your well-being or that of your office in time to come.

Given under our signet at my Lord's city of London the sixth day of June.

LAW AND ORDER

During the Middle Ages the function of the Church was to ensure that men and women obeyed God's law, while it was the task of kings to administer justice. The following letters reveal the diversity of law enforcement and law-breaking which were dominated by the omnipotence of God's law and the inevitability of the final judgement, all men were to be treated equally regardless of their standing on earth. The law of God, therefore, was the only certainty, the only permanent force in a period of dramatic change and development.

Medieval canon law, the law of the Christian Church in Europe, delineated the responsibilities of the clergy and concerned itself with the moral welfare of all Christians. Canon law was enforced through ecclesiastical tribunals and it became increasingly important that churchmen possessed a good knowledge of its precepts. By the early twelfth century canon law was being taught at Bologna, which had been the centre of classical, Roman law studies since the eleventh century. Consequently canon law incorporated many ideas from Roman law, especially in terms of the value of written law and the systematization of judicial procedure. It was through canon law that the influence of Roman law made itself felt in most European legal systems.

The study of Roman law helped satisfy the growing demand for trained administrators and judges. It was also applied to circumstances which had no legislative precedents such as commerce.

Important as Roman law was as an ingredient in promoting the authority of the secular prince, it was more influential in providing a clear and systematic procedure by which judges and lawyers could be guided in the welter of confused custom which passed for law.

In England in the mid twelfth century a school of Roman law was established at Oxford. It prompted the codifying and organization of English local custom as common law which was administered by royal courts for the entire country. Roman law also encouraged the opinion that ownership of property was an absolute right and many changes in secular law emerged from the need to establish rights to land.

The judicial system in England was centralized soon after the Norman Conquest with the establishment of the King's Court. This restricted the powers of local customary courts since serious crimes were now dealt with by royal judges travelling around the country 'on circuit'. So common law usurped customary law. During Henry II's reign a basic jury system was developed which was to become an essential feature of most European legal systems and by the late thirteenth century the office of judge had become a profession in its own right; legal training was concentrated at the Inns of Court in London. However, The Wars of the Roses led to the collapse of the English legal system, the king's judges had little impact when faced with powerful lords and private armies, corruption was rife and despite efforts to consolidate English law few advances were made. Nevertheless, by the end of the century 'England and Wales had an elaborate and workable system of judicial bureaucracy.' (Post, p.149).

Despite the development of legal systems throughout our period law enforcement and the nature of crime remained primitive. Kings placed the responsibility of capturing criminals and maintaining law and order with each locality, and heavy fines were used to punish members of a community harbouring an offender. A letter expressing Henry VII's concern about murders in Lincolnshire shows that this method was not entirely effective.

Trial by ordeal and battle remained common practice until the early thirteenth century, when the Church's dissaproval led to their abolition, with solid evidence and fact coming to be relied upon rather than divine intervention. Death was the penalty for crimes such as murder, high treason, blasphemy and heresy; mutilation was frequently imposed on thieves. Imprisonment became more widespread, but the use of fines as a punishment prevented the number of prisoners escalating to an uncontrollable level and provided the Crown with a substantial income, as did the granting of pardons, to the extent that profit became an additional impetus to law enforcement.

Many medieval punishments involved public spectacle to a greater or lesser extent, whether it be an execution or a day in the pillory. This hardly acted as a deterrent but made it quite plain that crime and sin were unacceptable, both legally and morally.

The following letters reveal some personal reactions to lawbreaking, judicial procedure and/or punishment, by individuals involved in upholding the law and breaking it.

The Archdeacon of Gloucester had asked the Bishop of London's advice concerning a woman who was accused of adultery. Usually the accused was put on oath, but under threat from her husband the woman in question had promised to suffer the ordeal of red-hot metal. Since the woman was only suspected of adultery, rather than caught in the act, the Bishop of London considers that the oath 'will suffice'; promises made 'under duress' should never be accepted.

• • •

From Gilbert Foliot, Bishop of London to Matthew, Archdeacon of Gloucester.

1163-77.

Latin.

To Matthew, Archdeacon of Gloucester, greetings.

This is the question that you have expressed, to which you ask for an opinion: whether you should admit the woman whom it concerns to the oath, as has been adjudged to her, or whether you ought legally to permit the red-hot iron plate to be carried as she promised to her husband under threat of death. Various cases often arise, and a woman is sometimes caught in the act, and is sometimes supposed guilty though not so caught but suspected. The Law of Moses had the woman who was caught in the act stoned, but the law of jealousy put the suspected woman to the test The suspected woman drank the bitter waters in which the priest had compounded accursed things, but these did not harm the innocent though they burst the guilty asunder on the spot. The Roman Law punished the adulterer and the adulteress, and threatened many kinds of penalties against wretched mortals whose condition is dubious. Thanks be to the Lord Jesus who, making all things new, has changed them for the better, and has tempered the hard and bitter things of the law by mixing in the Waters of Bitterness the Wood of the Cross; he freed the woman who had been caught in the act and brought before him as guilty of the crime, and changed the hard stones of the Law into those other stones of which it was said: 'Because his stones have pleased thy servants'. For these are our stones: the admonition and reproof of the sinner, and calling her to tears, to groans, to confession and to making up for the offence in all ways. The adulteress is well stoned with these, when she dies to sin, receiving inner life from him who said: 'Neither do I condemn you; go, and sin no more.' From the death of the soul, which she had incurred, she is raised to newness of life. There is no doubt that when a good man sees his wife being stoned in this way, he himself must die along with her, weep with her when she mourns, be generous so that the penitent may have to hand the means to remedy her necessities while redeeming the sin from the sufferer, so that the two may be found not only in one flesh, but also in one spirit. If she is only suspected, then to destroy suspicion and reconcile her in peace with her husband, the appropriate oath will suffice, since Paul declares that an oath is the end of all dispute.

For if she promised anything under duress, let it never happen that an ecclesiastical judge should accept it, when he is aware that secular judges reject it. For that which is done or said because of force or fear has no validity, and according to Pope Alexander, if anything is extorted from someone by force, fear or fraud, it counts for nothing to their prejudice or harm.

Farewell.

• • • • •

William of York began his career as a clerk at the court of Henry III, and in 1226 he accompanied Martin de Pateshull, the Chief Justice, on the second eyre of the king's reign. The eyre was a circuit by judges from Westminster who attemped to assert royal control throughout the country. They visited each county, accompanied by administrators, and reviewed all the local crime which had occurred since the last visit. William of York later became a senior justice and Bishop of Salisbury in 1246.

In William's letters to his patron the Chancellor, Ralph Neville, he complains of travelling to remote areas and the heavy duties that working for the diligent Martin de Pateshull implied. The first letter was written at the end of an eyre in Lincolnshire, when it had been proposed that this particular circuit would continue to Yorkshire, Northumberland, Cumberland, Westmorland and Lancashire but William was eager to visit his recently acquired living at Kirk Deighton and reluctant to accompany Pateshull further north. A dispensation was required in order to hold two livings, William already held that of King's Ripton in Huntingdonshire. William Ralege was a fellow clerk whose career followed a similar path to that of William of York, becoming a senior justice and then obtaining a bishopric.

The various eyres took longer than had been anticipated and in the following August William again writes to Ralph Neville, trying to excuse himself from the impending visit to Cumberland; he did go in fact but as a justice in his own right. William's domestic concerns, combined with fears of civil war and requests for gossip provide an insight into his day-to-day concerns and the general isolation and weariness of life on the judicial circuit. After the death of Henry III the eyre system disintegrated and quarterly sessions were established.

• • •

From William of York to the Chancellor Ralph Neville.

1226-7.

Latin.

1 October 1226.

My Lord, please let me, your devoted servant, know by return of messenger if you want me to go on eyre with Martin of Pateshull farther than to Yorkshire. If I do go farther with him it will be a great nuisance, because of the heavy expense and enormous labour, for Martin works from sunrise to nightfall and has worn out all his fellows, above all William of Ralege and myself. Don't doubt, however, that I am ready to obey your command, even to my own cost and hurt. Your excellency might like to know that I've recently been presented to a living in Yorkshire, which suits me very well since it is near to another of my rents. The Archbishop has just committed it to my custody: he estimates its value at £20 a year. I'd like your advice about getting a dispensation for it, since I intend to send to Rome about it this Christmas. Long may you flourish.

2 August 1227.

My Lord, I implore you to arrange that I do not have to go on eyre in Cumberland. It would mean a long journey and the climate there disagrees with my constitution. I have discussed it with the Bishop of Carlisle [Walter Mauclerk] and told him that I won't go, even if I have a royal mandate, unless I get a special order from you. If the eyres are beginning again, and if you want me to go on them, please let me go to Cambridge and Huntingdon, with a grant for expenses. I've got a good store of provisions in that district. If there are any fresh troubles, please let me know by letter if I ought to return to Court or to await better times in my home country, at Scarborough or Knaresborough castles or on one of my rents. For God's sake don't forget to tell me how things go with you and the Court. Long may you flourish. If you have to stay in London and war breaks out, there are three casks of wine at my lodgings, near yours, which you can have. Again goodbye.

• • • • •

The Mayor and sheriffs of London had been delegated the responsibility of maintaining law and order during Edward III's absence. The king writes to commend them on the prompt execution of two offenders and urges them to imprison any other criminals or trouble-makers. Enforcing the law and arresting offenders was an onerous task, especially when rioting and large scale affray were at hand.

• • •

From King Edward III, commending Andrew Aubrey, the Mayor, for his prompt execution of two offenders, in Chepe.

6 December 1340 (Ghent).

Probably French.

Edward, by the grace of God, King of England and of France, and Lord of Ireland, to our well-beloved, the Mayor, Aldermen, Sheriffs, and Commons, of our city of London, greeting.

We do remember how, before our first passage to the parts beyond sea, you did undertake in our presence the keeping of our said city at all risks; and thereupon we did strictly charge you, that you should inflict punishment upon misdoers and disturbers of our peace in our said city, if any such should there be found; and we since have heard that there has been a conflict in our said city between the Pelterers and the Fishmongers thereof; to put an end to the which conflict, and appease the same, you, the aforesaid Mayor and Sheriffs, together with other our servants of our said city, did attach some of the misdoers; against the which attachment arose other misdoers, and rescued them, and upon you, the aforesaid Mayor and Sheriffs, and other our servants, made assault. And that one Thomas, son of John Haunsard, fishmonger, with his sword drawn, seized you, the aforesaid Mayor, by the throat, and would have struck you on the neck, if he had been able; and one John le Brewere, a porter, wounded one of our serjeants of our said city, so greatly that his life was despaired of; in contempt of us, and in great affray of the good folks of our said city: by reason whereof, the aforesaid Thomas and John were forthwith taken and brought to the Guildhall and there before you of their violence and excess were arraigned, and thereof by their own admission convicted; and by your award were condemned to death, and beheaded in Chepe. Wherefore we do signify unto you, that upon what has been so done to the said misdoers, to the punishment of the bad, and to the comforting of the good, we do greatly congratulate you; and your doing therein do accept, and so much as in us lies, do ratify the same. And we do let you know for certain, that contempts and outrages so committed against our servants, we do hold as being committed against ourselves: and if you had not acted in such manner therein, we should have taken the same so grievously as towards yourselves and the franchise of our said city, that it would have been for an example to you, and to all your successors in time to come. We do therefore command and charge you, that if any one in our said city by the good folks thereof, or by good inquisition, shall be found to be a maintainer or abettor thereof, or to menace you or other our servants, or any other person of the commonalty, or to excite others among the people to make riot or conflict in our said city, in disturbance of the peace, either for the reason aforesaid, or for any other reason, to the offence of our royal dignity, you will cause him to be taken, and in our prison safely kept, until you shall have other commands from us thereon. And this you are in no manner to omit. Given under our Privy Seal, at Ghent, the 6th day of December, in the 14th year of our reign in England, and in France the first.

• • • • •

The royal courts dealt with civil cases by means of writs, in the king's name, which ordered the defendant to appear and face charges. Different types of writ were used for particular complaints, and they had become vital in proving land ownership since the reign of Henry II.

• • •

From Philippa of Hainault, Queen of Edward III, to Sir John de Edington, her attorney.

14 May 1354.

French.

Philippa, by the grace of God Queen of England, Lady of Ireland, and Duchess of Aquitaine, to our dear clerk Sir John de Edington, our attorney in the exchequer of our very dear lord the king, sends greeting.

We command you, that you cause all the writs which have been filed from the search lately made by Sir Richard de Cressevill to be postponed until the octaves of Easter next ensuing; to the end that, in the meantime, we and our council may be able to be advised which of the said writs are to be put in execution for our profit, and which of them are to cease to the relief of our people, to save our conscience. And we will that this letter be your warrant therefore.

Given under our privy seal, at Westminster, the 14th day of May, in the year of the reign of our very dear lord the king of England the twenty-eighth.

• • • • •

Imprisonment had long been used for custodial purposes but it was not until the thirteenth century that it became a form of punishment in itself. Medieval prisons ranged from crude village cells to purpose-built town gaols and castle dungeons. A prisoner's quality of life depended largely on his status, since he was expected to support himself; an affluent prisoner would at least avoid starvation and possibly manage to secure his release by bribing the gaoler or purchasing a pardon, the poor could do little more than depend on alms to relieve their needs and pray for a rapid end to their confinement.

The following supplication to King Henry IV illustrates the situation whereby:

If the King chose, for whatever reason that might come into his head, to pardon someone, there was in principle nobody who could quarrel with him. (McCall, p 80).

The King was viewed as the earthly overseer of God's law and technically irreproachable.

Johanna de Kynnesley writes that her husband has 'long lain' within the walls of the castle; sentences varied from a few days to several years, although many captives died from disease or malnutrition during their incarceration.

• • •

From Joanna de Kynnesley to King Henry IV.

1399-1413.

French.

To our most excellent and most redoubted lord the king.

Supplicates most humbly a poor and simple woman, Joanna de Kynnesley; that whereas John de Kynnesley, her husband, by hate and malice, was put in prison within the castle of Norwich, where he has long lain through false suggestions, that it would please your most gracious lordship, for the love of God, and for the souls of your most noble father and mother, whom God assoil, to grant and give to your said suppliant your gracious letters, sealed under your seal, made in due form, directed to the sheriff of the county of Norfolk, charging and straitly commanding him to deliver up the body of the said John out of prison, that he may go at large, to answer before your royalty, in case any one should accuse him; and she will pray God for you and for your progenitors for ever.

• • • • •

During the fifteenth century piracy was a constant problem for coastal Europe, but it was particularly rife during the 1440s and 1450s. In some areas of England, notably the West Country, it was aided and abetted by men of standing, and most ports had either sufferred or benefited from piracy. It posed a threat to merchants, was the bane of customs officials and a source of friction between England and its neighbours. Nevertheless, 'in an age where any successful law enforcement was largely a matter of chance, the elusive mobility of shipping made it virtually immune to arrest.'

• • •

From Agnes Paston to her son John Paston.

12 March 1450.

English.

To John Paston, dwelling in the Inner Inn of the Temple, at London, be this Letter delivered in haste.

Son, I greet you, and send God's blessing and mine; as for my daughter your wife she fareth well, blessed be God! as a woman in her plight may do, and all your Sons and Daughters.

And for as much as ye will send me no tidings, I send you such as be in this Country; Richard Lynsted came this day from Paston and let me weet, that on Saturday last past, Dravell, half-brother to Warren Harman, was taken with enemies, walking by the Sea side, and have him forth with them, and they took two Pilgrims, a man and a woman, and they robbed the woman and let her go, and led the man to the Sea; and when they knew he was a Pilgrim they gave him money, and set him again on the land; and they have this week taken four vessels of Winterton, and Happisborough and Eccles.

Men be sore afraid for taking of men, for there be ten great Vessels of the Enemy's; God give grace that the sea may be better kept than it is now, or else it shall be a perilous dwelling by the sea coast.

I pray you greet well your brethren, and say them that I send them God's blessing and mine, and say William that if Janet Lauton be not paid for the Crimson Coat which Alson Crane wrote to her for in her own name, that then he pay her, and see Alson Crane's name stricken out of her book, for she saith she will ask no man the money but Alson Crane. And I pray you that ye will remember the Letter that I sent you last, and God be with you.

Written at Norwich, the Wednesday next before Saint Gregory

(12th March).

By your Mother, Agnes Paston.

• • • • •

Not only were requests for pardons directed to the King but also to other members of the royal family who were felt to possess influence. This example, conveying genuine despair, was written by the prisoner herself rather than by a friend or relation.

Lord Abergavenny, Edward Neville, sixth son of Ralph Earl of Westmorland, had been a fervent Lancastrian and his quarrel with the petitioner probably originated in political persecution.

• • •

From Joanna Conway to Cecilia Duchess of York.

1461+ ?

English.

To the most gracious and excellent princess the Duchess of York.

Most piteously, and with incessant lamentation, complaineth unto your most gracious ladyship your continual and poor beadwoman Joanna Conway; forasmuch as she hath been long in the miserous prison of Ludgate, at the suit of the right noble lord the Lord of Abergavenny, to her confusion and mortal destruction forever, without your most *mercyable* grace be benignly to her enlarged in that behalf. Wherefore pleaseth it your most excellent gracious ladyship the premises tenderly to consider, and for the relief of your said beseecher to send of your most abundant grace to the said Lord of Abergavenny, and to will and desire him to release and withdraw all such suits as he hath willed to be done against your said beseecher, as conscience and law of God requireth. And your said beadwoman shall incessantly pray to God of his *influent* grace for to preserve your most benign and gracious estate, and to send your most royal estate many prosperous days.

• • • • •

This letter provides another instance of a Justice of the Peace being admonished for his inability to maintain order and administer the law. JPs had to answer to the royal courts which dealt with the most serious offences, and they were reprimanded when details of their negligence came to light, especially, as in this case, when trouble was caused by men under their own personal command.

• • •

From the King to the Lord Zouche.

Before 1494.

English.

By the King to the Lorde Zouche

Right trusty etc.

This is to tell you that we have been informed that one of your servants, called Nicholas B., with employees and other adherents of his, has riotously assaulted our liegeman and tenant T. W. of the county of Northampton, and hurt him severely, and injured one of his employees, called N. and does them further injury every day, in breach of our law and peace in our said county. And, in as much as you are our Justice of the Peace in the said county, whose business is to prevent such anarchic and riotous behaviour, especially among people under your control, we are therefore writing to you now, asking you, and also charging you that, according to your duty in this regard, you order and see to it that the said B. and his employees observe our peace with the said T. and his employees. And henceforth, for their greater security, you bind over the said B. and his servants, in whatever amount is suitable, to keep our peace with our people, and especially with the said T. And we trust you not to fail in this.

Given etc.

• • • • •

This letter of reproof from Queen Margaret of Anjou, addressed to John Forester, lists the accusations the people of Hertingfordbury Manor had filed against him. The Queen orders him to desist from persecuting and wrongfully imprisoning her tenants and to allow those that had fled through fear of harassment to return to their homes. Forester's abuse of his role as Justice of the Peace will be forgiven if he puts an end to this intimidation and the Queen assures him that any legitimate offenders will be dealt with accordingly.

• • •

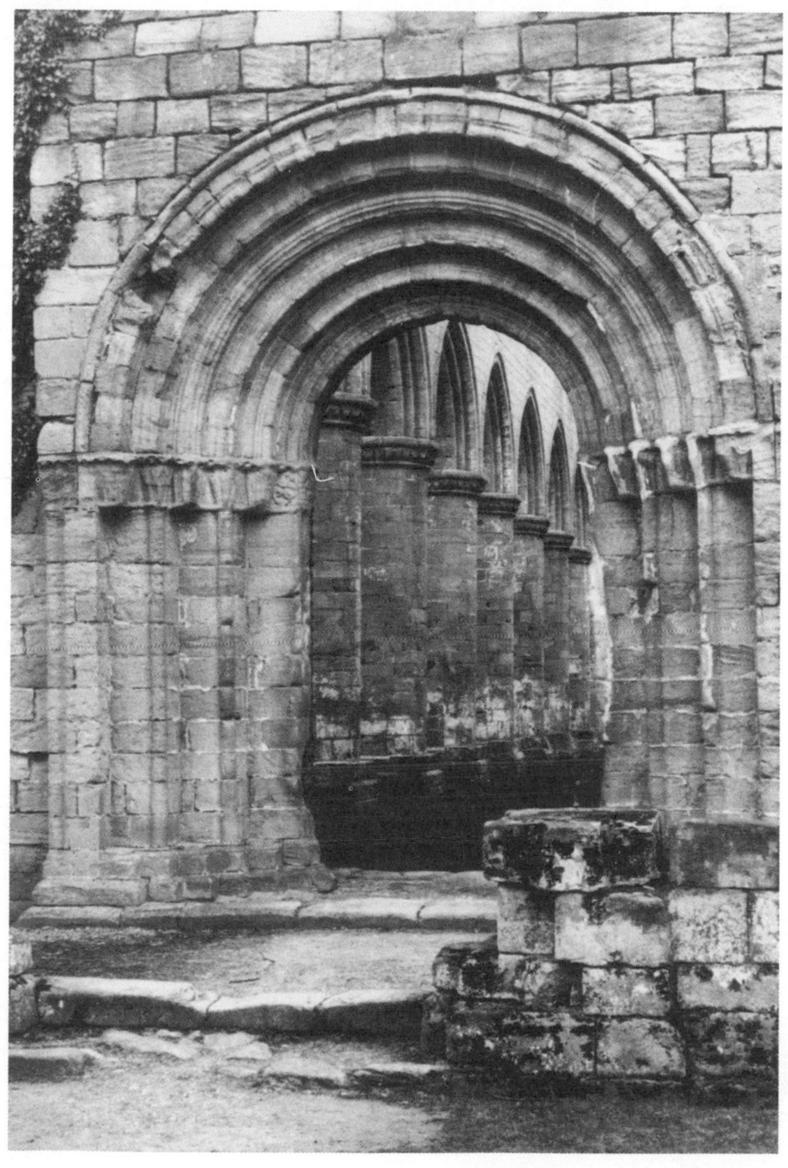

FOUNTAINS ABBEY, YORKSHIRE
Its foundation as a rigorous alternative to the more lax St.Mary's, York, led in 1133 to an involved correspondence between Geoffrey, Abbot of St.Mary's and St.Bernard of Clairvaux.

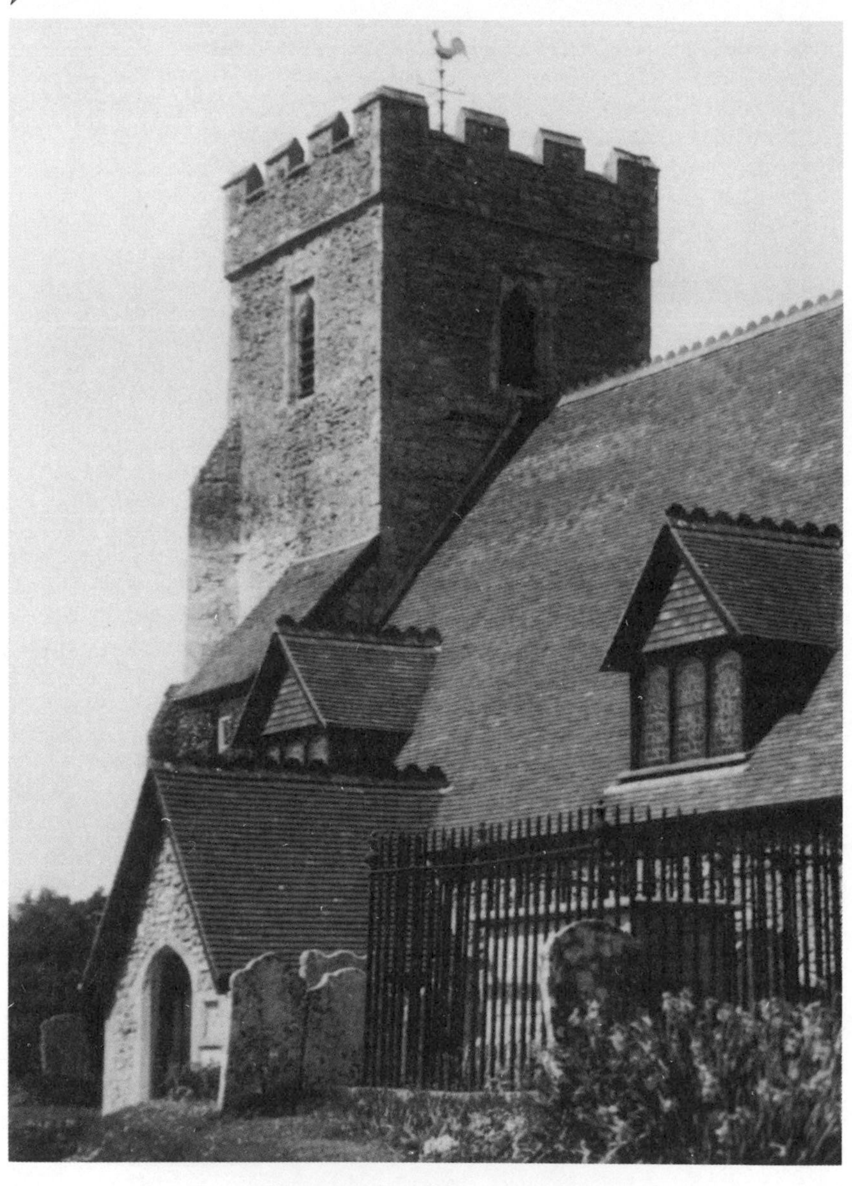

MUNDEHAM CHURCH, SUSSEX
Its bigamous vicar was the subject of a series of letters between Simon de Senlis and the Bishop of Chichester, around 1220.

QUEEN ELEANOR OF CASTILE
Wife of Edward I, who was the recipient of a sorrowful petition from the nuns of St.Mary's, Chester, in 1253.

BERSTED CHURCH, ESSEX
In 1465, Thomas Walton, its priest, found it against his conscience to sing Mass twice daily, and wrote to the Prior of Canterbury to say so.

CHESTER CATHEDRAL
When still Chester Abbey in the 1360's, it suffered from the rapacious misrule of the Prior Seynesbury, whose career of escapades and outrages in the Northwest led to a dispairing correspondence with the Prince of Wales.

HENRY IV

He received complaints from the Prioress of Rowney concerning the misdemeanors of a wayward nun who 'wanders and roams abroad from country to country, in a secular habit, despising her vows of obedience....'

QUEEN ELIZABETH
Wife of Henry VII. In 1499 she wrote to the Prior of Christ Church, Canterbury, demanding a blank letter of appointment to the benefice of All Saints, Lombard Street, so that she could appoint 'whichever of our chaplains we will think able and suitable'.

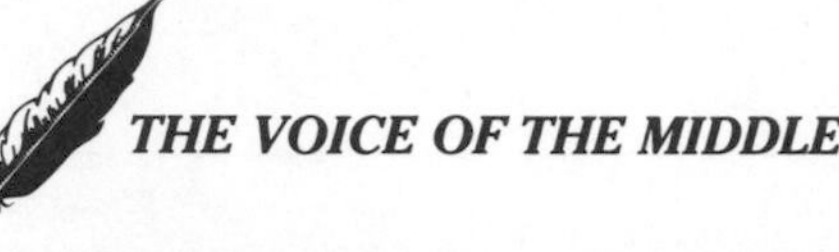

QUEEN PHILIPPA OF HAINAULT

Wife of Edward III. In 1354, she wrote to her attorney, Sir John de Edington, postponing the legal activities of Sir Richard de Cresseville.

From Queen Margaret of Anjou to Sir John Forester, Knight.
Before 1482.
English.

By the Queen to Sir John Forester

Trusty and well-beloved.

This is to tell you that today there have come before us a great number of men and women, tenants of our lordship of Hertingfordbury, complaining that you have been and still are daily setting about their destruction and permanent undoing; specifically, that you have caused many of them to be wrongfully indicted for felonies before the Coroner on the words of your own close employees and adherents, not having discovered the truth of the matter; and you have put many of them in prison, and the remainder of our tenants dare not remain in their houses for fear of death or other injuries, that you do them daily; and all on account of a farm of ours which you rent there, and that, it is said, for your own sole benefit, you wrongfully expand so that it consumes all the livelihood of our tenants; not only to the great disadvantage and undoing of our tenants, but also to the dishonour and prejudice of our lordship and ourself. We are greatly surprised by this, especially that you who are a judge should tolerate so complaisantly the destruction of our said tenants.

Therefore we wish, and expressly exhort and require, that you cease from such activities, and especially against ourselves and our said tenants, until such time that you have replied and explained yourself to us in this matter; and that meanwhile, you allow our tenants who are in prison to be released under reasonable bail; and the remainder of our tenants, who are guiltless and have fled for fear of being destroyed by yourself, may come home to our said lordship [i.e., manor]. And if any of our tenants have offended against the law, it is our intention that when the truth is known they shall be severely punished and chastised, as is justified by the circumstances. And you will advise us by the messenger that brings you this what reaction you intend to make to this, which we trust you will fulfil, if you intend in future to stand in our tender and favourable regard.

Given at Windsor etc.

• • • • •

Marsilio Ficino's letter to Angelo Niccolini, an eminent Florentine lawyer who became ambassador to Pope Innocent VIII in 1484 and King Charles VIII in 1494, acts as a reminder of the essential values the profession had to uphold. Lawyers, especially those of great influence and standing, were particularly prone to corruption through their desire for privilege and favour. Ficino overlooks the lawyer's pragmatic and worldly concerns to highlight a fundamental truth, 'justice remained an aspect of divine order, an attribute of the very harmony by which the sun and stars were moved.' (Green, p.234.)

• • •

From Marsilio Ficino to Angelo Niccolini.

Before 1499.

Latin.

The goodness and dignity of the lawyer

Marsilio Ficino to Angelo Niccolini, son of the distinguished lawyer Ottone, and the distinguished heir to the art of his father: greetings.

A painter who makes corrupt use of his art is not necessarily a bad painter because of this, but he is a bad man. Thus a good painter is not the same as a good man. This is evident, for there is a great deal of difference between goodness and painting. And the same applies to the rest of the arts. But a lawyer who makes unlawful use of the law, is both a bad lawyer and a bad man; while the upright lawyer is also an upright man and citizen. The relationship between the profession of civil law and the virtue of man is as close as this.

He who defaces a coin, a thing of very little value, dug from the bowels of the earth, is punished by human law, as you know, with the severest penalty. Thus how sternly is the man punished by divine law who corrupts the most precious law itself, which has been sent to us from heaven!

So I charge you, my Angelo, use the law lawfully. Persist in this, I beseech you. With a noble heart spurn threats and bribes; Almighty God, who is the maker and master of law and who is also its aim and reward, will not desert you. Persevere, my friend; be sure you will store up incorruptible riches with God. High also is the office of lawyer among men. He is the defender of the citizens as a whole, the general oracle of the state, and the interpreter of the divine mind and will.

Farewell. Greet your, or rather our, Renato Pazzi, a just and learned citizen.

• • • • •

King Henry VII had received complaints from the ambassadors of England's allies; instead of helping to tackle the problems caused by Danish pirates the citizens of Hull had been allowing them to land and obtain supplies as well as relieving them of some of their ill-gotten gains. The King demands an end be put to this racketeering and that any future offenders be imprisoned. The urgency of this letter suggests that the situation in Hull had caused a considerable diplomatic embarrassment.

• • •

From the King (Henry VII) to the Mayor of Hull.

Late fifteenth century.

English.

By the King to the Mayor, Excisemen and Comptroller of Hull

Trusty and well beloved, we greet you well.

And as the Danes, under cover of the affection we have for our cousin the King of Denmark, their sovereign lord, rob and plunder by sea the servants of our cousins of France, Spain and Portugal, and of other kings, princes and commonwealths with which we have allegiance and are at peace, and come into our harbours and creeks with their robberies and pillages to sell them on the dockside, and to refit and take on food and other necessaries; we, hearing daily the great representations, imprecations and complaints made to us by our allies or confederates on one side, and on the other, the requests of our own servants, because the processes of trade are greatly hindered by the pillages of the said Danes, . . . and to no small loss of our own customs and duties, with other inconveniences . . . . other hand, may equally observe . . . our treaties with the said kings, princes . . . subjects of any of our confederates, to rob or make war on the others, and . . . there must not be any such sale, nor shelter to such pirates and despoilers upon . . . will, and strictly command and charge you, that from now on you give neither help, relief, nor . . . . to any Dane who makes war by sea, or to any other robber, neither by purchasing nor bartering for any goods violently robbed from the allies or subjects of any of our friends, even though the same subjects should permit it or wish you to do so: but you take the said Danes, whenever they come up with any prizes into our harbours or creeks, and send the captains and two or three of their officers to us, to answer for it, you keeping all the ships and property of the takers and what they have taken, until such time as you shall have knowledge of our further pleasure.

And apart from this, we desire and charge you that you give no sort of supplies nor anything necessary to make war to Danish pirates nor to any other pirates or sea robbers in this connection, under the penalty that any subject of ours who buys from, barters with, supplies or aids any such sea robber makes restitution of the whole of what has been robbed, and suffers confiscation of as much of his own goods that he has gained from buying from, bartering with, supplying or aiding the pillagers, and that he himself be committed to prison, there to remain as long as we please. And that this should be more certain, cause this to be publicly known, and not dissimulated; we give and grant to whoever exposes such people half of what is forfeited, to have and enjoy himself forever.

Given under our signet, at the manor of Shene, the twenty-third day of May.

• • • • •

Henry VII had heard of some particularly gruesome murders and urges the local justices to capture the offenders swiftly and to punish them accordingly. Between the lines we detect his suspicions that not every possible effort was being made to find the murderers and that maybe some sort of cover up was in operation. The references to God's view of the affair, since when all was said and done offenders and accomplices would eventually have to face His judgement, underlines the medieval view that if the consequences of breaking the law of the land were not a satisfactory deterrent the fear of hell was sometimes more effective.

• • •

From King Henry VII.

Late fifteenth century.

English.

By the King to our trusty and well-beloved the Justices of our peace in the Parts of Lindsay within the county of Lincoln. For murders.*

Trusty and well-beloved, we greet you.

This is to let you know that it has come to our notice that certain cruel and indisputable murders have been recently committed at various places in our county of Lincoln, in the Parts of Lindsay, and

* The northern Trithing of the county of Lincolnshire.

there has been no lawful redress or punishment to be had there. Therefore, not wishing that such hateful offences should go unpunished, bearing in mind how abominable they are before the face of God, we strictly command you that you make haste to have the said murderers investigated until such time as they are found out, and having done so, you shall, without favour, affection, fear or partiality see to it that the offenders are fiercely punished, according to the severity of our laws. And if you fail to act with the utmost diligence at your command in this matter, you will be in danger of answering to God and ourselves.

Given under our signet at our city of Lincoln, the fifth day of April.

• • • • •

King Henry VII had been informed of a possible attack upon the King of the Romans on his imminent arrival in England. Henry orders that precautions be taken to detect any devious activity since, 'we shulde provide for the worst'. The towns' governors probably had enough troubles to contend with let alone scouring every inlet of the Humber for suspicious characters.

• • •

From King Henry VII to the officers 'of the Towne and Creke of Grymesby'.

Late fifteenth century.

English.

By the King to our trusty and well-beloved the officers of the town and creek of Grimsby

Trusty and well-beloved, we greet you well.

Since we are reliably informed that our cousin the King of the Romans has come to Mechlyns, or will be there: and since because if this, it is said certain rebels take heart, and noise it about, saying that in this realm of ours there are certain people who will not stay away from them for long, but go to them in haste, on hearing that the King of the Romans is coming: and since, whether what is written above is true or not, good policy holds that it is as well to prepare for the worst: we therefore require that you hold yourself in constant readiness for all sorts of vessels within your jurisdiction, and especially in the creeks and other small rivers navigable by boats or curraghs to the sea, and that no sort of suspicious persons should be permitted to pass, but arrested, and thereupon be sent to us under guard, with the appearance and grounds for suspicion against him; and we will meet your reasonable expenses in this connexion.

So do not fail in this regard, if you hope to avoid our most grievous displeasure, and such jeopardy as this may entail for yourselves.

Given under our signet, at our castle at Windsor, the twenty-first day of July.

• • • • •

The final letter in this section illustrates how very little things may change in the course of four centuries. It comes from the reign of Henry VIII and is technically beyond the scope of this book, but the events portrayed constitute a piquant sixteenth-century example of the rapacious behaviour of some members of monastic communities, which surely must have contributed to local pockets of enthusiasm for the Dissolution of the monasteries.

• • •

From Margery Clerke to Thomas Cranmer.

1526.

English.

To Thomas, Archbishop of York and Chancellor of England

It is the humble complaint of your beadswoman Margery Clerke of Cheshire, once the wife of William Clerke that, although her late husband and his ancestors had for many years enjoyed undisturbed tenancy of a property in the parish of St Werberga, at the discretion of the Abbot of St Werberga in Westchester, according to immemorial tradition, at an annual rent of forty shillings, John, the late abbot, although there had been nothing done to forfeit the tenancy and though there was no other reason, in the eighth year of the current reign sent certain of his servants to the said property and evicted from it your present petitioner, her late husband, and five small children, this being the coldest part of the winter. They were forced by necessity to go to their parish church for relief and remained there three weeks, as they had no house to stay in, until the abbot, out of his yet further malice, ordered the vicar of the church to evict them from there as well.

The same servants took all the farm stock, and they took all the furniture and household effects and threw it into a deep pond. As a result of brooding about this her husband fell into depression and shortly died.

Your petitioner has complained about this to your highness on various occasions, and your grace has appointed certain gentlemen to examine her case, and bring it to a conclusion, as their commissions direct; but the said abbot, has delayed and extended the investigation by improper means, so that the said commissioners were unable to conclude it. And now the said abbot has recently resigned from his post, and another has been elected. Your petitioner has made representations to him, but he refuses redress unless ordered to make it by the King's writ, which your beadswoman has not the ability or power to deploy against him, she being an poor woman and he a great lord in these parts, high in both rank and office.

TRADE AND TRAVEL

From the twelfth century onwards massive commercial expansion in Europe stimulated industry and technology, encouraged the development of new financial systems and initiated international cooperation. The Hanseatic League, a federation of towns established purely to protect mercantile interests, epitomized the increased power and wealth of the merchant class, and had an enormous influence on the economy of Northern Europe. Medieval towns were natural markets, being centres of merchandise and manufacturing. Trade supplied industries with raw materials and distributed the end product, and became increasingly organized throughout the period, with traditional methods of exchange and distribution, such as fairs, declining as towns came to monopolize commerce. Foodstuffs were primary commodities, particularly grain, salt and wines, whilst textiles were the most important manufacturing industries of the Middle Ages.

Trade contracted after the Black Death and became more specialized, the affluence of royal courts and leading churchmen creating a market for luxury goods which made a significant contribution to the medieval economy. Rich fabrics, jewels and exotic foods were the most obvious means of manifesting wealth.

The traffic on medieval roads was heavy; in addition to local movement national and international commerce passed, by means of pack horses or carts, along the highways, which were generally in poor condition despite sporadic efforts to repair them by local landowners or the clergy. The road system of Europe, despite its failings, managed to remain in working order and the building of stone bridges where the Romans had sufficed with fords, indicated the commercial and civil nature of medieval traffic as opposed to military.

Alongside merchants, crowds of pilgrims, messengers, itinerant craftsmen, wandering students, preachers, pedlars and churchmen on ecclesiastical and legal business contributed to the density of road users in the Middle Ages. Thieves regularly attacked travellers on roads especially in remote areas. Only the foolish journeyed during the night, the nobility and ruling classes stopped at castles, the middle classes at inns and the remainder at monasteries and guesthouses if room could be found to accommodate them.

Large quantities of raw materials were transported on water

routes, which usually worked out considerably cheaper than by land, as many important towns grew up alongside rivers and sea coasts. Improvements in ship design, such as the carrack, a development of Mediterranean and north European innovations, improved the efficiency of trade by sea, as did navigational advances, yet the threat of piracy and shipwrecks were a constant hazard.

The movement of people played a major part in the spread of knowledge during the Middle Ages. Petrarch's 'tourism' illustrates the greater understanding of life that travel was thought to encourage; the hardships of movement contributed to the symbolic association of travelling as a spiritual quest, most evident in pilgrimages and the Crusades.

• • • • •

The next letter was written after the Battle of Stirling Bridge in 1297 to inform the merchants of Lubeck and Hamburg that they could once again enjoy 'safe access' to Scotland's harbours. The defeat of the English had 'secured freedom of entry to the Forth' but Andrew Moray later died from the wounds he had suffered achieving this victory.

• • •

From Andrew Moray and William Wallace to the Senate and Commoners of Lubeck and Hamburg.

11 October 1287 Haddington.

Latin.

To the Senate and Commoners of Lübeck and Hamburg.

Andrew Moray and William Wallace, leaders of the Scotch army, and the commonwealth of the same kingdom send to the prudent and discreet men, our good friends, the Senate and the commoners of Lübeck and of Hamburg greeting and a continuous increase of sincere affection.

We have been informed by trustworthy merchants of the said kingdom of Scotland, that you on your own behalf have been friendly in counsel and deed in all things and enterprises concerning us and our merchants, though our own merits did not occasion this. We are therefore the more beholden to you, and wishing to prove our gratitude in a worthy manner we ask you to make it known among your merchants that they can now have safe access with their merchandise to all harbours of the Kingdom of Scotland, because the Kingdom of Scotland has, thanks be to God, by war been recovered from the power of the English. Farewell.

Given at Hadsington [Haddington] on the eleventh day of October in the year of Grace one thousand two hundred and ninety seven.

We also pray you to be good enough to further the business of John Burnett and John Frere, our merchants, just as you might wish that we should further the business of your merchants. Farewell, Given as above.

• • • • •

London was the major trading centre in England. Exports and imports were distributed here and the urban population depended on the supply of food from rural areas. Any impediment to the movement of merchants could have serious effects and warranted the intervention of high authority.

• • •

From the Mayor and Citizens of London to the Countess of Gloucester.

1301.

Norman French.

To the most noble lady, and wise, my Lady Johanna, daughter of the noble King of England, Countess of Gloucester and Hertford, her servants Elias Russel, Mayor of London, and the Citizens of the same city, greeting, with all manner of reverence and honour.

Whereas, my Lady, our fellow citizens, certain merchants, resorting to Henley, in passing through Marlowe and elsewhere in your domain, have been grievously distrained, and their merchandise detained, which ought to come to the City of London for their sustenance; through which distresses and grievances, the people dwelling in and repairing to the said city have received, and do still receive, from one day to another, grievous damage; we do pray your goodness, dear lady, and do request, that you will command your bailiff of Marlowe that he cause to be delivered up the distresses made upon our fellow-citizens aforesaid, and that he cease to make such distresses, until the return of our Lord the King, your [father], to the neighbourhood of London. And if anything be done to him, or to you, my Lady, by any persons of the City, which shall displease you - the which may God forfend - amends shall be made to you, high and low, at your good pleasure. Greeting.

• • •

Edward II to the Mayor of London.

21 May 1326.

Norman French.

Edward, by the grace of God, King of England etc., to our well-beloved Hamon de Chigewelle, Mayor of our City of London, greeting.

We have read the letters that you have sent us, in the which you have signified unto us that Flemings, Brabanters, and other aliens, have been suddenly buying throughout our land all the teasels that they can find; and also are buying butter, madder, woad, fullers' earth, and all other things which pertain to the working of cloth, in order that they may disturb the staple and the common profit of our realm; and further, that you have stopped twenty tuns that were shipped and ready for going beyond sea, at the suit of good folks of our said city; upon your doing the which we do congratulate you, and do command and charge you, that you cause the said tuns well and safely to be kept; and, if any such things come into our said city from henceforth, to be sent beyond sea by merchants, aliens or denizens, cause them also to be stopped and safely kept, until you shall have had other mandate from us thereon; and you are not to allow any such things to pass through your bailiwick, by reason whereof the profit of our staple may be disturbed. We have also commanded our Chancellor, that by writs under our Great Seal he shall cause it everywhere to be forbidden that any such things shall pass from henceforth out of our realm, in any way whatsoever. given under our Privy Seal, at Saltwode [near Hythe], in Kent,* the 21st day of May, in the 19th year of our reign.

• • • • •

John de Grandisson congratulates his cousin on the latter's safe journey home after a visit to the Bishop in Exeter.

• • •

From John de Grandisson, Bishop of Exeter to his Cousin the Earl of Devon.

c.1329.

French.

---

* The Archbishop of Canterbury had a fine castle there.

Greetings as to his son, with the blessing of God, and ours.

My dear Lord, we are much bound to be thankful that God has saved you in yesterday's tempest, and we pray to him that he will always safeguard you in safety. And know, my Lord, that it was much against our will that you left our household. By which, my Lord, it is good to work always after good advice.

My Lord, whenever we can hear anything concerning your honours, we shall write to you about it, as we beg you to do the same for us when you conveniently can.

My Lord, may Our Lord have you in his protection.

•••••

England's power at sea depended greatly on the support of merchant vessels. The Admiral grants a mariner permission to deliver a cargo of wool before joining the fleet for naval duties.

•••

Letter of Geoffrey de Say, Admiral, granted to John Pope, mariner.

12 August 1336.

Norman French.

Geoffrey de Say, Ameraille for our Lord the King from the mouth of the Thames as far as the parts of the West, to all who this letter shall see or hear, greeting in God.

Know that I have given leave unto John Pope to take his ship, which is called 'Cokiohan,'* laden with wool, to Flanders; so that he be with us in the Douns on the tenth day after the date hereof. And he begs of all people, that he [John] may safely go there and return. In witness whereof, to these letters patent I have set my seal. Given at Berlynge, the 12th day of August.

•••••

Petrarch believed travel to be an education and the sign of an enquiring mind. The observation and assimilation of new lands, the people and their customs was an essential ingredient of a deeper understanding of the world. In his youth Petrarch travelled for pleasure,

* Probably meaning "Coggjohn".

he has been described as 'the first tourist' and was stimulated by change and movement, he enjoyed hunting for ancient works in foreign libraries and meeting new and exciting acquaintances, many of which developed into deep friendships. Later in his life travel was an essential and sometimes irksome consequence of his fame and prestige. In his letter to Andrea Dandolo Petrarch writes of his love of travel; compared to most men of his time Petrarch could be described as having extraordinarily itchy feet.

• • •

Petrarch to Andrea Dandolo, Doge of Venice.

26 February 1352.

Latin.

To Andrea Dandolo, Doge of Venice; from Vaucluse, 26 February 1352.

I had suspected, and now I learn from your words, that you are amazed that I keep wandering here and there, never settling down, never choosing a secure base for my existence, and that after hardly a year in Italy I migrate to France and then after two years return to Italy. As I can't deny the fact, I must report the reason, to you for your pity, to men of good will for their pardon, to the public for its information. I applaud the words of Annaeus Seneca, that "the first mark of a well-ordered mind is that it can stand still and commune with itself." But I am also aware that many who have never stepped outside of their own hometowns are nevertheless vague of mind and incoherent in thought, while some who were constantly in movement have been serious, logical thinkers. Many great generals and philosophers have been travelers, as you well recall; whereas Vatia exists as if buried alive in his country house, and Buta snores all day and lies awake all night, and never sets foot beyond his bedroom door. You know of them from Seneca's famous letters, which in mockery made them immortal. The Apostle`s traveled far, and barefoot journeyed to the most distant lands. One or another was sent to Ephesus, to Syria, Greece, Rome, India, Egypt. Their bodies wandered in the most rugged regions; they suffered all the misadventures of land and the wide waters; but their hearts were fixed upon heaven. Today, indeed the bodies of our "apostles" rest on golden beds, while they send their thoughts afar over land and sea. To which group shall we adjudge the "mark of the well-ordered mind"? To those who never change their location, or to those who never change their purpose?

I must repeat what I have often said, what I still take pleasure in saying, that Homer and his great Latin follower, who are to be ranked among the first observers of human affairs, in describing the character and actions of the perfect man show him as a world-wanderer, everywhere learning something new. They thought that the kind of man they portrayed could not be formed if perpetually limited to a single spot. But since perhaps such lofty examples do not apply to me I shall omit excuses which might suggest pride and provoke to envy, and return to my statement that you should pity me.

You have always been a partisan of virtue; you have travelled far and are familiar with many places, many things; and now while still underage you have gloriously ascended to the highest post of your very noble Republic, and for the common good and common liberty you have entered the sumptuous prison of eminence. And I know that I should answer your desires if, after the long campaigns of my life I should pitch my tent beside you, there to pass in peace the remainder of my existence. Nothing could be more pleasant for me; nothing would better fulfill my hopes; and yet nothing appears more difficult of achievement. I have long set my helm on this course, but violent seas have swept me otherwhere, despite my struggles. And since I recognize your kind condescension in lending an ear, in the midst of your occupations, to the talk of your humble friend, I shall confess that it was my purpose in youth to follow Homer's advice, to inspect the manners of many men and their high cities, "to gaze upon new lands, mountain peaks, famous seas, lauded lakes, secluded founts, mighty rivers, and all the world's varied sites. I thought that thus I might become learned, most expeditiously and briefly, and not only at expense of trouble but with great pleasure. To know more was always among the first of my desires; and I seemed somehow to be overcome with ignorance by mere agitation of mind and body. But far enough have I wandered now; enough have I gone round and round, enough has bowed to my desires. Now it may be time for me to say to my special guide the words of the Roman centurion: "Standard-bearer, plant the banner; here we shall do well to remain." Perhaps I am sated by travel, with rambling through many lands; perhaps my youthful is relaxing and cooling, turning naturally to a love of peace, suitable for my occupations. At any rate I am losing my love of roving.

So what shall I do? You must believe me, if I have ever proved trustworthy. If I should ever find under the sun any good place - or at least not a bad place, if not perfectly awful - I should remain there gladly, and permanently. But now I keep turning over and over like a man on a hard bed, and I can obtain no rest in spite of my desire; and since I can find no softness in my bed I try to ease my weariness by constant shifting; and so I stray hither and yon and I seem to be a wanderer forever. Tired of the hardness of one place, I try another; and though it's no softer it seems so because it's different. Thus I am tossed about, well aware that though there is no resting-place for me, I must seek it out forever with pain and labour, and - this is the worst of it - with the consciousness that in all life's toils and fiery passions we must fear eternal straits and toils and everlasting fires. 'Well,' you may say, 'where you tremble and quake, many another sits quietly and comfortably!' I reply: 'How many more live there in great distress of mind, and cannot for a moment be still!'

I shan't speak of the celestial origin of souls, according to Virgil, nor shall I quote Cicero to the effect that our spirits come to us from the everlasting fires that we call stars and heavenly bodies. And Seneca has it that the changeableness of our souls, born from the rapid whirl of the celestial fires, is thereby to be excused. But I do say this: that our souls are created by God and by him are at once infused in our bodies; that God's throne is in heaven, as the Psalmist says; that the movement of the heavens is perpetual, as we see with our own eyes; so it is not surprising that we have some relation of likeness with the home of our Creator. Whatever its origin, I know that in men's minds, especially in superior minds, resides an innate longing to see new places, to keep changing one's home. I don't deny that this longing should be tempered and held in bounds by reason. Your own experience will lead you to agree with me that this taste for wandering about the world mingles pleasure with its pains, while those who sit forever on one spot experience a strange boredom in their repose. Which is the better course, in this as in man's other problems? God alone knows. If one thinks that reward is to be found not in the spirit but in some particular place, if one calls immobility constancy, then the gouty must be extremely constant, and the dead are more constant still, and the mountains are the most constant of all.

Enough of this. Perhaps I shall be accused of hunting out arguments to excuse my own diseased character. Well, I grant that I am stricken with a very serious disease - I pray it be not mortal. But I protest that I cannot blame my disease on the bed whereon I lie. I repeat, I am sick; this must be apparent to anyone, even though I should not reveal it in words. Cure me, and I shall be stronger, but my bed will be no smoother and softer. I refer to the bed of this life on which I lie exhausted. This bed is, rather, rough, uncomfortable, foul, evil, lumpy; it tortures any occupant in the best of health. I do not know how some can rest quietly thereon, unless, in their drugged slumber, they do not feel what oppresses me, or unless they find in what tortures me some strange pleasure, to me unknown. One may of course freely presume that my mind is in fever, while theirs is healthy. I could believe this of learned men, but I can't believe that base folk are more healthy than I or than anyone else; I think rather that they are torpid and insensible. Let others ascribe their peace to what cause they will; let it suffice that I have indicated the reasons for my agitation. Unless I am much mistaken, I am not sick to such a degree that I could not find rest if freed from the inconveniences of place and circumstance. It will be well if I can apply to my own case a remedy that I have recommended to others; that is, to seek within oneself a peace one cannot find without, and to find my repose, not in this spot or that, but in the spirit, or rather in the master and enlightener of the spirit.

But more of this at another time. Wisest of rulers, you who were moved by affection to worry about my own affairs, this must be for the moment my reply. Farewell.

• • • • •

The Cinque Ports played an important role in England's defence and continental trade. Raw materials, especially wool, corn and metals were exported and exchanged for spices, wine and luxurious fabrics. Travel by land was hazardous and limited, ships were an essential means of transport. Vessels used by merchants in peacetime were adapted to carry troops and weapons in times of war.

The first letter, from Sir John Devereux, Warden of the Cinque Ports, was sent to Rye and included a communication by King Richard II expressing concern about the selling of warships abroad, which posed a threat to the defence of the realm. The King's order was communicated to Sir John in Latin who in turn sent on the information in Latin to each port, it was then 'publicly proclaimed'.

• • •

From Sir John Devereux, Constable of Dover Castle and Warden of the Cinque Ports to the authorities of the Cinque Ports. Containing a communication by writ of the Privy Seal.

1390.

Latin.

Richard, by the grace of God King of England and France, and Lord of Ireland, to his well-beloved and faithful Constable of his Castle of Dover and Warden of his Cinque Ports, or to his lieutenant there, greeting.

Hearing, and understanding for certain, that certain merchants and other liege people of our Kingdom of England have sold, and are still selling, various ships of war and other vessels to aliens who are in friendship with us, and that these same aliens are reported often to have sold such ships and vessels before this time to our notorious enemies, for the sake of the excessive profit proceeding from the same; from which in process of time inestimable losses undoubtedly threaten to befall us and all our kingdom, unless we swiftly apply our hands to [measures] for preventing it;

And because we wish it to come to the notice of our people that with a view to avoiding such losses and dangers, and particularly with a view to resisting the preconceived malice of our said enemies, by whom we are embanked around, if they presume to attack us or our said kingdom in future times, we desire the navy of our aforesaid kingdom to be preserved whole in so far as we can, and we intend to employ all our diligence about it with the help of God, we command you, enjoining you as strictly as we can, that forthwith on seeing these presents, you cause it to be publicly proclaimed on our behalf in such particular places of the said ports as shall seem most expedient to you, that no master or possessor of such ships or vessels, or merchant, or other liege subject of ours, of whatsoever estate, degree or condition he may be, shall sell, or presume to exchange for other goods or merchandise to any aliens, secretly or openly, any ship of war or other vessel, greater or leases, on pain of [double the value] of the same ship as vessels, without our special licence, and our will is that the same double value shall be exacted and levied for our use, from the goods and chattels of all those who henceforth seek to sell, or exchange for other goods and merchandise, such ships or other vessels, greater or less, against our present command; and this you are on no account to omit.

Witness ourself at Westminster, the 8th day of June in the thirteenth year of our reign.

By writ of Privy Seal. Burton.

• • •

John Devereux, Constable of Dover Castle and Warden of the Cinque Ports, to all and singular the Mayors, Bailiffs and ministers of our Lord the King of the aforesaid Cinque Ports and their members, greeting.

We send to you a certain writ of our Lord the King, directed to us and sewn on to these presents, ordering on behalf of the same Lord King and of ourselves, and firmly enjoining that you have the said writ publicly proclaimed and observed [according to the tenor] and effect of the same, and [this upon pain and peril of the penalty therein mentioned].

Given at the aforesaid Castle under [our official] seal there, the

20th day of June in the [13th] year of the reign.

• • • • •

No doubt, John Wikham, the subject of the next letter would have been aware of these measures from the oral interpretation, since he probably only possessed an elementary ability to read.

Letter testimonials had come into widespread use. In England, during the thirteenth century, they were carried especially by the lower classes of society as guarantees of trustworthiness, written by the local bailiff or other noteworthy individual. The following example is typical, being addressed to whosoever should read it, stating the holder's occupation and length of residence or acquaintance.

• • •

From the Mayor and Barons of Rye.

18 January 1392.

Latin.

To all Christ's faithful people to whose notice the present letters shall come, the Mayor and Barons of the town of Rye send greeting.

Because John Wikham, shipwright of the same, the bearer of these presents, has besought us to provide testimony as to his stay in our community, we notify all of you by these presents that the same John has dwelt honestly in the said community in good fame and irreproachable behaviour, for twenty years before the date of these presents, of which he lived for the space of sixteen years to the benefit of the liberty there by the upkeep of the ships of the port of the aforesaid town, paying scot and lot with us from his goods, and bearing the other burdens there as each of us has hitherto been accustomed to do.

And lest the effect of the aforesaid testimony should in future come into doubt, we the aforesaid Mayor and Barons have with the consent of the same community caused our Common Seal to be affixed to our present letters patent.

Given at Rye, the eighteenth day of the month of January in the fifteenth year of the reign of King Richard the Second.

• • • • •

Men working together in the same craft banded together to form craft guilds which included the master craftmen and their employees. During the twelfth and thirteenth centuries guilds were little more than support groups for craftsmen who had similar economic interests and which provided funds for widows, orphans and elderly members. In large cities where there were many specialized trades and many more men practising them the guilds developed into a force to be reckoned with, which eventually acquired the right to define codes of conduct, quality control, terms of apprenticeship and hours of work.

• • •

From Henry IV to the Mayor, Recorder and Aldermen of City of London.

21 January 1409.

Norman French.

Henry, by the grace of God etc., to our very dear and well-beloved, the Mayor, Recorder, and Aldermen, of our City of London, greeting.

We do send you enclosed herein a Petition, delivered unto us by our well-beloved lieges the men of the trade of *Cordewaneres* in our said city, touching a certain dissension and dispute that has been pending for some time past between them and the *Cobelers* in the same city residing, as by the same Petition may unto you more fully appear. And we do will and command you, that upon the matter contained in the same Petition you do cause due inquisition to be taken, and such government between the said trades to be ordained and established, for the ease and quiet of both parties, as is befitting, and ought to be befitting, according to the custom of our City aforesaid; that so, we may not have reasonable cause to provide any other remedy in this case. Given under our Privy Seal, at Westminster, the 21st day of January, in the 10th year of our reign.

• • • • •

The Archbishop of Canterbury, Thomas Arundel, exhorts the Mayor of London to ensure that Sunday is preserved as a day of rest and to punish the barbers who have been openly operating their businesses on this day and contravening God's law. He deplores the growing tendency for men to fear physical punishment or fines, rather than Divine retribution, but suggests that 'scourge inflicted upon their purse' may well have the desired effect.

• • •

From the Archbishop of Canterbury, to the Mayor of London.
13 July 1413.
Latin.

Sons in Christ and dearest friends

We know that you do seek for the things which are of above, and that you will the more readily incline to our desires, the more surely that the things as to which we write are known to tend to the observance of the Divine law, the maintenance of public propriety, and the rule of the Christian profession. We do therefore write unto you on this occasion, to intimate that when we were presiding of late in our Provincial Council, held at London, with our venerable brethren, the Suffragan Bishops, and our clergy of the Province of Canterbury, it was publicly made known unto us with universal reprobation, that the Barbers of the City of London, over the governance of which city you preside, being without zeal for the law of God and not perceiving how that the Lord has blessed the seventh day and made it holy, and has commanded that it shall be observed by no abusive pursuit of any servile occupations, but rather by a disuse thereof, in their blindness do keep their houses and shops patent and open on the seventh day, the Lord's Day, namely, and do follow their craft on the same, just as busily, and just in the same way, as on any day in the week, customary for such work. Wherefore we, with the consent and assent of our said Suffragans and clergy, in restraint of such temerity as this, have determined that there must be made solemn prohibition thereof in the City aforesaid, and that, of our own authority, and that of our said Provincial Council; and not there only, but also throughout the Diocese of London, and each of the cities both of our own Diocese and of our Province of Canterbury; to the effect, that such barbers must not keep their houses and shops patent or open, or follow their craft, on such Lord's Days for the future, on pain of the greater excommunication; in the same manner as it has been enacted and observed of late in our time as to the City and Diocese of York, as we do well recollect. But, dearest children, seeing that so greatly has the malice of men increased in these days - a thing to be deplored - that temporal punishment is held more in dread than clerical, and that which touches the body or the purse more than that which kills the soul, we do heartily entreat you, and, for the love of God and of His law, do require and exhort you, that, taking counsel thereon, you will enact and ordain a competent penalty in money, to be levied for the Chamber of your city, or such other purpose as you shall think best, upon the barbers within the liberty of your City aforesaid, who shall be transgressors in this respect, that so at least, those whom fear of the anger of God does not avail to withhold from breach of His law, may be restrained by a scourge inflicted upon their purse, in the way of pecuniary loss; knowing that we in the meantime, after taking counsel hereon, will devise measures for the prevention of this, and for the due publication of our Provincial enactment aforesaid.

Fare you well always in Christ. Written at Ikham, on the 13th day of the month of July.

Thomas, Archbishop of Canterbury.

• • • • •

Margaret de Lacy and Sir Robert de Vere, the fifth Earl of Oxford were cousins. Her father was Robert de Quincy, the first son of Seher de Quincy, Sir Robert's maternal grandfather. Knife handles were most commonly set with coral, silver and jasper, they were also engraved, most precious stones being imported via Italy and France.

The second letter refers to the extraction of silver from the Mendip lead mines. England and Germany were the main sources of lead during the Middle Ages.

• • •

Margaret de Lacy to Sir Robert de Vere.

1245-1266.

French.

Margaret de Lascy, Countess of Lincoln and of Pembroke, to her dear friend Sir Robert de Vere, greeting and friendship.

I beg and require you that you will, if you please, send me by the bearer of these letters the knife with the jasper handle that my Lord lent to us for the use of our Lord my father, for I should like to send it to my Lord beyond the sea together with other things that I shall send him. In witness of this I send you my letters patent. Greeting.

• • •

A landreeve to the Bishop of Bath and Wells.

Early 14th century.

French.

Know, my lord, that your workmen have found a splendid mine of lead on the Mendips to the east of Priddy, and one that can be opened up with no trouble, being only five or six feet below the ground. And since these workmen are so often thieves, craftily separating the silver from the lead, stealthily taking it away, and when they have collected a quantity fleeing like thieves and deserting their work, as has frequently happened in times past, therefore your bailiffs are causing the ore to be carried to your court at Wookey where there is a furnace built at which the workmen smelt the ore under supervision of certain persons appointed by your steward. And as the steward, bailiffs, and workmen consider that there is a great deal of silver in the lead, on account of its whiteness and sonority [ringing sound], they beg that you will send them as soon as possible a good and faithful workman upon whom they can rely. I have seen the first piece of lead smelted there, of great size and weight, which when it is struck rings almost like silver, wherefore I agree with the others that if it is faithfully worked the business should prove of immense value to yourself and to the neighbourhood, and if a reliable workman is obtained I think that it would be expedient to smelt the ore where it is dug, on account of the labour of carrying so heavy a material such a distance. The ore is like grains of sand.

• • • • •

Jewellery and other valuables were frequently used as surety of payment when cash could not readily be found, and it seems likely that the spoils of war were sometimes put to use in this way. Bruges was one of the great ports of medieval Europe and a major commercial centre attracting trade of all kinds, especially wool merchants and Italian bankers who based themselves here, making Bruges the chief financial centre of northern Europe.

• • •

A letter from one of Ducal rank, respecting jewels of his in pawn to merchants at Bruges.

Nov. 1432?-April 1433.

English.

Right trusty and well-beloved, we greet you well.

And as it has recently pleased our blessed Creator to take our late wife the duchess out of this world into his everlasting bliss, or so we trust, may God pardon her soul; we therefore urgently need to repossess our jewels, which are still in Bruges, held by Carles Giles and Johan Martin, merchants of Ligny established in Bruges, for the sum of 2904 Flemish crowns, or equal value, this being what they are worth in London.

We request you urgently that you will hasten and apply your good offices with all possible diligence to the release of our said jewels, taking them into your own keeping, and retaining them until such time as you have been fully paid by us for all your expenses in this connection. And see that you do not fail in any aspect of this matter, if you wish to retain our custom, for you know that you can assist us in our reputation and our peace of mind. And may God bless you etc.

Given under our signet etc.

• • • • •

England was the main importer of wine during the Middle Ages since all classes of society drank it. In 1453 the loss of Gascony had caused a decline in the wine trade but by the end of the fifteenth century vintners were once again making a very good living especially if they supplied large institutions such as Christ Church; John Fawne is evidently eager to maintain good relations with the Prior.

• • •

From John Fawne to the Prior of Christ Church.

c.1479.

English.

Right reverend and my best Lord, I ask your lordship's favour, hoping to hear that you are in good health, prosperity and fortune. I would have come to see your lordship before now, but my wife has been very ill. I trust in God that I will see your lordship before long, and I understand from Nicholas Grevell of Sandwich that your butler has been there and has seen those wines of mine that are kept there. I will be most gratified if your lordship will take whatever you like at £4 or £5 a tun, or whatever you like; as to the price, your lordship and I can agree that well enough when next I see your lordship, by the grace of God, may He keep you.

Written at London the seventh of April.

By your servant,

John Fawne, Vintner.

• • •

From Queen Margaret of Anjou in aid of letters patent of safe-conduct granted to Guille Alany, master of a ship of Brittany named the Jenet.

1448-1449.

English.

Margaret, by the grace of God, etc., to all sorts of admirals, captains, lieutenants, excisemen, investigators, harbour-masters, mayors, sheriffs, bailliffs, constables, all other officers of my lord and true liege subjects, greetings.

As it has pleased my lord's highness, to grant, by special favour, letters-patent of safe-conduct to Guille Alany, master of the Breton ship *Jenet* (fifty tons deadweight) to come into this kingdom with certain wines for our use, we request you earnestly that you should show good will, friendship and favour to the said Guille and his seamen according to the statement and intention of my said lord's letters of safe conduct, and do not on the other hand allow them to be harassed, interrupted or arrested; instead consider our request, as we trust you, and as you hope to please us.

Given, etc. in the twenty-seventh year of my lord's reign.

• • • • •

In the second letter Queen Margaret of Anjou ensures that the arrival of her personal supply of wine will not be delayed, and in the following example uses her influence to inform the port authorities that a merchant bringing valuables for her own personal use should not be detained in any manner or required to pay duty.

• • •

From Queen Margaret of Anjou to the Officers of the King's Ports, respecting Antony Hewet of Rome.

Before 1482.

English.

Margaret, etc, to other officers of my lord's ports whom this concerns, greeting.

Be advised that we have issued commands to Antony Hewet of Rome to bring us certain silver vessels, jewels, rings and other objects of art and virtu, for gifts at the New Year and other celebrations. We request you therefore that as the said goods are ours, and for our own use, you will give passage to them and the said Antony without levying any customs on them, and without any delaying arrest, or interference of any kind, as we trust you, and as you hope to please us.

Given, etc.

• • • • •

The Cely family were prosperous city wool traders, merchants of the Staple, who bought raw wool in the Cotswolds and then sold it in either London or Calais. Traditionally most raw wool was exported to Flemish cloth producers but from the late fourteenth century cloth manufacturing began to develop in England, in an attempt to increase profits and to avoid the taxes levied on wool exports. The export of English wool which had suffered a serious decline in the early fourteenth century, continued to be of great importance to the English economy.

In the following letter Richard Cely writes to his son George who was conducting business across the Channel. Hanham has written: 'It was usual for the senior members of the family to spend most of their time in England, buying the wool and fell and seeing to its packing and shipping, while a junior member of the firm attended to affairs in Calais. (Hanham p.xi.)

Letters were vital in communicating details of business transactions within the family firm. The Cely letters provide a detailed insight into the late fifteenth century wool trade, but also portray the characters of the individuals involved and their relationships with one another. This letter reveals the family's concern for their son George whom they had heard was unwell. William Maryon was godfather to George's brother Richard, who also participated in the family business.

• • •

From Richard Cely the elder at London to George Cely at Calais or Bruges.

6 November 1479.

English.

Let this letter be delivered to George Cely at Calais or Bruges. [endorsement]

I greet you well, wishing to hear if you need anything, since I understand from John Rose that you were very ill in Bruges, so that your mother and both your brothers and Wyll Maryon and I were all sorry and concerned for you. I got your letter written in Bruges, and dated October twenty-third, on the last day of October and understand it well. I hope to God that you have now recovered and are fully healed.

Your letter reached me in London at dinnertime on the Sunday before All Hallows, when Wyll Eston the mercer and Wyll Midwinter of Norleach were dining with me, and I was so pleased by your letter that I bought forty sacks of Cotswold wool from Wyll Midwinter, which is currently lying at Norleach.

John Cely has been in Cotswold and made up a consignment of thirty-seven sacks altogether, in sacks, tods and half-sacks, for which I will need a good lot of canvas, in respect of which you can buy for me four or five lengths of Burgen canvas, or Barras good quality, as long as it's as broad as Normandy canvas, and three dozen trade packs of Calais thread, as I will need them. If you can't, I will have to negotiate for them in London, as I'm advised to pack the wool between Christmas and Candlemas. I hope to God that you will be at Cotswold to see to the packing of the wool. I'm advised not to ship any wool before March.

I'll write nothing more for the present, but may Jesus keep you.

Written in London in haste, the sixth day of November.

pp Richard Cely.

• • • • •

Although the life and work of Leonardo da Vinci is rightfully viewed in terms of the Renaissance, rather than the Middle Ages, the following letter is included in this collection since it illustrates the explosion of activity and discovery which took place in almost every field of endeavour, towards the end of our period.

Leonardo da Vinci (1452-1519) had trained as a painter under Verrocchio in Florence. He then moved to the court of Ludovico Il Moro, Duke of Milan, lured by the opportunities to develop his scientific and technical knowledge. Vasari tells how the Duke was keen to witness Leonardo's talents as a musician. Leonardo was an accomplished player of the lyre and 'the most talented improviser in verse of his time.'* Leonardo's letter to his prospective patron describes his skill as a military engineer, maybe to emphasize his many capabilities and possible usefulness other than as a court entertainer. Kenneth Clark wrote of this letter:

The fact that Leonardo only speaks of himself as an artist in six lines out of thirty-four is so much at variance with the opinion of posterity as to seem

* Vasari, *Lives of the Artists*, translated by George Bull, 1965, p. 262.

like a piece of elaborate irony. We may be sure that it was not so intended. In the Renaissance war was the most vitally important of all the arts, and demanded the services of the most skilful artists. *

The bronze monument of a horse, dedicated to the memory of Ludovico's father, Francesco Sforza, was never completed. Leonardo made an enormous clay model which proved impossible to cast due to its size and complicated form; it later disintegrated. Leonardo remained in Milan until the French invaded the city in 1499, he then returned to Florence.

• • •

From Leonardo da Vinci to the Duke of Milan.

1428.

Italian.

Having, most illustrious lord, seen and considered the experiments of all those who pose as masters in the art of inventing instruments of war, and finding that their inventions differ in no way from those in common use, I am emboldened, without prejudice to anyone, to solicit an appointment of acquainting your Excellency with certain of my secrets.

1. I can construct bridges which are very light and strong and very portable, with which to pursue and defeat the enemy; and others more solid, which resist fire or assault, yet are easily removed and placed in position; and I can also burn and destroy those of the enemy.

2. In case of a siege I can cut off water from the trenches and make pontoons and scaling ladders and other similar contrivances.

3. If by reason of the elevation or the strength of its position a place cannot be bombarded, I can demolish every fortress if its foundations have not been set on stone.

4. I can also make a kind of cannon which is light and easy of transport, with which to hurl small stones like hail, and of which the smoke causes great terror to the enemy, so that they suffer heavy loss and confusion.

5. I can noiselessly construct to any prescribed point subterranean passages either straight or winding, passing if necessary underneath trenches or a river.

6. I can make armoured wagons carrying artillery, which shall break through the most serried ranks of enemy, and so open a safe passage for his infantry.

---

* Clark, K. *Leonardo da Vinci*, 1963 reprint, p. 46.

7. If occasion should arise, I can construct cannon and mortars and light ordnance in shape both ornamental and useful and different from those in common use.

8. When it is impossible to use cannon I can supply in their stead catapults, mangonels, *trabocchi*, and other instruments of admirable efficiency not in general use - in short, as the occasion requires I can supply infinite means of attack and defence.

9. And if the fight should take place upon the sea I can construct many engines most suitable either for attack or defence and ships which can resist the fire of the heaviest cannon, and powders or weapons.

10. In time of peace, I believe that I can give you as complete satisfaction as anyone else in the construction of buildings both public and private, and in conducting water from one place to another.

I can further execute sculpture in marble, bronze or clay, also in painting I can do as much as anyone else, whoever he may be.

Moreover, I would undertake the commission of the bronze horse, which shall endue with immortal glory and eternal honour the auspicious memory of your father and of the illustrious house of Sforza.

And if any of the aforesaid things should seem to anyone impossible or impracticable, I offer myself as ready to make trial of them in your park or in whatever place shall please your Excellency, to whom I commend myself with all possible humility.

• • • • •

On August 3rd 1492 Christopher Columbus sailed from Palos on the south coast of Spain on his first voyage across the Atlantic; he landed on one of the Bahama Islands on October 12th. Columbus had believed he would reach Asia if he sailed far enough west but unknowingly discovered America.

King Ferdinand and Queen Isabella of Spain had supported his expedition, after much persuasion, and in this letter to them Columbus describes what he found when he first came ashore. The King and Queen immediately demanded his presence at court, where they bestowed great honours upon the explorer and urged him to return to the West Indies as soon as possible. By 1504 Columbus had made three more voyages but it was not until the discoveries of John Cabot on the north coast of America and of Amerigo Vespucci in South America that the idea of a New World, which lay to the west between Europe and Asia, began to be seriously considered.

During the fifteenth century the Portuguese had pioneered

exploration along the West African coast, with the eventual discovery of the Cape of Good Hope in 1487 by Bartholomew Diaz. The Italians had long monopolized trade from the East and the Portuguese hoped to discover alternative routes by sea to the wealth of the Orient. The discoveries of the fifteenth century heralded the dramatic transformation of European trade in the sixteenth century and contributed to the broadening of men's ideas and understanding.

• • •

From Christopher Columbus to Gabriel Sanchez, Treasurer of King Ferdinand of Spain.

14 March 1493.

Spanish.

Because my undertakings have attained success, I know that it will be pleasing to you: these I have determined to relate, so that you may be made acquainted with everything done and discovered in this our voyage. On the thirty-third day after I departed from Cadiz, I came to the Indian sea, where I found many islands inhabited by men without number, of all which I took possession for our most fortunate king, with proclaiming heralds and flying standards, no one objecting.

To the first of these I gave the name of the blessed Saviour,* on whose aid relying I had reached this as well as the other islands. But the Indians called it Guanahany. I also called each one of the others by a new name. For I ordered one island to be called Santa Maria of the Conception,† another Fernandina,§ another Isabella,‡ another Juana, and so on with the rest.

As soon as we had arrived at that island which I have just now said was called Juana, I proceeded along its coast towards the west for some distance; I found it so large and without perceptible end, that I believed it to be not an island but the continental country of Cathay; seeing, however, no towns or cities situated on the sea-coast, but only some villages and rude farms, with whose inhabitants I was unable to converse, because as soon as they saw us they took flight.

I proceeded farther, thinking that I would discover some city or large residences. At length, perceiving that we had gone far enough,

* In Spanish, San Salvador, one of the Bahama Islands. It has been variously identified with Grand Turk, Cat, Watling, Mariguana, Samana, and Acklin islands. Watling's Island seems to have much in its favour.

† Perhaps Crooked Island or, according to others, North Caico.

§ Identified by some with Long Island; by others with Little Inagua.

‡ Identified variously with Fortune Island and Great Inagua.

that nothing new appeared, and that this way was leading us to the north, which I wished to avoid, because it was winter on the land, and it was my intention to go to the south, moreover the winds were becoming violent, I therefore determined that no other plans were practicable, and so, going back, I returned to a certain bay that I had noticed, from which I sent two of our men to the land, that they might find out whether there was a king in this country, or any cities. These men travelled for three days, and they found people and houses without number, but they were small and without any government, therefore they returned. . . .

This island is surrounded by many very safe and wide harbours, not excelled by any others that I have every seen. Many great and salubrious rivers flow through it. There are also many very high mountains there. All these islands are very beautiful, and distinguished by various qualities; they are accessible, and full of a great variety of trees stretching up to the stars; the leaves of which I believe are never shed, for I saw them as green and flourishing as they are usually in Spain in the month of May; some of them were blossoming, some were bearing fruit, some were in other conditions; each one was thriving in its own way. The nightingale and various other birds without number were singing, in the month of November, when I was exploring them.

There are besides in the said island Juana seven or eight kinds of palm-trees, which far excel ours in height and beauty, just as all the other trees, herbs and fruits do. There are also excellent pine-trees, vast plains and meadows, a variety of birds, a variety of honey, and a variety of metals, excepting iron. In the one which was called Hispana, as we said above, there are great and beautiful mountains, vast fields, groves, fertile plains, very suitable for planting and cultivating, and for the building of houses.

The convenience of the harbours in this island, and the remarkable number of rivers contributing to the healthfulness of man, exceed belief, unless one has seen them. The trees, pasturage, and fruits of this island differ greatly from those of Juana. This Hispana, moreover, abounds in different kinds of spices, in gold, and in metals.

On this island, indeed, and on all the others which I have seen, and of which I have knowledge, the inhabitants of both sexes go always naked, just as they came into the world except some of the women, who use a covering of a leaf or some foliage, or a cotton cloth, which they make themselves for that purpose.

All these people lack, as I said above, every kind of iron; they also are without weapons, which indeed are unknown; nor are they competent to use them, not on account of deformity of body, for they are well formed, but because they are timid and full of fear. They carry for weapons, however, reeds baked in the sun, on the lower ends of which they fasten some shafts of dried wood rubbed down to a point; and indeed they do not venture to use these always; for it frequently happened when I sent two or three of my men to some of the villages, that they might speak with the natives, a compact troop of the Indians would march out, and as soon as they saw our men approaching, they would quickly take flight, children being pushed aside by their fathers, and fathers by their children. And this was not because any hurt or injury had been inflicted on any one of them, for to everyone whom I visited and with whom I was able to converse, I distributed whatever I had, cloth and many other things, no return being made to me; but they are by nature fearful and timid.

Yet when they perceive that they are safe, putting aside all fear, they are of simple manners and trustworthy, and very liberal with everything they have, refusing no one who asks for anything they may possess, and even themselves inviting us to ask for things. They show greater love for all others than for themselves; they give valuable things for trifles, being satisfied even with a very small return, or with nothing; however, I forbade that things so small and of no value should be given to them, such as pieces of plate, dishes and glass, likewise keys and shoestraps; although if they were able to obtain these, it seemed to them like getting the most beautiful jewels in the world. . .

In all these islands there is no difference in the appearance of the people, nor in the manners and language, but all understand each other mutually: a fact that is very important for the end which I suppose to be earnestly desired by our most illlustrious king, that is, their conversion to the holy religion of Christ, to which in truth, as far as I can perceive, they are very ready and favourably inclined. . . .

In all these islands, as I have understood, each man is content with only one wife, except the princes or kings, who are permitted to have twenty. The women appear to work more than the men. I was not able to find out surely whether they have individual property, for I saw that one man had the duty of distributing to the others, especially refreshments, food, and things of that kind. . . .

Truly great and wonderful is this, and not corresponding to our merits, but to the holy Christian religion, and to the piety and religion of our sovereigns, because what the human understanding could not attain, that the divine will has granted to human efforts. For God is wont to listen to His servants who love His precepts, even in impossibilities, as has happened to us on the present occasion, who have attained that which hitherto mortal men have never reached.

For if anyone has written or said anything about these islands, it was all with obscurities and conjectures; no one claims that he had seen them; from which they seemed like fables. Therefore let the king and queen, the princes and their most fortunate kingdoms, and all other countries of Christendom give thanks to our Lord and Saviour Jesus Christ, who has bestowed upon us so great a victory and gift. Let religious processions be solemnized; let sacred festivals be given; let the churches be covered with festive garlands. Let Christ rejoice on earth, as He rejoices in heaven, when He foresees coming to salvation so many souls of people hitherto lost. Let us be glad also, as well on account of the exaltation of our faith as on account of the increase of our temporal affairs, of which not only Spain but universal Christendom will be partaker. These things that have been done are thus briefly related. Farewell. Lisbon, the day before the ides of March.

Christopher Columbus, admiral of the Ocean fleet.

• • • • •

The central tower of Canterbury Cathedral, referred to in this letter, was built c.1494-1504. Prior Sellyng asks the Archbishop's opinion on the details of one of the pinnacles: the mason, John Wastell, was primarily concerned with the structural problems of erecting the edifice, leaving the finishing touches to his superior's judgement. Newman described it thus:

John Wastell's majestic crossing tower perfectly sets the seal on the cathedral, lofty enough to weigh against the enormous length of the building, magisterially forceful of outline, yet profusely decorated. *

• • •

Draft letter from Prior Sellyng to Archbishop Morton.

c. 1494.

English.

Most reverend father in God, and my sole good lord, with all favours and humble obedience.

May you be pleased to know that the Master Surveyor and I have spoken with your mason John Wastell, the bearer of this letter, to find out from him what forms and shapes he will employ in raising the pinnacles of your new tower here. He drew for us two patterns. The first was of a double finial, without crockets, the other was of a single finial

---

* John Newman, *North East and East Kent* - 2nd edition 1976. Pevsner, N. and Nairn, J. *The Buildings of England.*

with crockets. Will your good lordship please graciously command the said John Wastell to draw the two patterns and show them to you, and having seen them your Grace may advise him which of the two it is your pleasure to have constructed, or if any other sort should be designed to please your Lordship. Moreover, if your grace requires it of the said John Wastell, I think he would be able to arrange for the pinnacles to be built and finished by next summer, and if it can be done, then the outward appearance of your tower will be that of a completed work.

• • • • •

The role of the Cinque Ports has been discussed in other letters. As well as providing centres of merchant and wartime shipping they had long been familiar and actively involved with piracy. Traditionally acts of piracy were frequently overlooked but the following letter describes an instance when this was far from the case and great consideration shown to the victim.

• • •

To the Mayor, Bailiffs and Jurats* of Rye from the Privy Seal.
21 and 26 December 1495.
Latin and English.

[Latin]

To all and singular Christ's faithful people to whom the present writing shall come, the Mayor, Bailiffs and Jurats of the Town and Port of Rye in the Kingdom of England wish eternal salvation in the Lord.

You are to know that we, the aforesaid Mayor, Bailiffs and Jurats, have inspected and read, and have after mature deliberation in all things understood, the letters of the Lord King lately directed to us under his Privy Seal, of which the tenor follows, in these words:

[English]

Henry, by the grace of God King of England and of France, and Lord of Ireland, to the Mayor, Bailiffs and other Officers of our Town and Port of Rye, and to all manner other our Officers, Ministers and true subjects, and to every of them our letters hearing or seeing, greeting.

Forasmuch as one Piers le Daulfyn of Crosic [le Croisic] in Brittany hath

* Municipal officers, roughly equivalent to J.P.s.

done to be showed unto us and our Council, by bill of supplication, how that one John Whalle of our Town of Sandwich, by mean of our letters of marque heretofore by us granted unto him upon the inhabitants of the town of Penmark [Penmarch] in Brittany aforesaid, lately arrested the ship and goods of the said Piers there in our said Port, which as yet, by force of the said arrest, remain under your jurisdiction as it is said; it is so, that upon the complaint of the said Piers in this behalf, it has been lawfully proved and recorded by divers honest and credible persons in our said Council, that the said Piers is of the town of Crosic, which is 140 miles from the said Penmark or more, as they say. Whereby, it hath been adjudged by the same our Council that he is not, nor ought to be, bound to answer for them of Penmark aforesaid in this part.

We therefore, willing right to be ministered as well herein as in all other causes, as reason is, straitly charge and command you that, incontinently upon the sight hereof, you do the said ship of the said Piers, with all the goods, tackling and apparels of the same, cause to be delivered unto him without anything taking, embezzling or retaining thereof; suffering him with the same, and with his company, freely to depart at his pleasure and liberty, the said arrest, or any other cause you moving to the contrary, notwithstanding. And if any other impediment were made unto the said Piers for this matter, we eftsoons will and command you that you incontinently discharge him thereof. And that you not fail of the premises, as you purpose to avoid our high indignation, and will answer unto us in that behalf at your perils.

Given under our signet at our Palace of Westminster, the 21st day of December, the 11th year of our reign.

[Latin]

Wherefore, we have had the meaning and tenor of the said letters exemplified and sealed at the instance of the aforesaid Piers le Daulfyn, under the Official Seal of our Mayoralty of the aforesaid Town and Port of Rye.

Given in the aforesaid Port, on the day of Saint Stephen the Martyr, in the year of our Lord One thousand four hundred and ninety five, and in the eleventh year of the reign of the aforesaid lord King Henry the Seventh of England.

•••••

Roger de Marlowe, Rector of Harwell in Berkshire, writes to his friend at Hailes Abbey explaining how he is in need of a horse and that

Winchombe fair has been recommended. Rural communities and small towns were comparatively self-sufficient in the early medieval period, a weekly market satisfied most local needs whilst annual fairs catered for more irregular demands and attracted traders from further afield. The most important fairs in England during the thirteenth century were held at Winchester, Northampton, St Ives and Boston, smaller fairs such as that at Winchcombe were held throughout the country. As the towns grew merchants began to dominate trading practices, the dependency on fairs decreased as methods of supply and distribution became more sophisticated.

• • •

From Roger de Marlowe to a monk at Hailes Abbey.

Late fifteenth century.

Latin.

To the religious man and his beloved friend Sir J ... de H... monk of the Abbey of Hayles, R. de Marlowe chaplain of H. sends greeting in Him Who is the true safety and Saviour of the world.

As I should like to hear good news of your health and safety I am writing to you, as my particular friend, eagerly desiring you to send me by the bearer news of yourself and the brethren and my friends in the neighbourhood. Also, since having lost some of my horses I am hardly able to go about, and there is at present a fair at Winchcombe near you, where as I have often heard, many horses are to be found, I earnestly beg you to look about and get some of your people to give their advice and help to the bearer and Sir Thomas de Sandford, canon, and also to assist them yourself, so that I may be provided with some suitable horse there, costing not more than four or five marks. May you fare well, as I would fare well. Greet your brethren and companions from me.

WAR

War was considered to be both inevitable and honourable throughout the Middle Ages. It was the means of extending and defending territories and all classes of medieval lay society were required to undertake military duties of some description. War was blessed by the Church and armed conflict resulted from religious as well as political strife. Participation in a just war, especially a holy war, could enhance a man's likelihood of reaching heaven, yet the rules by which wars were fought were exacting. Out and out total warfare was the exception and the letters detailing specific battles indicate the conventions of war, a mixture of Church doctrine and the laws of chivalry, which were closely adhered to by opposing armies.

Generally, wars were fought between sovereign princes, by small armies, over questions of honour and rights which were combined with the attraction of loot and handsome ransoms. Great land-owning lords were obliged to provide a specified number of knights at their sovereign's request but this was a far from satisfactory procedure and was replaced by the payment of a sum of money, or scutage, which the king would use to pay mercenaries. The Pope and large cities, particularly those in Italy, also recruited mercenaries often from abroad. 'Fief-rente' or money rent was another means of supplementing an army. A noble was paid a certain sum on the agreement that he would become the King's vassal and provide him with a fixed number of armed men whenever requested to do so.

The idea that armies should consist of able-bodied citizens, called to arms when necessary, developed gradually. During the fourteenth century the efforts of mounted knights together with men drawn from the indigenous population as foot soldiers and bowmen proved to be a formidable combination. By the fifteenth century most armies were semi-professional with soldiers being paid actual wages.

Wars tended to take the form of sieges and raids rather than pitched battles, and although conventions existed the conduct of individuals in the fury of a raid could not be guaranteed. Princes and knights were as likely to commit savage and murderous acts as common soldiers. Canon law forbade clerics to participate in wars and the letter from Henry V's chaplain is significant because, written by an individual who had never participated in armed combat, it expresses the image of glorious war and the nobility of victory prevalent throughout the medieval period.

• • • • •

Simon de Montfort was created Governor of Gascony in 1248. Although born and bred in France he had arrived in England seventeen years previously to claim the earldom of Leicester which he had inherited from his mother. The Earl rapidly became one of King Henry III's favourites and married his sister Eleanor. De Montfort's experiences in Gascony were an important factor in the developing conflict between himself and the King which resulted in de Montfort leading the barons in the troubles of 1258 and the ensuing civil war. Ironically, it was largely Henry's activities abroad which led to so much disagreement and bloodshed with his formerly highly trusted and respected ambassador.

In this letter, which was written shortly after his appointment as governor, de Montfort expresses concern about his reputation at home and it was reports such as these which encouraged Henry's distrust. De Montfort did return to England but the King almost immediately sent him back to Gascony to contend with warring barons possesed of highly fickle loyalties. In 1249 the Earl could write that he was 'ready to do that which you command me', but it was only nine years later that he was making his own demands on the King.

• • •

From Simon de Montfort, Earl of Leicester to Henry III.

3 April 1249.

Latin.

Sir, since your envoys the bishop, Sir Antony, and the lord Robert left Paris, I have heard for certain that some knights of Gascony whom your envoys saw there, because they do not recover their lands by the Lord Gaston, which lands I hold in your hands by judgement, and because they know well that they will lose if they demand right in the court of Gascony, have provided themselves with everything to demand their lands by war. And they are certainly leagued together, they and their friends; and I fully understand that they will begin soon after Whitsuntide to overrun the land; but what force they will have I cannot as yet be at all sure. And because the great men of the land bear me such ill will, because I uphold your rights and those of the poor against them, there would be danger and shame to me, and great damage to you, if I were to return to the land without instructions from you and without speaking to you. For if I were there, and they made war on me, it would be needful for me to return to you, because I have not and cannot have a penny of your revenues, because the king of France holds all, and I cannot trust much to the people of the land. And on the other hand one cannot stay such men by an army in the kind of war which they will make, for they will do nothing but rob the land, and burn and plunder, and put the people to ransom, and ride by night like thieves by twenty or thirty or forty, in different parts; wherefore it is needful in every way, if you please, that I should speak to you, before I go into the country. For I heard that they have given you to understand many sinister things of me; they will tell you soon that I was the cause of their war. Therefore, sir, if you please, do not take it amiss if, when I have finished your business in this parliament of Paris, which is going well, thank God, I return towards you to know your advice, ready to do that which you command me. And your castles and your lands and your men are well supplied, for that matter, to hold out until I come. And I have sent the lord Bidau de Coupenne there, to aid and advise them and I have told them that I shall be there, if God will, by Whitsuntide. Given at Paris, this Easter Eve.

• • • • •

At the time this letter was written King Henry III was absent on an expedition to Gascony. He had concluded a truce with Alphonso X, King of Castile, by arranging a marriage between his young son Edward and Alphonso's sister, Eleanora. Henry hoped that he would still be able to extract funds for his wars with the Castilians, which he could then enjoy himself, by keeping the treaty a secret, but the news must have reached the English magnates who agreed to provide aid only if Alphonso attacked first, and in the form of personal service rather than squanderable cash. The clergy also distrusted the King's demands for finances, they had been asked to contribute to a projected crusade which Henry had little intention of performing. Queen Eleanora informs her husband of the scepticism felt by the lords and the clergy but outlines their enthusiasm to assist with *bona fide* causes.

Nevertheless, Henry III, by his wilful obstinacy in persevering in his infringements on the liberties of his subjects, rushed with open eyes on his own destruction. The character of Queen Eleanora, as depicted in this letter, is that of an affectionate and faithful wife and a clear-sighted politician. *

---

* Wood, p. 37.

• • •

Eleanor Queen-Regent of England and Richard Earl of Cornwall to Henry III.

13 February 1254.

Latin.

To their most excellent lord, the Lord Henry, by God's grace the illustrious King of England, Lord of Ireland, Duke of Normandy and Aquitaine and Earl of Anjou, his most devoted consort Eleanora, by the same grace Queen of England, and his devoted and faithful Richard Earl of Cornwall, send health with all reverence and honour.

Be it known to your revered lordship that the lords the earl marshall and John de Bailiol, being hindered at sea by a contrary wind during twelve days, came to us in England on the Wednesday after the Purification of Blessed Mary last past.*

We had been treating with your prelates and the magnates of your kingdom of England before the advent of the said Earl and John, on the quinzaines of St. Hilary last past† about your subsidy, and after the arrival of the said Earl and John, with certain of the aforesaid prelates and magnates, the archbishops and bishops answered us that if the King of Castile should come against you in Gascony each of them would assist you from his own property, so that you would be under perpetual obligations to them; but with regard to granting you an aid from their clergy, they could do nothing without the assent of the said clergy; nor do they believe that their clergy can be induced to give you any help, unless the tenth of clerical goods granted to you for the first year of the crusade, which should begin in the present year, might be relaxed at once by your letters patent, and the collection of the said tenth for the said crusade, for the two following years, might be put in respite up to the term of two years before your passage to the Holy Land; and they will give diligence and treat with the clergy submitted to them, to induce them to assist you according to that form with a tenth of their benefices, in case the King of Castile should attack you in Gascony; but at the departure of the bearer of these presents no subsidy had as yet been granted by the aforesaid clergy.

Moreover, as we have elsewhere signified to you, if the King of Castile should come against you in Gascony, all the earls and barons of your kingdom, who are able to cross the sea, will come to you in Gascony, with all their power; but from the other laymen who do not

* 4 February. † 27 January.

sail over to you we do not think that we can obtain any help for your use, unless you write to your lieutenants in England firmly to maintain your great charters of liberties, and to let this be distinctly perceived by your letters to each sheriff of your kingdom, and publicly proclaimed through each county of the said kingdom; since, by this means, they would be more strongly animated cheerfully to grant you aid; for many persons complain that the aforesaid charters are not kept by your sheriffs and other bailiffs as they ought to be kept. Be it known, therefore, to your lordship, that we shall hold a conference with the aforesaid clergy and laity at Westminister, in the quinzaines of Passover next, about the aforesaid aid, and we supplicate your lordship that you will write us your good pleasure concerning these affairs with the utmost possible haste. For you will find us prepared and devoted, according to our power, to solicit the aforesaid aid for your use, and to do and procure all other things . . . which can contribute to your convenience and the increase of your honour. Given at Windsor, the 13th of February, in the thirty-eighth year of your reign.

Endorsed, 'A certain letter directed to King Henry by the queen his wife, about a cerain subsidy for the said king, when the king was in Gascony.'

• • • • •

When the boy king Henry III attained his majority in 1222 his rule was characterized by a desire for peace at home and an increasing ambition for power and influence abroad. His foreign exploits sapped the financial strength of England and encouraged discontent amongst the barons. In 1258, as a result of a petition by rebellious barons led by Simon de Montfort demanding political changes and a reduction of the king's authority, the Provisions of Oxford were drawn up. In the following letter King Henry III declares his intention to agree to the Provisions.

In 1215 Magna Carta had stated basic principles of government but had not provided a means for ensuring that these were upheld. The Provisions of Oxford were an attempt to rectify this, by the introduction of a baronial council and a reorganization of government. The twenty-four men referred to in Henry's letter consisted of twelve from his own side and twelve from the barons'. The king was obliged to uphold its wishes, and prevented from taking action which might harm the nobility or the country as a whole. Nevertheless discontent was widespread and Henry was able to regain control in 1261 with the support of Pope Alexander IV and Louis IX of France.

• • •

Letters Patent of Henry III.
4 August 1258.
Probably French.

Henry, by the grace of God King of England, etc., to all those, etc.

Know ye that for the profit of our realm, and at the request of our chief men and wise men, and of the commons of our realm, we grant that twenty-four of our men shall have power that all which they shall ordain concerning the estate of our realm shall be firm and stable, and this we have caused to be sworn on our soul, and have given thereto our letters patent. And this same Edward our eldest son has sworn, and has given thereto his letters patent.

And the above-named twenty-four have chosen four, to the which four they have given their power of election our council of the wise men of our land. The which council we have promised and do promise to create for the redressing and amending of all the affairs which belong to us and our realm. And we will that the aforesaid council, or the greater part of it, may elect a wise man or wise men to be members of it in place of him or of them who may fail. And we will hold firm and stable whatever the aforesaid council or the greater part of it shall do. And we command firmly that all our lieges and our men also be firmly held to keep all the enactments, which they shall make to the honour of God and our faith, and to the profit of our realm. And in witness of this thing we have caused our seal to be set to this present letter.

This thing was done at London the Sunday after Lammas day, in the forty-second year of our coronation.

This letter is duplicated, and delivered to the earl marshal by the king and his council.

• • • • •

Lady Havisia de Neville's first husband, John de Neville, died in 1246. She later married Sir John Gatesden whom she refers to as her son's father-in-law.

Hugh de Neville had been brought up at Windsor with other children of the nobility. He then participated in expeditions to Wales and Scotland and actively supported the Barons in the civil war. His possessions were escheated in 1265 for the part he had played against Henry III but in 1266 he was pardoned, his lands were restored to him and later in the year Hugh went to the Holy Land, appointing his mother and brother as attorneys to oversee his property during his absence. At this time England was in a state of agitation and 'the probability of an exodus, to follow the Crusades, of many of the greater ones of the realm, the consequent difficulty of obtaining assistance from the funds, specially raised for the furtherance of these Holy Wars, for one who was in real need of such help,* forms the background to Lady Neville's letter to her son.

• • •

From Lady Havisia de Neville to her son, Hugh de Neville.

c.1258.

French.

Havisia de Neville to her very dear son, Hugh de Neville, wishes health and the blessing of God and her own.

Know, dear son, that I am well and hearty, thanks to God, and am much rejoiced at the news that William Fitz Simon brought me of your health. God be thanked for it! Know, dear son, that our necessities of receiving the returns from your lands can avail nothing, on account of the great rule your adversary has in the king's court, unless you yourself were present. Wherefore your father-in-law and I, and all your other friends, agree that you should come to England, and we pray and entreat you, by the faith and love that you owe us, that you will not by any means fail in this; since you ought once again to return. For we know well that it would be a very great dishonour and we consider it a great sin, to suffer us and ours to be disinherited by your indolence. Therefore I anxiously pray you, dear son, that you will travel with all possible haste, and also, according to the counsel of all your friends, that you go to the court of Rome, and procure if you can the letter of the pope, express and stringent, to the king of England, that he should restore your lands, and have them restored. And that you may make a proper understanding at the court of all our needs, without omitting or concealing anything; that is, how you are placed with the king, and that you are compelled by a writing to hold the (obligation), without contradiction and without ever making an acquisition to the contrary. For wise persons have said the acquisition would be worth nothing, unless it made express mention of this, that it was through no fault of yours that you made this the aforesaid obligation when in war, and through fear of prison.

* Guiseppi, M.S. 'On the Testament of Sir Hugh de Nevill, written at Acre, 1267' *Archaeologia*, vol. lvi, p. 361. 1899.

And know, good son, that the first acquisition you got at Rome for our lands was not such as you understood, for it was only a loving petition for your rights of the money which you ought to have had of the crusade allowance. The legate, thanks to him, has granted us that he would let us have it if we could espy out where it is, but we have not as yet found any, except what is in the hands of such as themselves would wish to go into the Holy Land; but as much as we may be able to acquire now or henceforth, between this and St. John's day, we will then send you by the messengers of the Temple, who will bring their own money. And for God's sake, good son, guard against making such an obligation as you have made for Sir Ingelram de Umfranville; for I was grieved that it was proper to have it paid from our own demesne. And good, sweet, dear son, I anxiously pray you that you will send us word how much money you have really had by my command, for the thing is not in my power, for I could never spy a man who went to that part, that I might send you letters, that weighs no little upon me. For if it could be that I could often have good news of you, and comfort you again often by my messages, there would be nothing that could more rejoice me, expect it were to see and speak to you. And know, dear son, that my heart is grieved and alarmed day and night, since William Fitz Simon brought me news that you were so poorly provided with money; but God who is Almighty, if it please him, give you speedy amendment, and I will do it to my utmost power.

Dear son, I pray you not to trust too much to the money of the crusade allowance, for they say that more great lords of England will take the cross; and they will take away as much as shall be raised for the crusade, as certain friends have given me to know. But do not ever cease, as you dearly love me, for no waiting for money, to borrow all the money that you can, and to go to the court of Rome to acquire for our necessities, and to hasten to come to England to accomplish our needs. For I hope, by the help of God, if you could well accomplish what you have to do about the acquisition of our lands, that you will see such change in England, that never in our time could you have better accomplished your wish, or more to your honour. Wherefore cease not to solicit again about your coming, since you can here best serve God. I commend you to the true body of God, who give you life and health. Sir Walter de la Hide, Joanna your sister, and all our household, salute you. And know, dear son, that my counsel is that you obtain the letters of request of the legate of that country, and the letters of the master of the Temple and of the Hospital, to the legate of England and to other rich men, for your needs, and in testimony of your deeds in that country on the occasion of your coming. And ever take care of your house that you have there, if God give you courage to return.

To Sir Hugh de Neville.

Endorsed in Latin, in a later hand, 'The letter of the Lady Havisia de Neville, directed to the Lord Hugh her son, being in the Holy Land.'

• • • • •

During the first half of the thirteenth century, Llywelyn the Great had established a powerful Welsh state which threatened the security of the Lords of the Marches and denied King Henry III's authority in the region. The Welsh problem lay dormant after the death of Llywelyn the Great but re-emerged during the English Civil War of 1257-67, when Llywelyn Ap Gruffydd reassumed the title of Prince of Wales and took control over the entire Kingdom and much of the Marches, to the great anger of barons with land in these areas. It was due to the great loss of life, such as that mentioned in the letter, and continuing struggle needed to maintain his Kingdom, that Llywelyn sought acknowledgement of his title and a peace treaty from Henry III. The Lords in the area were also heartily sick of maintaining expensive armies to counteract the Welsh attack which increased in vigour at the time this letter was written. On 29th September 1267 Llywelyn's title and his authority over the Welsh Lords was recognized by Henry III and Edward with the treaty of Montgomery. Llywelyn's rule was not to last long due to the energy Edward I expended on reclaiming the lost territory. Llywelyn was killed in battle in 1282, becoming the last native Prince of Wales and its last independent ruler.

From Peter de Montfort to Roger le Bigod, Earl of Norfolk, and others.

2 October 1262.

Probably Norman French.

To the noble brothers and his very dear lords and friends, my Lord Roger le Bigod, Earl of Norfolk and Marshal of England, my Lord Philip Basset, Justiciar of England, Sir John Mauncel and Robert Waleraund, Peter de Montfort health and all honour.

Know that the Thursday next after the feast of St. Matthew the Apostle, Wienoch ap Edenavet, Llewellyn's seneschal, Meredut ap Res, Res Vachan, and Meredut ap Owein, with all the pride of Wales, save the person of Llewellyn and his brother, and with a very great host from the south, went to the land of our lord the king and of my lord Edward, which is in my keeping, to pillage and destroy; and we with our people and the aid of friends from the neighbouring lands, of which I . . . . defended the waters of Esk Water the two days until the Saturday about noon, and then came my lord John de Grey, Sir Roger de Mortemer, my lord Renald Fitz Peter, and my lord Humphry de Boun, and I led them to a guardhouse above the town of Bergaveny, where we crossed to encounter these Welshmen, who had already burnt a part of the land of Bergeveny below Bloreis; and when they saw us approach them, they dismounted their horses and fled across the mountain of Bloreis, in a place which is by no means suitable for men on horseback to pass. And since we saw well that we could never reach them, we turned along the valley to their plunderers and foragers, who were there in great numbers, so that there perished, God be praised, in the day between killed and taken, more than three hundred. And still on the Monday following, when this letter was written, there was the greater part of them, both on foot and on horseback, scattered over the monasteries of the country and the moors everywhere, and men are searching them out constantly.

And know, fair lords, that now and heretofore full five times we have met there and kept all at our cost as many as three thousand or four thousand at one time of men on foot, and as many as eighty horses mounted, to guard and defend the land of the king and my lord Edward. Wherefore I pray and request you, fair lords, since you are of the council of our lord the king, that you will tender counsel to the king and the queen and my lord Edward, or one of them, that these expenses be repaid to me, and that counsel be taken how the land is to be defended henceforth; for know assuredly, that if counsel be not taken thereon, it behoves me to leave my castle furnished and go away, and leave the land to make terms and perish; for if all the land were in good peace and were it all mine, beside the three lands which I have, I should not have power to maintain the great expense which I have on it. And know that if they descend another time, as I know well that they will do before long in very great force to revenge themselves . . . . and if they are not stopped they will destroy all the land of our lord the king as far as the Severne and W . . . . and they ask nothing but to have the land of Went. Farewell in God.

• • • • •

It was quite unusual for women to have a career other than as a wife and mother or outside the nunnery. Women worked on the land, and in towns and cities frequently helped with the running of a family business; some women were skilled in crafts or trades but they were usually excluded from guilds unless a close male relative was already a member.

Petrarch's 'mighty female soldier' is an interesting exception particularly since she appears to have been treated with a great deal of respect among her male counterparts. Petrarch's mention of this woman is, however, as pure novelty value, women rarely enjoyed the same opportunities or recognition as did men.

Women nevertheless were expected to assist with the defence of towns and castles when under attack. In the next letter the Lord of Pembroke entrusts his wife with the defence of Winchester Castle and stresses that the knights he is sending will be under her command. Henry III had recently added new residential quarters to the castle and lavishly refurbished the interior to provide a greater degree of comfort and aesthetic pleasure. Yet in spite of this upgrading, the castle retained its primary defensive function.

From William de Valence, Earl of Pembroke, to his Lady.

29 May 1267.

Probably Norman French.

William de Valence, lord of Pembroke, to his dear consort and friend, health.

Know that we are sending Sir Robert de Immer to supply the castle of Winchester with corn and provisions, and to stay with you to defend the aforesaid castle with Sir Martin de Roches and Philip le Clerk. And do you command them on our behalf that they act in all things with one accord and one counsel. And we give you power over them all and of them all, to ordain and arrange in all things according to that which you shall see to be best to do. In witness whereof we send these our letters patent.

Given at Berking, the Sunday next after the Ascension, in the year of king Henry, son of king John, the fifty-first.

• • • • •

Towards the end of his reign King Edward I was occupied with two great obsessions, the recovery of the Holy Land and the subjection of Scotland. He was determined to become overlord of Scotland and reduce the King of Scotland to his vassal. The premature deaths of Alexander III in 1286 and his grand-daughter, the Maid of Norway in 1290 marked the end of a long period of peace between Scotland and England.

The Scottish magnates were divided in their choice of an heir to the throne and sought advice and support from King Edward. In 1291 at Norham he demanded that they submit to his overlordship whilst the Scottish throne was unoccupied, and lacking any better alternative the Scottish magnates agreed.

The following year Edward decided that John Balliol had the strongest claim and crowned him King of Scotland at Scone, but Edward's humiliation of this inadequate and feeble sovereign led to the outbreak of war between the two kingdoms culminating in the seige of Berwick in 1296. Balliol surrendered his crown and left Scotland forever, the Scottish magnates submitting to Edward's overlordship once again. The Stone of Scone was transferred to London and Edward left three Englishmen in charge of the country.

The next year William Wallace, an outlawed knight, began his attacks to reclaim Scottish territory. He was remarkably successful and fought with the aim of returning John Balliol to the throne. Wallace's achievements were short-lived due to the success of the English at the Battle of Falkirk.

The letter below, from the Bishop of Lichfield and Coventry, describes the battle which took place on 22nd July 1298 and the huge loss of life suffered by the Scots. The letter was sent on 26th July and received in London on 1st August. The messenger received 26 shillings for his speedy journey south; travelling was certainly easier in the summer months than in the middle of winter.

• • •

From the Bishop of Lichfield and Coventry to the Mayor, Aldermen and Barons of London.

26 July 1298.

Norman French.

To his dear friends, the Mayor and the Barons of London, Walter; by the grace of God, Bishop of Chester, greeting and true friendship.*

Because we well know that you willingly will hear good tidings of our Lord the King and of his affairs in Scotland, we give you to understand that on the Monday next before the Feast of Saint James [25 July], there came tidings unto our Lord the King where he was staying, six leagues

* Walter Langton, Bishop of Coventry and Lichfield from 1295 to 1322, is frequently termed the Bishop of Chester, also from the fact of the see having been moved there in 1075.

beyond Edeneburg, that the Scots were approaching, directly towards him. As soon as he heard this, he moved with his host towards the parts where the Scots were; and on the morrow the King arrived in good time, and found his enemies prepared to give battle. And so they engaged, and, by the grace of God, his enemies were soon discomfited, and fled; but nevertheless, there were slain of the enemy in the day's fight 200 men-at-arms, and 20,000 of their foot-soldiers; wherefore we do hope that affairs yonder will go well from henceforth, by the aid of our Lord. Unto God [we commend you]. Written at Acun, on Sunday after the Feast of St. James, in the 26th year of our Lord, the King Edward.

• • • • •

The Bishop's hopes that 'affairs yonder will go well from henceforth' were not fulfilled even though King Edward again placed Scotland under the rule of three regents and secured his power by regular campaigns during the next seven years. The three regents he chose were Bishop Lamberton of St Andrews, John Comyn and Robert Bruce, whose grandfather had rivalled John Balliol for the Scottish throne in 1292. King Edward's letter to Robert Bruce was written during the last campaign in 1304; it illustrates his obsession in that parliament or 'any other thing' could be neglected if it meant a chance of 'Scotland gained'.

The colloquial expression 'whereas the robe is well made you will be pleased to make the hood' derives from the long robes worn at this time which were not complete without a hood. It also indicates that perhaps this letter was spontaneously dictated by the King himself in his eagerness to have Bruce fight rather than having been carefully worked upon by a secretary who is unlikely to have used such a term. Other letters of King Edward I and his father Henry III contain phrases of this sort which gives their correspondence a vitality often lacking in other royal letters.

• • •

From King Edward I to Robert Bruce.

3 March 1304.

French.

Edward, by the grace of God, King of England, Lord of Ireland and Duke of Aquitaine, to our faithful and liege Robert de Brus, Earl of Carrick, and to all our other good people who are in his company, greeting.

We have heard that it is agreed between you and Sir John de Segrave, and our other good people of his company, to follow the enemy, and that you desire we should hold you excused if you come not to us on the day appointed: Know that for the great diligence and ...... that you have used and do use in our affairs from day to day, and for that you are thus agreed to follow the enemy we thank you as earnestly as we can, and pray and require especially, as we confide in you, who are our good people, and have well begun the said business, that you will complete it, and that you leave not either for Parliament or for any other thing until you ...... diligently your intention to pursue the enemy, and to put an end to affairs before your departure from those parts. For if ...... * that which you have there begun, we shall hold the war ended by your deed, and all the land of Scotland gained. So we pray you again, as much as we can, that whereas the Robe is well made you will be pleased to make the Hood. And by your letters, and by the bearer of these, send back unto us your answer hereupon without delay, together with the news of your parts. Given under our privy seal at Aberdour, the third day of March, the thirty second year of our reign.

• • • • •

Two years later Robert Bruce murdered John Comyn at Dumfries. The latter had refused to support Bruce who had now decided to claim the Scottish throne as his own. He was crowned King of Scotland at Scone on the 27th March 1306.

King Edward's health was rapidly deteriorating yet he insisted on participating in the consequent attacks on the new Scottish King, and died on his way northwards at Burgh-upon-Sands on 27th July 1307. He had requested that his bones be carried by his son in future Scottish campaigns but this never came about as his body was immediately taken to Westminster Abbey.

King Edward II neglected the gains made by his father in Scotland. A campaign in 1310-11 had no effect and this offer of financial aid from the mayer and commonality of London did little to prevent Robert Bruce consolidating his kingdom. It was not until 1314 that Edward II made his first determined attack against Bruce although this was more to gain prestige in England rather than through any real desire to rule Scotland. The massive English defeat at the Battle of Bannockburn 'brought an end to all English claims to overlordship of Scotland'. †

• • •

* Probably 'you accomplish'.
† Chancellor, *The Life and Times of Edward I* p. 199.

From Richer de Refham, Mayor of London to King Edward II
25 April 1311.
Norman French.

To the most noble Prince, and their very dear liege lord, our Lord the King of England, his lieges, Richer de Refham, Mayor of his city of London, and the commonalty of the same city, all manner of reverence, service, and honour, as unto their liege lord.

Whereas, Sire, we have heard good news of you, Sire, and of your successful prosecution of your war in Scotland, God be thanked; we do send you, by the bearers of these letters, one thousand marks, in aid and in prosecution of your war; and we do pray you, as being our most dear lord, that you will be pleased to accept the same; and that, if aught shall please you as regards your said city, you will signify your will unto us, as being your liege men. Our Lord have you in his keeping, body and soul; and may he give you a good life, and long.

• • • • •

Dante had been in exile for fifteen years when he wrote this letter. An amnesty had been declared for all those who had been banished from Florence but Dante considered its conditions a humilation which he was not prepared to accept after all the years he had suffered for his beliefs. He had looked to Emperor Henry VII to restore the Florentine exiles to their homes and to put an end to the anarchy in Italy.

The recipient of this letter was probably Dante's brother-in-law Teruccio di Manetto Donati, and the nephew referred to, Niccolò Donati.

• • •

From Dante to a Friend in Florence.
May 1315.
Latin.

From your letter, which I received with due respect and affection, and have diligently studied, I learn with gratitude how my recall to Florence has been the object of your care and concern; and I am the more beholden to you therefor, inasmuch as it rarely happens that an exile finds friends. My reply to what you have written, although perchance it be not of such tenor as certain faint hearts would desire, I earnestly beg may be carefully examined and considered by you before judgement be passed upon it.

I gather, then, from the letter of your nephew and mine, as well as from those of sundry other friends, that, by the terms of a decree lately promulgated in Florence touching the pardon of the exiles, I may receive pardon, and be permitted to return forthwith, on condition that I pay a certain sum of money, and submit to the stigma of the oblation - two propositions, my Father, which in sooth are as ridiculous as they are ill-advised - ill-advised, that is to say, on the part of those who have communicated them, for in your letter, which was more discreetly and cautiously formulated, no hint of such conditions was conveyed.

This, then is the gracious recall of Dante Alighieri to his native city, after the miseries of well-nigh fifteen years of exile! This is the reward of innocence manifest to all the world, and of the sweat and toil of unremitting study! Far be from a familiar of philosophy such a senseless act of abasement as to submit himself to be presented at the oblation, like a felon in bonds, as one Ciolo and other infamous wretches have done! Far be it from the preacher of justice, after suffering wrong, to pay of his money to those that wronged him, as though they had deserved well of him!

No! my father, not by this path will I return to my native city. If some other can be found, in the first place by yourself and thereafter by others, which does not derogate from the fame and honour of Dante, that will I tread with no lagging steps. But if by no such path Florence may be entered, then will I enter Florence never. What! Can I not anywhere gaze upon the face of the sun and the stars? Can I not under any sky contemplate the most precious truths, without I first return to Florence, disgraced, nay dishonoured, in the eyes of my fellow-citizens? Assuredly bread will not fail me!

• • • • •

Petrarch, whilst on a visit to Baia, near Naples, meets Maria, a mighty female soldier. His description of Maria, as a novelty and exception, affords us an insight into how most women were perceived: gentle, concerned about their appearance, restricted to the domestic sphere and altogether excluded from the preoccupations and activities of men.

• • •

From Petrarch to Cardinal Giovanni Colonna.
23 November 1343 (from Baia, near Naples).
Latin.

Of all the wonders of God, 'who alone doeth great wonders,' he has made nothing on earth more marvelous than man. Of all we saw that day, of all this letter will report, the most remarkable was a mighty woman of Pozzuoli, sturdy in body and soul. Her name is Maria, and to suit her name she has the merit of virginity. Though she is constantly among men, usually soldiers, the general opinion holds that she has never suffered any attaint to her chastity, whether in jest or earnest. Men are put off, they say, more by fear than respect. Her body is military rather than maidenly, her strength is such as any hardened soldier might wish for, her skill and deftness unusual, her age at its prime, her appearance and endeavour that of a strong man. She cares not for charms but for arms; not for arts and crafts but for darts and shafts; her face bears no trace of kisses and lascivious caresses, but is ennobled by wounds and scars. Her first love is for weapons, her soul defies death and the sword. She helps wage an inherited local war, in which many have perished on both sides. Sometimes alone, often with a few companions, she has raided the enemy, always, up to the present, victoriously. First into battle, slow to withdraw, she attacks aggressively, practises skilful feints. She bears with incredible patience hunger, thirst, cold, heat, lack of sleep, weariness; she passes nights in the open, under arms; she sleeps on the ground, counting herself lucky to have a turf or a shield for pillow.

She has changed much in a short time, thanks to her constant hardships. I saw her a few years ago, when my youthful longing for glory brought me to Rome and Naples and the king of Sicily. She was then weaponless; but I was amazed when she came to greet me today heavily armed, in a group of soldiers. I returned her greeting as to a man I didn't know. The she laughed, and at the nudging of my companions I looked at her more closely; and I barely recognized the wild, primitive face of the maiden under her helmet.

They tell many fabulous stories about her; I shall relate what I saw. A number of stout fellows with military training happen to have come here from various quarters. (They were diverted from another expedition.) When they heard about this woman they were anxious to test her powers. So a great crowd of us went up to the castle of Pozzuoli. She was alone, walking up and down in front of the church, apparently just thinking. She was not at all disturbed by our arrival. We begged her to give us some example of her strengh. After making many excuses on account of an injury to her arm, she finally sent for a heavy stone and an iron bar. She then threw them before us, and challenged anyone to pick them up and try a cast. To cut the story short, there was a long, well-fought competition, while she stood aside and silently judged the contestants. Finally, making an easy cast, she so far outdistanced the others that everyone was amazed, and I was really ashamed. So we left, hardly believing our eyes, thinking we must have been victims of an illusion.

The story goes that Robert [of Naples], that noblest of kings, was once sailing along these shores with a great fleet, and, tempted by the stories of this woman, he came ashore at Pozzuoli only to see her. This does not seem very likely, since, living so nearby, it would seem easier for him to summon her. But perhaps he landed for some other reason and was eager to inspect this great novelty. He has a very curious mind. Let the tale-tellers bear the responsibility for the truth of this story, as of many others we have heard. For me the sight of this woman makes more credible not only the tales of the Amazons and their famous feminine kingdom, but also those of the Italian virgin warriors, led by Camilla, whose name is celebrated above all. For what hinders us from believing of many what I could hardly have credited of one, if I had not seen it? And that ancient Camilla was born not far from here, at Piperno, at the time of the fall of Troy; while our modern girl was born at Pozzuoli. I wanted to give you this report in my little letter.

Farewell and prosper.

• • • • •

Petrarch writes to his friend Barbato Sulmoma describing Parma under a state of seige and his own traumatic escape. Bishop has assessed the causes for the unrest:

Two aggressive powers were rising in northern Italy: Milan under Luchino Visconti and Verona under Mastino della Scala, nephew of the four Correggio brothers. The Correggi had gained control of Parma with the aid of Luchino Visconti . . . . . . and had secretly promised to turn over the city to him in four years. But Azzo had a better idea. Without informing his brothers, he sold the lordship of Parma to Obizzo d'Este, commander of the Veronese troops, for 60,000 gold florins, and decamped. This was about November 1, 1344. The three Correggio brothers gave up, and Obizzo entered Parma, with the usual acclamations and announcements that mercy, pity, peace, and love had at length begun their reign. But Obizzo fell into an ambush by the Milanese, who then laid siege to Parma. Naturally Mastino della Scala of Verona was shocked at the outrage. He *sent an army to besiege the besiegers. In the circumstances, life in Parma, within its double blockade, was very uncomfortable during the winter of 1344-1345.* *

Petrarch refers to Vaucluse, his valley retreat north of Avignon where much of his writing was done, but instead of returning there to recuperate Petrarch travelled on to Verona and it was here, in the cathedral library, that he found a manuscript of Cicero's *Letters to Atticus,* mentioned in an earlier letter. The injury to his arm had made it difficult for Petrarch to write and he explains why he is having to employ the services of a scribe which was not his usual practice.

• • •

Petrarch to Barbato da Sulmoma.

25 February 1345.

Latin.

To Barbato da Sulmona, a friend in Naples; from Bologna, 25 February 1345.

I am of a mind to share with you my toils and fortunes, as is my custom. War has come to Parma, as you know. We are surrounded, pressed within the limits of a single city, by a large army, not from Liguria alone but from all Italy. It is not that our men lack the spirit to fight - we have proved that often by our vigorous sorties - but the enemy's strategy is not to allow us peace or war; he trusts to conquer by mere persistence, weakening our spirits by the tedium of a long siege. Thus with various ups and downs the besieger sometimes becomes the besieged. The outcome is not yet certain. Anyway, the issue is fiercely fought, and unless I am much mistaken the day of decision is near at hand. My mind wavers, inclining toward compromise, trying to fend off both empty hope and useless fear.

In this state of affairs the siege, not the least of war's calamities, has oppressed us not for a few days but for many months. In the circumstances, I have been longing for liberty, that liberty which I always earnestly entreat and ardently embrace, though it flee me over land and sea. I had long been possessed by the desire for Vaucluse, my transalpine Helicon, since my Italian Helicon was ablaze with the wars. But what could I do? The road to the west had become impassable, so I looked to the east. Although this region swarmed with enemy troops, it seemed safer than the long roundabout way through Tuscany.

* M. Bishop, *Petrarch and His World*, 1963, p. 227.

To cut it short, at sunset on 23 February I ventured forth from the city with a few companions. We succeeded in dodging the hostile pickets. About midnight we got near Reggio, held by the enemy. Suddenly a band of marauders burst out of ambush, threatening us with death. It was no time for deliberations; the time, the place, the ring of enemies were too terrifying. Few in number, unarmed unprepared, what could we do against so many armed men, practised in violence? Our only hope lay in flight under cover of darkness. 'The comrades scatter, and black night covers them,' as Virgil puts it. I too fled, I confess, escaping death and the whistling arrows.

But when I thought that I had got safe - when, pray is man ever safe? - my trusty horse stumbled into a hole or against a tree trunk or a rock; I couldn't tell what in that black, cloudy night. I was thrown to the ground, shattered and almost unconscious. But I assembled my wits and stood up. Fear gave me strength to remount my horse - though for some time now I haven't been able to raise my hand to my mouth. Some of my companions turned back to Parma, but some, after their vain wanderings, remained fixed in purpose. Our two guides, tired, fearful, and totally lost, forced us to halt in a retired spot, where, to add to our terror, we could hear the voices of sentinels on unidentifiable walls. Add to this a heavy rain mixed with hail; amid the lightning flashes our fear of a dreadful death increased.

The story is much too long to recount in detail. We spent that really hellish night in the open, lying on the ground, while the swelling and pain of my injured arm increased. No grassy turf invited us to sleep, no leafy boughs or rock, cave gave us shelter. We had only bare earth, foul weather, Jupiter in anger, and the fear of men and wild beasts, and I had my injuries into the bargain. You will perhaps be surprised and sympathetic to learn that there was one comfort in our distresses; we stationed our horses across the path, and used their backs as shelter against the storm. Though before they were shying and nervous, now they became quiet, as if they were aware of their own sorry pass; and so they did us a double service. Thus in toil and terror we reached daybreak. When the dim, dubious light revealed to us a way among the underbrush we left that ominous region in all haste. Received within the walls of a friendly town named Scandiano, we learned that a large force of horse and foot had been lying in wait outside the walls to seize us, and shortly before our arrival had made off, driven by the storm. Now go and deny the power of Fortune, which can turn wise counsel to disaster and our errors to salvation! I am joking, my dear Barbato. You know my judgement of Fortune; that is a formidable name. In any case, our straying was advantageous, and so was the storm; our misfortunes saved us from worse.

So when it was day I revealed for the first time my wounds to my companions; they were moved to tears. And since it did not seem safe to stay here, I had my arm temporarily bound up, and took a mountain path to Modena, and the next day I went on to Bologna. From there I am dictating (contrary to my custom) this letter, to inform you of my own case and of the general situation. My body will receive all the care humanly possible; cure is certain, though it will be slow. The doctors expect recovery by summer; I look for aid from Almighty God. In the meantime my stiff right arm will not obey orders, but my mind is strengthened by adversity. Farewell.

• • • • •

Edward, the eldest son of King Edward III and Philippa of Hainault was born in 1330 at Woodstock. He was made Prince of Wales in 1343 but is better known as the Black Prince.

His father had encouraged the Prince's military prowess by allowing him to take major responsibilities in his first campaign and where he achieved great honour at the Battle of Crecy in 1346. He was present at the Seige of Calais in 1344, and in 1356 the Prince led the English army to Gascony.

In the following letter he traces his movements up to the victory of Poitiers, a battle which revealed the Prince's skill as a soldier and the superiority of the English army. The French King was captured and held for an enormous ransom whilst the Black Prince achieved great fame and glory. He personified the knightly ideals of the time and was considered to be 'the flower of chivalry of all the world'.

• • •

From Edward, Prince of Wales, announcing his victory at Poitiers.

22 October 1356.

Norman French.

Letter of Edward, Prince of Wales, sent to the Mayor, Aldermen, and Commonalty, of the City of London, as to the battle fought near Peyters.

Very dear and very much beloved. As concerning news in the parts where we are, know that since the time when we certified unto our most dread lord and father, the King, that it was our purpose to ride forth against the enemies in the parts of France, we took our road through the country of Peregord and of Lymosyn, and straight on towards. Burges in Wene,* where we expected to have found the King's son, the

* Bourges in Vienne.

Count of Peyters; and the sovereign cause for our going towards these parts was, that we expected to have had news of our said lord and father, for us to assent thereto, for there we were more fully certified that the King had prepared in every way to fight with us.

Whereupon, we withdrew ourselves from thence towards Chastel Heraud, by passage over the stream of the Vivane;* where we remained four days, waiting to know for greater certainty of him. And the King came with his force to Chaveny† five leagues from us, to pass the same river, in the direction of Peytiers And thereupon, we determined to hasten towards him, upon the road along which he would have to pass, so as to have a fight with him; but his battalions had passed before we had come to the place where we intended to meet him, save a part only of their people, about 700 men-at-arms, who engaged with ours; and there were taken the Counts de Sousseire and de Junhy, the Sieur de Chastillon, a great number of others being both taken and slain, both on their side and ours. And then our people pursued them as far as Chaveny, full three leagues further; for which reason we were obliged that day to take up our quarters as near to that place as we could, that we might collect our men. And on the morrow we took our road straight towards the King, and sent out our scouts, who found him with his army; [and he] set himself in battle array at one league from Pieters, in the fields; and we went as near to him as we could take up our post, we ourselves on foot and in battle array, and ready to fight with him.

Where came the said Cardinal, requesting very earnestly for a little respite, that so there might parley together certain persons of either side, and so attempt to bring about an understanding and good peace; the which he undertook that he would bring about to a good end. Whereupon, we took counsel, and granted him his request; upon which, there were ordered certain persons of the one side and the other, to treat upon this matter; which treating was of no effect. And then the said Cardinal wished to obtain a truce, by way of putting off the battle at his pleasure; to which truce we would not assent. And the French asked that certain knights on the one side and the other should take equal shares, so that the battle might not in any manner fail: and in such manner was that day delayed; and the battalions on the one side and the other remained all night, each one on its place, and until the morrow, about half Prime§; and as to some troops that were between the said main armies, neither would give any the King, as to his passage; and seeing that we did not find the said Count there, or any other great force, we turned towards Loyre‡ and commanded our

* The Vienne.
† Chauvigny.
§ Half past seven A.M.
‡ The river Loire.

people to ride forth and reconnoitre if we could find a passage anywhere: the which people met the enemy, and had to enter into conflict, so that some of the said enemies were killed or taken; and the prisoners so taken said that the King of France had sent Grismotoun, who was in that company, to obtain for him certain news of us, and of our force; and the said king, for the same purpose, had sent in another direction the Sieur de Creon, Messire Busigaut, the Mareschal de Clermount, and others. And the same prisoners declared that the King had made up his mind for certain to fight with us, at whatever time we should be on the road towards Tours, he meeting us in the direction of Orliens.

And on the morrow, where we were posted, there came news that the said Sieur de Creon and Busigaut were in a castle very near to our quarters; and we determined to go there, and so came and took up our quarters around them; and we agreed to assault the said place, the which was gained by us by force, and was quite full of their people, both prisoners and slain, and also some of ours were killed there; but the said Sieurs de Creon and Bursiguad withdrew themselves into a strong tower which was there, and which occupied us five days before it was taken; and there they surrendered. And there we were certified that all the bridges upon Leyre were broken down, and that we could nowhere find a passage; whereupon, we took our road straight towards Tours; and there we remained four days before the city, in which were the Count d'Angeo* and the Mareschal de Clermount, with a great force of troops. And upon our departing from thence, we took the road so as to pass certain dangers by water, and with the intention of meeting with our most dear cousin, the Duke of Lancaster, of whom we had had certain news, that he would make haste to draw towards us. At which time the Cardinal de Peregort came to us at Monbezon, three leagues from Tours, where he spoke to us fully as to matters touching a truce and peace. Upon which parley we made answer to him, that peace we had no power to make, and that we would not intermeddle therewith, without the command and the wishes of the King, our most dear lord and father; nor yet as to a truce were we at that time of opinion that it would be the best thing advantage in commencing the attack upon the other. And for default of victuals, as well as for other reasons, it was agreed that we should take our way, flanking them, in such manner that if they wished for battle or to draw towards us, in a place that was not very much to our disadvantage, we should be the first; and so forthwith it was done. Whereupon battle was joined, on the Eve of the day before St. Matthew; and, God be praised for it, the enemy was discomfited, and the King was taken, and his son; and a great number of other great

* D'Anjou.

people were both taken and slain; as our very dear Bachelor Messire Neele Loereng, our Chamberlain, the bearer hereof, who has very full knowledge thereon, will know how more fully to inform and shew you, as we are not able to write to you; to whom you do give full faith and credence; and may Our Lord have you in His keeping. Given under our Privy Seal, at Burdeaux, the 22nd day of October.

• • • • •

Edward III's reign was characterized by his claim to the French throne and the victorious battles of Sluys (1340), Crecy (1346) and the conquest of Calais in 1374. In later years the King's sons, Edward and John of Gaunt the Duke of Lancaster, took on the responsibility of attempting to maintain power across the Channel, but by 1375 only Calais, Bordeaux, Bayonne and Brest remained under English control.

In 1373, when he was twenty-one years old, Lord Welles accompanied the Duke of Lancaster on his historic but disastrous march from Calais to Bordeaux. In later years he was regularly abroad serving in the French wars of Richard II, as well as participating in the expedition to Scotland in 1385. Lord Welles married twice and when his long and active life ended in 1421, he was aged eighty-seven.

• • •

From John Lord Welles to Monsieur John Helyng.

c. 1374.

Old French.

Dear companion and most faithful friend, know that our redoubtable King has by royal letter bid me join him in France with one of his garrisons on the first day of June, and naturally I desire your company. If it would please you to join me there, come with all speed to my manor at Hellowe that we may properly consider the matter in hand, and where between us, with God's help, we will resolve it.

I would be most grateful if you would send me word of your decision by the bearer of this letter, and of when you wish to come.

May God preserve you always, most dear companion and faithful friend.

Hellowe manor, this last day of January, John Welles.

• • • • •

The three following letters relate to Henry V's campaigns in France. Since the loss of Normandy in the early thirteenth century successive Kings of England had longed to assert their power across the Channel. Edward III had claimed the French crown through his mother, and although he had some success his forces were never strong enough to achieve substantial control.

Henry V's enthusiasm and energy posed the greatest threat the French had ever had to face. In a speech he made prior to his first campaign he declared:

We do intend with no small army to visit the parts beyond sea, that so we may duly re-conquer the lands pertaining to the heirship and crown of our realm, and which have been for long, in the times of our predecessors, by enormous wrong witheld.

In the first letter the King describes the capture of the city of Harfleur, a well-fortified centre of trade, 'considered to be the key to Normandy'. It was his very first act of aggression against the French. The English army had landed in mid August 1415 but it was not until five weeks later that they took possession of Harfleur. The letter describes a feature of seige warfare which was characteristic of this period and especially common in Henry V's campaigns. Rather than suffer a full-scale sack by the aggressors, or incur their monarch's wrath by submitting too readily, a town's garrison would agree with the enemy to suspend hostilities until additional troops arrived to engage in a more fairly balanced battle. In this instance the people of Harfleur were unlucky since Sieur de Hankeville returned from King Charles VI and the Dauphin 'without any rescue being offered', and Harfleur had little alternative but to surrender.

The letter conveys how pleased the English King was with his first success, but winter was approaching and instead of penetrating farther into Normandy he decided, as a show of strength, to march to Calais through Picardy and Artois.

• • •

From King Henry V, announcing the capture of Harfleur.

22 September 1415.

Norman French.

On the King's behalf.

Very dear and trusty, and well-beloved.

We do greet you oftentimes, in signifying unto you, for your consolation, that we are in very good health as to our person, thanks be to God who grants unto us the same, and that, after our arrival on this side, we came before our town of Harefleu on Saturday, the 17th day of August last past, and laid siege thereto, in manner as we have writen heretofore in our other Letters sent to you. And by the good diligence of our faithful lieges at this time in our company, and the strength and position of our cannon, and our other ordnance, the people who were within the town made great urgency to have divers parleys with us; yet this notwithstanding, it was our full purpose to make assault upon the town on Wednesday the 18th day of this month of September; but those within the town had perceived it, and made great instance, with means which they had not employed theretofore, to have conference with us.

And to avoid the effusion of human blood on the one side and on the other, we inclined to their offer, and thereupon we made answer unto them, and sent to them the last conclusion of our will; to the which they agreed, and for the same we do render thanks unto God, for we thought that they would not have so readily assented to the said conclusion. And on the same Wednesday there came by our command out of the said town the Sieurs de Gaucourt, d'Estouteville, Hankeville, and other lords and knights, who had the governance of the town, and delivered hostages; and all those, as well the lords and knights as the hostages, of whom some are lords and knights, and some notable burgesses, were sworn upon the body of Our Saviour that they would make unto us full deliverance of our said town, and submit the persons and goods therein to our grace, without any condition, if they should not by the Sunday then next ensuing, at one of the clock in the afternoon, have been rescued by battle given to us by our adversary of France, or his eldest son, the Dauphin. And thereupon, we gave our letters of safe conduct to the said Sieur de Hankeville and others, to the number of twelve persons, to go to our said adversary, and his son, to declare unto them the treaty so made.

The which Sieur de Hankeville, together with the others of his company, returned on the day* at eight of the clock in the forenoon, into our said town, without any rescue being offered by our said adversary, his son, or any other of their party; and the keys of the town were then fully delivered and rendered into our hand, and all those within were submitted to our grace without any condition, as above stated; praised be our Creator for the same; and we have put in our said town our very dear uncle, the Earl of Dorset† and have made him

* The day of final surrender, probably.

† Thomas Beaufort, youngest natural son of John of Gaunt, by Katherine Swynford.

Captain thereof, with a sufficient staff of people, as well of the one rank as the other. And we do will that you render humble thanks unto our Lord Almighty for this news; and do hope by the divine power, and the good labour and diligence of our faithful people on this side, to do our duty still further in gaining our right in these parts; and we do desire also, that by those passing between us you will certify us from time to time as to news as regards yourselves. And may Our Lord have you in His holy keeping.

Given under our Signet in our said town of Harflu, the 22nd day of the said month of September.

• • • • •

The next letter was written sometime after the battle of Agincourt which took place on 25th October 1415. Henry's army, which had suffered delays and sickness since leaving Harfleur, finally encountered the French force as they began the last part of their march to Calais. Although outnumbered, the King's strategy and organized soldiers, inspired by a great faith in God, routed the French who suffered terrible loss of life. The battle greatly added to Henry's prestige. After a generation of peace the English were delighted to have a victory to celebrate and were more eager to fund future campaigns.

The next letter written by one of the King's chaplains, immediately after the battle of Agincourt illustrates this enthusiasm in an highly effusive manner.* He refers to the capture of Harfleur 'a fortress of great strength, generally esteemed impregnable', the march through 'so many spacious and hostile provinces', and finally the glory of Agincourt. The chaplain's caution concering the lust for power yet urging further victories seems rather ambiguous but ties in with the highly complicated attitude towards warfare and etiquette of chivalry which was so dominant throughout the period and especially characteristic of King Henry V.

• • •

To King Henry V from one of this chaplains.

Between 25 October and 18 November 1415.

Latin.

* Munro suggests that the chaplain may have been Henry, Bishop of Winchester, later Cardinal Beaufort, who was the king's chancellor at this time.

Most Glorious Prince, and invincible Lord, the devoted chaplain, in as humble wise as he can or may, recommends himself to his supreme Lord on earth.

To the omnipotent King of Kings, whose judgements are ever just, I humbly address such daily thanksgivings as I can. Now, what I long hoped for and wished to see before I left this world, I behold before my eyes, whereby I feel my heart warmed with special delight, viz. the glory and honour of the famous realm of England, for a long time wholly lulled to sleep and forgotten, roused from its heavy slumber. For now winter is gone - the winter, that is, of sloth and idleness, that I say not timidity or madness. Flowers have appeared - the flowers of vigorous and warlike youth; and flourishing vines - whereby I understand that noble progeny of kings and nobles of England, which, rooted in virtuous arts, formerly spread their branches throughout the world, have given forth the odours of fame and of worthiest probity and of victory unheard of in all time; which to all the wellwishers of the realm are a savour of rare sweetness, to its enemies a terror, and deprives those who would cripple the rights of England of all courage for further resistance. National justice has required, the wisdom of the combatants has struggled, the prayers of the population have worked for [this consummation]. He whose victory is neither to the many or the few - who, the supreme judge of all, resists the proud and gives grace to the humble - hath looked on the combatants. What wise man, I ask, beholding, in future times, the success of such an expedition, will not marvel, and ascribe it to the power of God himself? How great are the events that have happened! When it is considered that, within nine weeks, a fortess of great strength, generally esteemed impregnable, and the safest port of the glorious realm of France, were taken; a progress opened through so many spacious and hostile provinces; and, finally, a victory obtained, which may well be deemed glorious in royal annals. Nothing like it has been heard or read of in all time. Not in the time of the Maccabees, whose history is still read in the church; not in that of Saul, the anointed of the prophet; not in that of David, the chosen king of the Israelitish people; not in that of Solomon, the wisest of men; not in that of Alexander, the most fortunate, has anything similar been read. Thy royal majesty deems and firmly holds, as I presume, that not thy hand, but the outstretched hand of God, hath done all these things, for His own praise, the honour and glory of the English nation, and the eternal memory of the royal name. In which it is chiefly to be considered what God has done for us; that whilst it was His will, perchance, to punish us to some extent, on account of our sins, he did not deliver us into the hands of our enemies, who know not how to spare; but he sent among us a plague, the rod of His displeasure; and lest the glory of such a victory should be claimed by the men who perchance did not deserve it, it was His will that they should be absent, that the glory of the victory should be to Him, and to you as His minister. Chiefly let us beware lest, after such victories, the accompaniments of victory vanquish the victors - such as pride, vainglory, boasting, swelling words, cruelty, rage, and the fury of revenge; all of which are enemies greatly to be dreaded by conquerors, and by which the most famous victors have been themselves conquered. Much more let humility, modesty, giving of thanks, piety, clemency, and a warm desire to pardon, prevail. There remains, therefore, invincible prince, that, with our inmost affections, praises be rendered to God for these great things; and, living righteously and serving him, let us suppliantly pray that He may bring so glorious a work to an end pleasing to Him. And you, most dread Prince, receive not the glory of God in vain, but for the prosecution of your right, casting away the lust of power, go forward manfully (the false dealings of the adversary being retarded and put to flight) and insist, with the utmost vigilance, that he shall not regain his strength. No man putting his hand to the plough, and looking back, is fit for the kingdom [of heaven]; but continued effort usually leads to success; and, according to Tully, it is the part of true virtue not to look on what has been done, but what remains to be done; not what a man has, but what he is wanting in. Moreover, it is fitting that your royal highness should not boast of the past, but be anxious for the future; neither let the power of our enemies drag us back; let not their astuteness disturb us; nor let any fair promises seduce anyone. Until you may be able to bring about and establish, on a basis of justice, a permanent peace, which has so long been the fixed desire of your heart . . . . .fitting matter will not be wanting, nor ought a careful executor [of the divine will] to falter, who, as far as possible, should spare Christian blood, and, tempering all things with mercy, bring them happily to an end. Truly, most worthy Prince, it behoveth you not to fear for the subsidies of your realm, both spiritual and temporal, to be raised in this matter; because your faithful people so delight in their present happy auspices, that they offer to you themselves and their goods, and pour out for you unceasingly their devout prayers; and therefore they are now met together in Parliament; and the devout clergy of your realm will meet in London, on the Octave of St. Martin next coming. At which time, I doubt not that they will so regard their Prince - (I allude to the phrase lately used by certain persons, 'the Prince of Priests,') that it will appear plainly, that they not only laud you with their voices, but rather gloriously magnify you with their deeds, and heartily desire that you may long reign over them. To the honour of your realm of England may the great God safely preserve your glory and majesty! Written, &c.

• • • • •

The next letter concerns Henry's second campaign. The King and his army left Southampton on July 30th 1417 accompanied by smiths, carpenters and other skilled men, as well as many servants. The destination remained a secret and many agreed that the fleet would probably land at Harfleur but, 'after two smooth days at sea the English sailed into the haven at the mouth of the little river Touques, on the south side of the estuary of the Seine,* a small force was waiting for them but it was rapidly dispersed.

After a day or two of preparation the King moved into the town of Touques with the aim of capturing the castle of Bonneville, which Henry describes as the castle of Touque in the following letter. As at Harfleur the garrison was unable to obtain assistance from the Dauphin, who was at Rouen, and was forced to surrender. In this instance the Dauphin ordered the messenger from Bonneville to be hanged for bringing such bad news. The French government also felt that the castle had been too ready to submit and beheaded an important citizen of the town.

King Henry at once communicated his success to the mayor of London in a letter which was received with transports of joy. The capture of Bonneville laid open all the rich vicomté of Auge.†

He then set about capturing Caen and all of Lower Normandy then succumbed to his might. After further victories Henry married Charles VI's daughter and was recognized as heir to the French throne in 1420. His premature death in 1422 marked the end of English domination in northern France.

• • •

From King Henry V, announcing the surrender of the Castle of Touque.

10 August 1417.

Norman French and Middle English.

By the King to our very dear and trusty, the mayor, Sherriffs, Aldermen and good people of our city of London.

Trusty and well-beloved, we greet you as always.

This is for you to have the pleasure of knowing that by God's grace we have safely arrived in our country of Normandy, and it has been arranged for all our subjects to come with us on the first crossing.

* Wylie p. 53. † Wylie p. 54.

Today, the Eve of St Lawrence, the Castle of Toucques was surrendered to us, having been besieged by our well-beloved cousin the Earl of Huntingdon, so that the keys of the castle were given to us with no shedding of Christian blood, nor any defence being offered by our enemies. The said castle is an honour,* and the Viscountcy and all the manors of Auge go with it, as we have been told by such people as were in it. So we humbly thank God that it pleased him of his high grace to give us such a fine beginning to our current expedition, and we also wish you to thank God for it by the best means you know; and that from time to time you send us news from your side of the sea, as between comrades.

Given under our signet, at our said castle of Toucques, the ninth day of August.

• • • • •

Petrarch's words make a fitting conclusion to this section. Judging by the previous letters it would be easy to imagine that in the medieval period war was revered by all. His anecdote provides a refreshing contrast to the bitter nationalistic and religious antagonisms which have so far been revealed.

• • •

Petrarch to Gasparo Squaro dei Broaspini of Verona.

22 November 1372.

Latin.

To Gasparo Squaro dei Broaspini of Verona; from Padua.

I received your note, full of affection and solicitude, like your other letters; I thank you; I am in your debt. Do not worry, and don't interrupt your worthy labours. My family, for which I feared much more than for myself, has fortunately escaped the thunderbolts of Mars, and is here with me, thank God. I have nothing else to write to you about; but it occurs to me that, to fill out the page, I might put in a somewhat comic story, perhaps new to you, about a fool and his far from foolish remark. It was when the great troubles between the Florentines and the Pisans were raging. (These occur almost annually, thanks to the sins of both sides.) The army of Florence was marching out of the gates; and a certain fool, who wandered nearly naked about the streets, was struck

* An honour was a collection of manors.

by the sight. He asked what it was all about. A bystander answered: "Don't you know, fool, that war has been declared against the Pisans?"

Said the fool: "And after this war there will be peace?"

"How can you think of peace, you idiot? Now the great war is just beginning."

"I still wonder," said the fool, "Won't there be a peace sometime after this war?"

"Well, certainly. No war lasts forever. Of course there will be peace sometime; but now there is war."

"Well then," said the fool, "wouldn't it be better to make the peace now, before the war begins to rage?"

What shall I say to that? Merely, if it were permissible, that the fool was very wise. Would that our warmakers might ponder his words! So might a war never be begun, or it might be ended before we should sink under war's ravages and calamities, after which indeed peace will come. That peace will be good, though it be all too late; it would be much the best, if it could come in time. But men's ears are shut against wise counsels. The ultimate triumph of war they say, is total madness. And surely the cause of all our evils is man's sin. We shall see this clearly at the war's end. Till then we can merely await God's will. Farewell.

LOVE AND MARRIAGE

During the Middle Ages the institution of marriage was influenced by both the requirements of lay society and the attitude of the Church. The former regarded marriage as a vital tool in developing and safeguarding the social order, the latter was more concerned with the interests of the divine order. In medieval times households, consisting of two parents, their children and domestic servants, formed the structure of society. Marriage, between households, reinforced this pattern, and therefore, 'more than at any other time in history, procreation was the main purpose of marriage.'

A marriage was usually arranged by the head of each household involved, rather than the bride and groom, primarily because so much was at stake. The bride's household lost a female member of the family whereas the groom's household gained one, along with her ancestral background, her inheritance, if any, and her 'anticipated motherhood'.

Royal marriages acted as an example to the rest of society by their desire to safeguard the family power and wealth through the careful marriage of the eldest son; the remaining sons were generally discouraged from marrying in order to tighten the pattern of lineage and to prevent a large number of heirs fragmenting the family fortune. On the other hand, daughters were encouraged to marry, especially within the nobility, either for political reasons, to create alliances, to end feuds or to encourage trade. Inevitably there were more women seeking husbands than men seeking wives and this meant that an elder son could often attract a wife of a higher rank and dynastic quality than himself.

At the other end of the social scale the value of a serf's daughter and her ability to have children, or rather potential workers, was recognized by feudal lords who were reluctant to allow women to marry away from their own estates at times when labour was scarce. This led to the establishment of the 'merchet' which was a payment made by the serf to his lord if his daughter married away from the locality, in order to obtain his consent and as compensation for the potential loss to the workforce.

The Church recognized man's need to reproduce and viewed marriage as the necessary state by which this should be achieved, and also as a vehicle for restraining carnal desires. Marriage was regarded as a sacred bond with both partners mutually consenting, symbolizing

God's union with mankind. The Church prohibited adultery in both partners, disapproved of widows remarrying and incest.

Incest was considered to have occurred if husband or wife had a common ancestor during the last seven generations. In practice this rule was not always observed, partly due to the desire to maintain a closely knit family lineage, and also because few people could trace their family so far back. In 1251 the Fourth Lateran Council decreased the prohibited degrees from seven to four, illustrating how lay attitudes to marriage were gradually absorbed into ecclesiastical policy.

The lifestyle of a medieval woman was primarily dependent upon her marital status. A single woman was under her parents' control but as soon as she married she became her husband's partner and responsible for the running of her own household.

Wealthy widows were sought after and once again family pressure might persuade a woman to remarry, despite the Church's ruling. Some opted for the nunnery and some, such as Agnes and Margaret Paston, were able to enjoy considerable independence. Marriages were not always inhibited by the restrictions of family influence and love played a vital part, frequently overcoming such obstacles. Personal choice is particularly evident in the Paston letters and whilst accepted procedures were followed, the individuals concerned were far from powerless. Although good marriages had contributed greatly to the family's standing, love was recognized as a force to be reckoned with; despite the hard-headed practicality which dominated the marriage market, romance was often present.

When a wife was left in charge of the household during her husband's absence, as a soldier or merchant perhaps, letters were essential for conveying not only domestic news but strength of feeling also. Chaucer's *Franklin's Tale*, which contains an excellent analysis of the rules of courtly love, describes how a husband, whilst posted abroad, writes to his wife to revive her spirits.

And eek Arveragus, in al this care,
Hath sent hir lettres hoom of his welfare,
And that he wol come hastily agayn;
Or elles hadde this sorwe hir herte slayn.

• • • • •

Peter Abelard was born at Le Pallet near Nantes in 1097, and became a great scholastic philosopher, logician and highly controversial theologian. His studies and teaching career were mainly based in Paris. Peter the Venerable and John of Salisbury were amongst his pupils as was Heloise, the niece of Fulbert, a canon at the cathedral in Paris. The tragedy of Heloise and Abelard's passion is well known, and the following letters have been selected since they illustrate their ideas and experiences of love and marriage.

Heloise and Abelard's love was all-consuming and ecstatically passionate. Heloise was totally devoted to Abelard in every way although he later admitted that he had only felt lust for her. When Heloise became pregnant Abelard agreed with Fulbert to marry her as long as the marriage remained a secret so that his reputation as a serious scholar would not be harmed. Heloise realized that such a marriage would not pacify her uncle in the face of public scandal and rejected any form of marriage outright, basically because it would contradict their fundamental belief in the insignificance of 'human ties' and because she considered Abelard's career to be more important than her reputation or her uncle's wrath.

The marriage took place and in order to avoid Fulbert's unabated anger, as well as to maintain the clandestine nature of their union, Abelard removed Heloise to a convent on the outskirts of Paris where he knew he would be able to make regular visits.

Fulbert believed that Abelard was encouraging Heloise to take the veil in order to free himself from any further responsibilities, and it was then that he ordered Abelard's castration. Both Abelard and Heloise then entered the monastic life. To appreciate the whole story the correspondence of Abelard and Heloise should be read in its entirety. Abelard resumed his teaching career although his rivals felt that a monk should not teach philosophy or encourage a critical analysis of traditional theological writings and beliefs. Abelard dedicated the Hermitage of the Paraclete, which he had founded in 1122 to Heloise and her fellow nuns, but he himself found it difficult to cope with the pressures of a monastic life, particularly his role as abbot of the unruly monastery of St Gildas, where he continued to attract antagonism until his death in 1142.

• • •

Heloise to Abelard.

1132-1142.

Latin.

To her master, or rather her father, husband, or rather brother; his handmaid, or rather his daughter, wife, or rather sister; to Abelard, Heloise.

Not long ago, my beloved, by chance someone brought me the letter of consolation you had sent to a friend. I saw at once from the superscription that it was yours, and was all the more eager to read it since the writer is so dear to my heart. I hoped for renewal of strength, at least from the writer's words which would picture for me the reality I have lost. But nearly every line of this letter was filled, I remember, with gall and wormwood, as it told the pitiful story of our entry into religion and the cross of unending suffering which you, my only love, continue to bear.

In that letter you did indeed carry out the promise you made your friend at the beginning, that he would think his own troubles insignificant or nothing, in comparison with your own. First you revealed the persecution you suffered from your teachers, then the supreme treachery of the mutilation of your person, and then described the abominable jealousy and violent attacks of your fellow-students, Alberic of Rheims and Lotulf of Lombardy.* You did not gloss over what at their instigation was done to your distinguished theological work or what amounted to a prison sentence passed on yourself. Then you went on to the plotting against you by your abbot and false brethren, the serious slanders from those two pseudo-apostles, spread against you by the same rivals, and the scandal stirred up among many people because you had acted contrary to custom in naming your oratory after the Paraclete. You went on to the incessant, intolerable persecutions which you still endure at the hands of that cruel tyrant and the evil monks you call your sons, and so brought your sad story to and end.

No one, I think, could read or hear it dry-eyed, my own sorrows are renewed by the detail in which you have told it, and redoubled because you say your perils are still increasing. All of us here are driven to despair of your life, and every day we await in fear and trembling the final word of your death. And so in the name of Christ, who is still giving you some protection for his service, we beseech you to write as often as you think fit to us who are his handmaids and yours, with news of the perils in which you are still storm-tossed. We are all that are left you, so at least you should let us share your sorrow or your joy.

It is always some consolation in sorrow to feel that it is shared, and any burden laid on several is carried more lightly or removed. And if this storm has quietened down for a while, you must be all the more prompt to send us a letter which will be the more gladly received. But whatever you write about will bring us no small relief in the mere proof that you have us in mind. Letters from absent friends are welcome indeed, as Seneca himself shows us by his own example when he writes

* See *Historia calamitatum*, p. 79.

these words in a passage of a letter to his friend Lucilius.

Thank you for writing to me often, the one way in which you can make your presence felt, for I never have a letter from you without the immediate feeling that we are together. If pictures of absent friends give us pleasure, renewing our memories and relieving the pain of separation even if they cheat us with empty comfort, how much more welcome is a letter which comes to us in the very handwriting of an absent friend.

Thank God that here at least is a way of restoring your presence to us which no malice can prevent, nor any obstacle hinder; then do not, I beseech you, allow any negligence to hold you back.

You wrote your friend a long letter of consolation, prompted no doubt by his misfortunes, but really telling of your own. The detailed account you gave of these may have been intended for his comfort, but it also greatly increased our own feeling of desolation; in your desire to heal his wounds you have dealt us fresh wounds of grief as well as re-opening the old. I beg you, then, as you set about tending the wounds which others have dealt, heal the wounds you have yourself inflicted. You have done your duty to a friend and comrade, discharged your debt to friendship and comradeship, but it is a greater debt which binds you in obligation to us who can properly be called not friends so much as dearest friends, not comrades but daughters, or any other conceivable name more tender and holy. How great the debt by which you have bound yourself to us needs neither proof nor witness, were it in any doubt; if the whole world kept silent, the facts themselves would cry out. For you after God are the sole founder of this place, and sole builder of this oratory, the sole creator of this community. You have built nothing here upon another man's foundation. Everything here is your own creation. This was a wilderness open to wild beasts and brigands, a place which had known no home nor habitation of men. In the very lairs of wild beasts and lurking-places of robbers, where the name of God was never heard, you built a sanctuary to God and dedicated a shrine in the name of the Holy Spirit. To build it you drew nothing from the riches of kings and princes, though their wealth was great and could have been yours for the asking: whatever was done, the credit was to be yours alone. Clerks and scholars came flocking here, eager for your teaching, and ministered to all your needs; and even those who had lived on the benefices of the Church and knew only how to receive offerings, not to make them, whose hands were held out to take but not to give, became pressing in their lavish offers of assistance.

And so it is yours, truly your own, this new plantation for God's purpose, but it is sown with plants which are still very tender and need watering if they are to thrive. Through its feminine nature this plantation would be weak and frail even if it were not new; and so it needs a more careful and regular cultivation, according to the words of the Apostle: 'I planted the seed and Apollos watered it; but God made it grow. The Apostle through the doctrine that he preached had planted and established in the faith the Corinthians, to whom he was writing. Afterwards the Apostle's own disciple, Apollos, had watered them with his holy exhortations and so God's grace bestowed on them growth in the virtues. You cultivate a vineyard of another's vines which you did not plant yourself and which has now turned to bitterness against you, so that often your advice brings no result and your holy words are uttered in vain. You devote your care to another's vineyard; think what you owe to your own. You teach and admonish rebels to no purpose, and in vain you throw the pearls of your divine eloquence to the pigs. While you spend so much on the stubborn, consider what you owe to the obedient; you are so generous to your enemies but should reflect on how you are indebted to your daughters. Apart from everything else, consider the close tie by which you have bound yourself to me, and repay the debt you owe a whole community of women dedicated to God by discharging it the more dutifully to her who is yours alone.

Your superior wisdom knows better than our humble learning of the many serious treatises which the holy Fathers compiled for the instruction or exhortation or even the consolation of holy women, and of the care with which these were composed. And so in the precarious early days of our conversion long ago I was not a little surprised and troubled by your forgetfulness, when neither reverence for God nor our mutual love nor the example of the holy Fathers made you think of trying to comfort me, wavering and exhausted as I was by prolonged grief, either by word when I was with you or by letter when we had parted.* Yet you must know that you are bound to me by an obligation which is all the greater for the further close tie of the marriage sacrament uniting us, and are the deeper in my debt because of the love I have always borne you, as everyone knows, a love which is beyond all bounds.

You know, beloved, as the whole world knows, how much I have lost in you, how at one wretched stroke of fortune that supreme act of flagrant treachery robbed me of my very self in robbing me of you; and how my sorrow for my loss is nothing compared with what I feel for the manner in which I lost you. Surely the greater the cause for grief the

* This sentence, often mistranslated as if it refers to the present and so suggesting that Abelard has never visited nor written to her at the Paraclete, has been used as evidence that the letters are a forgery because it contradicts what Abelard says in the *Historia calamitatum* (p. 98). But the tense (*movit*) is past, translated here as 'I was troubled,' and Heloise must be referring to his failure to help her by word before they separated and by letter after she had entered the convent.

greater the need for the help of consolation, and this no one can bring but you; you are the sole cause of my sorrow, and you alone can grant me the grace of consolation.

You alone have the power to make me sad, to bring me happiness or comfort; you alone have so great a debt to repay me, particularly now when I have carried out all your orders so implicitly that when I was powerless to oppose you in anything, I found strength at your command to destroy myself. I did more, strange to say - my love rose to such heights of madness that it robbed itself of what it most desired beyond hope of recovery, when immediately at your bidding I changed my clothing along with my mind, in order to prove you the sole possessor of my body and my will alike.

God knows I never sought anything in you except yourself; I wanted simply you, nothing of yours. I looked for no marriage-bond, no marriage portion, and it was not my own pleasures and wishes I sought to gratify, as you well know, but yours. The name of wife may seem more sacred or more binding, but sweeter for me will always be the word mistress, or, if you will permit me, that of concubine or whore. I believed that the more I humbled myself on your account, the more gratitude I should win from you, and also the less damage I should do to the brightness of your reputation.

You yourself on your own account did not altogether forget this in the letter of consolation I have spoken of which you wrote to a friend,* there you thought fit to set out some of the reasons I gave in trying to dissuade you from binding us together in an ill-starred marriage. But you kept silent about most of my arguments for preferring love to wedlock and freedom to chains. God is my witness that if Augustus, Emperor of the whole world, thought fit to honour me with marriage and conferred all the earth on me to possess for ever, it would be dearer and more honourable to me to be called not his Empress but your whore.

For a man's worth does not rest on his wealth or power; these depend on fortune, but worth on his merits. And a woman should realize that if she marries a rich man more readily than a poor one, and desires her husband more for his possessions than for himself, she is offering herself for sale. Certainly any woman who comes to marry through desires of this kind deserves wages, not gratitude, for clearly her mind is on the man's property, not himself, and she would be ready to prostitute herself to a richer man, if she could. This is evident from

* This suggests that Heloise believed the *Historia calamitatum* tobe a genuine letter to a real person, and not an example of a conventional epistolatory genre, unless she is writing ironically.

the argument put forward in the dialogue of Aeschines Socraticus* by the learned Aspasia to Xenophon and his wife. When she had expounded it in an effort to bring about a reconciliation between them, she ended with these words: 'Unless you come to believe that there is no better man nor worthier woman on earth you will always still be looking for what you judge the best thing of all - to be the husband of the best of wives and the wife of the best of husbands.'

These are saintly words which are more than philosophic; indeed, they deserve the name of wisdom, not philosophy. It is a holy error and a blessed delusion between man and wife, when perfect love can keep the ties of marriage unbroken not so much through bodily continence as chastity of spirit. But what error permitted other women, plain truth permitted me, and what they thought of their husbands, the world in general believed, or rather, knew to be true of yourself; so that my love for you was the more genuine for being further removed from error. What king or philosopher could match your fame? What district, town or village did not long to see you? When you appeared in public, who did not hurry to catch a glimpse of you, or crane his neck and strain his eyes to follow your departure? Every wife, every young girl desired you in absence and was on fire in your presence; queens and great ladies envied me my joys and my bed.

You had besides, I admit, two special gifts whereby to win at once the heart of any woman - your gifts for composing verse and song, in which we know other philosophers have rarely been successful. This was for you no more than a diversion, a recreation from the labours of your philosophic work, but you left many love-songs and verses which won wide popularity for the charm of their words and tunes and kept your name continualy on everyone's lips.† The beauty of the airs ensured that even the unlettered did not forget you; more than anything this made women sigh for love of you. And as most of these songs told of our love, they soon made me widely known and roused the envy of many women against me. For your manhood was adorned by every grace of mind and body, and among the women who envied me then, could there be one now who does not feel compelled by my misfortune to sympathize with my loss of such joys? Who is there who was once my enemy, whether man or woman, who is not moved now by the compassion which is my due? Wholly guilty though I am, I am also, as you know, wholly innocent. It is not the deed but the intention of the doer which makes the crime, and justice should weigh

* Aeschines Socraticus, a pupil of Socrates, wrote several dialogues of which fragments survive. This is however no proof that Heloise knew Greek, as the passage was well known in the Middle Ages from Cicero's translation of it in *De inventione*, 1.31.

† None of Abelard's secular verse survives.

not what was done but the spirit in which it is done. What my intention towards you has always been, you alone who have known it can judge. I submit all to your scrutiny, yield to your testimony in all things.

Tell me one thing, if you can. Why, after our entry into religion, which was your decision alone, have I been so neglected and forgotten by you that I have neither a word from you when you are here to give me strength nor the consolation of a letter in absence? Tell me, I say, if you can - or I will tell you what I think and indeed the world suspects. It was desire, not affection which bound you to me, the flame of lust rather than love. So when the end came to what you desired, any show of feeling you used to make went with it. This is not merely my own opinion, beloved, it is everyone's. There is nothing personal or private about it; it is the general view which is widely held. I only wish that it were mine alone, and that the love you professed could find someone to defend it and so comfort me in my grief for a while. I wish I could think of some explanation which would excuse you and somehow cover up the way you hold me cheap.

I beg you then to listen to what I ask - you will see that it is a small favour which you can easily grant. While I am denied your presence, give me at least through your words - of which you have enough and to spare - some sweet semblance of yourself. It is no use my hoping for generosity in deeds if you are grudging in words. Up to now I had thought I deserved much of you, seeing that I carried out everything for your sake and continue up to the present moment in complete obedience to you. It was not any sense of vocation which brought me as a young girl to accept the austerities of the cloister, but your bidding alone, and if I deserve no gratitude from you, you may judge for yourself how my labours are in vain. I can expect no reward for this from God, for it is certain that I have done nothing as yet for love of him. When you hurried towards God I followed you, indeed, I went first to take the veil - perhaps you were thinking how Lot's wife turned back when you made me put on the religious habit and take my vows before you gave yourself to God. Your lack of trust in me over this one thing, I confess, overwhelmed me with grief and shame. I would have had no hesitation, God knows, in following you or going ahead at your bidding to the flames of Hell. My heart was not in me but with you, and now, even more, if it is not with you it is nowhere; truly, without you it cannot exist. See that it fares well with you, I beg, as it will if it finds you kind, if you give grace in return for grace, small for great, words or deeds. If only your love had less confidence in me, my dear, so that you would be more concerned on my behalf! But as it is, the more I have made you feel secure in me, the more I have to bear with your neglect.

Remember, I implore you, what I have done, and think how much you owe me. While I enoyed with you the pleasures of the flesh, many were uncertain whether I was prompted by love or lust; but now the end is proof of the beginning. I have finally denied myself every pleasure in obedience to your will, kept nothing for myself except to prove that now, even more, I am yours. Consider then your injustice, if when I deserve more you give me less, or rather, nothing at all, especially when it is a small thing I ask of you and one you could so easily grant. And so, in the name of God to whom you have dedicated yourself, I beg you to restore your presence to me in the way you can - by writing me some word of comfort, so that in this as least I may find increased strength and readiness to serve God. When in the past you sought me out for sinful pleasures your letters came to me thick and fast, and your many songs put your Heloise on everyone's lips, so that every street and house echoed with my name. It is not far better now to summon me to God than it was then to satisfy our lust? I beg you, think what you owe me, give ear to my pleas, and I will finish a long letter with a brief ending: farewell, my only love.

• • •

Abelard to Heloise.

1132-1142.

Latin.

To the bride of Christ, Christ's servant.

The whole of your last letter is given up to a recital of your misery over the wrongs you suffer, and these, I note, are on four counts. First you complain that contrary to custom in letter-writing, or indeed against the natural order of the world, my letter to you put your name before mine in its greeting. Secondly, that when I ought to have offered you some remedy for your comfort I actually increased your sense of desolation and made the tears flow which I should have checked. This I did by writing 'But if the Lord shall deliver me into the hands of my enemies, so that they overcome and kill me . . .' Thirdly you went on to your old perpetual complaint against God concerning the manner of our entry into religious life and the cruelty of the act of treachery performed on me. Lastly, you set your self-accusations against my praise of you, and implored me with some urgency not to praise you again.

I have decided to answer you on each point in turn, not so much in self-justification as for your own enlightenment and encouragement, so that you will more willingly grant my own requests when you understand that they have a basis of reason, listen to me more attentively on the subject of your own pleas as you find me less to blame in my own, and be less ready to refuse me when you see me less deserving of reproach.

What you call the unnatural order of my greeting, if you consider it carefully, was in accordance with your own view as well as mine. For it is common knowledge, as you yourself have shown, that in writing to superiors one puts their name first, and you must realize that you became my superior from the day when you began to be my lady on becoming the bride of my Lord; witness St Jerome, who writes to Eustochium 'This is my reason for writing "my lady Eustochium". Surely I must address as "my lady" her who is the bride of my Lord.' It was a happy transfer of your married state, for you were previously the wife of a poor mortal and now are raised to the bed of the King of kings. By the privilege of your position you are set not only over your former husband but over every servant of that King. So you should not be surprised if I commend myself in life as in death to the prayers of your community, seeing that in common law it is accepted that wives are better able than their households to intercede with their husbands, being ladies rather than servants. As an illustration of this, the Psalmist says of the queen and bride of the King of kings: 'On your right stands the queen,' as if it were clearly stated that she is nearest to her husband and close to his side, and moves forward with him, while all the rest stand apart or follow behind. The bride in the Canticles, an Ethiopian (such as the one Moses took as a wife) rejoices in the glory of her special position and says: 'I am black but lovely, daughters of Jerusalem; therefore the king has loved me and brought me into his chamber.' And again, 'Take no notice of my darkness, because the sun has discoloured me.' In general it is the contemplative soul which is described in these words and especialy called the bride of Christ, but your outer habit indicates that they have particular application to you all. For that outer garb of coarse black clothing, like the mourning worn by good widows who weep for the dead husbands they had loved, shows you to be, in the words of the Apostle, truly widowed and desolate and such as the Church should be charged to support. The Scriptures also record the grief of these widows for their spouse who was slain, in the words: 'The women sitting at the tomb wept and lamented for the Lord.'

The Ethiopian woman is black in the outer part of her flesh and as regards exterior appearance looks less lovely than other women; yet she is not unlike them within, but in several respects she is whiter and lovelier, in her bones, for instance, or her teeth. Indeed, whiteness of teeth is also praised in her spouse, in reference to 'his teeth whiter than milk'. And so she is black without but lovely within; for she is blackened outside in the flesh because in this life she suffers bodily affliction through the repeated tribulations of adversity, according to the saying of the Apostle: 'Persecution will come to all who want to live a godly life as Christians.'

As prosperity is marked by white, so adversity may properly be indicated by black, and she is white within in her bones because her soul is strong in virtues, as it is written that 'The king's daughter is all glory within'. For the bones within, surrounded by the flesh without, are the strength and support of the very flesh they wear or sustain, and can properly stand for the soul which gives life and sustenance to the flesh itself in which it is, and to which it gives movement and direction and provision for all its well-being. Its whiteness or beauty is the sum of the virtues which adorn it.

She is black too in outward things because while she is still an exile on life's pilgrimage, she keeps herself humble and abject in this life so that she may be exalted in the next, which is hidden with Christ in God, once she has come into her own country. So indeed the true sun changes her colour because the heavenly love of the brideroom humbles her in this way, or torments her with tribulations lest prosperity lifts her up. He changes her colour, that is, he makes her different from other women who thirst for earthly things and seek worldly glory, so that she may truly become through her humility a lily of the valley, and not a lily of the heights like those foolish virgins who pride themselves on purity of the flesh or an outward show of self denial, and then wither in the fire of temptation. And she rightly told the daughters of Jerusalem, that is, the weaker amongst the faithful who deserve to be called daughters rather than sons, 'Take no notice of my darkness, because the sun has discoloured me.' She might say more openly: 'The fact that I humble myself in this way or bear adversity so bravely is due to no virtue of mine but to the grace of him whom I serve.' This is not the way of heretics and hypocrites who (at any rate when others are present) humiliate themselves to excess in hopes of earthly glory, and endure much to no purpose. The sort of abjection or tribulation they put up with is indeed surprising, and they are the most pitiable of men, enjoying the good things neither of this life nor of the life to come. It is with this in mind that the bride says 'Do not wonder that I do so;' but we must wonder at those who vainly burn with desire for worldly praise and deny themselves advantages on earth so that they are as unhappy in their present life as they will be in the next. Such self denial is that of the foolish virgins who found the door shut against them.

And she did well to say that, because she is black, as we said, and lovely, she is chosen and taken into the king's bedchamber, that is, to that secret place of peace and contemplation, and into the bed, of which she says elsewhere. 'Night after night on my bed I have sought my true love.' Indeed, the disfigurement of her blackness makes her choose what is hidden rather than open, what is secret and not known to all, and any such wife desires private, not public delights with her husband, and would rather be known in bed than seen at table. Moreover it often happens that the flesh of black women is all the softer to touch though it is less attractive to look at, and for this reason the pleasure they give is greater and more suitable for private than for public enjoyment, and their husbands take them into a bedroom to enjoy them rather than parade them before the world. Following this metaphor, when that spiritual bride said 'I am black but lovely,' she rightly added at once 'Therefore the king has loved me and brought me into his chamber.' She relates each point to the other: because she was lovely he loved her, and because she was black he brought her into his chamber. She is lovely, as we said before, with virtues within which the bridegroom loves, and black outside from the adversity of bodily tribulation. Such blackness of bodily tribulation easily turns the minds of the faithful away from love of earthly things and attaches them to the desire for eternal life, often leading them from the stormy life of the world to retirement for contemplation. Thus St Jerome writes that our own, that is, the monastic life, took its beginning from Paul.

The humiliation of coarse garments also looks to retirement rather than to public life, and is to be preserved as being most suitable for the life of humility and withdrawal which especially befits our profession. The greatest encouragement to public display is costly clothing, which is sought by none except for empty display and worldly ceremony, as St Gregory clearly shows in saying that 'No one adorns himself in private, only where he can be seen.' As for the chamber of the bride, it is the one to which the bridegroom himself in the Gospel invites anyone who prays, saying 'But when you pray, go into a room by yourself, shut the door and pray to your Father'. He could have added 'not like the hypocrites, at street corners and in public places'. So by a room he means a place that is secluded from the tumult and sight of the world, where prayer can be offered more purely and quietly, such as the seclusion of monastic solitude, a place where we are told to shut the door, that is, to close up every approach, lest something happen to hinder the purity of prayer and what we see distract the unfortunate soul.

Yet there are many wearing our habit who despise this counsel, or rather, this divine precept, and we find them hard to tolerate when they celebrate the divine offices with cloister or choir wide open and conduct themselves shamelessly in full view of both men and women, especially during the Mass when they are decked out in valuable ornaments like those of the worldly men to whom they display them. In their view a fast is best celebrated if it is rich in external ornament and lavish in food and drink. Better to keep silence, as it is shameful to speak of their wretched blindness that is wholly contrary to the religion of Christ which belongs to the poor. At heart they are Jews, following their own custom instead of a rule, making a mockery of God's command in their practices, looking to usage, not duty; although, as St Augustine reminds us, the Lord said 'I am truth' not 'I am custom.' Anyone who cares to may entrust himself to the prayers of these men, which are offered with doors open, but you who have been led by the King of heaven himself into his chamber and rest in his embrace, and with the door always shut are wholly given up to him, are more intimately joined to him, in the Apostle's words, 'But anyone who is joined to the Lord is one spirit with him.' So much the more confidence, then, have I in the purity and effectiveness of your prayers, and the more urgently I demand your help. And I believe these prayers are offered more devoutly on my behalf because we are bound together in such great mutual love.

But if I have distressed you by mentioning the dangers which beset me or the death I fear, it was done in accordance with your own request, or rather, entreaty. For the first letter you wrote me has a passage which says: 'And so in the name of Christ, who is still giving you some protection for his service, we beseech you to write as often as you think fit to us who are his handmaids and yours, with news of the perils in which you are still storm-tossed. We are all that are left you, so at least you should let us share your sorrow or your joy. It is always some consolation in sorrow to feel that it is shared, and any burden laid on several is carried more lightly or removed.' Why then do you accuse me of making you share my anxiety when I was forced to do so at your own behest? When I am suffering in despair of my life, would it be fitting for you to be joyous? Would you want to be partners only in joy, not grief, to join in rejoicing without weeping with those who weep? There is no wider distinction between true friends and false than the fact that the former share adversity, the latter only prosperity.

Say no more, I beg you, and cease from complaints like these which are so far removed from the true depths of love! Yet even if you are still offended by this, I am so critically placed in danger and daily despair of life that it is proper for me to take thought for the welfare of my soul, and to provide for it while I may. Nor will you, if you truly love me, take exception to my forethought. Indeed, had you any hope of divine mercy being shown me, you would be all the more anxious for me to be freed from the troubles of this life as you see them to be intolerable. At least you must know that whoever frees me from life will deliver me from the greatest suffering. What I may afterwards incur is uncertain, but from what I shall be set free is not in question. Every unhappy life is happy in its ending, and those who feel true sympathy and pain for the anxieties of others want to see these ended, even to their own loss, if they really love those they see suffer and think more of their friends' advantage than of their own. So when a son has long been ill a mother wants his illness to end even in death, for she finds it unbearable, and can more easily face bereavement than have him share her misery. And anyone who takes special pleasure in the presence of a friend would rather have him happy in absence than present and unhappy, for he finds suffering intolerable if he cannot relieve it. In your case, you are not even permitted to enjoy my presence, unhappy though it is, and so, when any provision you are able to make for me is to your own advantage, I cannot see why you should prefer me to live on in great misery rather than be happier in death. If you see your advantage in prolonging my miseries, you are proved an enemy, not a friend. But if you hesitate to appear in such a guise, I beg you, as I said before, to cease your complaints.

However, I approve of your rejection of praise, for in this very thing you show yourself more praiseworthy. It is written that 'he who is first in accusing himself is just* and 'Whoever humbles himself will be exalted.' May your written words be reflected in your heart! If they are, yours is true humility and will not vanish with anything I say. But be careful, I beg you, not to seek praise when you appear to shun it, and not to reject with your lips what you desire in your heart. St Jerome writes to the virgin Eustochium on this point, amongst others: 'We are led on by our natural evil. We give willing ear to our flatterers, and though we may answer that we are unworthy and an artful blush suffuses our cheeks, the soul inwardly delights in its own praise.' Such artfulness Virgil describes in wanton Galatea, who sought what she wanted by flight, and by feigning rejection led on her lover more surely towards her:

She flees to the willows and wishes first to be seen.

Before she hides she wants to be seen fleeing, so that the very flight whereby she appears to reject the youth's company ensures that she obtains it. Similarly, when we seem to shun men's praise we are directing it towards ourselves, and when we pretend that we wish to hide lest anyone discovers what to praise in us, we are leading the unwary on to give us praise because in this way we appear to deserve it. I mention this because it is a common occurrence, not because I suspect such things of you; I have no doubts about your humility. But I want you to refrain from speaking like this, so that you do not appear

---

* Proverbs xviii, 17. The N.E.B. translates the whole verse: 'In a lawsuit the first speaker seems right, until another steps forward and cross-questions him.' The Knox translation of the Vulgate has a note on the obscurity of the Hebrew, and translates the Latin as 'An innocent man is the first to lay bare the truth.' Neither seems to suit the interpretation given by Abelard.

to those who do not know you so well to be seeking fame by shunning it, as Jerome says. My praise will never make you proud, but will summon you to higher things, and the more eager you are to please me, the more anxious you will be to embrace what I praise. My praise is not a tribute to your piety which is intended to bolster up your pride, and we ought not in fact to believe in our friends' approval any more than in our enemies' abuse.

I come at last to what I have called your old perpetual complaint, in which you presume to blame God for the manner of our entry into religion instead of wishing to glorify him as you justly should. I had thought that this bitterness of heart at what was so clear an act of divine mercy had long since disappeared. The more dangerous such bitterness is to you in wearing out body and soul alike, the more pitiful it is and distressing to me. If you are anxious to please me in everything, as you claim, and in this at least would end my torment, or even give me the greatest pleasure, you must rid yourself of it. If it persists you can neither please me nor attain bliss with me. Can you bear me to come to this without you - I whom you declare yourself ready to follow to the very fires of hell? Seek piety in this at least, lest you cut yourself off from me who am hastening, you believe, towards God; be the readier to do so because the goal we must come to will be blessed, and our companionship the more welcome for being happier. Remember what you have said, recall what you have written, namely that in the manner of our conversion, when God seems to have been more my adversary, he has clearly shown himself kinder. For this reason at least you must accept his will, that it is most salutary for me, and for you too, if your transports of grief will see reason. You should not grieve because you are the cause of so great a good, for which you must not doubt you were specially created by God. Nor should you weep because I have to bear this, except when our blessings through the martyrs in their sufferings and the Lord's death sadden you. If it had befallen me justly, would you find it easier to bear? Would it distress you less? In fact if it had been so, the result would have been greater disgrace for me and more credit to my enemies, since justice would have won them approval while my guilt would have brought me into contempt. And no one would be stirred by pity for me to condemn what was done.

However, it may relieve the bitterness of your grief if I prove that this came upon us justly, as well as to our advantage, and that God's punishment was more properly directed against us when we were married than when we were living in sin. After our marriage, when you were living in the cloister with the nuns at Argenteuil and I came one day to visit you privately, you know what my uncontrollable desire did with you there, actually in a corner of the refectory, since we had nowhere else to go. I repeat, you know how shamelessly we behaved on that occasion in so hallowed a place, dedicated to the most holy Virgin. Even if our other shameful behaviour was ended, this alone would deserve far heavier punishment. Need I recall our previous fornication and the wanton impurities which preceded our marriage, or my supreme act of betrayal, when I deceived your uncle about you so disgracefully, at a time when I was continuously living with him in his own house? Who would not judge me justly betrayed by the man whom I had first shamelessly betrayed? Do you think that the momentary pain of that wound is sufficient punishment for such crimes? Or rather, that so great an advantage was fitting for such great wickedness? What wound do you suppose would satisfy God's justice for the profanation such as I described of a place so sacred to his own Mother? Surely, unless I am much mistaken, not that wound which was wholly beneficial was intended as a punishment for this, but rather the daily unending torment I now endure.

You know too how when you were pregnant and I took you to my own country you disguised yourself in the sacred habit of a nun, a pretence which was an irreverent mockery of the religion you now profess. Consider, then, how fittingly divine justice, or rather, divine grace brought you against your will to the religion which you did not hesitate to mock, so that you should willingly expiate your profanation in the same habit, and the truth of reality should remedy the lie of your pretence and correct your falsity. And if you would allow consideration of our advantage to be an element in divine justice, you would be able to call what God did to us then an act not of justice, but of grace.

See then, my beloved, see how with the dragnets of his mercy the Lord has fished us up from the depth of this dangerous sea, and from the abyss of what a Charybdis he has saved our shipwrecked selves, although we were unwilling, so that each of us may justly break out in that cry: 'The Lord takes thought for me.' Think and think again of the great perils in which we were and from which the Lord rescued us; tell always with the deepest gratitude how much the Lord has done for our souls. Comfort by our example any unrighteous who despair of God's goodness, so that all may know what may be done for those who ask with prayer, when such benefits are granted sinners even against their will. Consider the magnanimous design of God's mercy for us, the compassion with which the Lord directed his judgement towards our chastisement, the wisdom whereby he made use of evil itself and mercifully set aside our impiety, so that by a wholly justified wound in a single part of my body he might heal two souls. Compare our danger and manner of deliverance, compare the sickness and the medicine. Examine the cause, our deserts, and marvel at the effect, his pity.

You know the depths of shame to which my unbridled lust had

consigned our bodies, until no reverence for decency or for God even during the days of Our Lord's Passion, or of the greater sacraments could keep me from wallowing in this mire. Even when you were unwilling, resisted to the utmost of your power and tried to dissuade me, as yours was the weaker nature I often forced you to consent with threats and blows. So intense were the fires of lust which bound me to you that I set those wretched, obscene pleasures, which we blush even to name, above God as above myself; nor would it seem that divine mercy could have taken action except by forbidding me these pleasures altogether, without future hope. And so it was wholly just and merciful, although by means of the supreme treachery of your uncle, for me to be reduced in that part of my body which was the seat of lust and sole reason for those desires, so that I could increase in many ways; in order that this member should justly be punished for all its wrongdoing in us, expiate in suffering the sins committed for its amusement, and cut me off from the slough of filth in which I had been wholly immersed in mind as in body. Only thus could I become more fit to approach the holy altars, now that no contagion of carnal impurity would ever again call me from them. How mercifully did he want me to suffer so much only in that member, the privation of which would also further the salvation of my soul without defiling my body nor preventing any performance of my duties! Indeed, it would make me readier to perform whatever can be honourably done by setting me wholly free from the heavy yoke of carnal desire.

So when divine grace cleansed rather than deprived me of those vile members which from their practice of utmost indecency are called 'the parts of shame' and have no proper name of their own, what else did it do but remove a foul imperfection in order to preserve perfect purity? Such purity, as we have heard, certain sages have desired so eagerly that they have mutilated themselves, so as to remove entirely the shame of desire. The Apostle too is recorded as having besought the Lord to rid him of this thorn in the flesh, but was not heard. The great Christian philosopher Origen provides an example, for he was not afraid to mutilate himself in order to quench completely this fire within him, as if he understood literally the words that those men were truly blessed who castrated themselves for the Kingdom of Heaven's sake, and believed them to be truthfully carrying out the bidding of the Lord about offending members, that we should cut them off and throw them away; and as if he interpreted as historic fact, not as a hidden symbol, that prophecy of Isaiah in which the Lord prefers eunuchs to the rest of the faithful: 'The eunuchs who keep my sabbaths, and choose to do my will I will give a place in my own house and within my walls and a name better than sons and daughters. I will give them an everlasting name which shall not perish.' Yet Origen is seriously to be blamed because he sought a remedy for blame in punishment of his body. True, he has zeal for God, but an ill-informed zeal, and the charge of homicide can be proved against him for his self mutilation. Men think he did this either at the suggestion of the devil or in grave error but, in my case, through God's compassion, it was done by another's hand. I do not incur blame, I escape it. I deserve death and gain life. I am called but hold back; I persist in crime and am pardoned against my will. The Apostle prays and is not heard, he persists in prayer and is not answered. Truly the Lord takes thought for me. I will go then and declare how much the Lord has done for my soul.

Come too, my inseparable companion, and join me in thanksgiving, you who were made my partner both in guilt and in grace. For the Lord is not unmindful also of your own salvation, indeed, he has you much in mind, for by a kind of holy presage of his name he marked you out to be especially his when he named you Heloise, after his own name, Elohim. In his mercy, I say, he intended to provide for two people in one, the two whom the devil sought to destroy in one; since a short while before this happening he had bound us together by the indissoluble bond of the marriage sacrament. At the time I desired to keep you whom I loved beyond measure for myself alone, but he was already planning to use this opportunity for our joint conversion to himself. Had you not been previously joined to me in wedlock, you might easily have clung to the world when I withdrew from it, either at the suggestion of your relatives or in enjoyment of carnal delights. See then, how greatly the Lord was concerned for us, as if he were reserving us for some great ends, and was indignant or grieved because our knowledge of letters, the talents which he had entrusted to us, were not being used to glorify his name; or as if he feared for his humble and incontinent servant, because it is written 'Women make even the wise forsake their faith.' Indeed, this is proved in the case of the wisest of men, Solomon.

How great an interest the talent of your own wisdom pays daily to the Lord in the many spiritual daughters you have borne for him, while I remain totally barren and labour in vain amongst the sons of perdition! What a hateful loss and grievous misfortune if you had abandoned yourself to the defilement of carnal pleasures only to bear in suffering a few children for the world, when now you are delivered in exultation of numerous progeny for heaven! Nor would you have been more than a woman, whereas now you rise even above men, and have turned the curse of Eve into the blessing of Mary. How unseemly for those holy hands which now turn the pages of sacred books to have to perform degrading services in women's concerns! God himself has thought fit to raise us up from the contamination of this filth and the pleasures of this mire and draw us to him by force - the same force whereby he chose to strike and convert Paul - and by our example perhaps to deter from our audacity others who are also trained in letters.

I beg you then, sister, do not be aggrieved, do not vex the Father who corrects us in fatherly wise; pay heed to what is written: 'Whom the Lord loves he reproves' and 'He lays the rod on every son whom he acknowledges.' And elsewhere: 'A father who spares the rod hates his son.' This punishment is momentary, not eternal, and for our purification, not damnation. Hear the prophet and take heart: 'The Lord will not judge twice on the same issue and no second tribulation shall arise.' Listen too to that supreme and mighty exhortation of the Truth: 'By your endurance you will possess your souls.' Solomon, too: 'Better be slow to anger than be a fighter; and master one's heart rather than storm a city.' Are you not moved to tears or remorse by the only begotten Son of God who, for you and for all mankind, in his innocence was seized by the hands of impious men, dragged along and scourged, blindfolded, mocked at, buffeted, spat upon, crowned with thorns, finally hanged between thieves on the Cross, at the time so shameful a gibbet, to die a horrible and accursed form of death? Think of him always, sister, as your true spouse and the spouse of all the Chruch. Keep him in mind. Look at him going to be crucified for your sake, carrying his own cross. Be one of the crowd, one of the women who wept and lamented over him, as Luke tells: 'A great crowd of people followed, many women among them, who wept and lamented over him.' To these he graciously turned and mercifully foretold the destruction which would come to avenge his death, against which they could provide, if they understood. 'Daughters of Jerusalem,' he said, 'do not weep for me; no, weep for yourselves and your children. For the days are surely coming when they will say, "Happy are the barren, the wombs that never bore a child, the breasts that never fed one." Then they will start saying to the mountains, "Fall on us," and to the hills, "Cover us." For if these things are done when the wood is green, what will happen when it is dry?'

Have compassion on him who suffered willingly for your redemption, and look with remorse on him who was crucified for you. In your mind be always present at his tomb, weep and wail with the faithful women, of whom it is written, as I said, 'The women sitting at the tomb wept and lamented for the Lord.' Prepare with them the perfumes for his burial, but better perfumes which are of the spirit, not of the body, for this is the fragrance he needs though he rejected the other. Be remorseful over this with all your powers of devotion, for he exhorts the faithful to this remorse and compassion in the words of Jeremiah: 'All you who pass by, look and see if there is any sorrow like my sorrow.' That is, if there is some sufferer for whom you should sorrow in compassion when I alone, for no guilt of mine, atone for the sins of others. He himself is the way whereby the faithful pass from exile to their own country. He too has set up the Cross, from which he summons us, as a ladder for us to use. On this, for you, the only begotten Son of God was killed; he was made an offering because he wished it. Grieve with compassion over him alone and share his sufferings in your grief. Fulfil what was foretold of devout souls through the prophet Zachariah: 'They shall wail for him as over an only child, and shall grieve for him as for the death of a first born son.'

See, sister, what great mourning there is amongst those who love their king over the death of his only and first begotten son. Behold the lamentation and grief with which the whole household and court are consumed; and when you come to the bride of the only son who is dead, you will find her wailing intolerable and more than you can bear. This mourning, sister, should be yours and also the wailing, for you were joined to this bridegroom in blessed matrimony. He brought you not with his wealth, but with himself. He bought and redeemed you with his own blood. See what right he has over you, and know how precious you are. This is the price which the Apostle has in mind when he considers how little he is worth from whom the price was paid, and what return he should make for such a gift: 'God forbid that I should boast of anything but the Cross of our Lord Jesus Christ, through whom the world is crucified to me and I to the world!' You are greater than heaven, greater than the world, for the Creator of the world himself became the price for you. What has he seen in you, I ask you, when he lacks nothing, to make him seek even the agonies of a fearful and inglorious death in order to purchase you? What, I repeat, does he seek in you except yourself? He is the true friend who desires yourself and nothing that is yours, the true friend who said when he was about to die for you: 'There is no greater love than this, that a man should lay down his life for his friends.'

It was he who truly loved you, not I. My love, which brought us both to sin, should be called lust, not love. I took my fill of my wretched pleasures in you, and this was the sum total of my love. You say I suffered for you, and perhaps that is true, but it was really through you, and even this, unwillingly; not for love of you but under compulsion, and to bring you not salvation but sorrow. But he suffered truly for your salvation, on your behalf of his own free will, and by his suffering he cures all sickness and removes all suffering. To him, I beseech you, not to me, should be directed all your devotion, all your compassion, all your remorse. Weep for the injustice of the great cruelty inflicted on him, not for the just and righteous payment demanded of me, or rather, as I said, the supreme grace granted us both. For you are unrighteous if you do not love righteousness, and most unrighteous if you consciously oppose the will, or more truly, the boundless grace of God. Mourn for your Saviour and Redeemer, not for the seducer who defiled you, for the Master who died for you, not for the servant who lives and, indeed, for the first time is truly freed from death. I beg you, beware lest Pompey's reproach to weeping Cornelia is applied to you, to your shame:

The battle ended, Pompey the Great
Lives, but his fortune died. It is this you now mourn
And loved. *

Take this to heart, I pray, and blush for shame, unless you would commend the wanton vileness of our former ways. And so I ask you, sister, to accept patiently what mercifully befell us. This is a father's rod, not a persecutor's sword. The father strikes to correct, and to forestall the enemy who strikes to kill. By a wound he prevents death, he does not deal it; he thrusts in the steel to cut out disease, he makes to live what he should have destroyed, cuts out impurity to leave what is pure. He punishes once so that he need not punish forever. One suffers the wound so that two may be spared death; two were guilty, one pays the penalty. That, too, was granted by divine mercy to your weaker nature and, in a way, with justice, for you were naturally weaker in sex and stronger in continence, and so the less deserving of punishment. For this I give thanks to the Lord, who both spared you punishment then and reserved you for a crown to come, and who also by a moment of suffering in my body cooled once and for all the fires of that lust in which I had been wholly absorbed through my excessive incontinence, lest I be consumed. The many greater sufferings of the heart through the continual prompting of the flesh of your own youth he has reserved for a martyr's crown. Though you may weary of hearing this and forbid it to be said, the truth of it is clear. For the one who must always strive there is also a crown; and the athlete cannot win his crown unless he has kept to the rules. But no crown is waiting for me, because no cause for striving remains. The matter for strife is lacking in him from whom the thorn of desire is pulled out.

Yet I think it is something, even though I may receive no crown, if I can escape further punishment, and by the pain of a single momentary punishment may perhaps be let off much that would be eternal. For it is written of the men, or rather, the beasts of this wretched life, 'The beasts have rotted in their dung.' Then too, I complain less that my own merit is diminished when I am confident that yours is increasing for we are one in Christ, one flesh according to the law of matrimony.

* Lucan, *Pharsalia*, 8. 84-5. this is the nearest Abelard comes to a direct rebuke to Heloise for indulging in her memories.

Whatever is yours cannot, I think, fail to be mine, and Christ is yours because you have become his bride. Now, as I said before, you have as a servant me whom in the past you recognized as your master, more your own now when bound to you by spiritual love than one subjected by fear. And so I have increasing confidence that you will plead for us both before him and, through your prayer, I may be granted what I cannot obtain through my own; especially now, when the daily pressure of dangers and disturbances threaten my life and give me no time for prayer. Nor can I imitate that blessed eunuch, the high official of Candace, Queen of Ethiopia, who had charge of all her wealth, and had come from so far to worship in Jerusalem. He was on his way home when the apostle Philip was sent by the angel to convert him to the faith, as he had already deserved by his prayers and his assiduous reading of the Scriptures. Because he did not want to take time from this even on his journey, although he was a man of great wealth and a gentile, it came about through the great goodness of Providence that the passage of Scripture was before him which gave the apostle the perfect opportunity for his conversion.

So that nothing may delay my petition nor defer its fulfilment, I hasten to compose and send to you this prayer, which you may offer to the Lord in supplication on our behalf:

God, who at the beginning of human creation, in forming woman from a rib of man didst sanctify the great sacrament of the marriage bond, and who didst glorify marriage with boundless honours either by being born of one given in marriage, or by the first of thy miracles; thou who moreover didst grant this remedy for the incontinence of my frailty, in such manner as pleased thee, despise not the prayers of thy humble handmaid which I pour out as a suppliant in the presence of thy majesty for my own excesses and those of my beloved. Pardon, O most gracious, who art rather graciousness itself, pardon our many great offences, and let the ineffable immensity of thy mercy test the multitude of our faults. Punish the guilty now, I beseech thee, that thou mayst spare them hereafter. Punish now, lest thou punish in eternity. Take to thy servants the rod of correction, not the sword of wrath. Afflict their flesh that thou mayst preserve their souls. Come as a redeemer, not an avenger; gracious rather than just; the merciful Father, not the stern Lord. Prove us, Lord, and test us, in the manner in which the prophet asks for himself, as if he said openly: First consider my strength and measure accordingly the burden of my testing. This is what St Paul promises to the faithful, when he says 'God keeps faith, and he will not allow you to be tested beyond your powers, but when the test comes he will also provide a way out, so that you are able to sustain it.' Thou hast joined us, Lord, and hast parted us, when and in what manner it pleased thee. Now, Lord, what thou hast mercifully begun, most mercifully end, and those whom thou hast parted for a time on earth, unite forever to thyself in heaven: thou who art our hope, our portion, our expectation and our consolation, O Lord, who art blessed world without end. Amen.

Farewell in Christ, bride of Christ; in Christ fare well and live in Christ.

• • • • •

The letters of Abelard and Heloise are of course of great length; other medieval writings on love and marriage were somewhat shorter. In the next letter, King Edward I asks the Archbishop of Auch to exhibit no partiality when considering the abduction of the Lord of Lescune's daughter by the Countess of Foix.

• • •

From Edward I to the Archbishop of Auch.

18 August 1299.

Latin.

The King to the Reverend Father, &c. by the same grace Archbishop of Auch, greeting, and the feeling of sincere affection.

We do most earnestly request and beg your reverence that, by reason of the Countess of Foix having caried off the daughter of the Lord of Lescune, and having given her in marriage, contrary to the will of the same lord, as it is reported, that you be pleased, at our entreaties and for love of us, to inflict the full amount of justice upon her, without favour, in the Ecclesiastical Court.

Given at Certesye, the 18th day of August, 1299.

• • • • •

In 1301 Dante was exiled from his native city of Florence. His belief that the papacy should concern itself solely with the spiritual wellbeing of mankind whilst the empire oversaw secular concerns 'as an ideal world government'* led him to support the White Guelfs (pro-imperialists) and oppose the Black Guelfs who approved the papacy's thirst for political power. The Black Guelf victory ended the clashes within Florence, but many pro-imperialists were persecuted and forced

* Barber, p. 191.

to flee.

Dante favoured a policy of reconciliation between the two parties rather than continued aggression. He spent the rest of his life in exile, moving from place to place in northern Italy. The next letter was probably written whilst he was in Casentino, the region north of Arezzo, and it was addressed to a Guelf leader, Moroello Malaspina. Dante had helped conduct peace negotiations between the Malaspina family and their neighbour the Bishop of Luni.

In the letter Dante apologizes for his silence since leaving the Malaspina court and sets about explaining the reasons for this, so as to put an end to any rumours. He describes an apparition of a woman who materialized in front of him, and falling instantly in love with her caused all other matters to be subordinated. The following poem examines 'the manner in which Love exercises his tyranny.'*

In the *Vita Nuova*, which Dante wrote c.1294, he considered the 'spiritual qualities and internal effects of love'† and he continued to develop traditional European ideas about courtly love 'in radically new directions. The simile comparing Dante's love to the rage of a 'despot expelled from his fatherland' indicates that his own exile was very much on his mind despite his consuming passion.

• • •

From Dante Alighieri to Lord Moroello, Marquis Malaspina.

1308-10.

Latin.

Lest the lord should be ignorant of the bonds of his servant, and of the spontaneity of the affection by which he is governed, and lest reports spread abroad at variance with the facts, which too often are wont to prove seed-beds of false opinion, should proclaim to be guilty of negligence him who is a captive, it has seemed good to me to address to the eyes of your Magnificence this present epistle.

It befell, then, that after my departure from the threshold of that court (which I since have so yearned for), wherein, as you often remarked with amaze, I was privileged to be enrolled in the service of liberty, no sooner had I set foot by the steams of Arno, in all security and heedlessness, than suddenly, woe is me! like a flash of lightning from on high, a woman appeared, I know not how, in all respects

* Toynbee, p. 33.

† Hallam pp. 154-5

answering to my inclinations both in character and appearance. Oh! how was I dumbfounded at the sight of her! But my stupefaction gave place before the terror of the thunder that followed. For just as in our everyday experience the thunder-clap instantaneously follows the flash, so, at the sight of the blaze of this beauty, Love, terrible and imperious, straightway laid hold on me. And he, raging like a despot expelled from his fatherland, who returns to his native soil after long exile, slew or expelled or fettered whatsoever within me was opposed to him. He slew, then, that praiseworthy resolve which held me aloof from women and from songs about women; and he pitilessly banished as suspect those unceasing meditations wherein I used to ponder the things of heaven and of earth; and finally, that my soul might never again rebel against him, he fettered my free will, so that it behoves me to turn me not whither I will, but whither he wills. Love, therefore, reigns within me, with no restraining influence; and in what manner he rules me you must inquire from what follows below outside the limits of this present writing.

[*Canzone.*]

Love, since 'tis meet that I should tell my woe,
That men may list to me,
And show myself with all my manhood gone,
Grant that I may content in weeping know;
So that my grief set free
My words may utter, with my sense at one.
Thou will'st my death, and I consent thereon;
But who will pardon if I lack the art
To tell my pain of heart?
Who will believe what now doth me constrain?
But if from thee fit words for grief are won,
Grant, O my Lord, that, ere my life depart,
That cruel fair one may not hear my pain,
For, of my inward grief were she made ware,
Sorrow would make her beauteous face less fair.
I cannot scape from her, but she will come
Within my phantasy,
More than I can the thought that brings her there:
The frenzied soul that brings its own ill home,
Painting her faithfully,
Lovely and stern, its own doom doth prepare:
Then looks on her, and when it filled doth fare
With the great longing springing from mine eyes,
Wroth with itself doth rise,

That lit the fire where it, poor soul! doth burn.
What plea of reason calms the stormy air
When such a tempest whirls o'er inward skies?
The grief it cannot hold breaks forth in sighs,
From out my lips that others too may learn,
And gives mine eyes the tears they truly earn.
The image of my fair foe which doth stay
Victorious and proud,
And lords it o'er my faculty of will,
Desirous of itself, doth make me stray
There, where its truth is showed,
As like to like its course directing still.
Like snow that seeks the sun, so fare I ill;
But I am powerless, and I am as they
Who thither take their way
As others bid, where they must fall as dead.
When I draw near, a voice mine ears doth fill,
Which saith: Away! seek'st thou his death to see?
Then look I out, and search to whom to flee
For succour: to this pass I now am led
By those bright eyes that baleful lustre shed.
What I become when smitten thus, O Love,
Thou can'st relate, not I;
For thou dost stay to look while I lie dead,
And if my soul back to my heart should move,
Blind loss of memory
Hath been with her while she from earth hath fled.
When I rise up, and see the wound that bled,
And cast me down sore smitten by the blow,
No comfort can I know
To keep me from the shuddering thrill of fear;
And then my looks, with pallor o'er them spread,
Show what that lightning was that laid me low.
For, grant it came with sweet smile all aglow,
Long time all clouded doth my face appear,
Because my spirit gains no safety clear.
Thus thou hast brought me, Love, to Alpine vale,
Where flows the river bright,
Along whose banks thou still o'er me dost reign.
Alive or dead thou dost at will assail,
Thanks to the fierce keen light
Which flashing opes the way for Death's campaign.
Alas! for ladies fair I look in vain,
Or kindly men, to pity my deep woe.
If she unheeding go,

I have no hope that others help will send,
And she, no longer bound to thy domain,
Cares not, O Sire, for dart that thou dost throw;
Such shield of pride around her breast doth go,
That every dart thereon its course doth end;
And thus her heart against them doth defend.
Dear mountain song of mine, thou goest thy way,
Perchance thou'lt Florence see, mine own dear land,
That drives me doomed and banned,
Showing no pity, and devoid of love.
If thou dost enter there, pass on, and say,
'My Lord no more against you can wage war,
There, whence I come, his chains so heavy are,
That, though thy fierce wrath placable should prove,
No longer freedom hath he thence to move'. *

• • • • •

Adultery, as much as romance, was a perrenial feature of the affairs of the heart, and in the letter below Petrarch outlines its evils in no uncertain terms. He uses shocking examples from literature and personal knowledge to highlight the downfall of man's soul resulting from acts of adultery and incest. Petrarch believed that adultery, a lapse into animal instincts, denies man's standing as the noblest of God's creatures, he derides such passions in the young and particularly in those mature enough to appreciate the significance of their actions.

The last paragraph refers to the chaste love of Petrarch's own life, Laura. He never revealed her identity or status but it is possible that she was a married woman. His love for her inspired his great Italian poems and her inaccessibility probably contributed to the strength of his feeling concerning adultery.

• • •

From Petrarch, addressee unknown.

1348-1351.

Latin.

Fear and grief force me to speak; perhaps in the face of either alone I should have kept silent. I know very well what it is that allures you and all who are dazzled by a certain way of life to leave the level course for

* Plumptre's translation.

the rugged one. You are blinded by false judgements, captured by evil customs. Everything easy of attainment seems base to you; you delight in the difficult, the more so the nearer it seems to approach the impossible. You despise what lies wide open; you must have bolts and bars. Wherever a jealous husband, an anxious mother, a solicitous father is reported to keep his prize well guarded, wherever feminine virtue erects its own defences, a noble prey is scented out by our distinguished youths, to be captured with gifts or blandishments or some new variety of fraud. It is the custom of hunters not to touch a sleeping deer or a hare crouching in the bushes; he must rouse the quarry in order to take it in flight. Similarly your love, as Horace elegantly puts it, 'disregards what lies at hand to chase what flees away.' Dandified but vigilant wooers, you desert your own spouses and seek out those of others. Thus everywhere one may see fulfilled the words of Jeremiah: 'They are become as amorous horses, and stallions; every one neighed after his neighbor's wife.' Truly, neighing, bestiality, lust, abound unchecked; the occupation of our young men is well described by the Prophet. And another sings, though vainly: 'Be ye not as the horse, or as the mule, which have no understanding'

I must say it with bitter disgust - equine lust has sometimes shown more restraint, more (how shall I put it?) sense of shame than does man's lewdness. Indeed we read of many men who have coupled with their sisters and have attempted conjunction with their unhappy mothers. Of these it is unpleasant to speak, as of the famous case of Semiramis, who, when already advanced in years, sought concourse with her son and was by him, in his anger and shock, put to death. And there was recently a creature - I don't know if I should call him a man - well known to me by name and by face, but hardly to be counted of our kind, who attempted to commit incest on his daughter, already married and a mother; and when she repelled his horrid violence, he so tore her with his teeth and nails that she died. Set against this the story we read in very good authorities of a stallion who, by a hostler's cunning, had his eyes blindfolded and was put to stud to his own dam; and when the bandage was removed and he recognized his mother, as if in horror at his crime he jumped into a pit and so injured himself that he died. We read in Varro's *Res rusticae* of another stallion who was similarly tricked, and who wreaked punishment not on himself but on his deceiver. When the blindfold was removed, says Varro, the horse attacked the man and bit him to death. How much better might these stories be told of men, and my previous examples be told of beasts! But the fact is that no animal is nobler than man, as long as he remembers his manhood; but as soon as he begins to forget his quality, nothing is more vile, more base, more abject than one driven by nature's impulses with no restraint of reason.

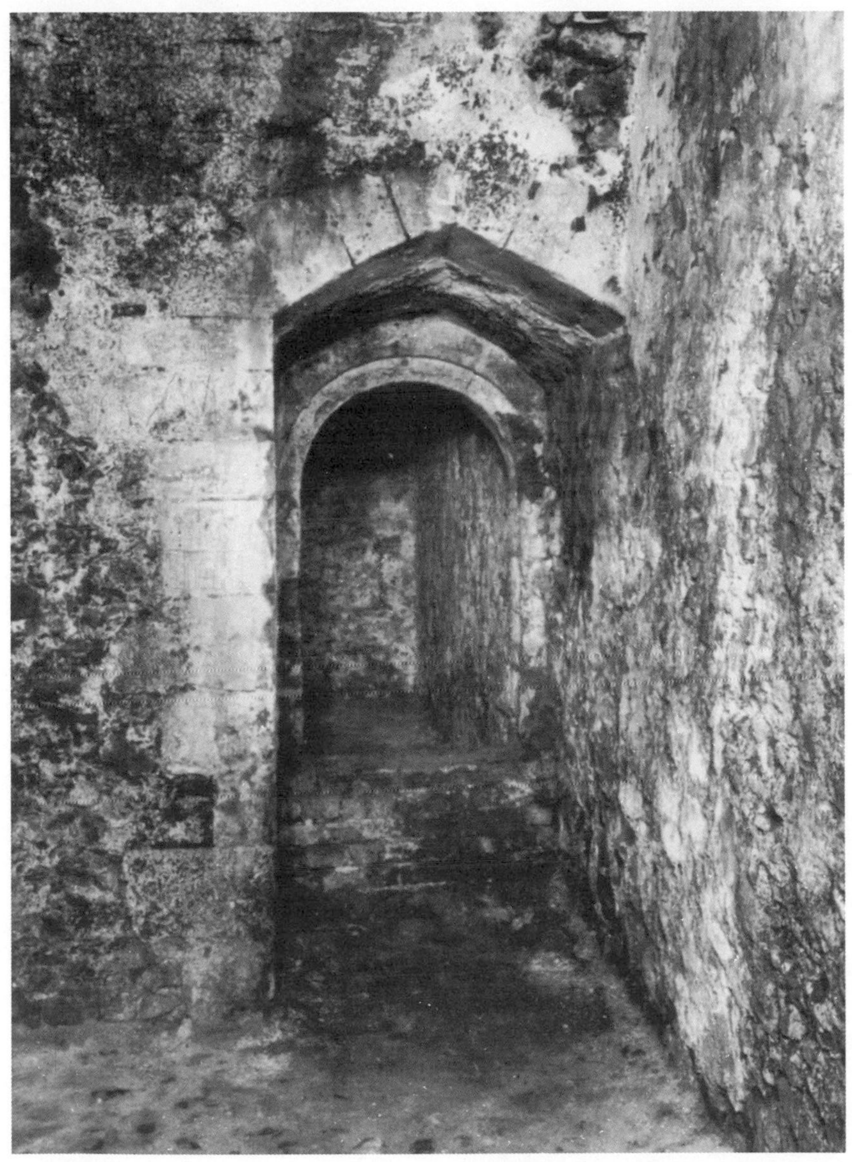

NORWICH CASTLE, THE DUNGEONS
Here was imprisoned John de Keynnesley, whose wife, Joanna, writing as a 'poor and simple woman', petitioned Henry IV for his release, in around 1400.

HENRY VII
Ever mindful of invasion, he commanded the Mayor of Hull to be vigilant against the attacks of the Danes, who 'under cover of the affection we have for our cousin the king of Denmark, their sovereign lord, rob and plunder by sea...'.

HAILES ABBEY, GLOUCESTERSHIRE
Its proximity to the fair at Winchcombe led Roger de Marlowe to write to a friend, a monk at Hailes, urging him to buy on his behalf 'a suitable horse there, costing no more than four or five marks'.

CANTERBURY CATHEDRAL, THE BELL HARRY TOWER
Prior Sellyng of Canterbury wrote to Archbishop Morton, around 1494, asking him to choose from two possible designs for the tower, proposed by John Wastell, the mason.

WINCHESTER CASTLE, HAMPSHIRE

In 1267, William de Valence, Earl of Pembroke, entrusted its defence to 'his dear consort and friend', his wife. He made it clear that the knights that he sent to her were to be completely at her command.

EDWARD, PRINCE OF WALES, THE BLACK PRINCE
In 1356 he wrote to the City of London, describing his victory over the French at the Battle of Poitiers.

RICHARD II
In 1399, he received a courteous and polite request from Joanna of Navarre, then Duchess of Brittany, complaining that Richard's forces held lands that were rightfully hers. Ironically, in 1402, she married Henry IV, Richard's murderer.

THOMAS CROMWELL

Architect of the Reformation, at the very close of the Middle Ages, Cromwell was petitioned in order to save the de la Warr chantry at Boxgrove Priory in Sussex.

But let us drop these weighty considerations and return to modern youth and its vaunts and purposes. I am talking of adultery, a filthy crime that disguises itself with a veil of love, profiting by that lovely name. It's familiar not only in our own times, abounding in every evil, but it was so common in many previous periods that it was very justly written. 'This is something that can be neither permitted nor prohibited.' And Annaeus Seneca could include in his observations: 'If a man has boasted of no lady friend and has persuaded no one else's wife to wear his ring, the matrons call him a poor creature who discharges his sordid lusts with serving-maids.' This plague, beginning in those days, is now so widespread that a young man with no adultery to his credit, though rich, handsome, and noble, is regarded as pitiable by his fellows, as though he were repulsed not by a lady's virtue but by her contempt, and as though the chastity of his beloved were a censure of the lover. Hence proceeds the ardour of the young, their impudent pursuit, as if they were in search of glory, not impelled by lust; hence come labours and regretful sighs, and often success which turns out to be still more bitter. For while all stands well, with Venus favoring and Cupid propitious, what is that ardour with its stings of suspicion, that hour-long, day-long distress of spirit, that continual alternation of peace and war in the realm of love! If these are now, by an evil usage, numbered among the delights of noble souls, what then are the punishments that cannot be concealed, administered by public justice or by the private revenges of husbands? For how many has that longed-for night not turned out to be their last on earth! How many have we not seen or heard of who found that their sensuous sweet embraces finished in deadly wounds!

If I wanted to collect examples, I should not need to go to history; I shall find them by visiting any street, any house. One case, I grieve to say, was so recent and so celebrated that, even though no other ancient or modern examples existed, this single calamity of a distinguished man should deter all others from following in his steps. In this wretched affair I deplore the undeserved fate of a man who had loved us much, and the spot upon the army, and the irreparable harm suffered by his friends; but above all I grieve for the indelible, eternal infamy staining the name of so great a man. He subjected himself to a woman, not merely ardently and avidly - that is the common case of all lovers - but blindly, witlessly, prudent though he was in all else. What chiefly outrages me is that the woman was not faithful to him, but was free of her favours to many, and his infatuation was not fresh, but had lasted long; if he had had any sense, he would have been disgusted with her. Unhappy man, he was lighter than the wind; perhaps he did not reflect that the wind does not enter a place from which it cannot issue, for he ran into a retreat where there was no room for defence, no chance of escape, no chance for an honourable death. Thus unarmed and naked he fell, an eminent victim of the enraged spoüse, to the shame and grief of us all.*

I miss that man we have lost, but no less do I miss the good fortune which he destroyed in destroying himself. In mourning him I judge as did the Roman people, mourning Claudius Marcellus. I deplore not his death, which is the same for all men, not his sword wounds, which many have borne with great glory, but his great errors at an age when he should long since have emerged from youth and outlived its stormy impulses. I think that some infernal Alecto kindled the chilling heart of our friend, or that some dire Furies from Tartarus, hovering before the light on their creaking wings, hid from him the face of imminent death. Truly this calamity is one of those that it is proper to bewail but was impossible to avert. Let me then set aside my irremediable grief and turn to your case, briefly touching on my fear of what may occur.

It would be vain pretension for me to say much about love to you, whom experience and art have made the Ovid, the Catullus, the Propertius, the Tibullus of our time. Repeat to yourself what these and others have said, and especially Horace in his well-known *Sermo* on the casual loves of matrons and young men. To cite it would make queasy one who is already replete. But I shall quote something you may not know, to point out how ancient is that passion which human folly makes forever new. Plautus in his play called *Cistellaria* has two common women talking, one of them ignorant, unschooled in love, the other really learned in the subject. The first one inquires of the second: 'Is it disagreeable to begin loving, if you please?' The other replies: 'Dear me, love abounds in both honey and gall; is has a sweet taste, and then it piles up bitterness until you can hardly bear it.' But one might say that this applies only to the sex that struggles vainly against the spirit's passions. Hear then what one of the stronger sex has to say a little later: 'I think that love was sent to be men's first torturer. I conclude this from my own personal experience, I don't need to look elsewhere. I surpass all men, I beat everybody in torturability of soul. I am tossed, tortured, agitated, turned upside down on fortune's wheel! I'm done in and done for! I'm distracted, distressed, distraught and depressed; I seem to have no mind left. Where I am, I'm not; and where I'm not, there are all my thoughts. Thus love tricks my tired soul; it chases, drives, seeks, seizes, holds back, deceives, confers bounty! What it gives it doesn't give; it cheats me; what it has just persuaded me to do it now forbids; and what it has forbidden it now commands.'

So he speaks. Well? Do these seem to you the words of a tranquil

* The episode to which Petrarch refers is not known.

spirit? Believe me, one who talks thus is in a pretty pass. But, you may say, this is just a poetic fiction. Of course; but the law of poetry permits nothing to be invented without the consent of nature; and - believe one who knows - nothing can be invented more in accordance with nature than this, nothing can be spoken more truly. I confess the truth; I am deeply alarmed for fear that you may swallow the baited hook, that the sweet songs of the sirens may entice you, that the snares may be cast about your feet. I beg and conjure you, for your salvation, to be warned by the fate of that friend which so distressed us, to learn caution in your own case, drawing some good from his calamity, than which there could be no sadder or more conspicuous example. When your neighbour's house is burning, don't delay to douse your own with water. Fire is fast-spreading; it leaps from house to house when the high winds blow; and you can make the evident application.

But enough for now, though I might have much to say to you in person that I fear to write down. I shall close with a quotation from another play of Plautus: 'No one keeps you from walking on the public highway, provided you don't make a path across fenced-in property.' Also what follows the quotation.* You want to know the source? The name of the play is *Curculio.*

In short, I want to convince you of something of which I have already convinced myself. What smoldering sparks still remained of my own old flame have been subdued by reflection, allayed by time, and extinguished by a recent death. You know that in this war of my life I have sounded the retreat. I shall say nothing further. You know who I am and whence I write; you understand my warnings; you recognize my fears. Farewell; be careful; and be on your guard.

• • • • •

Elisabetta, daughter of Barnabo Visconti, Lord of Milan, and wife of Ernest, Duke of Bavaria, writes to the recently crowned Henry IV of England, suggesting a marriage with her niece. Henry rejected this proposal as he had already formed a deep attachment to Joanna of Navarre, the Duke of Brittany's wife, whom he married in 1402 after the Duke's death; he also felt his sons were too young to consider marriage, Prince Henry the eldest being only twelve years old at the time.

Whilst in exile Henry had regarded Elisabetta's younger sister, Lucia, as a possible bride but the Visconti family objected to such a

* 'Provided you keep away from married women, widows, virgins, young people, and respectable children, love anyone you wish.' *Curculio*, II 37-38, translated by George E. Duckworth, Random House, N.Y., 1912.

match, having little faith in Henry's prospects. As soon as he became king his attractions instantly increased and the Duchess was not afraid to take the initiative and vouch for the qualities of her unattached niece, Magdalena.

• • •

From Elisabetta, Duchess of Bavaria to King Henry IV.

24 November 1400.

Latin.

Most illustrious Prince and gracious Lord.

The intention of our present letter is to make known to your Highness that there is a certain damsel of wondrous beauty, and held in such high regard by all for her many good qualities, that she could not fail to be desired and sought after as an object of legitimate and dear embrace by yourself or any other prince of the earth who should know of her elegance of person, her superiority of mind, and her admirable bearing in the world. She is the daughter and beloved offspring of the late most illustrious Frederic Count Palatine of the Rhine, Duke of Bavaria, born to him of his rightful consort the illustrious Magdalena, our dear sister.

Very many magnates and princes of the land have already made suit to us for her hand, in person, or by message. But we know of none in this world to whom it would be more our wish and urgent inclination to unite her in marriage than to yourself or one of your sons. For we should consider it an alliance highly suitable and honourable to the house of Bavaria.

If the Almighty, who is the beginning and end of every good thing, and who brings all things to pass according to His will, should render you disposed to carry out this matter, we shall be delighted to receive your letter to that effect; and it will give us unbounded joy.

May the Creator of all nature keep and confirm you in health, for our consolation!

Given in our town of Wasserburg,* the 24th day of November, in the year Fourteen Hundred.

Elisabetta de' Visconti, of Milan, by the grace of God Countess Palatine of the Rhine, and duchess of Bavaria.

(*Indorsed.*)– To the most illustrious Prince, the lord Henry, Lord of

* A town in Upper Bavaria, situated on the river Inn, east of Münich.

England and Ireland, our gracious lord.

Letter of the Viscountess of Milan.

• • • • •

Philippa Queen of Portugal was the eldest daughter of John of Gaunt and his first wife Blanche of Lancaster. In 1387 Philippa married John I of Portugal and proceeded to provide him with a large family, nevertheless the King had numerous illegitimate children which the Queen nobly accepted.

The next letter concerns Beatrix, one of King John's illegitimate daughters, who had accompanied Queen Philippa on a visit to England. Philippa had persuaded the heir to the earldom of Arundel to marry Beatrix and in 1404 the wedding took place in the presence of King Henry IV and Queen Joan.

In his youth the the young Fitz-Alan had abhorred the thought of marrying against his will as a political, diplomatic or financial tactic, and had promised a large sum of gold to the King for the privilege of choosing his own wife. Such romantic intentions must have vanished with age since Queen Philippa had suggested that if he married Beatrix, a match approved by the King, he would not have to pay the bribe as he would be satisfying the King's wishes. However, the King did demand the gold and the Earl was placed in a difficult situation because if he refused to pay it he would be admitting that Beatrix was not the wife he truly desired. In an attempt to solve the problem he sent an ambassador to Queen Philippa who had encouraged the marriage in the first place, and she then sent the following letter to her brother.

• • •

From Philippa Queen of Portugal to her brother King Henry IV.

4 November 1405.

French.

Most high and most puissant prince, my most supremely beloved brother,

I recommend myself to your high nobleness as humbly and entirely as I can or know how with all my entire heart, supremely desiring to hear and know often of your estate and health; and in special of the prosperity of your most genteel person, as good, pleasant, and joyous news as you yourself, most noble prince, could best devise, or in any manner desire, for your sovereign ease and comfort. And because I am certain that you would most willingly hear similar things from here, I signify to you that the king my sovereign lord, all my children, your own nephews, who wish always to be most humbly recommended to you, and I their mother, your own sister, at the making of these presents were all well and hearty of body, thanks to our Creator, who ever maintain you in honour and prosperity according to your desire.

Most high and puissant prince, my best beloved brother, please it you to know that by Mr John Wiltshire, knight and ambassador of our cousin the Earl of Arundel, I am here informed how a sum of gold is yet owing to you by the said earl, which he pledged himself to pay you for the license which it pleased your gracious lordship to grant and give him in his nonage, that he might marry according to his wish, and in whatever place he saw fitting to his estate. And since you know well, my supremely best-loved brother, that he is now married not after his own seeking but as by your commandment, in part at my instance, I therefore supplicate you, since you are so great and noble a prince, as entirely as I know how, that it will please you to quit claim to the said sum at this my request, in order that I, who am in part the cause of his marriage, may be the cause of the acquittal of the said sum. And if there be anything in these parts which might give you pleasure, may it please you to command and certify it to me, and I will do it to my utmost power without hypocrisy. So I pray our sovereign Lord Jesu ever to give you prosperity, pleasaunce, and joy, and very long to endure. Written at the palace of Lisbon, the 4th day of November.

Your entire and loyal sister, P. DE P.

To the most high and puissant [prince my best] beloved brother the King of England.

• • • • •

The following letter contributes to the evidence that medieval men and women did marry purely 'for downright love' but outlines the difficulties which occurred when considerations of financial security were neglected. Nevertheless, the Countess evidently feels great sympathy for the couple in question.

Joanna Beaufort was the only daughter of John of Gaunt by his third wife Catherine Swynford. She married Ralph Neville, Earl of Westmorland in 1396: her youngest daughter, Cicely, wife of Richard Duke of York, was the mother of Edward IV and Richard III.

• • •

From Joanna Countess of Westmorland to her brother, King Henry IV.

1406.

French.

Most high and puissant prince, and most excellent sovereign lord,

I recommend myself to your royal and high lordship in the most obedient manner which, with my whole, entire, and simple heart, I can most humbly do, as she who desires to know of you, and of your most noble estate and most perfect health, such prosperity as your royal and most honourable heart can desire. And may it please your high nobleness to understand that I write now to your royal presence in behalf of your loyal liege and esquire, Christopher Standith, who, as he has certified me, has been in your service in Wales every time you have been there against your enemies, and besides, in all your most honourable journeys since your coronation, in which he has expended the substance that he could acquire of his own and of his friends, in such wise that, whereas he and my well-beloved his wife Margaret (daughter to Mr. Thomas Fleming, who was chancellor and servant during is life to my most honoured and redoubted lord your father, whom God assoil) kept house and establishment, they have left it, and the said Margaret is lodged very uncomfortably with her children, of whom she has many, having one or two every year; and all this on account of the great charge which her said husband has incurred and still incurs in your service; to whom, of your gracious goodness and gentleness, you have aforetime promised guerdon of his labour, whenever he should spy out [something] from which [he could have a living] of 40 marks or of 40 pounds. And, most puissant and excellent prince and my most sovereign lord, he is the youngest [and his father has dismissed him from] his serv[ice], and that merely because he and his wife married each other for downright love, without thinking this time [what they should have to live upon. Wherefore I] entreat your most high and puissant lordship to consider that the said Margaret should dwell [in some suitable place, or else with the queen] your wife, whom God protect; and that she is come to me trusting that my [intercession] might avail her with you. May it please you to be gracious lord to her and her said husband, and of your guerdon [assist them] to support in their persons poor gentility, that their affiance may turn to good effect for them, and to my honour, if it please you, by their finding succour from your royal and most excellent nobility, on account of this my most effectual supplication.

Most high and puissant prince and most excellent sovereign lord, I pray God to grant you a most honourable and long life, and preserve you in his most excellent keeping, and give entire joy and gladness as much as your gentle and most noble heart would choose or desire. Written at the castle of Raby.

Your most humble and obedient subject, if it please you, J. DE W.

• • • • •

Thomas Beckington, 'one of the most famous English churchmen of the fifteenth century', was at this time Secretary to King Henry VI. He had been sent on a mission to negotiate a marriage between the King and one of the daughters of John IV, Court of Armagnac, one of the princes rebelling against the French King Charles VII.

Beckington had little faith in the success of this matchmaking and his letter to the king tells of a meeting with Sir Edmund Hull, just returned from France, who warned that Charles VII was planning an attack on Gascony. Beckington made his way to Plymouth where on July 10th, at six in the evening he embarked on board a vessel, called the *Katherine of Bayonne*, his main purpose to reassure the people of Bordeaux that aid would be provided in the event of a French attack, and to obtain portraits of all three of the Count's daughters.

• • •

From Thomas Beckington to King Henry VI.

16 June 1442.

English.

To the most mighty and most Christian Prince, our most redoubtable and sovereign lord the King.

Most Gracious and most Christian prince, our most redoubtable sovereign lord, with the most humble approaches made to your royal majesty, may it please your high and noble grace to be advised that in the course of my journey towards the coast on the embassy which it has pleased your highness to send me on, getting towards Taunton, I had news of the arrival of Sir Edmund Hull from the country of Guienne. On hearing the news I immediately sent a servant of mine to him overnight, asking him to remain for a little while the next day, so that I might visit him and learn from him how things stood in that country.

And therefore, sovereign lord, for the benefit of yourself and your embassy, he remained until today when I came to the house where he was staying in Taunton, where, out of respect for your highness he entertained me very hospitably, for which I, as your most humble servant, beseech your high and noble grace to thank him. And, as I feel, having heard his report, that the country which we should be visiting, according to your high command, is not in the condition which your highness had assumed it was in when I set out. I, your honest chaplain and servant, beseech your high and noble grace, that I should be fully informed of your intentions as to what I should do next, as quickly as your noble grace may do so. As to my own person, if it is to the benefit of yourself, sovereign lord (which I know very well is, and must be, the benefit of all your true subjects) I am prepared to place it in as much danger as I would that of a poor clerk, trusting always to have the good fortune of your own virtues, although I, a sinful creature, have no reason to trust to my own.

Most high and Christian prince, our most redoubtable and sovereign lord, I beseech our Saviour ever to have you in his gracious keeping, and send you as long and as good a life as ever had Christian prince on Earth.

Written etc.

Your most humble creature and poor chaplain.

T. B.

• • • • •

The second letter shows that the negotiations were not progressing and that the artist engaged to paint the portraits was also having problems. Later in the month Beckington returned home empty-handed but three years later Henry married the daughter of another French Count, Margaret of Anjou.

• • •

From Jean de Batute, Archdeacon of Saint-Antonin at Rodez, the Count of Armagnac's chancellor, to Sir Robert Roos, Sir Edmund Hull and Thomas Beckington.

3 January 1443.

Latin.

My honourable and most excellent Lords: After my humble and dutiful commendations. By the bearer of this letter I received on the twenty-ninth day of December, your two letters tied together, written with your own hand and sealed with your own seals, the first written on the last day but one of November, and the second on the nineteeth of December, just passed. If as you state, it gave you pleasure to learn from my last letter, the constant and unalterable disposition of my lord to bring the business to a happy termination, my lord and myself have received still greater pleasure from your letter and its contents, to find that your resolution is unchanged, and that you are determined to persevere with even greater vigour. My lord thanks you from his heart for continuing to entertain these sentiments, and entreats that you will persevere in them with your wonted zeal. He is grieved at heart that the business on which you came could not at present be brought to its desired consummation; but he used every means in his power to attain it, nor has be ceased from them ever since my arrival. He still hopes, and will continue to hope for its happy termination, but hitherto he has been prevented as you well know, *de facto* rather than *de jure*. After all, if the ability to proceed in the matter as we wish, should be denied, yet still, my lord will always preserve an ardent disposition towards it, according to the royal pleasure; and it will be right for you to make such provisions as will afford a facility to both parties, in which we will cooperate with you, as far as possible, unless our efforts should be resisted as they lately were. In this case we fear the matter may be longer protracted. We therefore entreat you to make the necessary provisions on your part for passing to the appointed place, and with God's help we intend to do the same on ours. My lord anticipated what you have written respecting the truce; he was sincerely earnest in the matter as he still is, and if he had obtained your consent, would, as I told you, have exerted himself in it with zeal; but it has so happened that he has been opposed on both sides. I believe in the Lord, if you would engage in the business with proper earnestness, it would not be without success. But a word to the wise, &c. Hans has finished one of the three likenesses. From the severe coldness of the weather which has prevented his colours from working, he could not finish it sooner, though he laboured with constant diligence. He is beginning to proceed with the other two, which, with God's help, he will finish in a shorter time, especially if the cold should subside, and give him greater facilities. But on this subject he has more fully written to you. I am constantly urging his operations, and shall continue to do so, as there is nothing on earth I more desire than to see them completed; and as soon as they are, which will be shortly, he shall be sent back to you in safety. I will write again by him, on some other points respecting our affair which do not now occur to me. May the lord deign to preserve you in all happiness and prosperity. From the island on the third of January, 1443. Do not be surprised that I have not written this time as usual with my own hand, for I have recovered my accustomed writer, and am hindered by other trifles. But when Hans returns, I will, with God's help, write to you more at large.

Your servant, as usual, Jo. &c. de B.

• • • • •

In 1445 King Henry VI of England and Margaret, the sixteen-year-old daughter of Rene I of Anjou, were married. Their union was part of a truce in the Hundred Years War between their respective countries. William de la Pole the Duke of Suffolk had organised the negotiations, 'neither money nor lands were demanded for the dowry of the bride, whose charms and high endowments were allowed by the gallant ambassadors of England "to outweigh all the riches in the world."'

The amusing incident the Venetian envoy relates involves the unorthodox use of a letter, as a ruse to enable the impatient king to catch a glimpse of his bride.

• • •

From a letter by Raffaelo de Negra, a Venetian envoy.

c. 1445?

Probably Italian.

I am writing to report what an Englishman told me about the magnificence of the Queen of England and how she was brought to England. I will tell you something of the King of England. First of all the Englishman told me that the King of England took her without a dowry and he even restored some lands which he held to her father. When the Queen landed in England the King dressed himself as a squire, the duke of Suffolk doing the same, and took her a letter which he said the King of England had written. When the Queen read the letter the King took stock of her, saying that a woman may be seen over well when she reads a letter, and the Queen never found that it was the King, because she was so engrossed in reading the letter, and she never looked at the King in his squire's dress who remained on his knees all the time. After the King had gone, the Duke of Suffolk said: 'Most serene Queen, what do you think of the squire who brought you the letter? The Queen replied: 'I did not notice him, as I was occupied in reading the letters he brought.' The duke remarked: 'Most serene Queen, the person dressed as a squire was the most serene King of England,' and the Queen was vexed at not having known it, because she had kept him on his knees.

• • • • •

Margaret Mautby married John Paston I, eldest son of Justice William Paston, in 1440. Margaret was a wealthy heiress and it was his wife's inheritance which formed the basis of John Paston's fortune.

Margaret has been described as, 'a capable and devoted wife, an admirable woman of business, a good friend and considerate mistress, held in high esteem by friends and neighbours, she proved herself a woman of intrepid courage and determination.* In this letter she begs her husband's forgiveness over some misunderstanding between them, and her true feelings are lucidly expressed. The rest of the letter concerns domestic matters which require her husband's attention.

• • •

From Margaret Paston to her husband John Paston.

March 1451?

English.

To my right worshipful Husband, John Paston, be this delivered in haste.

Right worshipful husband, I recommend me to you, beseeching you that ye be not displeased with me; by my truth it is not my will neither to do nor say that should cause you for to be displeased with me, though my simpleness caused you for to be displeased, and if I have done, I am sorry thereof, and will amend it; wherefore I beseech you to forgive me, and that ye bear no heaviness in your heart against me, for your displeasure should be too heavy to me to endure with.

I send you the Roll that ye sent for, ensealed by the bringer hereof; it was found in your trussing Coffer. As for Herring, I have bought a horse-load for 4s. and 6d. I can get none Eels yet; as for Bever† there is promised me some, but I might not get it yet. I sent to Joan Petche to have an answer for the windows, for she might not come to me; and she sent me word that she had spoken thereof to Thomas Ingham, and he said that he should speak with you himself, and he should accord with you well enough, and said to her it was not her part to desire of him to stop the lights; and also he said it was not his part to do it, because the place is his but for years.

And as for all other errands that ye have commanded for to be done, they shall be done as soon as they may be done. The blessed Trinity have you in his keeping.

Written at Norwich, on the Monday next after Saint Edward.

Yours,

Margaret Paston.

• • • • •

* Greenwood, p. xiii.

† Beverage; light drink, probably concocted from herbs, not ale.

Jane Carew was the widow of Sir Nicholas Carew who had died in 1447. She had married him when she was fourteen years old, being the sole heiress of her father's large inheritance which included seventeen manors; she bore him five sons.

Instead of Thomas Burneby, Jane married Sir Robert de Vere, brother to John, twelfth Earl of Oxford, in 1450. From this and the following letter Margaret of Anjou appears to have been something of a matchmaker, and evidently not an entirely successful one.

• • •

From the Queen, Margaret of Anjou to Dame Jane Carew.

1447-50.

English.

By the Queen

Right dear and well-beloved, we greet you well.

And since our trusty and well-beloved squire Thomas Burneby, our sewer*, as much for the ardent love and affection that he has for you personally, as for your reputation as virtuous and well-bred woman, wishes with all his heart to do you the honour of marrying you, in preference, as he says, to anyone else alive; we, hoping for the greater prosperity and advancement of our said squire, as he deserves for his many virtues, and for the good service that he has done and daily continues to do for ourselves and our lord, request you in a most affectionate spirit that, out of your respect for us, you will accept our special recommendation of our said squire in marriage, and favour his honest wish. And consider our request, in which we have the greatest confidence, that you will thereby do the right thing by yourself, and gain great honour and contentment, and cause us to hold you both in such tender favour of our good graces, that you will acknowledge that you are very pleased and happy. And advise us how well disposed you are to please us in this by the messenger who brings you this. As we have great confidence in you.

Given etc. at Eltham.

• • • • •

* This was a ceremonial position of some importance. At formal dinners he would have had the task of arranging the place-settings with due regard to favour and precedence, and acting as the Queen's food-taster, both to verify the quality and deter attempted assassination by poison.

Monro's introduction to this letter details the background of William Gastrick who had an only daughter, Elizabeth, the prospective bride in question. Elizabeth was to inherit her father's property and Thomas Fountains was probably attracted by this as much as her 'womanly and vertuous governance'. Despite the King and Queen's approbation Elizabeth did not marry Thomas but Henry Boothe, nephew of William Boothe, Archbishop of York

• • •

From Queen Margaret of Anjou to William Gastrick.

c. 1445.

English.

By the Queen to William Gastrick

Trusty and well-beloved.

Seeing that our well-beloved servant Thomas Fountains, yeoman of my lord's crown, as much for your daughter's reputation as a virtuous and well-bred woman as for the ardent love and affection that he has for her person, above anyone else alive, wishes, as he says, with all his heart to do her honour by way of marriage; for which reason, my lord has written to you in affectionate terms recommending him, which we are confident you have understood and taken to heart; we, also hoping for the enrichment, well-being and advancement of my lord's servant, who is also ours, and the achievement of his desires, most affectionately request that you, since you have your daughter under your orders and control, as is proper, will give your kindly assent, in friendship and good will, to persuade and encourage your daughter to accept my lord's servant (who is also ours) as her husband, bearing in mind his many great virtues, his high social standing, and the good and faithful service he has done my lord and ourself, so as to lead to an affectionate marriage, according to our complete trust in you.

In this way you will give us great pleasure, so that we will hold yourself and your household in high regard, and we will consequently do such things for you in time to come, in affectionate memory of your graciousness, as will make you very happy, and pleased with the power of God, may He hold you in his blessed keeping.

At our manor of P., etc.

• • • • •

The first two sons of John and Margaret Paston were both named John. The eldest brother, John II was knighted at the age of twenty-one and has been described as a 'typical young courtier'* who was frequently travelling with the royal household or visting Calais and Flanders with his patron Lord Hastings. The younger and more responsible brother became the head of the Paston family in 1479 when John II died at the age of forty-two.

This letter describes the wedding of Margaret of York, the King's sister, to Charles the Bold, Duke of Burgundy, in 1468. Margaret had ordered Sir John to attend her and his younger brother accompanied him. The marriage secured the support of the English for the Duke of Burgundy who was busy consolidating his kingdom and aggravating the French king Louis XI. At the time of his marriage to Margaret of York the Duke was enjoying great power and popularity, the young Paston brothers admired his chivalrous spirit regarding him as the embodiment of all knightly attributes. The Burgundian alliance with England came to an end in 1475 and contributed to the rapid decline of the Duke's fortunes and his untimely death two years later.

The closeness of the relationship between John III and his mother is revealed at the end of the letter, along with his genuine interest in the younger members of the family who must have greatly enjoyed reading the descriptions of the pageants, jousting and the awesome wealth of the Burgundian Court.

• • •

John Paston, the younger, to his mother, Margaret Paston.

1468.

English.

To my right reverend and worshipful Mother, Margaret Paston, dwelling at Caister, be this delivered in haste.

Right reverend and worshipful Mother, I recommend me unto you as humbly as I can think, desiring most heartily to hear of your welfare and heart's ease, which I pray God send you as hastily as any heart can think.

Please it you to weet, that at the making of this bill, my Brother, and I, and all our Fellowship, were in good hele, blessed be God.

As for the Guiding here in this country, it is as worshipful as all the world can devise, and there were never Englishmen had so good chear out of England, that ever I heard of.

* Greenwood, p. x.

As for Tidings here, but if it be of the Feast, I can none send you; saving, that my Lady Margaret was married on Sunday last past at a Town that is called The Damme, three miles out of Bruges, at five of the clock in the morning; and she was brought the same day to Bruges to her dinner; and there she was received as worshipfully as all the world could desire; as with procession with Ladies, and Lords, best beseen of any people, that ever I saw or heard of. Many Pageants were played in her way in Bruges to her welcoming, the best that ever I saw; and the same day my Lord, the Bastard,* took upon him to answer twenty-four Knights and Gentlemen with eight days at Justs of Peace; and when that they were answered, the twenty-four and himself should turney with other twenty-five the next day after, which is on Monday next coming; and they that have justed with him into this day, have been as richly beseen, and him self also, as cloth of Gold, and Silk, and Silver, and Goldsmiths work might make them; for of such Gear, and Gold, and Pearl, and Stones, they of the Duke's court, neither Gentlemen nor Gentlewomen, they want none; for without that they have it by wishes, by my truth, I heard never of so great plenty as here is.

This day my Lord Scales justed with a Lord of this country, but not with the Bastard; for they made promise at London, that none of them both should never deal with other in arms; but the Bastard was one of the Lords, that brought the Lord Scales into the field; and of misfortune an horse struck my Lord Bastard on the leg, and hath hurt him so sore, that I can think he shall be of no power to accomplish up his arms; and that is great pity, for by my truth I trow God made never a more worshipful Knight.

And as for the Duke's Court, as of Lords, Ladies and Gentlewomen, Knights, Esquires, and Gentlemen, I heard never of none like to it, save King Arthur's Court. And by my truth, I have not wit nor remembrance to write to you, half the worship that is here; but what lacketh, as it cometh to mind, I shall tell you, when I come home, which I trust to God shall not be long tofore. We depart out of Bruges homeward on Tuesday next coming, and all folk that came with my Lady of Burgoyn out of England, except such as shall abide here still with her, which I wot well shall be but few.

We depart the sooner, for the Duke hath word that the French King is purposed to make war upon him hastily, and that he is within four or five days journey of Bruges, and the Duke rideth, on Tuesday next coming, forward to meet with him; God give him good speed, and all his; for by my truth they are the goodliest fellowship that ever I came amongst, and best can behave them, and most like Gentlemen.

---

* The Bastard of Burgundy, half brother to Charles the Bold.

Other Tidings have we none here, but that the Duke of Somerset, and all his Bands departed well beseen out of Bruges a day before that my Lady the Duchess came thither, and they say here, that he is to Queen Margaret that was, and shall no more come here again, nor be holpen by the Duke.

No more, but I beseech you of your blessing as lowly as I can, which I beseech you forget not to give me every day once; and Mother, I beseech you that ye will be good Mistress to my little man, and to see that he go to school.

I sent my Cousin Dawbeney 5s. by Calle's man, for to buy for him such gear as he needeth; and Mother I pray you this bill may recommend me to my Sisters both, and to the Master, my Cousin Dawbeney, Sir James, Sir John Stylle, and to pray him to be good Master to little Jack, and to learn him well; and I pray you that this bill may recommend me to all your Folks, and to my Well Willers; and I pray God send you your heart's desire.

Written at Bruges the Friday next after Saint Thomas.

Your Son and Humble Servant, J. Paston, the Younger.

• • • • •

Richard Calle married Margery, daughter of John Paston and Margaret Mautby, in 1469. Calle was John Paston's bailiff and of a considerably lower rank than his patrons.

When this letter was written Margery had already betrothed herself to Calle which, in the eyes of the Church, was 'almost as binding as matrimony* and is why he addresses her as 'mine own Lady and Mistress, and, before God, very true wife'. Margery's family greatly disapproved of her marrying beneath her, especially to a member of the household. The attempts to divert letters between the couple are described and Calle expresses the misery these circumstances had caused him. After the marriage Margaret Paston refused to forgive her daughter's lack of prudence.

• • •

From Richard Calle to Margery Paston.

c. 1469.

English.

* Greenwood, p. 274.

To Mistress Margery Paston.

Mine own Lady and Mistress, and, before God, very true wife, I with heart full sorrowful recommend me unto you, as he that cannot be merry, nor nought shall be till it be otherwise with us than it is yet, for this life that we lead now is neither pleasure to God nor to the world, considering the great bond of matrimony that is made betwixt us, and also the great love that hath been, and as I trust, yet is betwixt us, and as on my part never greater; wherefore I beseech Almighty God comfort us as soon as it pleaseth him, for we that ought of very right to be most together, are most asunder, me seemeth it is a thousand year ago since that I spake with you, I had liever than all the good in the world I might be with you; alas, alas! good Lady, full little remember they what they do that keep us thus asunder, four times in the year are they accursed that let (*hinder*) matrimony; it causeth many men to deem in them they have large conscience in other matters as well as herein, but what Lady suffer as ye have done. And make you as merry as ye can, for I wis, lady, at the long way God will of his rightwiseness help his servants that mean truly, and would live according to his laws, &c.

I understand, Lady, ye have had as much sorrow for me as any Gentlewoman hath had in the world, as would God all that sorrow that ye have had had rested upon me and that ye had been discharged of it, for I wish, Lady, it is to me a death to hear that ye be entreated otherwise than ye ought to be; this is a painful life that we lead, I cannot live thus without it be a great displeasure to God.

Also like you to weet that I had sent you a Letter by my lad from London, and he told me he might not speak with you, there was made so great await upon him and upon you both; he told me John Thresher come to him in your name, and said that ye sent him to my lad for a Letter or a token, which I should have sent you, but he trust him not, he would not deliver him none; after that he brought him a ring, saying that ye sent it him, commanding him that he should deliver the Letter or token to him, which I conceive since by my lad it was not by your sending, it was by my Mistress and Sir James's [Gloys] advice; Alas, what mean they? I suppose they deem we be not ensured together, and if they so do I marvel, for then they are not well advised, remembering the plainness that I brake to my Mistress at the beginning, and I suppose by you both [*too*], and ye did as ye ought to do of very right, and if ye have done the contrary, as I have been informed ye have done, ye did neither consciencely nor to the pleasure of God, without ye did it for fear, and for the time to please such as were at that time about you; and if ye did it for this cause it was a reasonable cause, considering the great and importable calling upon that ye had, and many an untrue tale was made to you of me, which, God know it, I was never guilty of.

My Lad told me that my Mistress your mother asked him, if he had brought any Letter to you, and many other things she bare him on hand, and among all other at the last she said to him that I would not make her privy to the beginning, but she supposed I would at the ending; and as to that, God know it, she knew it first of me and none other, I wot not what her mistresship meaneth, for by my troth there is no gentlewoman alive that my heart tendereth more than it doth her, nor is loather to displease, saving only your person, which of very right I ought to tender and love best, for I am bound thereto by the law of God, and so will do while that I live, whatsoever fall of it; I suppose and ye tell them sadly the truth, they will not damn their souls for us; though I tell them the truth they will not believe me as well as they do you, and therefore, good Lady, at the reverence of God be plain to them and tell the truth, and if they will in no wise agree thereto, betwixt God, the Devil, and them be it, and that peril that we should be in, I beseech God it may lie upon them and not upon us; I am heavy and sorry to remember their disposition, God send them grace to guide all things well, as well [as] I would they did; God be their guide and send them peace and rest, &c.

I marvel much that they should take this matter so heedely [*grievously*] as I understand they do, remembering it is in such case as it cannot be remedied, and [remembering] my desert upon every behalf, it is for to be thought there should be none obstacle against it; and also the worshipful that is in them, is not in your marriage, it is in their own marriage, which I beseech God send them such as may be to their worship and pleasure to God and to their hearts ease, for else were it great pity. Mistress I am afraid to write to you for I understand ye have shewed my letters that I have sent you before this time; but I pray you let no creature see this Letter, as soon as ye have read it let it be burnt, for I would no man should see it in no wise. Ye had no writing from me this two year, nor I will not send you no more, therefore I remit all this matter to your wisdom; Almighty Jesu preserve, keep, and [give] you your heart's desire, which I wot well should be to God's pleasure, &c.

This Letter was written with as great pain as ever wrote I thing in my life, for in good faith I have been right sick, and yet am not verily at ease, God amend it, &c.

Richard Calle.

• • • • •

The following Valentines were sent to John Paston the youngest in 1477 by his future wife, Margery Brews. Margery's father had no intention of parting with more than one hundred pounds with his daughter but she hopes that John will marry her nevertheless, even though he had been expecting a larger dowry than this. After many negotiations and setbacks the wedding took place later in the year.

• • •

From Margery Brews to John Paston.

1477.

English.

To my Right Well beloved Cousin John Paston, Esquire, be this Letter delivered, &c.

Right worshipful and well beloved Valentine, in my most humble wise, I recommend me unto you, &c. And heartily I thank you for the Letter, which that ye send me by John Beckerton, whereby I understand and know, that ye be purposed to come to Topcroft in short time, and without any errand or matter, but only to have a conclusion of the matter betwixt my father and you; I would be most glad of any Creature alive, so that the matter might grow to effect. And thereas ye say, and ye come and find the matter no more towards you than ye did aforetime, ye would no more put my father and my Lady my Mother to no cost nor business for that cause a good while after, which causeth my heart to be full heavy; and if that ye come, and the matter take to none effect, then should I be much more sorry, and full of heaviness.

And as for myself I have done and understand in the matter [all] that I can or may, as God knoweth; and I let you plainly understand, that my father will no more money part withal in that behalf, but an 100l. and 50 marks, which is right far from the accomplishment of your desire.

Wherefore, if that ye could be content with that Good, and my poor Person, I would be the merriest maiden on ground; and if ye think not yourself so satisfied, or that ye might have much more Good, as I have understood by you afore; good, true, and loving Valentine, that ye take no such labour upon you, as to come more for that matter, But let [what] is, pass, and never more to be spoken of, as I may be your true Lover and Beadwoman during my life.

No more unto you at this time, but Almighty Jesu preserve you both body and soul, &c.

By your Valentine, Margery Brews.

• • •

From Margery Brews to John Paston.
February 1477.
English.

Unto my right well beloved Valentine, John Paston, Esquire, be this Bill delivered, &c.

Right reverend and worshipful and my right well beloved Valentine, I recommend me unto you, full heartily desiring to hear of your welfare, which I beseech Almighty God long for to preserve unto his pleasure, and your heart's desire.

And if it please you to hear of my welfare, I am not in good hele of body, nor of heart, nor shall be till I hear from you;

For there wots no creature, what pain that I endure,
And for to be dead I dare it not discure [discover].

And my Lady my Mother hath laboured the matter to my father full diligently, but she can no more get than ye know of, for the which God knoweth I am full sorry. But if that ye love me, as I trust verily that ye do, ye will not leave me therefore.

And if ye command me to keep me true wherever I go,
I wis I will do all my might you to love, and never no mo,
And if my Friends say, that I do amiss,
They shall not let me so for to do,
Mine heart me bids evermore to love you,
Truly over all earthly thing,
And if they be never so wrath,
I trust it shall be better in time coming.

No more to you at this time, but the Holy Trinity have you in keeping; and I beseech you that this bill be not seen of none earthly Creature save only yourself, &c.

And this Letter was endited at Topcroft, with full heavy heart, &c.

By your own, Margery Brews.

• • • • •

Sir William Stonor was a wealthy landed gentleman and head of a long-established Oxfordshire family. In 1475 he married Elizabeth Ryche, a moneyed widow of a prosperous London mercer, and entered into partnership with his wife's old friend Thomas Betson, a Merchant of the Staple in Calais.

Stonor's estates in the Chilterns and Cotswolds were ideal for sheep grazing, which was far more profitable than arable farming at this time, and he welcomed the opportunity to become more involved with the wool trade. Stonor was ambitious and active in public affairs receiving a knighthood in 1478. Thomas Betson was betrothed to Katherine, Elizabeth's eldest daughter from her first marriage, who was thirteen years old when the following letter was written. Eileen Power described it as a 'veritable gem . . . for it brings to warm life again both Thomas Betson and Katherine Riche.'

• • •

From Thomas Betson to Katherine Ryche.

1 June 1476.

English.

Let this letter be delivered in haste to my faithful and heartily beloved Cousin Katherine Ryche, at Stonor.

My own deeply beloved cousin Katherine, I seek your favour from my bottom-most heart. You will know that I recently received from you a token, which was and remains very welcome to me, and I was very glad to have it; and I received also a letter from Holake, your gentleman attendant, from which I was happy to learn that you were happy, and in good health. I pray fervently to God that he will keep you so, for it gives me great pleasure that you should be so, as Jesus will save me.

And if you please, always be a hearty eater of your food, so that you grow up, and soon become a woman, which will truly make me the happiest man in the world; for when I remember your favour towards me, and the affectionate manner you showed me, the thought of it greatly gladdens my heart – as it does also when I remember your early childhood. So see to it that you don't become a rejecter of your food, which ought to be of great help to your growth, for that would certainly make me very sad again. So I ask, you, my own sweet cousin, if you love me, be happy, and eat up like a woman.

And if you will do that for love of me, think what you might like me to do for you, and whatever it may be, I give you my oath I will try to do it, with God's help, if it lies in my power. I can say nothing more at present, but when I come home I will tell you a lot more, just between you and me and God. And while you, like a woman and like a lover, think of me with many favours of various kinds, leaving them to my discretion, to divide them as I see fit, for truly, my own sweet cousin, you will you will realise that kindly and with good will I save half of them for myself, and keep them with me; and the other half I send to you, my own sweet cousin, with fervent love and affection; and above that, I send the blessing that Our Lady gave her dear son, and may it go well with you forever.

Please say hello to my horse, and ask him to give you four years of his age, to help you along. And when I come home I'll give him four years of my age, and four horse loaves, to make up. Tell him that I asked him to. And cousin Katherine, I thank you on his behalf, and as my wife you will thank yourself for him later on, for I have heard that you value him very highly.

My own sweet cousin, I have heard that you were recently in Calais looking for me, but were unable to find me; truly, you might have come to my cash desk where you could have seen me and found me, and not missed me. But you were looking for me in the wrong Calais, and you would know very well if you were here, and saw this Calais, as I wish to God you were, as well as some of those who were with you at your own dear Calais.

I pray, dear cousin, give my regards to the clock, and ask him to improve his profligate ways: for he is always striking at the wrong time, and he is always fast, and this is a bad way to be in. Tell him that unless he mends his ways he will make strangers avoid him, and not come there any more. I trust you to see that he improves before I come, which will be soon by the grace of God, as fast as my feet can bring me, and my hands as well.

My most faithful Katherine, I leave it to you that although I have not mentioned my honourable mistress your mother before in this letter, you will out of your kindness remember me to her mistresship as often as you like. And if you like you can tell her that I intend to come to market in Whitsun Week. And I hope you will pray for me, for I will pray for you, and maybe no one could as well. And may Almighty Jesus make a fine woman of you, and be pleased to send you many good long years to live.

At great Calais, on this side of the sea, the first day of June, when everyone had gone to dinner, and the clock struck twelve, and all the household called after me to come down, 'Come down to dinner at once!' And you know of old what sort of answer I gave them.

From your faithful cousin and lover, Thomas Betson.

I send this ring for a token.

• • • • •

Two years later Katherine was old enough to marry and Thomas writes to Elizabeth regretting that he is far too occupied with business and preparations for the wedding, including shopping for Katherine's trousseau, to manage a visit to Stonor. His excitement is evident and 'Thomas Betson, it is true, seems to have married his child-wife for love* The wedding took place in either the following August or September. Katherine bore Thomas five children before his death seven years later. She was only twenty-two years old and married again but Katherine must have sorely missed her first husband and she was buried by his side upon her own death in 1504.

• • •

From Thomas Betson to Dame Elizabeth Stonor.

24 June 1478.

English.

Let this be delivered in haste to my most honourable good lady, Dame Elizabeth Stonor.

Most honoured and respected and to me most valued lady, I seek your ladyship's favour as affectionately as I can, always hoping that Almighty God will send your ladyship the best of health and as much prosperity as ever any good lady had in the world, if it pleases God, and to your heart's content. And may it please your good ladyship to know that today I received a letter from you by the hand of your brother Master John Croke, and a token, for which with all . . .ness of my heart I thank your ladyship, as well as for your constant . . . . kindly affection, which your good ladyship always shows me so generously, though for my own part I as yet deserve nothing from you or yours. But I trust in God's mercy to remember it in the future, and am so bound to please you, as God will save me. Also, my lady, if you please, I understand from your writing that it will be the latter end of August before your ladyship can come London; and if that is the case, I am very sorry, for I have a lot of work in hand, and can apply little skill towards anything belonging to the matter you know about.

However, if that is how my master your husband and you have settled it, I am content; it will be painful to me, but I must and shall comfort myself as well as I can. I shall do as the blind bear does, which is to say . . . and therefore I must beseech your ladyship to send me your advice, how I should conduct myself with regard to the things that

* Kingsford, vol. 1, p. xliii.

concern my Cousin Katherine, and how I am to obtain them. She must have at least three girdles, and I don't know how they should be made: and there are many other things she must have, you know what they are, by my faith, I don't: by my oath, I wish it were finished more than I wish it cost less. I don't want to cause trouble or annoy anyone, but I would whole-heartedly, and with a will, like to be helped along a bit further forward with my business, it would make me a lot happier.

Also, my lady, though your ladyship wishes me to come to Stonor to celebrate etc., in good faith, my lady, my business is at a stage where I cannot travel to suit my pleasure. I have a lot in hand with the Fellowship of the Staple, and a lot else to do with my own concerns . . . that in good faith, I cannot bring to a quick conclusion, though God knows, I would greatly like to speak to your ladyship about the matters I've mentioned, and by the grace of God, once I have finished with what I have in hand, I will not be away from you much longer. And as for sending my Cousin Katherine here, your ladyship may do so if you like. I certainly wish she knew as much as you do, for then she could be of use, helping me with many things when she came. My lady, your mother, is in good health and doing well, and she sends God's blessing and her own, and likewise to my Cousin Katherine, and you all . . . .

[On the back] Also, my lady, your mother sends her best regards to my master your husband, and she is very glad of his recovery, and she prays God to send him good health. Also, my lady, you write of the courteous behaviour of my master towards my Cousin Katherine etc., and I'm very glad of that, and I pray to God fervently to thank him for it: for he has always been very loving towards her, and so I beseech God for him always to continue so, and also that Cousin Katherine will always deserve it from him, on account of her good womanly temper and manners, which she can display very well if she wishes to, and everybody who praises her says this.

Also, my lady, Mistress Bevesse wishes to be remembered to your ladyship, and prays sincerely for your good health. And I beseech Almighty Jesus and his blessed mother to bring you comfort, and to help you in all your good works, Amen.

Written at London, the twenty-fourth day of June.

By your own servant, Thomas Betson.

• • • • •

William Paston writes from Eton to his elder brother John. His grandfather, Justice William Paston, had been sent to school even though his parents had had to borrow money to fund him, he in turn had been eager to ensure his sons were well educated, basing their studies at Cambridge University and at Clifford's Inn, London. Education, particularly the study of law, had played a significant part in the Pastons' rise to eminence and it continued to be regarded with great importance.

After acknowledging the receipt of money for his lodgings and explaining the delayed arrival of supplies, William describes how he met a young woman at a wedding. He suggests that his brother visit her himself to verify the dowry available and the likely inheritance upon her mother's death. Her physical qualities are mentioned last of all and although William appears to be keen to marry nothing came of it, maybe either his own family or Margaret's disapproved of the match. William never married and he died insane in 1504.

• • •

From William Paston, junior, to his brother John.
23 February 1479.
English.

To his Worshipful Brother, John Paston, be this delivered in haste.

Right reverend and worshipful Brother, after all duties of recommendation, I recommend me to you, desiring to hear of your prosperity and welfare, which I pray God long to continue to his pleasure, and to your heart's desire; letting you weet that I received a letter from you, in the which Letter was 8d. with the which I should buy a pair of slippers.

Farthermore certifying you as for the 13s, 4d, which ye sent by a Gentleman's man, for my board, called Thomas Newton, was delivered to mine Hostess, and so to my Creansor [*Creditor*] Mr. Thomas Stevenson; and he heartily recommended him to you; also ye sent me word in the letter of 12lb. of Figgs and 8lb. of Raisins, I have them not delivered, but I doubt not I shall have, for Alweder told me of them, and he said, that they came after in another Barge.

And as for the young Gentlewoman, I will certify you how I first fell in acquaintance with her; her father is dead, there be two sisters of them, the elder is just wedded; at which wedding I was with mine hostess, and also desired [*invited*] by the Gentleman himself, called William Swan, whose dwelling is in Eton. So it fortuned that mine hostess reported on me otherwise than I was worthy; so that her Mother commanded her to make me good Cheer; and so in good faith she did; she is not abiding where she is now, her dwelling is in London; but her Mother and she came to a place of hers five miles from Eton, where the wedding was, for because it was nigh to the Gentleman, which wedded her Daughter; and on Monday next coming, that is to say, the first Monday of clean Lent, her Mother and she will go to the Pardon at Sheene [Richmond], and so forth to London, and there to abide in a place of hers in Bow Church-Yard; and if it please you to enquire of her, her Mother's name is Mistress Alborow, the name of the Daughter is Margaret Alborow, the age of her is, by all likelyhood, 18 or 19 years at the farthest; and as for the money and plate it is ready whensoever she were wedded; but as for the Livelihood [*property*], I trow not till after her mother's decease, but I cannot tell you for very certain, but you may know by enquiring.

And as for her Beauty, judge you that, when you see her, if so be that ye take the labour; and specially behold her hands, for and if it be, as it is told me, she is disposed to be thick.

And as for my coming from Eton, I lack nothing but versifying, which I trust to have with a little continuance.

Quœritur, Quomodo nonvalet hora, valet mora ? Unde dicitur ?

Arbore jam videas exemplum. Non die possunt
Qmnia suppleri; sed tamen illa mora.

And these two verses aforesaid be of mine own making.

No more to you at this time, but God have you in his keeping.

Written at Eton the even of Saint Mathias the Apostle, in haste, with the hand of your Brother.

William Paston, Junior.

• • • • •

George Cely married Margery, the widow and sole heir of a London draper, Edmund Rygon, who owned property in Calais and its environs in May 1484. Like his brother Richard, George married well and their wives were prized for their wealth and business contacts as much as for their personal attributes.

In the next letter William Cely, a junior member of the household, broke off a guarded report on George's progress in one matrimonial negotiation to congratulate him on being 'at apoynt' with 'at oder gentyllwoman,* and assured him that his income was certainly superior to any other contender for the lady's hand; this indicates that Margery was just as interested in her future husband's financial assets as he was in hers, and that widows had greater freedom to dictate their own

* Hanham, p. xv.

terms and exploit the marriage market than single girls under parental control.

The introductory paragraph reveals how the Merchants of the Staple would approach Flemish as well as English authorities in order to safeguard their trade in times of political instability.

• • •

From William Cely at Calais to George Cely at London.
14 April 1484.
English.

Let this be delivered to my honourable master George Cely, merchant of the Staple at Calais, in Mart Lane, London.

Most honourable masters, I ask your masters' favour in all due humility and respect. May it please you to know that the wool fleet arrived in Calais on April 10 . . . and most of your wool was brought ashore and. . . . etc. Moreover, I understand from your letters that Peter Bayledelett has been with your masterships, and showed you how he would find guarantors for whatever wool John Delowpes buys from you at Calais. Sir, if the guarantees stand up I would advise you to accept them, or not, since I can't say what prospects we will have in the Flanders trade.

I'm afraid they intend to drop us, as the men who were sent by the Staple to the Lords of Ghent to negotiate guarantees for all the Fellows of the Staple have now come home empty-handed, for they were told that Flanders has suffered many injuries at English hands, and received no compensation, and they can't put up with any more. And as for guarantees, they refuse to give any.

Where this is tending I can't say, so, sir, if you can get a firm guarantee out of Peter Bayledelett, it will be worth doing, whatever chance brings later. And now, sir, please let me know what terms Peter has stipulated for your masterships in respect of the wool that I deliver here to John Delowpes, as Wyllykyn, John Delowpes's agent has arrived and says John Delowpes has a letter from your masterships about it; but I will deliver no wool to him until I hear from you again, even though the man would be sound enough if we were sure of peace between ourselves and Flanders. But sir, if you could be sure of your money there, it would be good business, for there's not a merchant who comes to buy new wool here who pays ready cash.

Sir, As regards the matter your mastership wrote to me about Thomas Whyte, the mercer: I most certainly spoke to him, and he dined at the home of my host, though he didn't know me, and there he showed how matters lay between yourself and another man, although he said she held you in greater esteem than the other man, but sir, you have his good wishes etc.

Next, William Salford has arrived, and I spoke to him and made him welcome, and he told me how your mastership and that other lady were at an advanced stage in the matter, which I was glad to hear, and he said he was too. But he has resolved no more questions so far. And sir, it's the opinion of many people here that you're sure of her, which pleases me well, and I'm very glad of it . . . who know you, both merchants and soldiers, speak very highly of you, saying that even if the lady were worth twice what she has, you deserve to have her.

As regards any investigation of your business here, I don't think any has been mounted. If they do they need look no further than the books in the counting house, where they will find that your turnover in less than a full year amounts to over £2,000 sterling, while the person who applied to be set above you here, and his brother, have not done half that in this town in twelve months.

Moreover, your mastership wrote to me that if there was any good Gascon wine you would like a tun of it. Sir, there is no good wine for any money yet, though I understand that there should be some from Bruges in ten or twelve days, and I reckon I should be able to get you a tun, or a pipe at least, which I shall send to you.

I sent a letter to you by the last passage by a Thomas Bland of Boston, in which I describe the sale of 1500 cotswold fleeces made to Adrian Williamson of Latham and his company, at fourteen nobles the hundred, which is seventy pounds sterling, in silver.

Sir, today, April fourteenth, three passengers came in from Dover, and two great French warships had chased them into the harbour mouth. If it had been a mile further, they would have been taken, and all our warships are laid up at Cambrai.

Nothing further for your mastership today, but may Almighty Jesus preserve you.

Written at Calais the fourteenth day of April.

by your servant,

William Cely.

• • • • •

In 1483 Richard Cely the younger married Anne Rowson, daughter of a wealthy Yorkshire mercer who had provided her with a substantial dowry. Richard had been looking for a wife since 1481 and the Cely letters include details of his efforts, such as the following example which has been reproduced on many occasions due to its vivid and amusing picture of an unsuccessful wooing. Bagley wrote, 'it furnishes us with interesting sidelights upon the mechanics of the wool trade, matrimonial skirmishes, the drinking habits of gentlewomen, and Edward IV's attempts to prevent the drain of silver from England.*

• • •

From Richard Cely the younger at London to George Cely at Calais or the mart.

13 May 1482.

English.

Let this be delivered to my most well-beloved brother George Cely, merchant of the Staple at Calais or at the market.

My most beloved brother, I send you my best regards, to tell you that as I write this our mother, our brother, my godfather and the whole household are well, thank the good Lord.

Sir, the same day that I left for Cotswold I received a letter from you written at Calais on April fourteenth, including an inventory of such of our father's goods and money as were on that side of the sea. I have not spoken to the Bishop's officers since I received it, but when I last spoke with them, they said everything should await your arrival. I reckon from your letter that you will get over £500. I have been in Cotswold for the last three weeks, and packed twenty-two sarpels and a poke† with William Midwinter. Four tons of this are middle quality only. William Bretton says this is the best year for wool he has ever known, and under the same contract I packed§ four sarples at Camden, two good, two middle. Including rejects, there should be twenty-seven or twenty-eight sarpels altogether.

Sir, I can't get William Midwinter's fleeces at under £3 3s 4d the hundred, and I shall go up to that price Please write to me soon. Sir, I have bought options on 7,000 reasonably good fleeces in Cotswold at three pounds, I can't get any for less than that. I'm also sending you details of a court action, and I pray that God will bring it to a favourable conclusion.

---

* Bagley, vol. 1, pp. 179-80

† Twenty-two bags of a ton apiece, and another half full.

§ This is the word in the text, and it's not inaccurate, though baled would probably give a better flavour of what was going on.

On the same Sunday that I came to Northleach from Burford, before Mattins, William Midwinter welcomed me, and in course of conversation asked me if I was actively looking for a wife. I said I was not, and he told me that there was a young lady, whose father was called Lemryke, and whose mother was dead, and who expects to inherit from her mother £40 per year, according to the local gossip, and her father is the biggest employer and greatest man in the district, and there have been some great gentlemen paying court to her, who would like to have her, etc.

And after Mattins William Midwinter pressed this matter very strongly, about Mr Lemryke, and told me all about it, and about the young lady. The following Saturday William Midwinter went to London, as all the wool-gatherers had been summoned by the Pettyt Council, to settle accounts and verify the tallies, and they are expected to come again at Michaelmas.

When I had finished packing at Camden, and William Midwinter had gone, I came back to Northleach to finish the packing there, and on the next Sunday following the same man that William Midwinter had spoken to first came to me, and told me he had mentioned it to his master, as Midwinter had wanted him to, and he said his master was very pleased about it. And he also said that if I cared to linger till Mayday, I could see the young lady. I said I would be happy to stay till then, and that day her father should have been attending the King at Northleach, but he sent a clerk instead and rode to Winchcombe. The same day the young lady came to Mattins with her stepmother, and William Bretton and I were already there when they came in. After Mattins was over, they went to join a female relation, and I sent them all a half-gallon of white Romanée, which they accepted gratefully, for they had come a mile on foot that morning.

After Mass I came over and made them welcome, and kissed them, and they thanked me for the wine and asked me to dinner. but I made my excuses, so they made me promise to have a drink with them after dinner. I sent them a gallon of wine for dinner, and they sent me a roast heron, and after dinner I went to drink wine with them and took William Bretton to keep me company, and we had a very pleasant conversation, and her person attracted me as much as the original description. She is young, slim, very well favoured and witty, and has a very good reputation in the district. But sir, it all waits on the return of her father to London, when we can find out how much money he will give as a wedding portion, and how well he likes me. He will be here in three weeks, and please send me a letter with your thoughts on this matter.

Michael Koke and his wife have come from York to visit my

mother, and my mother and I have made them very welcome, and my mother has given Michael's wife a crimson gown she used to wear herself, and she has asked me to write to you to buy her a calaber* forepiece to attach to it. And Coke's wife and she ask you to buy for them ten of the best lap-dogs† you can find in the market, and she will be pleased with them. I shall send the bill of 13s 4d to Calais by Robert Herrick at Whitsun. I comes to £25 6s 7d paid. I understand from William Cely's letter that you have heard from Lord St John. Please send me some news – I sent you the latest I had.

Sir, they have begun to ship into London, and all our wool and fleeces are still in Cotswold, except for four sarpels, so we can't do anything for the moment. Sir, I think it will be profitable to pay cash in this market, as the king has circulated the mercers, and let them know that there will be three cash counters: one at Bruges, one at Calais and the third in London: and I am informed that any merchant of the Staple who sells out may buy whatever he wants back. And those who buy nothing can bring their money to the king's counter at Bruges or Calais, and be paid in full a month and a day later, and the rate of exchange will be fixed at eight shillings. The mercers are not happy with this.

Please think of our boys.

No more. Written at London the thirteenth day of May.

pp Richard Cely.

• • • • •

William Wittcars's concern for this 'poore woman' and her illegitimate child provides a glimpse of the personal troubles experienced in the lives of the 'anonymous' population. The political events of the time are remote from our experience of life but this letter evokes emotions that easily transcend five centuries.

• • •

From William Wittcars to Sir Robert Plumpton.

c. 1495.

English.

---

* Italian fur, not necessarily from Calabria, and not from any specific species. Think of it as a superior grade of fun fur.

† I offer this gloss with little confidence. The word in the text, 'mynkys', is not to be found on OED, and my guess is that Cely intended to write 'mynksys'; even so, ten at a time seems excessive. The only obvious alternative meaning is monkeys, which would be excessive beyond belief.

To Sir Robert Plumpton, or to Master William his son.

Most honourable Master Plumpton, I ask your favour most urgently, hoping that you will be a good master to the poor woman who brings you this. Sir, an employee of yours has fathered a child on her, which God knows will die if it is not looked after. She maintained it as long as she could, though she hasn't a cloth to her back apart from what I have given her, since I took her into my service. And if you will be good enough to listen to this poor woman's story, I hope to God you will be a good master to her – and a better one yet, for my sake. If I had not been she would have run away. Meanwhile I have been keeping the child at my own expense, and God knows, I will continue to do so until I hear from you. God keep you.

By your own (to the limit of his power),

William Wittcars.

• • • • •

King Henry VII and King Ferdinand of Aragon and Queen Isabella of Castile had considered the possibility of a match between Arthur, infant son of the English King and Princess Catherine of Aragon, as early as 1488. Both parties felt that an alliance between England and Spain would be mutually advantageous and create a formidable opposition to the increasingly powerful House of Hapsburg.

The treaty of Medina del Campo was signed in 1489. King Ferdinand complained about Henry VII's excessive demands in terms of a dowry, but the marriage was agreed. Over the next few years, the Spanish and English kings mistrusted each other, each fearing that the other was planning alternative marriage arrangements, but in October 1496 yet another treaty was signed. Reports were sent between the courts concerning the progress of the betrothed and in 1497 Elizabeth of York sent the following letter to Queen Isabella to confirm her enthusiasm for the intended marriage. Two proxy marriages followed in 1498 and 1499, and Catherine of Aragon finally arrived in England in October 1501 to a rapturous welcome; King Henry VII was most impressed by the Spanish princess. The marriage took place in St Paul's followed by lengthy celebrations, after which the Prince and Princess of Wales set off for Ludlow Castle to govern the principality. Arthur died five months after the wedding 'of a consumption'. Catherine remained in England and eight years later married Arthur's younger brother, Henry VIII.

• • •

From Elizabeth of York, Queen of Henry VII, to Queen Isabella of Castile.

3 December 1497.

Latin.

To the most serene and potent princess the Lady Elizabeth, by God's grace queen of Castile, Leon, Aragon, Sicily, Granada, &c., our cousin and dearest relation, Elizabeth, by the same grace queen of England and France, and Lady of Ireland, wishes health and the most prosperous increase of her desires.

Although we before entertained singular love and regard to your highness above all other queens in the world, as well for the consanguinity and necessary intercourse which mutually take place between us, as also for the eminent dignity and virtue by which your said majesty so shines and excels that your most celebrated name is noised abroad and diffused everywhere; yet much more has this our love increased and accumulated by the accession of the most noble affinity which has recently been celebrated between the most illustrious Lord Arthur prince of Wales, our eldest son, and the most illustrious princess the Lady Catherine, the Infanta, your daughter. Hence it is that, amongst our other cares and cogitations, first and foremost we wish and desire from our heart that we may often and speedily hear of the health and safety of your serenity, and of the health and safety of the aforesaid most illustrious Lady Catherine, whom we think of and esteem as our own daughter, than which nothing can be more grateful and acceptable to us. Therefore we request your serenity to certify of your estate, and of that of the aforesaid most illustrious Lady Catherine our common daughter. And if there be anything in our power which would be grateful or pleasant to your majesty, use us and ours as freely as you would your own; for, with most willing mind, we offer all that we have to you, and wish to have all in common with you. We should have written you the news of our state, and of that of this kingdom, but the most serene lord the king, our husband, will have written at length of these things to your majesties. For the rest may your majesty fare most happily according to your wishes.

From our palace of Westminster, 3d day of December, 1497.

Elizabeth R.

To the most serene and potent princess the Lady Elizabeth, by God's grace queen of Castile, Leon, Aragon, Sicily; Granada, &c., our cousin and dearest kinswoman.

FAMILY AND DOMESTIC LIFE

Medieval patriarchal society was dominated by the father figure, be it a king in charge of the royal household and centre of government, a bishop responsible for the members of his see or an abbot in charge of the monks in his monastery. Being part of a family or household guaranteed a certain degree of respectability and security, as is most evident in the suspicion with which wanderers and vagrants were viewed. The letter from German Pole underlines the importance placed on being acknowledged as a member of a family unit.

Wives were primarily responsible for domestic management, husbands depended on their wives' ability to maintain food supplies, manage accounts and organize staff. Women were expected to identify with their husbands' interests and to provide wholehearted support. Husbands came before children or self, domestic management frequently included acting on one's husband's behalf.

Since food supplies were sporadic, depending on the season and availability, it took considerable foresight to ensure the household was adequately fed and clothed all year round. Many tasks were performed within the home itself such as baking, brewing, spinning and sewing. Local towns could generally meet most demands, but if a particular spice or type of cloth was required then these had to be fetched from London.

Children were expected to revere and obey their parents unequivocally. The overwhelming impression is that relationships between parents and their children were formal and lacking in affection. Few parents had any qualms about sending their offspring away from home or delegating their care to others. During the fifteenth century life became more family-orientated and children began to be valued as individuals in their own right rather than marital obligations and financial burdens. Nevertheless, as many of the letters in this book tend to show, there is a marked discrepancy between the way people are traditionally expected to have behaved and how they actually did.

Most forms of entertainment and recreation were organized within the home.

Households of every grade and size were the organs of society within which men, women and children dwelt and enjoyed their being according

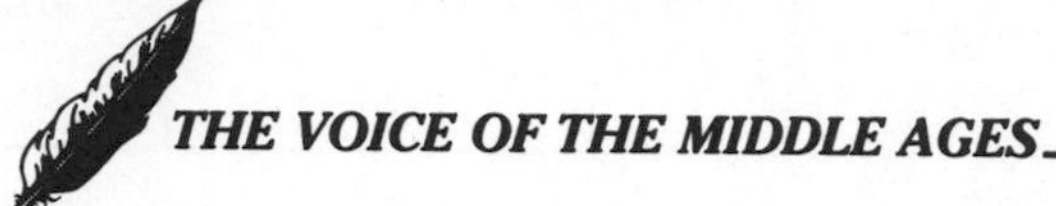

to degree and vocation. *

Social calls, religious duties, festivals and various pastimes occupied the leisure time of medieval lives. The lower ranks of society often resorted to alleviating their hardships by way of merrymaking or, at the other extreme, religious devotions. The higher ranks were able to pursue more extravagant and sophisticated activities including music, literature, and outdoor pursuits such as hunting and fishing.

The following letters show a variety of family relationships, everyday concerns, interests and entertainments.

•••••

The strong bonds between mothers and their children expressed in the next three letters provide a rare indication that loving relationships did exist between parents and their offspring during the Middle Ages, despite the tendency for children of the ruling classes to be brought up by others outside the immediate family from an early age.

•••

From Eleanor Queen-Dowager of England to her son, Edward I.
1286-1291.
French.

To the most noble prince and her very dear son, Edward, by God's grace King of England, Lord of Ireland, and Duke of Aquitaine, Eleanora, humble nun of the order of Fontevraud, of the convent of Amesbury, wishes health and her blessing.

Sweetest son, we know well how great is the desire that a mother has to see her child when she has been long away from him, and that dame Margaret de Nevile, companion of Master John Giffard, has not seen for a long time past her child, who is in the keeping of dame Margaret de Weyland, and has a great desire to see him. We pray you, sweetest son, that you will command and pray the aforesaid Margaret de Weyland, that she will suffer that the mother may have the solace of her child for some time, after her desire. Dearest son, we commend you to God. Given at Amesbury, the 4th day of March.

•••

* Du Boulay, p. 123.

Robert Lovell to his mother-in-law.

c. 1396.

French.

My lady and mother, most honoured and with all my heart most dearly well-beloved, I commend myself to you as utterly as I know how and best can, desiring earnestly to hear and truly know good and joyous news of you and of your honourable estate, entreating God, the heavenly king, most high and all-powerful, that he may grant me always to hear and know such [things] as you can indeed think and wish for and as my heart most earnestly desires, for certainly my joy is renewed when I have good news of you. Therefore I entreat you that, for the sincere joy and pleasure of my heart, it may please you to inform me of them very often by messengers. And, most-honoured lady and mother, because I am quite certain that it would please you much to hear of me and of my health, may it please you to know that at the time of sending this [letter] I am hale and hearty, thank God, and [that I] thank you again and again as much as I can for the very great affection and kindliness that you have had and still have for me, and for the countless other favours which it has pleased you in your very noble kindliness to do and to show me without my deserving any at all. I entreat you for your good and gracious encouragement to me forever. And if there be anything that I can do for your honour or pleasure, may it please you to communicate your gracious wishes and desires, which I am and always will be ready to obey and fulfil to the limit of my small ability, as I am assuredly held and obliged [to do]. My lady and mother, most honoured and with all my heart most entirely well-beloved, may the Blessed Trinity have you in its most holy keeping and grant you a good and very long life and the good fulfilment of all your noble desires. Written at Trim in Ireland, the third day of June.

Your humble son – so please you, Robert Lovell.

• • •

From Agnes Paston to her son, John Paston.

29 October 1458 (?)

English.

To my well beloved Son, John Paston, be this delivered in haste.

Son, I greet you well, and let you weet, that for as much as your brother Clement letteth me weet that ye desire faithfully my blessing; that blessing that I prayed your father to give you the last day that ever he spake, and the blessing of all saints under heaven, and mine mote come to you all days and times; and think verily none other but that ye have it, and shall have it, with that [*on condition*] that I find you kind and willing to the weal of your Father's soul, and to the welfare of your brethren.

By my counsel dispose yourself as much as ye may to have less to do in the world; your Father said, "In little business lyeth much rest." This world is but a thoroughfare, and full of woe; and, when we depart therefrom, right nought bear with us, but our good deeds and ill; and there knoweth no man how soon God will clepe him; and therefore it is good for every creature to be ready. Whom God visiteth him he loveth.

And as for your brethren they will I know certainly labour all that in them lyeth for you. Our Lord have you in his blessed keeping, body and soul. Written at Norwich, the 29th day of October.

By your Mother, Agnes Paston.

• • • • •

Lady Elizabeth Zouche was a widow whose second husband William, Lord Zouche, had died in 1396.

After describing her fears that her household at Eaton Bray in Bedfordshire is suffering from mismanagment, she lists her requirements from London – a gift of two gold rosary beads for her mother, whom she was intending to visit, white wine, and the price of black velvet.

The sumptuary law prescribed what different ranks of society could wear; velvet, silk, brocades and furs were the luxury of the nobility whilst peasants had to make do with homespun wool and linen. The social distinctions which dress expressed are alluded to in the letter where the Prince of Wales fears his appearance may not be indicative of his rank. Dress was a suitable vehicle for the display of wealth and therefore power; fortunes were rarely invested in capital assets which had little relevance in the volatile medieval world.

• • •

From Lady Elizabeth Zouche to her friend John Bore.

31 August 1402.

English.

Right well beloved friend, I greet you well, and gladly would I hear of your welfare, and I pray you that you will take a leisure that Frome* and you might come hither together and set, I pray, this house in better governance, for I think to God it is ever longer the worse; and that you would do it in haste, for I would prepare me to ride to my lady my mother. And also I would pray you that you would have ordered for me a pair of beads of gold for my lady my mother with the quaintest paternoster that you can find, whatsoever they cost; and also I pray you that you will order me a pipe of white wine as I spoke to you of; also I pray you that you will send me word what the price [is] of a whole cloth of black velvet and as my trust is in you, fail me not, especially of my beads. . . .

E. la Zouche.

[*Endorsed in French*]:

There was delivered by the said John Bore to Thomas, Chicheley's man, bearer of this letter, the fifth of September in the third year [of Henry IV] one pipe of white wine, which cost 35s. 8d.

And for barreling [?] the same, 7d. And for drawing out of the cellar, 12d. And for carriage of the same between the cellar and Smithfield, 12d. And delivered to the said Thomas for his charges, 8d.

Item, sent to my Lady la Zouche by the said bearer one pair of gold beads weighing one ounce and half an ounce save forty [sic] pennyweight, which cost in all 38s.

• • • • •

In this letter John Bore is burdened with the task of finding a suitably humble butler for the Lady Elizabeth.

• • •

Lady Zouche to John Bore.

29 May 1402.

English.

Right well beloved friend, I greet you well and desire to hear of your welfare. And I pray you for my love that you will think about my butler as you promised me, for you know well yourself that it is difficult for me

* One of her first husband's executors (Rickert).

to be so long without [one], and unless you can get me another and that he be humble, in any way, I pray you, and I trust that you will not fail me. I can say no more, but I commend you to God. Written at Eaton the twenty-ninth day of May.

• • • • •

The following letters are examples taken from a treatise on letter-writing which was a later adaptation of the earlier and widely used treatises such as that of Alberic of Monte Cassino discussed in the introduction.

In the first example an anonymous ambitious clerk writes how his promotion will allow him to help his family and friends. This is followed by a request from a clerk asking a friend to send him some plays which could be performed for his lord at Christmas. The last example is an offer to teach a student friend to play the harp.

• • •

Early 15th century.

Latin.

To remove your hesitancy altogether, I am writing this letter to explain that I have been in charge of drafting letters in the household of our most Serene Lady the Queen, in the office of clerk to her steward, in which by the aid (?) of God's mercy I hope shortly to rise higher, and to attain such a rank that I may be able honourably to help, and also to promote, my friends and kinsfolk.

May the Most High revive your friendship with the manifold increase of virtues, to our mutual comfort.

• • •

To his friend and companion H.H. sends kind greeting in everything.

Let it be known to you that I am in good estate, both of body and soul, blessed be God, and so I am much surprised that up to now I have had no letters, and that no reports of your health have come to my ears. Consequently, I beg you to let me know if you are well. I should also like you please to send me an 'interlude', or two or three of them, to be played in my Lord's hall at Christmas. I heartily request you to let me know of this in the aforesaid letter, and to do this by the first messenger if you can, because there can be nothing against it.

May no saint harm you, but may the new treaty of London, made in Saint M.'s week, allow you to do it.

I say no more for the present, but farewell in Christ, and may he increase your prosperous and happy success.

• • •

Greetings.

Dearest friend, by this present letter and with reference to our recent conversation, I declare to you that if you want to learn from me how to play the harp in accordance with the agreement made between us, namely for twenty shillings, you ought to know that I intend to call in at your house on Saint Thomas's Day, and stay with you all the autumn. I therefore advise you please to let me know your wishes, by letter, and if the agreement made between us is still to hold good, to be so kind as to forward 40 pence to buy a harp, knowing for certain that you will have as much from me for your ten shillings, as you would have to pay twenty shillings for in Oxford.

Farewell in God, etc.

• • • • •

Dunster castle had been bought by Sir Hugh Luttrell's mother during the reign of Edward III, the Luttrell seat having previously been at Irnham in Lincolnshire, and Sir Hugh became the head of a family said to have established itself in England at the time of William the Conqueror.

Sir Hugh had been a knight during Henry V's wars in France and held positions of responsibility for both Henry IV and Henry V, becoming Captain of Harfleur and Grand Seneschal of Normandy. He visited his family at Dunster once a year. Letters played an important role in maintaining contact with home for soldiers, merchants and ambassadors, often containing a combination of personal greetings and concerns about domestic management as well as requests for news and supplies.

• • •

From Sir Hugh Luttrell, of Dunster Castle to his son John Luttrell and Richard Arnold his receiver.

1419-20.

Let this be delivered to my most well-beloved son John Luttrell, and to Richard Arnold, my receiver at Dunster.

Most well-beloved son, I greet you well, with the blessing of Christ and my own.

This is to let you know that I now know that despite my expressed command in writing Philipot Stronge has not yet had his goods returned to him. I am astonished that my orders should be flouted, but whatever their position, some men play the part of lord for as long as they can get away with it. For by the grace of God, I shall be playing it before long, and then perhaps they will wish they had done as I told them, for when they begrudge such a small matter, which costs them nothing, it's not surprising that they disregard my orders in greater ones. But between you and Richard Arnold this letter and my instructions will . . . . be carried out, whoever speaks against it, and I don't need to write that. So no more of this, and consider that, thank God . . . alive, and by God's grace will come home, and better that than what some desire.

So summon Will Parson into your presence, and . . . mine by his Bible Oath if he had paid, and how much, and in respect of what, to my Receiver, and pay it back to him, and that Philipot have his goods returned to him, down to the last pennyworth that he can claim, and see that all this is done, Finally, dear friends, I can't . . . but may the Holy Trinity keep you. And Richard Arnold, this will be your warrant to claim in respect of the payment . . .

Written at Harfleur the eighteenth day of October.

Your father Hugh Luttrell, Knight, Lord of Dunster, and Great Seneschal of Normandy.

P.S. Also, dear friends, please send me post-haste enough fish for my household. Don't forget this.

• • • • •

During the medieval period hunting was such an important part of aristocratic life that expertise in this activity was considered to be the peacetime equivalent of skill in the battlefield.

The nobility took great care to ensure their forests and parks were well supervised, with plenty of game available during the summer and winter seasons, and that poachers were severely punished. A letter describes the penalty the Prince of Wales had to pay for poaching, but less distinguished offenders, probably desperate for food rather than entertainment, were lucky to escape with their lives.

than entertainment, were lucky to escape with their lives.

Wild boar and deer were the most highly prized game and bloodhounds were carefully reared for the chase. The letters emphasize how seriously hunting was regarded and reveal both these Queens' in-depth knowledge of this pursuit.

Edward, the second Duke of York, wrote *The Master of the Game*, a handbook of the hunt, between 1406 and 1413. It is the most detailed source on the subject.

• • •

From Queen Margaret of Anjou to the Parker of Ware.

1445-1455.

English.

*By the Queen to the Parker*of Ware*

Well-beloved, because we know very well that our cousin, the Earl of Salisbury, will be very happy and pleased if, when we come to our castle at Hertford, we take our pleasure and sport in his park at Ware, we make so bold as to request and desire that the game should be spared, protected and looked after with this in mind, with no one else being allowed to go there to hunt, shoot, course, or take part in any other sport which would destroy or reduce the game there, until you have a countermanding order from our cousin in that connexion.

As we trust you, etc.

• • •

From Queen Margaret of Anjou to Robert Hiberdon.

1445-1455

English.

By the Queen to Robert Hiberdon

Trusty and well-beloved, as we are informed that you are skilful in training bloodhounds to the highest standards, we desire and ask of you that you will, out of respect for us, go to the trouble and effort to train two bloodhounds for our use, keeping them securely and properly, under your personal training, control and guidance, until we send for them. And do not fail in this, if you wish to please us, and to enjoy our

* Chief game-warden

grace and favour for it in the future.

At Windsor, the sixteenth day of August.

• • •

From Elizabeth Woodville, Queen of Edward IV, to Sir William Stonor.

Before 1492

Probably French.

By the Queen to our trusty and well-beloved Sir William Stoner, Knight.

Trusty and well-beloved, we greet you well. And whereas we understand, by report made unto us at this time, that you have taken upon you now of late to make masteries within our forest and chace of Barnwood and Excill, and there, in contempt of us, uncourteously to hunt and slay our deer within the same, to our great marvel and displeasure; we will you wit that we intend to sue such remedy therein as shall accord with my lord's laws. And whereas we farthermore understand that you purpose, under colour of my lord's commission, in that behalf granted unto you as you say, hastily to take the view and rule of our game of deer within our said forest and chase; we will that you shew unto us or our council your said commission, if any such you have, and, in the mean season, that you spare of hunting within our said forest or chace, as you will answer at your peril. Given under our signet, at our manor of Greenwich, the first day of August.

Elizabeth.

• • • • •

Lucy was married to John Prynce, heir to the manors of Theydon Garnon and Gregories in Essex. This letter was most probably addressed to Thomas Clyfford, her husband's advisor. It reveals that the writing of letters, be they brief reminders, invitations or instructions, was common practice amongst the landowning classes for both men and women by the end of the fifteenth century. However, Thomas Clyfford's profession, other than acting as John Prynce's advisor, was as scrivener, so it is clear that some still felt a need for an intermediary in the letter-writing process, although 'scrivener' has increasingly being used to mean 'notary'. This was probably not due tq lack of ability but inclination, letter-writing was still a laborious task and few could use a pen with ease, consequently those that could afford to pay were probably glad

From Lucy Prynce for her cousin.

c. 1475.

English.

Right worshipful cousin,

I recommend me unto you and my cousin your wife, praying you and my Master Wretyll prays you, that ye will come a spell with him on Monday next ensuing, for to speak with him and them that will be with him; for you must come in any wise, and not fail. Also you must come, for Sir Thomas Mongumbere has sent letter and bill unto my Master Wretyll. Also, cousin, I pray you to send me word when ye will have your horse sent to you, [whether] on Saturday or else on Sunday, by the bringer of this bill.

No more at this time, but Jesus have you in his keeping.

Written at Theydon Garnon, Wednesday last past, in haste.

By your own cousin, Lucy Prynce.

• • • • •

Reynold Goldstone was appointed to the office of proctor representing the Chapter of Convocation shortly after William Sellyng became Prior of Christ Church in 1472. He was a trusted friend of long standing and when not engaged in his official duties performed various other services on behalf of the Prior, as this letter indicates. Goldstone rose in influence, 'filling every monastic office except the highest,* and died in 1504. Sir John Fyneux, with whom Goldstone was planning to stay, had been appointed seneschal of all the manors of Christ Church in 1476.

• • •

From Dom. Reynold Goldstone to Prior Sellyng.

c. 1476.

English.

To the reverend father in God, the Prior of Christchurch in Canterbury.

Reverend and honoured father in God, I send my humble regards.

* Sheppard, p. xxii.

This is to tell you, if you please, that I have expedited as many of your affairs as can be for the moment. On Wednesday we shall be going to the bar in the case of Robert Martyn the chandler, and on Thursday Master Fyneux and I intend to take the barge at six in the morning, and by the grace of God we should be with you by noon on Friday. I have received £30 in part payment today, and your jewel is in security until more comes in. It will cost you £5, and thank God for it, as I will explain to you when I come home.

Barnwell the fishmonger has died, and was buried today. Master Langton has ridden to the King – there's a Privy Council meeting being held today at Guildford. Please send me the horse soon. Master Fyneux wants me to spend Thursday night with him at Lynstead. I hope to God I will be fed better and more cheaply than by credit elsewhere.

I'll tell you about the other things when I get home, by the grace of God, may he keep you.

Written in haste in London, the twenty-fifth day of November.

Your Chaplain

Dom Reynold Goldstone

• • • • •

Sir John Paston's mother, Margaret Paston, had died in November 1484 and his wife is concerned that no inappropriate Christmas festivities should take place during a time of family mourning. Lady Morley's husband, William Lovel, had died in 1476 and she has recommended the more sober occupations her household engaged in after her own bereavement.

No doubt all the talk of death had made Margery long for her husband's return as her closing words reveal.

• • •

From Margery Paston to her husband Sir John Paston.

1484.

English.

To my right worshipful husband John Paston.

Right worshipful husband, I recommend me unto you; Please it you to weet, that I sent your eldest Son to my Lady Morley, to have knowledge what Sports were used in her house in Christmas next following, after the decease of my Lord her husband; and she said that that there were none Disguisings, nor Harping, nor Luting, nor Singing, nor none loud Disports; but playing at the Tables [*Back gammon*], and Chess, and Cards; such disports she gave her Folks leave to play and none other.

Your Son did his errant right well as ye shall hear after this. I sent your younger Son to the Lady Stapleton, and she said according to my Lady Morley's saying in that; and as she had seen used in places of worship thereas she hath been.

I pray you that ye will assure to you some man at Caister, to keep your Buttery, for the man that ye left with me, will not take upon him to breve (*keep accounts*) daily as ye commanded; he saith, he hath not used to give a reckoning neither of Bread nor Ale, till at the week's end, and he saith, he wot well that he should not content it and therefore I suppose he shall not abide, and I trow ye shall be fain to purvey another man for Symond, for ye are never the nearer a wise man for him.

I am sorry that ye shall not at home be for Christmas.

I pray you that ye will come as soon as ye may; I shall think myself half a Widow, because ye shall not be at home, &c. God have you in his keeping. Written on Christas Even.

By your Margery Paston.

• • • • •

Thomas Betanson writes from London and provides an assortment of interesting information. The Earl of Warwick, Edward Plantagenet, was a prisoner in the Tower at this time and Betanson reveals how events which we tend to regard as components of a dynastic struggle, were of great interest to the contemporary public. Despite 'many enimies on the see' and rampant plague he is busy making plans for Christmas.

• • •

From Thomas Betanson to Sir Robert Plumpton.

29 November 1486.

English.

Let this be delivered to his honoured master, Sir Robert Plumpton, Knight.

My most honourable and sole master, I send my regards to your mastership and both my ladies, and to all your colleagues, friends and servants. If your mastership is interested to hear from me, and where

I am, I'm serving in the church of St Sepulchre without Newgate, lodging with a woman from Selby.

I earn ten Marks without deduction, and in term time I eat at the table of Lord Brian, Chief Justice of the Common Pleas. I am to spend Christmas with him at his place in the country, and come back at the start of next term. It would give me great pleasure if your mastership would send me a letter, saying how you, and my ladies, and all your household are doing; and if there is anything I can or may do for you, just send the word, and I'll try to do it, as is my duty.

Sir, there is little news. The King and Queen are staying at Greenwich; Lord Percy is at Winchester; the Earl of Oxford is in Essex; the Earl of Derby and his son are with the King. There's little to be said of the Earl of Warwick at the moment, but it's expected there will be more after Christmas. Moreover, there are many pirates at sea, and various ships have been taken, and many have been taken from the King's house for thieves*. I have heard no other news, but people are beginning to die in London, there isn't a parish free of plague, and they die faster in summer. I intend to go to Yorkshire then, by the grace of God, may he keep you and all who love you forever.

At London, on the eve of St Andrew the Apostle† .

Your daily beadman,

Thomas Betanson

• • • • •

In this charming letter Edward Plumpton writes to his cousin explaining the dearth of wildfowl due to the bad winter and recommending a stout servant. The household of Lord Strange had enjoyed a merry Christmas and Edward's wife, Agnes sends her regards. Latham Hall in Lancashire was a seat of the Earls of Derby. The fluency of this letter reveals Edward's skill as a secretary.

• • •

From Edward Plumpton to Sir Robert Plumpton.

3 January 1489-90.

English.

* This is ambiguous. It may mean that some members of the King's household had been caught with their fingers in the till, something Henry VII would be the last man to tolerate; or it may mean some thieves had been taken from prison, presumably for execution.

† November 29.

From Edward Plumpton to Sir Robert Plumpton.
3 January 1489-90.
English.

To my only and most honoured master, Sir Robert Plumpton.

With the humblest and most deserved respects, may it please your lordship to present my deepest regards to my best of ladies. Please forgive me for sending you no wildfowl so far, but there are none to be had in Lancashire for any money. The snow and frost were so severe that they had all flown overseas, leaving none in the country, which is why I could send none, though I had promised.

Sir, my servant, Robert, is a faithful servant, but he is a big man to ride with my letters, and heavy on the horse, so he is very keen that I should write to your mastership on his behalf. He is an honest man in word and deed, and a good, kind man. If your mastership pleases to take him into your service, I beg you to be a good master to him, and even better by my own request.

Sir I have given him the black horse that he rode from the battlefield [Stoke]; and if you order me to do you any service, I am ready at your service, and will be till the end of my life, above any other obligations that may be on me.

My lord keeps as magnificent a Christmas as there ever was in this district, and is a very good lord to me, as I hope your mastership will discover soon. My artless bedfellow, your beadswoman and servant, sends her humble regards to your mastership, and to my good ladyship, and to your servants, as Jesus knows, may He preserve you.

Written at Latham, January the third.

Your most humble servant, Edward Plumpton.

Secretary to Lord Straung.

• • • • •

German Pole's parents had died when he was a young boy, he had later married Anne, daughter of Sir Robert Plumpton and this letter reveals the importance he placed on his 'new' family. German admits that 'the sole cause' of his letter, 'is but to hear of your good welfare' and explains that it is written in his own hand 'without the vise of any other body'. This provides further evidence that by the end of the fifteenth century letters were being written for purely personal reasons and without the aid of secretaries.

English.

Let these be delivered to his most honoured father, Sir Robert Plumpton, in the greatest haste.

Most honourable and honoured father and mother, in the humblest way I can, I ask to hear of your health and prosperity, which I pray that Almighty Jesus will please to maintain for a long time, to your joy, happiness and comfort. Moreover, my brother William earnestly and humbly asks your favour, and your lady my mother's, asking your daily blessing, which is as welcome to me as to any of your other children, for I have no other father but you, nor any other mother by my lady; for I put my highest trust in you. So I beg you to accept me as your poor son, a beadsman who will pray for you as long as I live.

If you please, Sir, on Monday my brother and I were at Thorntonbury, all in good health, thanks be to Almighty Jesus. And my sister Margaret, and my wife, and my sister Eleanor humbly ask favour of yourself and my lady, asking for your daily blessing, which they value more highly than any worldly goods. In fact, sir, neither Master Nevell nor Mistress Nevell was at home, but his brother was, and made us as welcome as possible. Sir, I'm very sorry to learn that death continues to strike at Plumpton, but I trust that Almighty Jesus, in his great mercy and grace . . . will send joy and comfort to my lady and all your friends, as shall be my daily prayer.

Sir, my reason for writing is only to hear of your good health, which is a great joy and comfort to me. And, sir, I humbly ask you and my lady, my mother, to be indulgent to this letter, for it is written in haste, in my own hand, and without the help of anyone else; for I know that you would rather have it by my own hand than anyone else's. Also, sir, John Tynderly sends you and my lady his regards, hoping to be gladdened by hearing that you are well. Nothing more to you, dear father and mother, at the moment, but I pray the holy Trinity to keep you in His holy protection.

Your good son and beadchild,

German Pole.

ROYALTY

Medieval kings constituted a class of men closely linked by intermarriage and political interests. Kingship was determined by divine right and right of blood, but effective rule depended to a great extent on personality, particularly strength of character and intelligence. A great king was considered to be one who could quash troublesome subjects and uprisings, introduce laws, establish administrations and extend territories by means of successful warfare. The following group of letters highlight some of these aspects, as well as relations between individual members of royal families, their subjects and their views on national achievements and disasters.

The Holy Roman Emperor was considered to be the secular equivalent of the Pope, other secular rulers recognized their superiority but this rarely inhibited their own power. The semi-divine nature of the role of the Holy Roman Emperor was characteristic of kings. A king's opinions and actions were regarded as a translation of God's will and could not easily be challenged. Treason and rebellions were punished severely and were considered to be fundamentally sinful. Any attack on the king's person, family or household was viewed far more seriously than attacks on other important individuals.

The power of medieval kings was limited by the laws and customs of the subjects over which they ruled, even though technically they were above the common law. Kings were expected to act with divine authority, if they failed to do this they could be viewed as inept and justifiably dethroned. As well as answering to God and obeying His law kings also needed to collaborate with other great men in their kingdoms, who accepted their authority and believed in their right to rule. On matters of great importance a king was wise to consult such individuals and to obtain their consent; his authority depended on their approval of his actions.

Royal power became increasingly centralized and kings had to depend far more on effective methods of government and individuals skilled at administering his demands. Those entrusted with the administering of royal justice were often closely allied to the king's household and the role of volatile magnates and nobles was kept to a minimum. Nevertheless, monarchs could be forced to listen to the views of the baronial class and to adapt their rule to their demands, Magna Carta being the most famous instance of this in England. Some letters illustrate the continued resistance to royal government and the need for increased involvement with the king's subjects. In England, by the middle of the fourteenth century parliament had become a regular institution.

• • • • •

Halliwell suggests in his footnote to this letter, 'It seems . . . that it was unlawful for a knight to indulge his chivalrous propensities at tournaments, when engaged on any business for royalty.' The English king urges Philip III to overlook John de Prye's diversion from his duty.

• • •

From Edward I to Philip III of France.

13 October 1279.

Latin.

To the noble prince, lord, and our very dear kinsman, the Lord Philip, by the grace of God King of France, the illustrious Edward, by the same grace, King of England, Lord of Ireland, and Duke of Aquitaine, greeting, with continued increase of sincere affection.

When John de Pryé, your knight, was lately coming towards England, a certain tournament happened to take place in those quarters through which he was travelling into England; and behold! when he had passed through those quarters, having unexpectedly heard the rumour of that tournament, he returned and took part in that meeting, as a knight becometh: and, because the same John feareth that he hath offended your highness, we affectionately request and beseech your serenity that you pardon him, and that (if it please you,) you be in no wise angered against him on this account, but that you be willing to excuse him for the same favourably; so far, at least, that he may feel that this, our urgent request, hath been to him of effectual service.

Given at Westminster, the 13th day of October, in the seventh year of our reign.

• • • • •

The three letters, written by Edward of Caernarvon, the first Prince of Wales, during the summer of 1305 are important in that they relate to an interesting dispute between the Prince and his father King Edward I. They refer to the people who had a great influence on the

Prince's life at this time and who were to continue to do so when he became king, they also convey something of his character and occupations.

During his teens Edward of Caernarvon had pleased his father, he had deputized on his behalf during absences and acquitted himsef well on the battlefield. All in all he had proved himself a capable and responsible heir but this harmony between the King and his son was suddenly broken.

On the 14th June 1305 the twenty-one year old Prince of Wales was banished from Court and his financial support suspended. His father, the King, had been informed of a quarrel between his son and the Bishop of Lichfield and Coventry, his favourite minister. The quarrel is believed to have developed when the Bishop discovered that the Prince, Peter de Gaveston and some other friends had broken into his park and hunted his deer.

Instead of demanding an apology from his son to the Bishop the King made him suffer a very harsh penalty indeed, 'it seems a likely explanation that his anger with the Prince came as the culmination of some build-up of tension between them.' The King is known to have been particularly intolerant concerning any disrespect shown to his officers and maybe he was making it very clear that such larking about, typical of young men throughout the ages, was not fitting behaviour for a Prince of Wales.

In the first letter the Prince describes the situation to the Earl of Lincoln and asks for his assistance. Four years earlier the Earl had advised the Prince during a campaign in Scotland when the King had entrusted his son with the command of half the English army. The Prince evidently felt that the Earl was a friend who would be sympathetic to his plight.

• • •

Edward, Prince of Wales to the Earl of Lincoln.

14 June 1305.

French.

*To the Lord Earl of Lincoln**

Edward, &c. to the Earl of Nicole, &c., heath and dear friendship; know, sire, that on Sunday, the 13th day of June, we came to Midhurst, where

* Henry de Lacy, (1251-1311), the last Earl of Lincoln in that family.

we found our lord the king our father, and on the following Monday, on account of certain words which were told him, that had been between us and the Bishop of Chester, he is so angry with us that he has forbidden us, that neither ourselves nor any one of our suite should be so bold as to enter within his household; and he has forbidden all his officers of his household and of the exchequer that they should neither give us nor lend us anything whatever for the sustenance of our household; and we have remained at Midhurst in order to wait for his good pleasure and his pardon, and we will at any rate proceed after him in the best manner that we shall be able, as at ten or twelve leagues from his household, until we may be able to recover his good pleasure, for which we have great desire. Wherefore we especially entreat you, that on your return from Canterbury, you would come towards us, for we have great need of your aid and your counsel. Given under (our privy seal at Midhurst, the 14th day of June).

• • • • •

Edward had followed his father's court at a respectful distance as it journeyed through Sussex. He had written many begging letters, mainly asking for church preferments for members of his household, in an attempt to generate some form of income. Later in the month he wrote to the treasurer of his household, Sir Walter Reynolds. Reynolds had been born the son of a Windsor baker, was fondly regarded by the Prince, and like others in this position the extent of Edward's kindness and readiness to grant favours excelled all reason and judgement. On Edward's accession to the throne in 1307 he appointed Reynolds Bishop of Worcester, in 1310 he became Chancellor and in 1315 Archbishop of Canterbury.

The letter concerns the impending arrival in England of Queen Mary, the Dowager Queen of France, widow of Philip III who had been dead for twenty years, and mother of the Prince's step-mother Margaret. Queen Mary's son Louis was also expected. The Prince of Wales did not wish to meet his foreign relations unsuitably attired and in the letter he lists requirements. He was physically very attractive and he must have made a noble sight clothed in luxurious garments and mounted on a splendid charger.

• • •

From Edward, Prince of Wales to Sir Walter Reynolds, treasurer of his household.

22 June 1305.

French.

To sire Wauter Renaud, Treasurer, &c., health

Inasmuch as we have heard that the Queen Mary of France and 'Monsire Lowys,' her son, will soon come to England, and that it will be our duty to meet them, and accompany them as long as they shall be in these parts, and therefore it will become us to be well mounted with palfreys, and well apparelled with robes and other things against their coming; wherefore we command you that you will cause to be bought for our use two palfreys, handsome and suitable for our riding and two saddles, with the best reins that we have in the care of Gilbert de Taunton, and the best and finest cloths that you can find for sale in London for two or three robes for our use, with fur, and satin, and all things proper for them. And these things, when you shall have procured them, cause them to come to us wherever we may be, and in the most haste you can - June 22.

• • • • •

During the rest of the summer the Prince had been ordered to stay close to Windsor, and although he occupied his time in outdoor pursuits and entertainments of diverse kinds he was sorely missing his beloved favourite Gaveston In early August he 'applied very circuitously through his sister, who was to ask the queen, to ask the king to grant this favour.'

The Prince puts Gaveston's name last on the list although he was probably first in his thoughts, as if hoping the King might not single his name out amongst the others. Yet the use of the diminutive 'Perot' revealed their intimacy. The indirect approach, as a way around domestic disputes is familiar to us all, and for once the King and his family are observed acting like any other.

The disagreement between the King and his son was eventually resolved and in the spring of 1306, the King knighted the Prince of Wales and granted him further territories. In future years King Edward II did not forget those who had helped him through the difficult summer of 1305, although he never forgave the Bishop of Lichfield and Coventry for the humiliation he had suffered as a result of their quarrel. As soon as he became King he ruthlessly persecuted the Bishop and imprisoned him. Ironically the Bishop remained loyal to Edward whilst Walter Reynolds who had enjoyed so much through his royal patron's favours deserted the King in his hour of greatest need. The role played by Gaveston in later years and his miserable fate is well known.

• • •

From Edward, Prince of Wales to his sister Elizabeth.
4 August 1305.
French.

Edward, &c. to his very dear sister my Lady Elizabeth, Countess of Holland and Hereford and of Essex, health and dear friendship.

Right glad are we of the good health of our lord the king our father, and of my lady the queen, and of yours, which we have learnt by your letters, and as to ours, we let you know that we were in good health, thanks to God, when these letters were written; and inasmuch as our lord the king has granted us two valets, whom we love and have loved, to dwell with us, that is to say, John de Hausted and John de Weston, we entreat and request you especially to be pleased to beg my lady the queen, our dear mother, that she would be pleased to beg the king to be pleased to grant two more valets to dwell with us; that is to say, Gilbert de Clare* and 'Perot' [Peter] de Gavaston; for if we had these two, with the others whom we have, we should be much relieved from the anguish which we have endured, and yet, daily suffer, from the restrictions at the pleasure of our lord the king. Very dear sister, may our Lord preserve you. Given under our privy seal, at the park of Wyndesore, the 4th day of August.

• • • • •

In 1324 war had broken out between England and France over Gascony. In March of the following year King Edward II sent Isabella to negotiate a treaty with her brother, the French King, Charles IV. Whilst performing this task however, Isabella was also planning revenge upon her cruel husband and the Despencers. She had secretly built up support for her cause and in September 1325 she persuaded Edward II to send their son, Prince Edward, to France to pay homage to the French King on his father's behalf. Isabella and Roger Mortimer had become lovers by this time.

Edward II's letter to his wife conveys panic and he is evidently aware that all is not as it should be. A number of devices are used in an attempt to persuade the Queen and heir to return, ranging from flattery to threats and ending feebly with an offer to pay for her travelling costs.

---

* The son of the Prince's sister, Princess Joan of Acre.

To increase her support in France Isabella married her son to Philippa of Hainault and persuaded him to withdraw his claims to the French kingdom. Together with Mortimer and an army of 1500 men Isabella landed in England in September 1326.

The second letter is one of several which Edward II sent to his son in order to induce him 'to tear himself away from the evil counsels by which he was surrounded'. The king was particularly anxious that his heir did not marry, yet seven years earlier he had ordered Bishop Stapledon to prepare an account of Philippa of Hainault as a prospective bride. Although warned by the king that if he acted against his orders the future Edward III would 'feel it all the days of [his] life,' he and Philippa enjoyed a successful marriage compared to the failure of that of his parents.

• • •

From Bishop Stapeldon to Edward II, Prince of Wales

1319.

French.

Inspection and Description of the Daughter of the Count of Hainault, Philippa by name.

The lady whom we saw has not uncomely hair, betwixt blue-black and brown. Her head is clean-shaped; her forehead high and broad, and standing somewhat forward. Her face narrows between the eyes, and the lower part of her face is still more narrow and slender than her forehead. Her eyes are blackish-brown and deep. Her nose is fairly smooth and even, save that it is somewhat broad at the tip and also flattened, and yet it is no snub-nose. Her nostrils are also broad, her mouth fairly wide. Her lips somewhat full, and especially the lower lip. Her teeth which have fallen and grown again are white enough, but the rest are not so white. The lower teeth project a little beyond the upper; yet this is but little seen. Her ears and chin are comely enough. Her neck, shoulders, and all her body are well set and unmaimed; and nought is amiss so far as a man may see. Moreover, she is brown of skin all over, and such like her father; and in all things she is pleasant enough, as it seems to us. And the damsel will be of the age of nine years on St. John's day next to come, as her mother saith. She is neither too tall nor too short for such an age; she is of fair carriage, and well taught in all that becometh her rank, and highly esteemed and well beloved of her father and mother and of all her meinie, in so far as we could inquire and learn the truth.

•••

From Edward II to his consort Isabella of France.
1 December 1325.
French.

Lady,

Oftentimes have we sent to you, both before and after the homage, of our great desire to have you with us, and of our grief of heart at your long absence; and, as we understand that you do us great mischief by this, we will that you come to us with all speed, and without further excuses.

Before the homage was performed, you made the advancement of that business an excuse; and now that we have sent by the Honourable Father the Bishop of Winchester our safe-conduct to you, you will not come, for the fear and doubt of Hugh le Despencer; whereat we cannot marvel too much, when we recall your flattering deportment towards each other in our presence, so amicable and sweet was your deportment, with special assurances and looks, and other tokens of the firmest friendship; and also, since then, your very especial letters to him of late date, which he has shown to us.

And, certes, lady, we know for truth, and so know you, that he has always procured from us all the honour he could for you, nor to you hath either evil or villany been done since you entered into our companionship; unless, peradventure, as you may yourself remember, once when we had cause to give you secretly some words of reproof for your pride, but without other harshness: and, doubtless, both God and the law of our holy church require you to honour us, and for nothing earthly to trespass against our commandments, or to forsake our company. And we are much displeased, now the homage has been made to our dearest brother, the King of France, and we have such fair prospect of amity, that you, whom we sent to make the peace, should be the cause (which God forefend!) of increasing the breach between us by things which are feigned and contrary to the truth. Wherefore, we charge you as urgently as we can that, ceasing from all pretences, delays, and false excuses, you come to us with all the haste you can. Our said bishop has reported to us that our brother, the King of France, told you in his presence, that, by the tenor of your safe-conduct, you would not be delayed, or molested, in coming to us as a wife should to her lord. And, as to your expenses, when it shall be that you will come to us as a wife should to her lord, we will provide that there shall be no deficiency in aught that is pertaining to you, and that you be not in any way dishonoured by us. Also, we require of you that our dear son Edward return to us with all possible speed, for we much desire to see him and to speak with him.

• • •

From Edward II to his son, Edward Prince of Wales.

1326.

French.

Edward, fair son,

We have seen, by your letters lately written to us, that you well remember the charges we enjoined you on your departure from Dover, and that you have not transgressed our commands in any point that was in your power to avoid. But to us it appears that you have not humbly obeyed our commands as a good son ought his father, since you have not returned to us, to be under government, as we have enjoined you by our other letters, on our blessing, but have notoriously held companionship, and your mother, also, with Mortimer, our traitor and mortal enemy, who, in company with your mother and others, was publicly carried to Paris in your train, to the solemnity of the coronation, at Pentecost just past, in signal despite of us, and to the great dishonour both of us and you; for truly he is neither a meet companion for your mother nor for you, and we hold that much evil to the country will come of it.

Also, we understand that you, through counsel, which is contrary both to our interest and yours, have proceeded to make divers alterations, injunctions, and ordinances, without our advice, and contrary to our orders, in the Duchy of Guienne, which we have given you; but you ought to remember the conditions of the gift, and your reply when it was conferred upon you at Dover. These things are inconvenient, and must be most injurious. Therefore, we command and charge you, on the faith and love you ought to bear us, and on our blessing, that you show yourself our dear and well beloved son, as you have aforetime done; and ceasing from all excuses of your mother, or any like those that you have just written, you come to us here with all haste, that we may ordain for you and your states as honourably as you can desire.

By right and reason, you ought to have no other governor than us, neither should you wish to have.

Also, fair son, we charge you by no means to marry till you return to us, nor without our advice and consent, nor for any cause either go to the Duchy, or elsewhere, against our will and command.

PS. Edward, fair son, you are of tender age; take our commandments tenderly to heart, and so rule your conduct with humility, as you would escape our reproach, our grief, and indignation, and advance your own interest and honour. Believe no counsel that is contrary to the will of your father, as the wise King Solomon instructs you. Understand certainly, that if you now act contrary to our counsel, and continue in wilful disobedience, you will feel it all the days of your life, and all other sons will take example to be disobedient to their lords and fathers.

• • • • •

In 1363 the Black Prince and his wife Joan, the Fair Maid of Kent, moved to Gascony and established their Court at Bordeaux and Angoulême where this letter was written to inform those in England of the birth of their first son, Edward in 1365.

A second son, Richard, was born at Bordeaux in 1367 who became King Richard II due to the deaths of his elder brother in 1371, his father in 1376 and his grandfather in 1377.

• • •

From Joan, Princess of Wales announcing the birth of a son.

4 February 1365.

Norman French.

Be it remembered, that a certain letter was delivered to Adam de Bury, Mayor, and the Aldermen, by Janian de Sharnefeld, on the last day of March, in the thirty-ninth year of the reign of King Edward etc., as to the birth of the first-born son of Edward, Prince of Gascoigne and of Wales, in the following words:

By the Princess of Gascoigne and Wales:

Dear and well beloved. Forasmuch as we do well know that you desire right earnestly to hear good tidings of us and of our estate, be pleased to know that on this Monday, the twenty-seventh day of January, we were delivered of a son, with safety to ourselves and to the infant, for the which may God be thanked for His might; and may He always have you in His keeping. Given under our seal, at the Castle of Engolesme, the 4th day of February.

•••••

After the battle of Poitiers there was relative peace in Gascony although relations with the nobles of the principality were uneasy. In 1367 the Black Prince led an expedition to Spain in order to help the deposed King of Castile but despite victory the campaign had proved expensive and taxes were imposed, much to the anger of the Gascon lords.

War broke out once more but the Prince's health was in decline and after the successful but merciless seige of Limoges he retired to England, leaving Aquitaine to the care of his brother John of Gaunt, the Duke of Lancaster. This letter of thanks was written by his wife, the Princess of Wales, in the year after their return to England.

•••

From the Princess of Aquitaine and Wales to the Mayor and Aldermen of London.

23 February 1372.

Latin and Norman French.

On Friday next after the Feast of St. Matthias the Apostle [24 February], in the forty-sixth year etc., our Lady the Princess of Aquitaine and Wales sent here a letter, directed to the Mayor and Aldermen, in these words.

Very dear and well-beloved. We have fully heard of the great gifts that of your own free will for us you have ordained; for the which we do thank you with all our heart, letting you know for certain that if you shall have any matter to transact with us, as to the which we may reasonably avail you, we will well remember the same, and to the best of our power will do it with good heart. And be pleased to credit hereupon our dear and well-beloved John de Chichestre and Sir Edward Chardestok, Keeper of our Wardrobe, as to that which on our behalf they shall say to you. Very dear and well-beloved, may God have you in His keeping. Given under our Signet, at Berkhampstede, on the 23rd day of February.

By reason of which letter, their credentials being heard, John de Cauntebrigge, the Chamberlain, delivered unto the said Edward five hundred marks, by precept of the Mayor and Aldermen, to make present thereof, and to pay the same, unto the Princess, on behalf of the Mayor, Aldermen, and Commonalty aforesaid.

•••••

Annabella, wife of Robert III of Scotland writes to Richard II, alluding to intended marriage negotiations between the royal families of England and Scotland as well as informing Richard II of the birth of a son, who was to become James I in 1406. The letter shows the Scottish Queen's interest in preserving good relations between her country and England, and she is felt to have had a considerable stabilizing influence on the volatile characters of her son and husband as well as the powerful Duke of Albany.

• • •

From Annabella Queen of Scotland to King Richard II.

1394.

French.

To the most high and mighty prince Richard, by the grace of God King of England, our very dear cousin, Annabella, by the selfsame grace Queen of Scotland, sends health and greeting.

We give you hearty and entire thanks for your loving letters presented to us by our well-beloved Douglas, herald-at-arms, from which we have learned to our great pleasure and comfort your good health and estate. And, dearest cousin, as touching the marriage-treaty to be made between some nearly allied to you by blood and some children of the king my lord and of us, be pleased to know that it is agreeable to the king my said lord and to us, as he has signified to you by these letters. And in especial, that, although the said treaty could not be held on the third day of July last past for certain and reasonable causes contained in your letters sent to the king my aforesaid lord, you consented that the treaty should in like manner take place another day, namely, the first day of October next coming, which is agreeable to the king my aforesaid lord and to us; and we thank you heartily and with good will, and affectionately pray you that you will continue the said treaty, and have the said day kept, for it is the will of my said lord the king and of us that as far as in us lies the said day should be kept without fail. And, dearest cousin, we affectionately require and entreat you that your highness will not be displeased that we have not sooner written to you; for we were lying in childbed of a male infant named James, of whom we are now well and graciously delivered, thanks to God and our Lady. And also, because, at the coming of your letters, the king my said lord was far away in the isles of his kingdom, we did not receive these letters sent to us on this matter till the last day of July last past. Most high and puissant prince, may the Holy Ghost ever keep you! Given under our signet, at the abbey of Dumfermline, the first day of August.

To the most high [and puissant prince Richard] by God's grace [king of England].

• • • • •

Joanna of Navarre's first husband, John V Duke of Brittany, died on November 1st 1399, and three years later she married Henry IV, King of England, whom she had met whilst he was in exile at Vannes. The first letter addressed to Richard II was written shortly before the Duke of Brittany's death and the withholding of lands, of which the Duchess complains, was probably, 'an act of retributive vengeance on the part of the English King for the counsel and protection which the rebel Henry Bolingbroke met with in the court of Bretagne.* Wood also points out the irony of this letter, in that Joanna, who writes so courteously to Richard II, was soon to become the wife of his murderer.

• • •

From Joanna of Navarre to Richard II.

c. 1399.

French.

My most dear and redoubted lord,

I desire every day to be certified of your good estate, which our Lord grant that it may ever be as good as your heart desires, and as I should wish it for myself. If it would please you to let me know of it, you would give me great rejoicings in my heart, for every time that I hear good news of you I am most perfectly glad at heart. And if to know tidings from this side would give you pleasure, when this was written my lord, I, and our children were together in good health of our persons, thanks to our Lord, who by his grace ever grant you the same. I pray you, my dearest and most redoubted lord, that it would ever please you to have the affairs of my said lord well recommended, as well in reference to the deliverance of his lands as other things, which lands in your hands are the cause why he sends his people promptly towards you. So may it please you hereupon to provide him with your gracious remedy, in such manner that he may enjoy his said lands peaceably; even as he and I have our perfect surety and trust in you more than in any other. And let me know your good pleasure, and I will accomplish it willingly and with a good heart to my power.

* Wood, p. 20.

My dearest and most redoubted lord, I pray the Holy Spirit that he will have you in his holy keeping.

Written at Vannes, the 15th day of March.

The Duchess of Bretagne.

• • • • •

The second letter which Wylie described as, 'brought by a Breton lady, and containing little else but general courtesies and compliments'* maybe indicates an increasing closeness between the Duchess and the new king who had last met in the summer of 1399 and were not to see each other again until January 1403 when Joanna landed at Falmouth as the new Queen of England. Letters must have played an important part in the courtship and marriage negotiations but unfortunately this is the only surviving example.

• • •

From Joanna Duchess of Bretagne, afterwards Queen of England, to her future husband Henry IV.

15 February 1400.

French.

My very dear and most honourable lord and cousin,

Since I am desirous to hear of your good estate, which our Lord grant that it may ever be as good as your noble heart knows best how to desire, and, indeed, as I would wish it for myself, I pray you, my most dear and honoured lord and cousin, that it would please you very often to let me know the certainty of it, for the very great joy and gladness of my heart; for every time that I can hear good news of you, it rejoices my heart very greatly. And if of your courtesy you would hear the same from across here, thanks to you, at the writing of these presents, I and my children were together in good health of our persons, thanks to God, who grant you the same, as Johanna of Bavalen, who is going over to you, can tell you more fully, whom please it you to have recommended in the business on which she is going over. And if anything that I can do over here will give you pleasure, I pray you to let me know it, and I will accomplish it with a very good heart, according to my power.

My dearest and most honoured lord and cousin, I pray the Holy Spirit to have you in his holy keeping.

---

* Wylie, vol. 1, p. 261.

Written at Vannes, the 15th day of February.

The Duchess of Bretagne.

• • • • •

Agnes Strickland relates how the marriage was never popular in England and that raids by the Breton fleet on Cornwall added to the nations dislike of their new Queen.*

Christine Dunbar was married to the influential Scottish noble, George Earl of March. A marriage had been arranged between their daughter and the heir to the Scottish crown the Duke of Rothesay, but due to the influence of the Douglas party the Duke broke the agreement and married instead Marjory, daughter of Archibald the Grim, Earl of Douglas.

The Earl of March requested aid from the English King, Henry IV, and along with his wife and children found refuge across the border.Having forfeited their estates in Scotland they were forced to live in comparative poverty. The earl's attempts to regain his position in Scotland were of no avail but he was active in the service of Henry IV, notably at the battle of Shrewsbury where Henry Percy, known as Hotspur, was killed. 'The death of this young nobleman, the flower of English chivalry, seems to have excited jealousy against the Scottish earl, of which the countess bitterly complains.'

'Feeling in the north of England was inflamed against the Earl of March for his share in Hotspur's fall.'

After several more years in exile the Earl returned to Scotland having come to an agreement with the Douglas faction, and spent the rest of his days in 'inglorious retirement'.

• • •

From Christine, Countess of March to Henry IV.

1403.

French.

My most excellent and redoubted sovereign lord,

I recommend myself to you as entirely as terrestrial creature can think or devise to the crowned king of the world, humbly thanking you on my

* Strickland, *Lives of the Queens of England* vol. II, Chapter 1, Joanna of Navarre, pp. 42-105.

knees for the high favours and benefits that you have conferred upon me before this time, piously supplicating for your gracious continuance, and particularly for the gracious refreshment which you lately sent. May God reward you for it, since I cannot.

My most gracious lord, may it please you to know that my lord my husband and I have been in such hardships and distress since we were banished from our country, that I am yet involved in heavy debt, from which without your gracious aid and succour I cannot deliver myself; and now the pestilence is so violent and severe where we are, that I am very fearful lest I should die in this great debt that I have incurrred. And by no intreaty that we can make can we obtain sufferance from our enemies to retire to our fortress of Colbrandspath, there to wait till the mortality has ceased. And for this cause I humbly entreat your high royal majesty that you will be pleased to have me in remembrance when you shall find leisure, and help me, that by your gracious relief I may be freed from the debt which makes me sad. Besides this, my most redoubted and gracious lord, we suffer great enmity on account of the death of Sir Henry Percy, which oftentimes is so heavy to my husband and his people, that they wish themselves dead, if they may not retire from this country, seeing that the people of the said Sir Henry Percy do nothing but hear comfortable news of you, in order then to do the malice that is in their hearts. And, my most gracious and sovereign lord, touching the capture of our people by those attending on the Earl of Douglas, deign to give credence to the bearer of this, and ordain such remedy as you please, according to what the said bearer shall tell you by word of mouth. And I pray most earnestly the ever-blessed God of Heaven to grant you a long life, with all increase of honour and joy, together with victory over your enemies; and after this mortal life may he grant you the kingdom of glory Amen.

Your humble oratrice, The Countess of March of Scotland.

To my most excellent and most redoubted lord, the king of England.

• • • • •

During the fourteenth century, the European states had grown richer and education increasingly widespread; the need for a church which was organized on an international scale declined and local clergy felt the papacy had lost touch with their spiritual requirements. Reform was sought on both political and spiritual levels.

In 1378, an Italian Pope, Urban VI was elected at Rome. He intensified dissent within the church and the French Cardinals pronounced him deposed and elected Clement VII who established himself at Avignon. Loyalty to the rival claimants was purely political. France and its allies supported Avignon whilst England, the Northern Italian states and many German states favoured Rome.

The council of Pisa in 1409 attempted to resolve the 'tragic and pestilent schism* by radically reforming the papacy, the rival popes† were both deposed and John XXII elected in their place. Neither side accepted this decision and Europe now had three popes.

The Council of Constance 1414-1418 finally ended the schism by deposing all three popes and declaring that from henceforth even a pope must obey a general council.

The frequent holding of general councils is one of the chief means of cultivating the Lord's field. It serves to uproot the briars, thorns and thistles of heresies, errors and schisms, to correct excess, to restore what is marred, and to cause the Lord's vine to bring forth fruit of the richest fertility.§

Pope Martin V was duly elected and the papacy, finally consolidated, was permanently moved to Rome. The following letter was sent to Henry V from the Council of Constance. It has been suggested that it was written by either Robert Hallam, Bishop of Salisbury or Thomas Polton, then a prebendary of York, 'the two most distinguished English ecclesiastics present at the Council', in December 1415.‡ The 'latest occurrences' first mentioned probably refer to John Huss, the Bohemian supporter of Wyclyf, who was burnt as heretic on July 6th 1415. The letter then refers to the Holy Roman Emperor, Sigismund, who had left Constance for Spain with the aim of persuading Benedict XIII to renounce his claim to the papal throne. This he refused to do and the capitulation of Narbonne declared his official deposition in December 1415.

Next the Turkish threat is discussed, Sigismund's efforts to end the schism and pacify Europe were partly inspired by his desire to lead a crusade against the Ottoman Turks who had established significant control in the eastern Mediterranean and had been encroaching on Sigismund's territories during his stay at Constance.

The writer goes on to inform the King of other significant news, the marriage of Joanna II, Queen of Naples to Jacques de la Marche and the execution of her former favourite Pandolfello Alopo, and also the

* Alexander V's confirmation of the Council of Pisa, January 22nd, 1410. Laffam, p. 193.

† By this time Urban VI and Clement VII had died, Boniface IX replaced the former and Petra de Luna (Benedict XIII), the latter.

§ From the Decree of Frequens, October 9th 1417. Laffam, p. 196.

‡ Monro, p. 7.

false report of the death of Ludovico Sforza, a 'great soldier of fortune', who was being tortured whilst imprisoned in Naples, but just about managed to escape with his life; and the arrival of the King of Poland's ambassadors. Gregory XII had agreed to renounce his claim to the papacy and had sent the Council a letter confirming this which was received on 7th December.

Henry V had just returned to England after the Battle of Agincourt and no doubt the writer's closing words refer to the King's achievement. This letter is important in that it unites various events, rather like a modern current affairs report; it provides an interesting picture of what was happening in Europe at one particular time, even though the individual issues are not easy to assimilate at once; the activity at Constance, the Turks in the east, Boniface XIII in Spain, the delegation from Poland, a marriage in Naples and the English victory in France, all communicating through letters and messengers and receiving news at a considerable interval after the event, in a haphazard manner and sometimes not at all.

• • •

A letter to King Henry V written from the Council of Constance.
December 1415.
Latin.

Invincible Sovereign, since the 19th day of the month of August, when I wrote to your Highness by Mr John Hervy the latest occurrences amongst us, very little has arisen, so far as the proceedings of the Council are concerned, worthy of mention. In fact, since the departure of the most Christian prince the King of the Romans, the matter of the reformation of the Church in its head and members is the only one which the Council has thought worthy to be taken in hand, and has treated of. Nor, at this time, when it has received certain intelligence of the success of the Prince himself in matters relating to the Church, striving lawfully for which he has borne in times past and still bears many wearisome labours, does it choose to entertain any other questions; being now engaged in establishing, in connection with this very reformation, things which, when, at the proper time, they shall be published to the world, will, as being acceptable to God and to the honour of the universal Church, be deservedly applauded as it is hoped, by all men. Nevertheless, most serene Prince, as touching any agreement come to with the King of Aragon and the Prince Peter de Luna, we have received no certain intelligence; although, from many written communications received by the Council, we have strong hopes of the desired issue. The illness, however, by which the King of Aragon is so much pulled down, is thought to be the cause of the delay. Furthermore, most serene Prince, we are informed *by a correspondent*, that the Turks, who with their immense power and the energy of their native ardour had invaded the lands of the Christians in times past, specially the dependencies of the King of the Romans, slaying with the sword (alas!) great numbers of Christians (as I presume your serenity will have understood by the writings of many, and by mine amongst others), have (praise be to God!) been, for the most part, destroyed by a Christian band; and this although some princes of Croatia and Dalmatia, men of great power, adhered to the aforesaid Turks, out of hatred to the King of the Romans, whose subjects, nevertheleess, they were or ought to have been; every one of whom has been destroyed by a sudden chance not less miraculous than wonderful. A wonderful circumstance, as is related, occurred. For the survivors of the infidels themselves are convinced, by a very ancient writing found amongst themselves, in which it is declared that, within the next five years, they will be wholly conquered by the Christians, or converted to the faith of the Christian religion. Of the survivors, those who had kept some order are, as it is said, returning, in different directions, to their homes. Moreover, most serene Prince, with regard to the condition of the Queen of Naples and the French Count de la Marche, who confirmed his marriage with her on the 10th of September, much news came the day before yesterday from one writing to the legate attending the Council in this city, which is in the schedule inclosed herein; the tenor of which, it is said, has been transmitted hither from the city of Naples by a man of high rank. And the legate himself directly informs the Council, from his later letters, that the General Pandolfello, and the great soldier of fortune there who was against the Church, as to both of whom also see the schedule, had lately died. Furthermore, most dread Lord, letters were received the day before yesterday from the King of Poland, by his ambassadors now present at the Council, of the firm hope he has of reducing the Greeks of his dominions to [the obedience of] the Roman Church, &c. amongst whom, the ambassadors say, there are two hundred bishoprics. To this end, and also for the purpose of bringing over permanently to our [mode of] life the simple population of that part of Russia, which is subject to his rule, which does not yet profess the Catholic faith, he has sent to the King of the Romans and the Council, on his own behalf, as a . . . writes, a Vicar General sufficiently versed in the Latin, Greek, and Tartaric languages, in order to gain certain favours and letters necessary for the aforesaid matters; who confidently hopes to be able shortly to bring to a prosperous end the business I have referred to above. And thus, most puissant Prince, let us firmly believe that the Most High, whose cause it is, means, in these last times, as promised of old, that His flock and empire shall form one fold, and that there shall be one shepherd of His Holy Church. The cardinals, lately adherents of Gregory, are all, without exception, expected at Constance within eight days. His other officials, now and for some time past with us, have been received, as was right, with honour. May your Highness long thrive and flourish in victory and success. Written &c.

• • • • •

Margaret Paston writes from Norwich where Margaret of Anjou, Queen of Henry VI had been staying. She describes with excitement her friend's audience with the queen and it seems that the ladies of Norwich were determined not to be outshone by their royal visitors. Margaret had had to borrow jewels from Elizabeth Clere and asks her husband to send a fitting necklace, 'for I durst not for shame go with my Beads amongst so many fresh Gentlewomen.'

• • •

From Margaret Paston to John Paston.

23 April 1453.

English.

To my right worshipful Master, John Paston, be this delivered in haste.

Right worshipful Husband, I recommend me to you, praying you to weet, &c. *(here follows some account of money received, &c.).*

As for tidings, the Queen came into this town on Tuesday last past after noon, and abode here till it was Thursday three [o'clock] afternoon; and she sent after my Cousin Elizabeth Clere,* by Sharinborn, to come to her; and she durst not disobey her commandment, and came to her; and when she came in the Queen's Presence, the Queen made right much of her, and desired her to have an husband, the which ye shall know of hereafter; but as for that, he is never nearer than he was before; the Queen was right well pleased with her answer, and reporteth of her in the best wise, and saith, by her truth, she saw no Gentlewoman since she came into Norfolk, that she liked better than she doth her.

Black, the bailey of Swaffham, was here with the King's Brother, and he came to me, weening that ye had been at home; and said, that the King's brother† desired him that he should pray you in his name to

* The wealthy widow of Robert Clere of Ormsby.

† Either Edmund or Jasper Tudor

come to him, for he would right fain that ye had come to him, if ye had been at home; and he told me, that he wist well that he should send for you, when he came to London, both for Cossey and other things.

I pray you that ye will do your cost on me against Whitsuntide, that I may have something for my neck; when the Queen was here, I borrowed by Cousin Elizabeth Clere's Device, for I durst not for shame go with my Beads amongst so many fresh Gentlewomen as here were at that time.

The blessd Trinity have you in his keeping.

Written at Norwich on the Friday next before Saint George *(23rd April).*

By yours, Margaret Paston.

• • • • •

One of the Archbishop of Canterbury's chaplain writes to the prior of Christ Church explaining how the King, Edward IV, had been particularly angry because a gift had failed to be presented to his sister, the Duchess of Burgundy, who had married Charles the Bold in 1468. It seems that the Archbishop,* although having made peace with the King, was highly embarrassed by the incident and feared the damaging effect vicious rumours might have on his reputation.

• • •

Edmond Lichfield to the Prior of Christ Church.

c. 1480.

English.

To the Right Reverend father in God my most excellent Lord, my Lord the Prior of Christ Church, Canterbury.

Right reverend father in God, and my sole lord, with due respects. I am informed that your good lordship has been told of the great displeasure that the King felt towards my Lord and us, his servants, in that my Lady the Duchess of Burgundy was not accommodated, in the sense of a handsome gift being made to her, when she was last with my lord. And it is certainly the case, in that the King expressed himself very forcibly on the subject. But his Grace has now been appeased, and is happy, and left in a very good temper with my lord.

* Thomas Bouchier 1454-86

I have explained the importance of this matter to my trusted and well-beloved Sir Robert Barton, his chaplain, who, if you wish, will explain everything to you; and I ask you to be a good lord to him, and to me as well. And we will not fail to be faithful and trustworthy chaplains and servants, God knows, may he always keep you, my best of lords, in his blessed protection.

Scribbled at Knoll by the hand of your said chaplain.

My Lord, I write to you in this connexion because I am sure that you enjoy my Lord's good wishes, and you are therefore sorry for any hurt that he takes, to his honour or reputation, or in any other way.

Edmond Lichfield.

• • • • •

The next three letters concern the internal troubles which King Henry VII had to overcome during the 1490s, and from which other European leaders hoped to profit. In 1491 a seventeen-year-old youth, employed by a Breton merchant who had landed at Cork, was the victim of a serious instance of mistaken identity. The Irish convinced themselves that Perkin Warbeck was Prince Richard of York, Edward V's younger brother, and set about supporting his claim to the English throne. The bodies of the princes in the Tower had never been found and soon Charles VII of France, James IV of Scotland, Margaret of Burgundy and the Emperor Maximilian, as well as latent Yorkists, were rallying to the pretender's cause.

In 1493 King Henry sent the following letter to Sir Gilbert Talbot, a loyal subect who had proved his worth at the Battle of Bosworth Field in 1485, instructing him to muster a company of men to counteract the threat to his realm. Margaret of Burgundy was already offering parts of it as rewards for assistance with the invasion. Warbeck had found refuge in the Burgundian court and in 1495 landed in Kent funded by his foreign allies. His force was rapidly defeated so he set sail to Waterford where he was similarly repulsed, and thence to Scotland. King James IV warmly welcomed the pretender, married him to his own cousin Lady Catherine Gordon and prepared to wage war with England. The Scottish King found little support from his subjects and only managed a small attack on the Borders in September 1496 which was easily quashed by the English. Nonetheless Henry VII was angered by this act of aggression and set out to humiliate the Scots.

It was agreed that the funding of the campaign would be met by taxes to be introduced at the next parliament which was to meet in January, in the meantime Henry set about procuring temporary loans from wealthy communities and citizens. In the following letter he demands funds from three subjects in order to revenge, 'the gret cruelte and dishonour that the Kyng of Scotts hath done'. Such demands were unpopular and in Cornwall an army of rebels began a march to London organized by men who were not prepared to pay for the King's war so many miles away in Scotland. The Cornishmen had reasonably peaceful intentions but Henry had had enough of threats to his kingdom and at the Battle of Blackheath more than two thousand protesters were killed.

James IV had sent Warbeck to the West Country to further his claim to the crown whilst discontent was rife but Warbeck did not arrive in Cornwall until after the Battle of Blackheath and meanwhile James IV and Henry had agreed a truce. At Bodmin Warbeck had himsef proclaimed King Richard IV and was able to raise an army of Cornishmen who had not forgiven Henry for the slaughter of their countrymen.

• • •

From King Henry VII to Sir Gilbert Talbot.

20 July 1493.

English.

To our trusty and well-beloved knight and councillor, Sir Gilbert Talbot.

Trusty and well-beloved, We greet you well: And not forgetting the great malice that the Lady Margaret of Burgundy beareth continually against us - as she showed lately in sending hither of a feigned boy, surmising him to have been the son of the Duke of Clarence, and cause him to be accompanied with the Earl of Lincoln, the Lord Lovel, and with great multitude of Irishmen and of Almains whose end, blessed be God! was as ye know well: And forseeing now the perseverance of the same her malice, by the untrue contriving eftsoon of another feigned lad called Perkin Warbeck, born of Tournay in Picardy (which at first [coming] into Ireland called himself the bastard son of King Richard; and after that the son of the said Duke of Clarence; and now the second son of our father [-in-law], King Edward the IVth, whom God assoil): Wherethrough she intendeth, by promising unto the Flemings and other of the archduke's obeissaunce - to whom she laboureth daily to take her way - and by her promise to certain aliens, captains of strange nations, to have [as reward] duchies, counties, baronies, and other lands within this our realm, to induce them thereby to land here to the destruction and disinheritance of the noblemen and other of our subjects the inhabitants of the same, and finally to the subversion of this our realm: In case she attaine to her malicious purpose - that God defend! - we therefore, and to the intent that we may be alway purveied and in readiness to resist her malice, write unto you at this time, and will and desire you that, preparing on horseback, defensibly arrayed, four score persons, whereof we desire you to make as many spears, with their custrells and demi-lances, well-horsed as ye can furnish, and the remainder to be archers and bills, ye be thoroughly appointed and ready to come upon a day's warning for to do us service of war in this case.

And ye shall have for every horseman well and defensibly arrayed, that is to say, for a spear and his custrel twelvepence; a demi-lance ninepence; and an archer, or bill, on horseback, eightpence by the day, from the time of your coming out unto the time of your return to your home again. And thus doing, ye shall have such thanks of us for your loving and true acquittal in that behalf as shall be to your weal and honour for time to come. We pray you herein ye will make such diligence as that ye be ready with your said number to come unto us upon any our sudden warning.

Given under our signet at our castle of Kenilworth, the twentieth day of July, 1493.

• • • • •

The next letter describes the events which followed, Warbeck's unsuccessful attack on Exeter, his final surrender at Beaulieu Abbey and confession at Taunton, as well as the rebels' pleas for mercy. The mayor and citizens of Waterford were no doubt pleased with this news since they had suffered an attack by Warbeck, albeit unsuccessful, two years earlier.

After having been treated comparatively leniently considering all the trouble he had caused, Warbeck tried to escape, and he was imprisoned in the Tower. A plot was then discovered which aimed to free Warbeck along with the Earl of Warwick, the last male Plantagenet, who had also been imprisoned. King Henry could not afford any more risks to his security and had both men hanged at Tyburn in 1499, even though Warwick had not been proved guilty.

• • •

King Henry VII to the Mayor and Citizens of Waterford.

17th October 1497.

English.

Trusty and well-beloved, We greet you well: And whereas Perkin Warbeck, lately accompanied by divers and many our rebels of Cornwall, advanced themselves to our city of Exeter, which was denied unto them, and so they came to the town of Taunton: at which town as soon as they had knowledge that our chamberlain, our steward of household, Sir John Chynie and other of our loving subjects with them, were coming so far forth towards the said Perkin as to our monastery of Glastonbury - the same Perkin took with him John Heron, Edward Skelton, and Nicholas Ashley, and stole away from his said company about midnight, and fled with all the haste they could make. We had well provided beforehand for the sea-coasts, that, if he had attempted that way (as he thought indeed to have done) he should have been put from his purpose, as it is coming to pass. For, when they perceived they might not get to the sea, and that they were had in a quick chase and pursuit, they were compelled to address themselves unto our monastery of Beaulieu; to the which, of chance and of fortune, it happened some of our menial servants to repair, and some we sent thither purposely.

The said Perkin, Heron, Skelton and Ashley, seeing our said servants there - and remembering that all the country was warned to make watch and give attendance, that they should not avoid nor escape by sea - made instances unto our servants to sue unto us for them, the said Perkin desiring to be sure of his life and he would come unto us, and show what he is; and, over that, do unto us such service as should content us. And so by agreement between our said servants and them, they [were encouraged] to depart from Beaulieu, and to put themselves in our grace and pity.

The abbot and convent hearing thereof demanded of them why and for what cause they would depart. Whereunto they gave answer in the presence of the said abbot and convent, and of many other, that, without any manner of constraint, they would come unto us of their free wills, in trust of our grace and pardon aforesaid. And so, the said Perkin came unto us to the town of Taunton, from whence he [had] fled; and immediately after his first coming, humbly submitting himself unto us, hath of his free will openly showed, in the presence of all the council here with us, and of other nobles, his name to be *Piers Osbeck*, (whereas he hath been named Perkin Warbeck), and to be none Englishman born, but born of Tournay, and son of John Osbeck, and sometime while he lived comptroller of the said Tournay; with many other circumstances too long to write, declaring by whose means he took upon him this presumption and folly.

And so, now this great abusion which hath long continued, is now openly known by his own confession: We write this news unto you, for we be undoubtedly sure, that calling to mind the great abusion that divers folks have been in, by reason of the said Perkin, and the great business and charges that we and our realm have been put unto in that behalf, you would be glad to hear the certainty of the same, which we affirm unto you for assured truth.

Sithence the writing of these premises, we be ascertained that Perkin's wife is in good surety for us, and trust that she shall shortly come unto us to this our city of Exeter, as she is in dole . . .

And sithence our coming to this our city of Exeter for the punition of this great rebellion, and for so to order the parts of Cornwall, as the people may live in their due obeisance to us and in good restfulness unto themselves for time to come; the commons of this shire of Devon come daily before us in great multitudes, in their shirts, the foremost of them having halters about their necks, and full humbly with lamentable cries for our grace and remission, submit themselves unto us; whereupon doing, first, the chief stirrers and misdoers [among them having been tried out] for to abide their corrections according, we grant to the residue our said grace and pardon. And our commissioners, the Earl of Devon, our chamberlain, and our steward of household, have done and do daily in likewise in our county of Cornwall.

Geven under our signet at our said city of Exeter, the 17th day of October.

To our trusty and well-beloved, the Mayor and his brethren of our city of Waterford.

• • • • •

Lady Margaret Beaufort, Countess of Richmond and Derby, and the grand-daughter of John of Gaunt, had given birth to the future King Henry VII in 1457. She had great ambitions for her only son and the two were rarely separated during Henry's childhood. Margaret, the heiress of the House of Lancaster had encouraged her son's marriage to Elizabeth of York, the heiress of the House of Plantagenet, realizing how formidable a union between the Red Rose of Lancaster and the White Rose of York would be. The King wrote this letter to his mother in c.1498. It reveals the affection he felt for her combined with genuine respect for her opinions and advice.

• • • • •

From King Henry VII to his mother Margaret Beaufort.

c. 1498.

English.

Madame, my most entirely Well-beloved Lady and Mother,

I recommend me unto you in the most humble and lowly wise that I can, beseeching you of your daily and continual blessings.

By your confessor, the bearer, I have received your good and most loving writing . . . I shall be as glad to please you as your heart can desire it, and I know well that I am as much bounden so to do as any creature living, for the great and singular motherly love and affection that it hath pleased you at all times to bear towards me. Wherefore, mine own most loving Mother, in my most hearty manner I thank you, beseeching you of your good continuance of the same.

And, madame, your said confessor hath moreover shown unto me, on your behalf, that ye, of your goodness and kind disposition, have given and granted unto me such title and interest as ye have - or ought to have - in such debts and duties which are owing and due unto you in France by the French king and others: wherefore, madame, in my most hearty and humble wise, I thank you. Howbeit, I verily think it will be right hard to recover it [the title] without it being driven by compulsion and force - rather than by any true justice - which is not yet, as we think, any convenient time to be put into execution. . . .

And verily, madame, an I might recover it at this time, or any other, ye be sure ye should have your pleasure therein, as I - and all that God has given me - am, and ever shall be, at your will and commandment, as I have instructed Master Fisher more largely herein, as I doubt not he will declare unto you. And I beseech you to send me your mind and pleasure in the same, which I shall be full glad to follow, with God's grace, the which send and give unto you the full accomplishment of all your noble and virtuous desires.

Written at Greenwich, the 17th day of July, with the hand of your most humble and loving son,

H. R.

. . . Madame, I have encumbered you now with this long writing, but think that I can do no less, considering that it is so seldom that I do write, wherefore I beseech you to pardon me: for verily, madame, my sight is nothing so perfect as it has been, and I know well it will appayre daily, wherefore I trust that you will not be displeased, though I write not so often with mine own hand, for on my faith I have been three days or I could make an end of this letter.

To My Lady

LITERACY AND LEARNING

The Church dominated education during the Middle Ages, when it was felt that knowledge would help men to understand God's law and to live their lives accordingly. Monasteries which had long been centres of learning played a valuable role in medieval education, providing schools for monks as well as copying books and establishing important libraries. The monastic schools taught the seven liberal arts which consisted of the Trivium; grammar, rhetoric and logic, and the Quadrivium; arithmetic, music, geometry and astronomy. This provided a basic system of education and was also used in the cathedral and urban schools which introduced the study of Roman and Canon law to the curriculum. New theories on philosophy, medicine and astronomy were developed in the twelfth century, largely due to progressive ideas spreading from Arab cultures.

Conflict between Church and State had encouraged new activity, not only in the study of Roman and Canon law but also in the study of science and theology. Men eager for knowledge had to travel in order to find masters at the forefront of learning in a particular subject. The first step in the development of universities was taken when masters, along with their various students, came together to exchange ideas and provide mutual support, often where cathedral schools were flourishing. Teaching began to be regulated as did the awarding of degrees, students and masters enjoyed certain privileges, and universities soon came to be recognized as influential institutions.

Bologna's reputation as a centre for legal studies and Paris as a hub of dialectical and theological thought led to the establishment of the two earliest universities. The University of Paris provided a model for universities in central and northern Europe, and also in England. Oxford and Cambridge both originated in the twelfth century and adopted the institution of colleges which gave the universities an identifiable character and permanence. By the early fifteenth century universities had been established across Europe, in cities as far apart as Glasgow, Seville, Nantes and Cracow.

A university education enabled a minority of medieval men to enjoy successful careers, not only within the Church, but also in the developing fields of public administration, which had become increasingly necessary to secular rulers.

It also led to an increase in the number of schools, notably grammar schools for boys which were connected to churches and cathedrals but were also founded by guilds and other mercantile bodies. Basic Latin grammar and rhetoric were widely taught, other subjects depended to a large extent on the teacher's own knowledge and training.

Apart from a minority of highly educated clerics and university graduates, most medieval people had a minimal experience of education. Parish priests were instructed to familiarize their charges with rudimentary Latin grammar but the lack of books inhibited teaching and the scriptures were used as texts for reading. John of Salisbury, who travelled to Paris to study, initially learnt to read through the efforts of a local priest and a copy of the Psalms.

Education in the urban schools was an expense few could afford, in terms of travel and lodgings. Sons were needed to help supplement the family income as soon as they were old enough rather than continuing to be a financial burden, and served apprenticeships or other forms of vocational training. The letters relating to Clement and William Paston's education reveal the high cost of schooling, be it board or books, and would have been inconceivable to less affluent families. The influential, land-owning families of fifteenth century England considered education to be a worthwhile investment and an important factor in the maintenance of the family's wealth and standing. Legal training, especially, was encouraged as a means of safeguarding rights to property and ensuring men had better control over their lives.

Royal and noble households had their own methods of educating their children. Boys served as pages, learning to aspire to the values of chivalry by observing the conduct and manners of their elders at court. As they grew older they gained experience of managing men and participated in hunts and other sports which provided ideal training for future experience on the battlefield. English kings from Henry I onwards were instructed in Latin, Henry II is known to have read for relaxation and was even able to write. He enjoyed the company of learned men and informal debating sessions were part of daily routine. Nunneries were a centre of culture and knowledge for women, some having schools which provided young children of both sexes with a rudimentary education, generally based on religious texts which were learnt by rote. Any other instruction depended on the nuns' own ability to read and write. Though during the thirteenth century some nuns were educated to a high standard, particularly in Germany, this was exceptional.

Daughters of the nobility and the enterprising bourgeoisie were educated at home, sometimes with the aid of treatises on ladylike conduct which encouraged good manners, familiarity with the scriptures and household management, as well as competence at suitable pastimes such as singing and poetry reading; all the qualities, in fact, which knights desired in a wife. Parents were keen to send grown up daughters to live with relatives or friends to act as understudies to the lady of the house. Some presumably welcomed the chance to move away from home but to others it was a miserable experience.

• • • • •

The following communication is one of the earliest records pertaining to St Paul's school, one of the first Grammar schools in London. Here the study of Latin grammar and dialectic took place; the choir school was completely separate. Bishop Richard (1108-1128) states that the schoolmaster is to act as the school's librarian with full responsibility for the books, the keys to the bookcases by the altar are to be given to him.

The tower that Canon Durand built was at the east end of St Paul's and detached from the main building. Its bell was used by the town as well as the church.

• • •

Richard de Belmeis to Dean William.

c. 1111.

Latin.

R[ichard de Belmeis], by the grace of God minister of the Church of London, to W[illiam] dean and all the assembly of brethren, greeting and paternal blessing.

Know ye beloved, my dearest sons, that I have confirmed to Hugh the schoolmaster, in right of the dignity of his mastership and to his successors in the same dignity, the station of Master Durand in the angle of the tower, namely, where Dean William placed him by my orders between Robert of Eu and Odo. I grant him also and to the privilege of the school the custody of all the books of our church. I will therefore and command you, Dean, to give him charge of them all when written in an indenture before the brethren, one part of which shall be safeguarded in the Treasury, and the other shall be kept by him, and give him seisin of their custody, making diligent inquiry under pain of excommunication whether any of the books, either secular or theological, have been taken out by anyone; and if there have been, I order them in virtue of their obedience to be returned.

Let him also have the keys of the cupboards by the altar, which I ordered to be made for the purpose.

NOTE. The schoolmaster ought to have the custody of the books in the cupboards.

• • • • •

St Bernard of Clairvaux, founder of the Cistercian order, devoted much of his time to exhorting, encouraging and guiding the Church in the form of letters and treatises. In the following letter to Abbot William of St Thierry, St Bernard paints a vivid picture of the richness of the decoration to be found in the medieval church, while warning against excess as a distraction to those engaged in the religious life.

• • •

Bernard of Clairvaux to William, Abbot of St Thierry (Excerpt).

1130.

Latin.

. . . But these are small things; I will pass on to matters greater in themselves, yet seeming smaller because they are more usual. I say naught of the vast height of your churches, their immoderate length, their superfluous breadth, the costly polishings, the curious carvings and paintings which attract the worshipper's gaze and hinder his attention, and seem to me in some sort a revival of the ancient Jewish rites. Let this pass, however: say that this is done for God's honour. But I say, as a monk, ask of my brother monks as the pagan [poet Persius] asked of his fellow-pagans: 'Tell me, O Pontiffs' (quoth he) 'what doeth this gold in the sanctuary?' So say I, 'Tell me, ye poor men' (for I break the verse to keep the sense) 'tell me, ye poor (if, indeed, ye be poor), what doeth this gold in *your* sanctuary? And indeed the bishops have an excuse which monks have not; for we know that they, being debtors both to the wise and the unwise, and unable to excite the devotion of carnal folk by spiritual things, do so by bodily adornments. But we [monks] who have now come forth from the people; we who have left all the precious and beautiful things of the world for Christ's sake; who have counted but dung, that we may win Christ, all things fair to see or soothing to hear sweet to smell, delightful to taste, or pleasant to touch - in a word, all bodily delights - whose devotion, pray, do we monks intend to excite by these things? What profit, I say, do we expect therefrom? The admiration of fools, or the oblations of the simple? Or, since we are scattered among the nations, have we perchance learnt their works and do we yet serve their graven images? To speak plainly, doth the root of all this lie in covetousness, which is idolatry, and do we seek not profit, but a gift? If thou askest: 'How?' I say: 'In a strange fashion.' For money is so artfully scattered that it may multiply; it is expended that it may give increase, and prodigality giveth birth to plenty; for at the very sight of these costly yet marvellous vanities men are more kindled to offer gifts than to pray. Thus wealth is drawn up by ropes of wealth, thus money bringeth money; for I know not how it is that, wheresoever more abundant wealth is seen, there do men offer more freely. Their eyes are feasted with relics cased in gold, and their purse-strings are loosed. They are shown a most comely image of some saint, whom they think all the more saintly that he is the more gaudily painted. Men run to kiss him, and are invited to give; there is more admiration for his comeliness than veneration for his sanctity. Hence the church is adorned with gemmed crowns of light - nay, with lustres like cart-wheels, girt all round with lamps, but no less brilliant with the precious stones that stud them. Moreover we see candelabra standing like trees of massive bronze, fashioned with marvellous subtley of art, and glistening no less brightly with gems than with the lights they carry. What, think you, is the purpose of all this? The compunction of penitents, or the admiration of the beholders? O vanity of vanities, yet no more vain than insane! The church is resplendent in her walls, beggarly in her poor; she clothes her stones in gold, and leaves her sons naked; the rich man's eye is fed at the expense of the indigent. The curious find their delight here, yet the needy find no relief. Do we not revere at least the images of the Saints, which swarm even in the inlaid pavement whereon we tread? Men spit oftentimes in the Angel's face; often, again, the countenance of some Saint is ground under the heel of a passer-by. And if he spare not these sacred images, why not even the fair colours? Why dost thou make so fair which will soon be made so foul? Why lavish bright hues upon that which must needs be trodden under foot? What avail these comely forms in places where they are defiled with customary dust? And, lastly, what are such things as these to you poor men, you monks, you spiritual folk? Unless perchance here also ye may answer the poet's question in the words of the Psalmist: 'Lord, I have loved the habitation of Thy House, and the place where Thine honour dwelleth.' I grant it, then, let us suffer even this to be done in the church; for, though it be harmful to vain and covetous folk, yet not so to the simple and devout. But in the cloister, under the eyes of the Brethren who read there, what profit is there in those ridiculous monsters, in that marvellous and deformed comeliness, that comely deformity? To what purpose are those unclean apes, those fierce lions, those monstrous centaurs, those half-men, those striped tigers, those fighting knights, those hunters winding their horns? Many bodies are there seen under one head, or again, many heads to a single body. Here is a four-footed beast with a serpent's tail; there, a fish with a beast's head. Here again the forepart of a horse trails half a goat behind it, or a horned beast bears the hinder quarters of a horse. In short, so many and so marvellous are the varieties of divers shapes on every hand, that we are more tempted to read in the marble than in our books, and to spend the whole day in wondering at these things rather than in meditating the law of God. For God's sake, if men are not ashamed of these follies, why at least do they not shrink from the expense?

The abundance of my matter suggested much more for me to add; but from this I am distracted both by my own anxious business and by the too hasty departure of Brother Oger [the bearer of this letter]..... This is my opinion of your Order and mine; nor can any man testify more truly than you, and those who know me as you do, that I am wont to say these things not about you but to your faces. What in your Order is laudable, that I praise and publish abroad; what is reprehensible, I am wont to persuade you and my other friends to amend. This is no detraction, but rather attraction: wherefore I wholly pray and beseech you to do the same by me. Farewell.

• • • • •

The late twelfth and thirteenth centuries were the great age of church building in France, a period of endeavour which was to witness the evolution of the Gothic style in architecture. The next two letters give a churchman's view of this period of architectural activity, which involved not only the labours of architects, masons and glaziers, but also the zeal and generosity of laymen. This was particularly marked at Chartres.

• • •

Abbot Haimon to the monks of Tutbury.

1145.

Latin.

Brother Haimon of the Company of Saint-Pierre-sur-Dives, humble servant of servants of the Blessed Mother of God, to his most dear brothers and fellow servants of Tutbury . . .

Who has ever seen! - Who has ever heard tell, in times past, that powerful princes of the world, that men brought up in honour and in wealth, that nobles, men and women, have bent their proud and haughty necks to the harness of carts, and that, like beasts of burden, they have dragged to the abode of Christ these waggons, loaded with wines, grains, oil, stone, wood, and all that is necessary for the wants of life, or for the construction of the church? But while they draw these burdens, there is one thing admirable to observe; it is that often when a thousand persons and more are attached to the chariots - so great is the difficulty - yet they march in such silence that not a murmur is heard, and truly if one did not see the thing with one's eyes, one might believe that among such a multitude there was hardly a person present. When they halt on the road, nothing is heard but the confession of sins, and pure and suppliant prayer to God to obtain pardon. At the voice of the priests who exhort their hearts to peace, they forget all hatred, discord is thrown far aside, debts are remitted, the unity of hearts is established.

But if any one is so far advanced in evil as to be unwilling to pardon an offender, or if he rejects the counsel of the priest who has piously advised him, his offering is instantly thrown from the waggon as impure, and he himself ignominiously and shamefully excluded from the society of the holy. There one sees the priests who preside over each chariot exhort every one to penitence, to confession of faults, to the resolution of better life! There one sees old people, young people, little children, calling on the Lord with a suppliant voice, and uttering to Him, from the depth of the heart, sobs and sighs with words of glory and praise! After the people, warned by the sound of trumpets and the sight of banners, have resumed their road, the march is made with such ease that no obstacle can retard it. . . . When they have reached the church they arrange the waggons about it like a spiritual camp, and during the whole night they celebrate the watch by hymns and canticles. On each waggon they light tapers and lamps; they place there the infirm and sick, and bring them the precious relics of the Saints for their relief. Afterwards the priests and clerics close the ceremony by processions which the people follow with devout heart imploring the clemency of the Lord and of his Blessed Mother for the recovery of the sick. . . .

• • •

Archbishop Hugo of Rouen to Bishop Thierry of Amiens.

1145.

Latin.

Hugo, priest of Rouen, to the Reverend Father Thierry, Bishop of Amiens, may he prosper always in Christ.

Great is the work of the Lord, excellent in all of His will. The inhabitants of Chartres have combined to aid in the construction of their church by transporting the material; our Lord has rewarded their humble zeal by miracles which have roused the Normans to imitate the piety of their neighbours. People of our land, therefore, having received blessing from us, set out continuously for that place and fulfil their vows. Since then, the faithful of our diocese and of other neighboring regions have formed associations for the same object; they admit no one into their company unless he has been to confession, has renounced enmities and revenges, and has reconciled himself with his enemies. That done, they elect a chief, under whose direction they conduct their waggons in silence and with humility, and present their oblations not without discipline and tears. These three things which we set forth, confession with penitence, concord in place of all malevolence, and humility with obedience - we require from those who are about to come to us; if they defer to these three, we receive them piously, absolve and bless them. While thus instructed they travel on their way, and whenever they bring their sick with them great miracles are very frequently wrought in our church, and they lead away as well those who came with them as invalids. And we allow our own people to go outside our regions, but we prohibit them from entering among the excommunicated or the interdicted. Given in this year of the Incarnate Word, 1145. Farewell.

• • • • •

The art of letter-writing was widely taught at medieval universities, and students' correspondence now largely exists in the form of collections which were compiled to assist the teaching of this skill. The collections were a combination of authentic letters and those composed by the *dictatores* as useful models. It is difficult to determine which are real and which are fictitious but as Haskins pointed out in his valuable study *Letters of Medieval Students*, 'even where they [letters] were the product of direct invention they would be likely to represent correctly the life of the academic environment in which they arose.'

Many of these letters are requests for money, food or clothing, others are from angry parents accusing their student sons of time-wasting, indulging in pastimes and neglecting their studies.

• • •

To a student at Orleans from his father.

Twelfth century.

Latin.

To his son G. residing at Orlean, Besançon sends greeting with paternal zeal.

It is written, 'He also that is slothful in his work is brother to him that is a great waster.' I have recently discovered that you lived dissolutely and slothfully, preferring license to restraint and play to work and strumming a guitar while the others are at their studies, whence it happens that you have read but one volume of law while your more industrious companions have read several. Wherefore I have decided to exhort you herewith to repent utterly of your dissolute and careless ways that you may no longer be called a waster and that your shame may be turned to good repute.

• • •

From two students at Orleans to their parents.

Twelfth century.

Latin.

To their very dear and respected parents M. Martre, knight and M. his wife, M. and S., their sons, send greetings and filial obedience.

This is to inform you that, by divine mercy, we are living in good health in the city of Orleans and are devoting ourselves wholly to study, mindful of the words of Cato, 'To know anything is praiseworthy,' etc. We occupy a good and comely dwelling, next door but one to the schools and market place, so that we can go to school every day without wetting our feet. We have also good companions in the house with us, well advanced with their studies and of excellent habits – an advantage which we well appreciate, for as the Psalmist says, 'With an upright man, thou wilt show thyself upright' etc. Wherefore lest production cease from lack of material, we beg your paternity to send us by the bearer, B., money for buying parchment, ink, a desk, and the other things which we need, in sufficient amount that we may suffer no want on your account (God forbid!) but finish our studies and return home with honour. The bearer will also take charge of the shoes and stockings which you have to send us, and any news as well.

• • • • •

The Bishop's request for a Doctor of Divinity to teach the monks at Gloucester is a particularly elegant letter. Whilst advocating the education of the monks, Godfrey is also demonstrating the advanced level of his own learning.

• • •

From the Bishop of Worcester to the Masters of Oxford University.
9 April 1283.
Latin.

To the venerable men and beloved in Christ, Sir. . . . Chancellor and the University of Masters of Oxford, Godfrey, by divine permission minister of the church of Worcester, fulness of health and eternal happiness.

The high vicar of Christ in the church though that the study of theology should be increased, so that by enlargement of the space of its tent it might make its ropes longer, and lo we hear of the laudable and divinely inspired devotion of the brethren of the abbey of St Peter's Gloucester, in our diocese, specially adhering to the same vicar of Christ, who are now disposed to put aside ignorance, the mother of error, and to walk in the light of truth, that they may become proficient in learning to the augmentation of their merits.

We therefore, helping all we can their so healthful purpose, put our earnest prayers before your University, asking you with all affection to permit and grant that in the house they possess in Oxford they may have a doctor in the sacred page to attend them, so that the way of learning may lie open to those thirsting for wisdom, and so at last they themselves becoming learned may be able to instruct the people in righteousness to the honour of God and the church.

May the most Highest always direct you in perfect love and the light of His love.

Dated at Henbury 9 April in the year aforesaid [1283].

• • • • •

Dante's letter to Can Grande was written two years before his own death in 1321. He explains how he had visited Verona in order to verify reports of Can Grande's fame and finding he more than lived up to his reputation, Dante declares himself to be his friend and servant. Dante dedicates the *Paradisio* which he had just begun, to his new friend and sets down the introduction of a commentary on it as well as the general framework and explanation of the *Commedia. La Commedia,* which later came to be known as the *Divine Comedy,* marked a new age in European literature which expressed contemporary values in new ways. It was written in Italian, rather than Latin, and has been described as 'a magificent synthesis of life and ideas in the Middle Ages,' it had a lasting influence, particularly on Petrarch and Boccaccio later in the fourteenth century.

• • •

From Dante to Can Grande, Lord of Verona.

1319.

Latin.

To the magnificent and most victorious Lord, the Lord Can Grande della Scala, Vicar-General of the most holy principality of Caesar in the city of Verona, and town of Vicenza, his most devoted servant, Dante Alighieri, a Florentine by birth, not by disposition, prayeth long and happy life, and perpetual increase of the glory of his name.

The illustrious renown of your Magnificence, which wakeful Fame spreads abroad as she flies, affects divers persons in divers ways, so that some it uplifts with the hope of good fortune, while others it casts down with the dread of destruction. The report whereof, overtopping all deeds of recent times, I erstwhile did deem extravagant, as going beyond the appearance of truth. But that continued uncertainty might not keep me longer in suspense, even as the Queen of the South sought Jerusalem, and as Pallas sought Helicon, so did I seek Verona, in order to examine with my own trusty eyes the things of which I had heard. And there was I witness of your splendour, there was I witness and partaker of your bounty; and whereas I had formerly suspected the reports to be somewhat unmeasured, I afterwards recognized that it was the facts themselves that were beyond measure. Whence it came to pass that whereas through hearsay alone, with a certain subjection of mind, I had previously become well disposed towards you, at the first sight of you I became your most devoted servant and friend.

Nor do I think that in assuming the name of friend I shall lay myself open to a charge of presumption, as some perchance might object; inasmuch as unequals no less than equals are united by the sacred tie of friendship. For if one should examine friendships which have been pleasant and profitable, it will be evident that in many cases the bond has been between persons of superior station and their inferiors. And if our attention be directed to true friendship for its own sake, shall we not find that the friends of illustrious and mighty princes have many a time been men obscure in condition but of distinguished virtue? Why not? since even the friendship of God and man is in no wise impeded by the disparity between them. But if any man consider this assertion unseemly, let him hearken to the Holy Spirit when it declares that certain men have been partakers of its friendship. For in *Wisdom* we read, concerning wisdom; 'For she is a treasure unto men that never faileth; which they that use are made partakers of the friendship of God.' But the common herd in their ignorance judge without discernment; and even as they imagine the sun to be a foot across, so they judge with regard to questions of conduct; and they are deceived by their foolish credulity with regard to both the one and the other matter. But it does not become us, to whom it has been given to know what is best in our nature, to follow in the footsteps of the common herd; nay, rather are we bound to oppose their errors. For those who have vigour of intellect and reason, being endowed with a certain divine liberty, are not restricted by precedent. Nor is this to be wondered at, for it is not they who receive direction from the laws, but rather the laws from them. It is manifest, therefore, that what I said above, namely that I was your most devoted servant and friend, in no wise savours of presumption.

Esteeming, then, your friendship as a most precious treasure, I desire to preserve it with assiduous forethought and anxious care. Therefore, since it is a doctrine of ethics that friendship is equalized and preserved by reciprocity, it is my wish to preserve due reciprocity in making a return for the bounty more than once conferred upon me. For which reason I have often and long examined such poor gifts and I can offer, and have set them out separately, and scrutinized each in turn, in order to decide which would be the most worthy and the most acceptable to you. And I have found nothing more suitable even for your exalted station than the sublime cantica of the *Comedy* which is adorned with the title of *Paradise*; this, then, dedicated to yourself, with the present letter to serve as its superscription, I inscribe, offer, and in fine commend to you....

• • • • •

In ancient Rome great poets had been crowned with laurel leaves in public recognition of their achievements. The tradition had almost been forgotten but Petrarch deeply desired the glory and status of the laureateship, and set out to influence King Robert of Rome and eminent members of the university of Paris. The innocent surprise Petrarch conveys in this letter is not all that it seems since he deliberately engineered events and used his friends and contacts to further his cause, particularly Cardinal Giovanni Colonna. Petrarch had approached the university of Paris in case no offer came from Rome, but faced with invitations from both there is little doubt as to which he treasured most. Petrarch was crowned poet on Easter Day 1341 on the Capitol by the Roman Senator. It was, 'a supreme event in Petrarch's life . . . . The laurel consecrated the work he had already done; it gave him confidence in the value of his own thoughts and words.'*

• • •

From Petrarch to Cardinal Giovanni Colonna.

1 September 1340.

Latin.

I am in a dilemma; I don't know which way to turn. The story is remarkable but short. Today, about nine a.m., I received letters from the Roman Senate, summoning me most urgently and persuasively to Rome to receive the laurel crown of poetry. Then this afternoon about four o'clock a messenger arrived on the same errand from the illustrious Roberto dei Bardi, Chancellor of the University of Paris. He is a fellow Florentine and very sympathetic to my purposes. He urges me, with very compeling arguments, to come to Paris.

Who, I ask you, would ever have guessed that such a thing could occur among our crags? Since in fact it seems almost incredible, I am sending you both letters, including the seals. One letter calls me eastward, the other westward; you will see how I am torn hither and thither by weighty considerations. I know that there is nothing secure in human affairs, and that assuredly in most of our concerns and actions we are deluded by shadows. And yet, as a young man's mind craves glory more than virtue, and as you have encouraged me in your intercourse to seek glory, why should I not admit my own desire for it? At least as much as did that mightiest of African kings, Syphax, when at the same time his friendship was besought by the world's two greatest cities, Rome and Carthage. No doubt the offers came to him because of his kingdom and his wealth; mine was for me alone. The ambassadors found him high on his haughty throne, adorned with gold and gems, and surrounded by his armed attendants; my couriers found me strolling by the banks of Sorgue, this morning in the woods, this afternoon in the fields. To me honour is offered; from him aid was sought.

* Bishop, *Petrarch and His World* p. 171.

But since joy is the enemy of good counsel, my happiness at the event is, I grant, mingled with uncertainty as to my choice. The charm of novelty tempts me to one side, reverence for antiquity to the other; on one side stands a friend, on the other my fatherland. One consideration weighs with me, that King Robert of Sicily is in Italy; he of all men is the one I would most confidently accept as a judge of my quality. You see how my thoughts waver. Will you, who have not disdained to guide them, now rule my fluctuating mind with your counsel?

With assurance of my most profound regard, I am, etc.

• • • • •

Zanobi da Strada, a friend of Petrarch's and a poor Florentine schoolmaster and scholar, was so affected by Petrarch's attack on his profession that he gave up teaching and became a government official. Zanobi continued to write poetry and was crowned Poet Laureate of Pisa in 1355. Petrarch was particularly annoyed by this since Zabobi was not a great poet and it diminished his own glory as the first to receive the laurel crown for many centuries; evidently Rome's initiative had prompted a trend in other Italian cities.

• • •

Petrarch to Zanobi da Strada.

1 April 1352 (or perhaps 1349).

Latin.

To Zanobi da Strada, a Florentine schoolmaster and poet; from Avignon.

. . . Let them teach who can do nothing better, whose qualities are laborious application, sluggishness of mind, muddiness of intellect, prosiness of imagination, chill of the blood, patience to bear the body's labours, contempt of glory, avidity for petty gains, indifference to boredom. You see how far these qualities are from your character. Let them watch boys' fidgety hands, their wandering eyes, their *sotto voce* whisperings who delight in that task, who enjoy dust and noise and the clamour of mingled prayers and tears and whimperings under the rod's correction. Let them teach who love to return to boyhood, who are shy of dealing with men and shamed by living with equals, who are happy to be set over their inferiors, who always want to have someone to terrify, to afflict, to torture, to rule, someone who will hate and fear them. That is a tyrannical pleasure, such as, according to the story, pervaded the fierce spirit of that old man of Syracuse, to be the evil solace of his deserved exile. But you, a man of parts, merit a better occupation. Those who instruct our youth should be like those ancient authors who informed us in our own early age; as those who first aroused our young minds with noble examples, so should we be to our successors. Since you can follow the Roman masters, Cicero and Virgil, would you choose Orbilius, Horace's 'flogging-master'? What is more, neither grammar nor any of the seven liberal arts is worth a noble spirit's attention throughout life. They are means, not ends . . .

• • • • •

Edward III did much to restore the prestige of English Kingship, tarnished by the unrest of his father's reign. He vowed to restore the Round Table of King Arthur and to that end founded a new chivalric order, the Order of the Garter. Edward undertook to reconstruct Windsor Castle as a fitting meeting place for the Knights, and the following letters concern the taking of masons to work on this endeavour.

• • •

Edward III to the sheriffs, mayors, bailiffs and ministers.

1359/60 and 1361.

Latin (?)

The King to the same [sheriffs, mayors, bailiffs and other ministers] greeting.

Know that we, trusting in the discretion and loyalty of Master Robert of Gloucester, our mason, have assigned and deputed him to take and arrest as many masons, as may be necessary for the erection of our works in our castle of Wyndesore, wherever he can find them, within liberties as without, and to place them in our works aforesaid at our wages, and to take and arrest all masons whom he shall find contrary or rebellious in this matter and bring them to the aforesaid castle there to be held in prison until they shall find security to remain at those works according to the instruction of the said Robert on our behalf. And therefore we command you that to the same Robert in these matters etc you be of assistance. In witness whereof etc. At Redyng, January 6th 1359/60.

The King to the sheriff of Norfolk and Suffolk greeting.

We command you as strictly as we can that immediately on sight of these present letters your cause to be chosen and attached with the said counties, whether within liberties or without, of the better and more skilled masons, forty masons for hewing freestone and forty masons for laying stone, and cause them to be brought or sent, with the tools belonging to their trade, to our castle of Windsor so that you have them there by the first of May next at the latest, to be delivered to our beloved clerk William of Wykeham*, clerk of our works there, to remain at our works for as long as may be necessary at our wages. And you shall take from all the same masons such sufficient security as you would be willing to answer for to us that they will remain continuously in our aforesaid works and will not depart therefrom without our special licence. And all masons whom the aforesaid William shall certify to you as having left our said works without leave and returned to the aforesaid counties you shall cause to be bodily taken and arrested wherever they may be found in your bailiwick, whether within or without, and kept securely in our prison, so that without our special mandate they shall in no wise be released from the same. And you shall inform us clearly and without concealment by the first of May of the names of masons aforesaid and of the security you take from each of them to remain at our works for as long as may be necessary at our wages. And you shall take from all the same masons such sufficient security as you would be willing to answer for to us that they will remain continuously in our aforesaid works and will not depart therefrom without our special licence. And all those masons whom the aforesaid William shall certify to you as having left our said works without leave and returned to the aforesaid counties you shall cause to be bodily taken and arrested wherever they may be found in your bailiwick, whether within liberties or without, and kept securely in our prison, so that without our special mandate they shall in no wise by released from the same. And you shall inform us clearly and without concealment by the first of May of the names of masons aforesaid and of the security you take from each of them to remain at our works aforesaid. And this you shall in no wise omit on pain of forfeiting everything you can forfeit us. Witness the King at Westminster.

• • • • •

Hugh, master of the Almonry school at Canterbury, had been transferred to the public school at Kingston, his town of origin, which was in the unfortunate position of lacking a teacher. Hugh's absence was sorely felt by the Almoner at Canterbury who used devious means to persuade him to return. The Bishop urges the Prior to put matters to right.

• • •

* Supervisor of king's works. Elected Bishop of Winchester in 1366.

The Bishop of Winchester to the Prior of Canterbury.
7 April 1364.
Latin.

William of Edyngdon, Bishop of Winchester, to the Prior of Canterbury.

My lord and dearest friend in Christ . . . We learnt some time ago, on the report of our beloved sons and parishioners of the town of Kingston, that they to their grief, being without a teacher or master of their boys and others coming to the said town, where a school has been accustomed to be kept, made an agreement and entered into a contract, confirmed by sureties, with one Hugh of Kingston, clerk, born in the said town, lately the worthy pedagogue, as it is said, of the scholars in the house of your Almonry, that he should undertake the instruction and teaching of the said boys and of other scholars in the said town and preside over the Public School there, first about Michaelmas, and again at Christmas last, as the said Hugh, who came before us and was sworn on the Holy Gospels, publicly confessed, offering faithfully to fulfil the same. But your fellow-monk, the Almoner of your house aforesaid, being, as we hear, troubled and annoyed at the said Hugh's leaving, seized or sequestrated some poor goods of his, and keeps them still under sequestration, thinking by these means to recall the said Hugh to his service. In the name of that friendship, in the soundness of which we have undoubting faith, we requre and ask your fatherhood, that you would be good enough with salutary warnings to order the said Almoner to restore and deliver the said goods to the said Hugh, or to the bearer of these letters in his name, and that he will hold the said Hugh excused for not returning; seeing, if it please you, that by law magistrates should be created from their own town, and the vinedressers of the people be chosen from the same place . . .

Written at Esher, 7 April.

• • • • •

Brother Edmund writes to his patron informing him of his eldest son's progress and welfare at school. The boy, who is recovering from an illness, is studying Latin grammar and Brother Edmund considers him to be in the best of hands, believing there to be, 'nothing serious in his condition'. Unfortunately Sir Edmund's son died soon after this letter was written.

• • •

From Brother Edmund to Sir Edmund Stonor.
c. 1380.
Latin.

To the Honorable Sir Edmund de Stonor.

Sir and God's servant:

Know, if you please, that I have seen your son Edmund and have observed his condition these two nights and a day. His sickness grows less from day to day, and he is no longer in bed. But when the fever returns, he is still a little out of sorts for two hours or so; after which he rises and, according to the demands of the time, goes to school and eats and walks about, well and jolly, so that there seems to be nothing serious in his condition. Of his own accord he himself sent his duty to you and to his lady, and greetings to all the others.

He is beginning to learn *Donatus* slowly, as is right enough so far. He has that copy of *Donatus* which I was afraid was lost.

Indeed, I have never seen a boy get such care as he has had during his illness. The master and his wife prefer that some of his clothes should be left at home, because he has far too many, and fewer would be enough; and his clothes, through no fault of theirs, might easily be torn and spoiled.

I enclose descriptive titles of the books in a volume which the owner will not sell for less than twelve shillings. In my opinion and that of others it is worth that; and if he sells it to us, he asks to be paid promptly.

And so, if you please, send me by your boy an answer of your wishes in these matters that I have mentioned.

Farewell, in the power of Christ and in the merits of the Virgin and Mother, Mary,

From your devoted, Brother Edmund.

• • • • •

Jan Van Eyck (1400?-1441), with his more obscure brother Hubert, is regarded as the founder of the Netherlandish school of painting. All great artists need the support of a great patron and in Philip the Good, Duke of Burgundy (1396-1467), Jan was to find a generous, wealthy and immensely powerful benefactor. The following letters reveal the environment in which a favoured painter could expect to work while in the employ of the Duke, and both demonstrate the high esteem in which Jan was held by his patron.

• • •

Letter patent from Duke Philip of Burgundy to the Audit Office at Lille.

1425/26.

French.

Jan van Eyck, former painter and equerry of the late Lord John,* Duke of Bavaria, was known for his ability and craftsmanship by my said lord† who had heard thereof from several of his people and which he knew to be true, being acquainted personally with the said Jan van Eyck. Confident of his loyalty and probity, my lord has retained said Jan as his painter and equerry, with the customary honours, prerogatives, franchises, liberties, rights, profits and usual emoluments pertaining to this position. And to the end that he shall be held to work for him in painting whenever it pleases him, my lord has ordered him to have and to take on his general receipt from Flanders, the sum of 100 parisis in Flemish money in two settlements yearly, half at Christmas and the other half at Saint John's, of which he wishes the first payment to be at Christmas 1425 and the other at Saint John's, and so from year to year and payment to payment, as long as it shall please him. Ordering to the masters of his household and his other officers that all his present honours, rights, prerogatives, profits and emoluments above mentioned they shall make and allow the said Jan to enjoy peaceably without prevention or disturbance; in addition ordering to his said receiver general of Flanders, present and future, that he shall pay, give and deliver every year the said sum of 100 Parisian pounds per year on the above declared terms to the said Jan, his painter and equerry, so all that is said on these matters may appear more plainly in the letters patent of my beforementioned lord, given in his city of Bruges, the 19th day of May in the year 1425. By virtue of that attestation is briefly given here to make payment for the term of Christmas 1425, and that which will follow to make a payment of 50 pounds on his quittance.

For the terms of St. John and Christmas 1426 together is made payment of 100 pounds on his quittance.

• • •

* John of Bavaria, Count of Holland and Zeeland (d. 1425). He had employed Jan at The Hague.

† i.e. Philip the Good.

Duke Philip of Burgundy to the Audit Office at Lille.

_1433._

French.

To our beloved and faithful keepers of our accounts at Lille.

Very dear and beloved

We have heard that you do not readily verify certain of our letters granting life pension to our well beloved equerry and painter, Jan van Eyck, whereby he cannot be paid said pension; and for this reason, he will find it necessary to leave our service, which would cause us great displeasure, for we would retain him for certain great works with which we intend henceforth to occupy him and we would not find his like more to our taste, one so excellent in his art and science. Therefore, we desire and expressly order that, according to these wishes, you do verify and ratify our said letters of pension and have this pension paid to the said Jan van Eyck, all according to the content of our said letters with no further talk or argument from you nor any omission, change, variation, or difficulty, as much as you would not anger and disobey [us].

For once and for all do so much so that we have no further need to write. This we would only do with great displeasure.

Very dear and well beloved, may the Holy Spirit have you in his Holy care. Written in our city of Dijon, the twelfth day of March, 1433.

• • • • •

The introduction to an earlier letter described the importance the Paston family placed on education. Clement's mother, Agnes, wife of Judge William Paston, requests information on her son's progress at Cambridge, advocating corporal punishment as a cure for reluctant students. She shows concern about the condition of Clement's clothing, possibly because of the season, and orders the purchase of some spoons. Finally, Agnes provides some words of advice for her daughter who was living away from home, at the household of Lady Pole, as was the custom.

• • •

From Agnes Paston.

28 January 1458.

English.

Errands to London of Agnes Paston, the 28th day of January, the year of King Henry VI. the 36th [1458].

To pray Greenfield to send me faithfully word by writing, how Clement Paston hath done his devoir in Learning. And if he hath not done well, nor will not amend, pray him that he will truly belash him, till he will amend; and so did the last Master, and the best that ever he had at Cambridge.

And say Greenfield, that if he will take upon him to bring him into good Rule and Learning, that I may verily know he doth his devoir, I will give him 10 Marks for his labour, for I had lever he were fairly buried than lost for default.

Item, to see how many Gowns Clement hath, and they that be bare, let them be raised.

He hath a short green Gown and a short musterdevelers* Gown were never raised.

And a short blue Gown, that was raised, and made of a side [*long*] Gown, when I was last at London; and a side Russet Gown furred with beaver was made this time two years. And a side Murrey Gown was made this time twelvemonth.

Item, to do make me six Spoons of eight ounces of troy weight, well fashioned and double gilt.

And say Elizabeth Paston that she must use herself to work readily, as other Gentlewomen do, and somewhat to help herself therewith.

Item, to pay the Lady Pole 26s and 8d. for her board.

And if Greenfield have done well his devoir to Clement, or will do his devoir, give him the noble.

Agnes Paston.

• • • • •

Sir John Paston II was an avid reader and collector of books. William Ebesham was the scribe he employed to copy books for him and the former's letter and account reveals the kinds of legal texts and instructive works on knightly conduct which his patron requested. John Paston II was also fond of French romances and was keen to own copies of printed books soon after their introduction to England in 1474. Book collecting had become fashionable at the court of Henry VI, so rich and educated men were eager to follow the royal initiative.

* A warm, mixed grey woollen cloth.

so rich and educated men were eager to follow the royal initiative.

The letter shows that the scrivening profession was not especially profitable despite Fenn's calculations. William Ebesham asks John Paston to pay his outstanding bill promptly and to send a gown which he no longer had any use for.

For a more detailed account of the Pastons and their books see Bennett, pp. 110-113, and A.I. Doyle, 'The Work of the late fifteenth century English scribe, William Ebesham', *John Rylands Library Bulletin*, XXXIX, 1957.

• • •

From William Ebesham to Sir John Paston.

c.1495.

English.

To my most worshipful Master, Sir John Paston, Knight.

My most worshipful and most special Master, with all my service, most lowly I recommend [me] unto your good Mastership, beseeching you most tenderly to see me somewhat rewarded for my labour in the Great Book* which I wrote unto your said good Mastership. I have often times written to Pampyng according to your desire, to inform you how I have laboured in writings for you, and I see well he speak not to your Mastership of it; and God knoweth I lie in Sanctuary at great costs, and amongst right unreasonable askers.

I moved this matter to Sir Thomas [Lewis] lately, and he told me he would move your Mastership therein, which Sir Thomas desired me to remember well what I have had in Money at sundry times of him.

(Then comes the Account, as stated more at large in the following Bill.)

And in especial I beseech you to send me for Alms one of your old Gowns, which will countervail much of the premises I wot well; and I shall be yours while I live, and at your commandment; I have greatly missed of it God knows, whom I beseech preserve you from all adversity; I am somewhat acquainted with it.

Your very man,

* i.e. A large volume containing several works, as was then usual.

Following appeareth, parcelly, divers and sundry manner of Writings, which I William Ebesham have written for my good and worshipful Master, Sir John Paston, and what money I have received, and what is unpaid.

First, I did write to his Mastership a little Book of Physic,
for which I had paid by Sir Thomas Lewis, in
Westminster 1s 8d
Item, I had for the writing of half the Privy Seal, of Pampyng 8d
Item, for the writing of the said whole Privy Seal of Sir
Thomas 2s 0d
Item, I wrote eight of the Witnesses in Parchment but after
14d. a-piece, for which I was paid of Sir Thomas 10s 0d
Item, while my said Master was over the sea in Midsummer
term; Calle set me at work to write two times the Privy Seal in
paper, and then after clearly in parchment 4s 8d
And also I wrote at the same time one or more of the longest
Witnesses, and other diverse and necessary Writings,
for which he promised me 10s. (whereof I had of Calle
but 4s. 8d.) due 5s 4d
Item, I received of Sir Thomas at Westminster
30 October 8 E. IV. 1468 ... ... 3s 4d
Item, I did write two Quires of paper of Witnesses,
every Quire containing 14 leaves after 2d. a leaf 4s 8d
Item, as to the Great Book
First, for writing of the Coronation; and other
Treatises of Knighthood, in that quire which containeth
a 13 leaves and more, 2d. a leaf 2s 2d
Item, for the Treatise of War in four books, which
containeth 60 leaves after 2d. a leaf 10s 0d
Item, for Othea, an Epistle, which containeth 43 leaves 7s 2d
"Item, for the Challenges, and the Acts of Arms
which is 28 leaves 4s 8d
"Item, for *D Regimine Principum*, which containeth
45 leaves, after I penny a leaf, which it is right well worth 3s 9d
"Item, for Rubrishing* of all the Book 3s 4d

65s 5d

---

* This either means ornamenting the whole with red Capital Letters, or writing the heads of the several Treatises or Chapters in red Letters. (F)

Sum received £1 2s 4d
Sum unpaid £2 1s 1d

Sum Total £3 3s 5d

William Ebesham

At this time the common wages of a Mechanic were, with diet, 4d. and without diet 5½d. or 6d. a day; we here see that a writer received 2d. for writing a folio leaf, three of which he could with ease finish in a day, [and] I should think that many quick writers at that time would fill four, five, or even six in a day, if so, the pay of these greatly exceeded that of common handicraft men.

• • • • •

Eton was founded by Henry VI in 1440 as a free grammar school. William Paston was educated there, and here he writes to his elder brother in typical schoolboy fashion, looking forward to the holidays and other possible diversions from his lessons. 'There is a curious modernity about this suggestion (to sport with his brother) which reminds us how little the character of youth is changed by the passing centuries.'*

• • •

From Wiliam Paston to his brother John Paston.

November 1478.

English.

To his worshipful Brother John Paston, be this delivered in haste.

Right reverend and worshipful brother, I recommend me unto you, desiring to hear of your welfare and prosperity, letting you weet that I have received of Alweder a letter and a noble in gold therein; furthermore my creasner [*creditor*] Master Thomas [Stevenson] heartily recommended him to you, and he prayeth you to send him some money for my commons, for he saith ye be 20s. in his debt, for a month was to pay for, when he had money last; also I beseech you to send me a hose cloth, one for the holydays of some colour, and another for the

*Bennett, p. 109.

working days how coarse soever it be it maketh no matter, and a stomacher [*a sort of ruff*], and two shirts, and a pair of slippers: and if it like you that I may come with Alweder by water, and sport me with you at London a day or two this term time, then ye may let all this be till the time that I come, and then I will tell you when I shall be ready to come from Eton by the grace of God, who have you in his keeping. Written the Saturday next after Allhallows day with the hand of your brother,

William Paston.

• • • • •

The founding of Canterbury College at Oxford has been outlined elsewhere. The following letter indicates how 'a university education was one of the few ways in which a man could overcome the disadvantages of plebeian birth.* Canterbury College, at this time, was able to accommodate seven secular clerks.

• • •

The Abbot of St Augustine's to the Prior of Christ Church, Canterbury.

Fifteenth century.

English.

My duty being assumed, I ask your fatherhood's favour, requesting urgently that if you intend to select more scholars to Oxford after Easter, you favour a subject of yours whose father, Richard Knight, is my servant, given that he is as apt to learn as any of your other subjects, assuming he behaves himself. I ask this not for myself, but in respect of the request of my servant, who would very much like his son to obtain preferment; so I would like to do whatever you please in this matter, and without sending me any written reply, unless you should choose, May Jesus preserve you.

By your beadsman John,

Abbot of St Augustine's.

• • • • •

* Green, p. 261.

Towards the end of the fifteenth century the traditional medieval systems of education were undergoing a transformation, particularly in Italy. The influence of humanist scholars placed increasing emphasis on classical studies and the development of the individual. Ficino's letter to Niccolo degli Albizzi illustrates both these aspects from a personal viewpoint.

• • •

From Marsilio Ficino to Niccolo degli Albizzi.

Late fifteenth century.

Latin.

An exhortation to pursue knowledge

Marsilio Ficino to Niccolo degli Albizzi: greetings.

You have heard that proverb, my dear Niccolo: Nothing is sweeter than profit. But what man does profit? He who takes possession of that which will be his. What we know is ours, everthing else depends on fortune. Let small-minded men envy the rich, that is those whose coffers are rich but not their minds. You should emulate those wise and good men whose mind is like God. Warn your fellow students to beware of Scylla and Charybdis; that is, the attractions of pleasure and the noisome fever of the mind given to opinion rather than knowledge. Let them remember that one day the highest delight for each will be that which is experienced in the highest part of the mind, in the supreme treasury of truth itself, when they discard the shadow of worthless pleasures for the sake of knowledge. The tree of knowledge, even if it seems to have rather bitter roots brings forth the sweetest possible fruit. Let them remember too that there will never be too much of this fruit because there is never enough.

He who still doubts has not yet learnt enough, yet we doubt as long as we live; and so as long as we live we should learn. Indeed we should imitate the wise Solon, who even when dying sought to learn something, for he was nourished by the food of truth and to him death was no more than rebirth. A man can never die who enjoys immortal nourishment. Socrates was first called the wisest of all men by Apollo, when he began to say publicly that he knew nothing. Pythagoras told his disciples that they should look at themselves in a mirror, not by the light of a lamp, but by the light of the sun. What is the light of a lamp, if it is not a mind as yet too little instructed by knowledge? What the light of the sun, if not the mind totally under its instruction?

When, therefore, anyone wants to know about the state of his mind, he should compare it not with the ignorant, but on the contrary with the wisest; thus he may see more clearly how much he has gained and how much remains. In feeding the mind we ought to imitate gluttons and the covetous, who always fix their attention on what is still left. What is there further?

The Lord of Life says, 'No man, having put his hand to the plough, and looking back, is worthy of reward.' You have heard too of that woman who, because she turned back, was changed into a pillar. You have also heard how Orpheus, when he looked back, lost Eurydice; in other words, his depth of judgement. Ineffective and empty-handed is the hunter who goes backwards rather than forwards.

Farewell.

• • • • •

Lorenzo de Medici writes from Pisa distressed by the lack of letters from his friend Marsilio Ficino. Lorenzo Medici was a more than competent poet and Latinist, the jesting metaphor of a trial in the fourth paragraph illustrates his confidence with written language. Of more significance is the importance he places on receiving and writing letters, 'correspondence, which is a duty of love', and that regardless of the informative purpose of letters it is their personal aspects, their ability to convey emotion and their entertainment value which he treasures the most.

• • •

From Lorenzo de' Medici to Marsilio Ficino

Before 1499.

Latin.

A request for a Letter

Lorenzo de' Medici to Marsilio Ficino, the Platonic philosopher: greetings.

Dearest Marsilio, when I was leaving for this place I urged you not to let me await your letters too long while I was away, and to this you agreed. But already four days have passed since our parting and there is still no letter from you; although a great many letters have been delivered to me from my household and other friends. Thus I am surprised and sorry at your delay in writing, because I fully believed that if good will were equally strong in us both there would be equal enthusiasm in correspondence, which is a duty of love.

I began at first to make an excuse for you, saying to myself on your behalf, 'Perhaps the study of philosophy, which demands the whole and undivided man, is the reason why Marsilio's letter has not reached me'; and my almost unbelievable love led me to make to myself the most honourable excuse of all. I had so much confidence in it that waiting for a few hours did not seem too difficult.

But since I saw that I must count in many days what I had thought should be measured in hours, there no longer appeared any room for excuse. Now I, who had taken up your defence, began to think only of how I should prosecute you, since many ways came to mind. I find so many varieties of offence in you that even if you engaged Demosthenes and our own Cicero as your own counsel for the defence, I am certain you would be condemned.

Now if you are not sorry for this – and I seek no other sign of repentance than your letters – know that you will undergo judgement at the court of our mutual love, for it is right that the case should be tried by such a judge. We shall find nobody fairer or more just, or anyone who could be a truer witness to our own soul. This judge gives you only the space of three days to write to me, and if these go by without your doing so, he promises you will be condemned.

'But,' you will say, 'what can I write to Lorenzo? I have no news of the Republic, no domestic issues to report.' I expect neither from you, since you have taken no heed of either. I know that you are no more solicitous about the affairs of others than about your own. Then what is there for you to write about? Anything that comes to mind. Everything that comes from you is good, everything that you think is right, and therefore everything that you write is profitable and delightful to me. What makes me so long for your letters is that in them humour appears so mixed with gravity that if considered lightheartedly everything seems full of humour, if seriously, then they seem more serious than anything else. So as soon as you have an opportunity to write, I beg you delay no longer, nor let me vainly wait so long for your letters.

Farewell.

Pisa.

• • • • •

Dorothy Plumpton has been placed in some 'menial situation' in the household of Lady Darcy, the mother of Dorothy's stepmother, and is not at all happy about her position. Dorothy's homesickness and distress about spiteful rumours, combined with her request for a new hat, provides a poignant view of the concerns of a young gentlewoman. Dorothy later married Henry Arthington, one of the Darcy's neighbours, distress about spiteful rumours, combined with her request for a new hat, provides a poignant view of the concerns of a young gentlewoman. Dorothy later married Henry Arthington, one of the Darcy's neighbours, which supports the view that part of the reason for sending grown-up daughters away from home was to improve their chances of meeting eligible bachelors.

• • •

Dorothy Plumpton to her father Sir Robert Plumpton.

c. 1500.

English.

Let this be delivered in haste to my most honoured and wholly beloved, good, kind father, Sir Robert Plumpton, presently staying at Plumpton in Yorkshire.

Most Honoured father, in the humblest manner I know I send you my respects, and to my lady mother, and to all my brothers and sisters, whom I beseech Almighty God to maintain and preserve in health, prosperity, and increasing honour, asking of you only your daily blessing; this is to let you know that I sent a message to you, by Wryghame of Knaresborough, about my feelings, how he should ask you, in my name, to send for me to return home to you, and as yet I have had no answers, and my lady has obtained knowledge of my desire.

Because of this she has become a better lady towards me than she ever was before, and she has promised to be my good lady as long as she lives; and if you or she can find anything more suitable for me in this district or any other, she will help to further my interests to the limit of her power. So I humbly ask you, to be so good and kind a father to me as to let me know your pleasure, how you would like me to be settled, as soon as you are pleased to.

And please write to my ladyship, thanking her good ladyship for the tender loving-kindness she has shown me, and asking her to continue it. Sir I beseech you to send a servant of yours to my lady and to me, and show by fatherly kindness that I am your child: for I have sent you various messages and letters, and have never had any answer. Because of this, it is believed in the district among those persons who would rather speak ill than good, that you have little feeling for me, an error which you can discredit, if it pleases you to be a good kind father to me.

And please send me a fine hat, and some good cloth to make headscarfs.

And I pray to Jesus that he will be pleased to have you in His blessed keeping, and bring you happiness and your heart's desire.

Written at the Hirst, the thirteenth day of May,

By your loving daughter,

Dorothy Plumpton.

• • • • •

Albrecht Dürer (1471-1528) was one of the most influential artists of his day. He travelled far more widely than was usual for a man of his time, spending the year after the completion of his apprenticeship to the artist Michael Wolgemut travelling in Germany and possibly Holland. He also went to Colmar, with the intention of studying with the engraver Martin Schongauer. Finding Schongauer dead, he went on to Basel and Strasbourg, centres of book illustration, an art he was to excel in. In 1494 Dürer was married, but also found time for a short trip to Venice, an experience he describes with evident enjoyment in the first letters.

• • •

Albrecht Dürer to Willibald Pirckheimer.

7 February 1506, Venice.

German.

First my willing service to you, dear Sir. If things are going well with you I am glad with my whole heart for you as I should be for myself. I recently wrote to you and hope that the letter reached you. In the meantime my mother has written to me, scolding me for not writing to you; and she has given me to understand that you hold me in displeasure because I do not write to you. She said I must apologize to you most seriously and she takes it very much to heart, as her way is.

Now I don't know what excuse to make except that I am lazy about writing, and that you have not been at home. But as soon as I heard that you were either at home or intended to come home, I wrote to you at once; after that I also very specially charged Kastell* to convey my service to you. So I humbly pray you to forgive me, for I have no other friend on earth but you, I don't believe, however, that you are angry with me, for I regard you in no other light than as a father.

I wish you were here at Venice! There are so many nice fellows

---

* Castulus Fugger

and they show me much honour and friendship. On the other hand there are also amongst them some of the most false, lying, thievish rascals, the like of which I should not have believed lived on earth. If one did not know them, one would think them the nicest men the earth could show. For my part I cannot help laughing at them whenever they talk to me. They know that their knavery is no secret but they don't care.

Amongst the Italians I have many good friends who warn me not to eat and drink with their painters. Many of them are my enemies and they copy my work in the churches and wherever they find it; and then they revile it and say that it was not in the *antique* manner and therefore not good. Giovanni Bellini,* however, has highly praised me before many nobles. He wanted to have something of mine, and himself came to me and asked me to paint him something and he would pay well for it. And all men tell me what a God-fearing man he is, so that I am well disposed toward him from the outset. He is very old, but still the best in painting. And those works of art which so pleased me eleven years ago please me no longer; if I had not seen it for myself I should not have believed it from anyone else. You must know too that there are many better painters here than Master Jacob† abroad, yet Anton Kolb would swear on oath that no better painter lives on earth than Jacob. The others sneer at him, saying 'If he were good he would stay here.'

I have only today begun to sketch in my picture,§ for my hands were so scabby that I could do no work, but I have got it cured . . .

. . . Given at Venice at the ninth hour of the night, on Saturday after Candlemass in the year 1506.

Give my service to Steffen Paumgartner and to Masters Hans Harstorfer and Folkamer.

• • • • •

Upon his return to Nürnberg in 1495 he established his own workshop. It is as an independent master that he writes the next two letters.

• • •

* Giovanni Bellini (1430-1516) Painter of Venice and teacher of Titian and Giorgio.
†Jacopo de' Barbari (1440-50) to 1515-1516).
§ The feast of the Rose Garlands. Painted for the Chapel of the German Merchants in Venice and now in the Prague Museum.

Albrecht Dürer to Jacob Heller.
24 August 1508 Nürnberg.
German.

Dear Herr Jacob, I have safely received your letter, that is to say, the last but one, and I gather from it that you wish me to execute your panel well, which is just what I myself have in mind to do. In addition, you shall know how far it has got on; the wings have been painted in stone colours on the outside, but they are not yet varnished; inside they are wholly underpainted, so that [the assistants] can begin to carry them out.*

The middle panel I have outlined with the greatest care and at cost of much time; it is also coated with two very good colours upon which I can begin to underpaint it. For I intend, so soon as I hear you approve, to underpaint it some four, five, or six times over, for clearness and durability's sake, also to use the very best ultramarine for the painting that I can get. And no one shall paint a stroke on it except myself, wherefore I shall spend much time on it. I therefore assume that you will not mind, and have decided to write you my proposed plan of work [but I must add] that I cannot without loss carry out said work [in such elaborate fashion] for the fee of 130 Rhenish florins; for I must spend such money and lose time over it. However, what I have promised you I will honourably perform: if you don't want the picture to cost more than the price agreed, I will paint it in such a way that it will still be worth much more than you paid for it. If, however, you will give me 200 florins I will follow out my plan of work. Though if hereafter somebody was to offer me 400 florins I would not paint another, for I shall not gain a penny over it, as a long time is spent on it. So let me know your intention, and when I have heard it I will go to the Imhofs† for 50 florins, for I have as yet received no money on the work.

Now I commend myself to you. I want you also to know that in all my days I have never begun any work that pleased me better than this picture of yours which I am painting. Till I finish it I will not do any other work; I am only sorry that the winter will so soon come upon us. The days grow so short that one cannot do much.

I have still one thing to ask you; it is about the Madonna that you

* The letter refers to the 'Assumption of the Virgin' ordered by Heller for the altar of St Thomas in the Dominican Church in Frankfurt am Main. It was removed to Munich and destroyed by fire in 1729.

† The great Nürnberg banking house.

saw in my house; if you know of any one near you who wants a picture pray offer it to him. If a proper frame were put to it, it would be a beautiful picture, and you know that it is neatly done. If I had to paint it for someone,* I would not take less than 50 florins. I will let you have it cheap. But as it is already done it might be damaged in the house. So I would give you full power to sell it for me cheap for 30 florins, indeed rather than that it should not be sold I would even let it go for 25 florins. I have certainly lost much food over it.

Many good nights. Given at Nürnberg on Bartholomew's day 1508.

• • •

Albrecht Dürer to Jacob Heller.

26 August 1509 Nürnberg.

German.

First my willing service to you, dear Herr Jacob Heller. In accordance with your last letter, I am sending the picture well packed and seen to in all needful points. I have handed it over to Hans Imhof and he has paid me another 100 florins. Yet believe me, on my honour, I am still losing my own money over it besides losing the time which I have bestowed upon it. Here in Nürnberg they were ready to pay 300 florins for it, which extra 100 florins would have done nicely for me had I not sent [the picture] in order to please and serve you. For I value keeping your friendship at more than 100 florins, I would also rather have this painting at Frankfurt† than anywhere else in all Germany.

If you think that I have behaved unfairly in not leaving the payment to your own free will, you must bear in mind that this would not have happened if you had not written by Hans Imhof that I might keep the picture as long as I liked. I should otherwise gladly have left it to you even if thereby I had suffered a greater loss still. But I have confidence in you that, supposing I had promised to make you something for about 10 florins and it cost me 20, you yourself would not wish me to lose by it. So pray be content with the fact that I took 100 florins less from you than I might have got for the picture - for I tell you that they wanted to take it from me, so to speak, by force.

I have painted it with great care, as you will see, using none but the best colours I could get. It is painted with good ultramarine under,

* i.e., to order.

† One of the largest fairs, in Europe.

I have painted it with great care, as you will see, using none but the best colours I could get. It is painted with good ultramarine under, and over, and over that again, some five or six times; and then after it was finished I painted it again twice over so that it may last a long time. Since you will keep it clean I know it will remain bright and fresh 500 years, for it is not done as men are wont to paint. So have it kept clean and don't let it be touched or sprinkled with holy water. I feel sure it will not be criticized, or only for the purpose of annoying me; and I believe it will please you well.

No one shall ever compel me to paint a picture again with so much labour. Herr Georg Tausy besought me of his own accord to paint him a Madonna in a landscape with the same care and of the same size as this picture, and he would give me 400 florins for it. That I flatly refused to do, for it would have made a beggar of me. Of ordinary pictures I will in a year paint a pile which no one would believe it possible for one man to do in the time. But painstaking drudgery does not get along so speedily. So henceforth I shall stick to my engraving, and had I done so before I should today have been a richer man by 1000 florins.

I may tell you also that, at my own expense, I have had for the middle panel a new frame made which has cost me more than 6 florins The old one I have broken off, for the joiner had made it crudely; but I have not had it gilded, for you would not have it. It would be a very good thing to have the bands unscrewed so that the picture may not crack.

If the picture is set up, let it be made to hang forward two or three finger breadths, for then it will be well visible, on account of the glare. And when I come over to you, say in one, or two, or three years' time, the picture must be taken down [to see] whether it has dried out, and then I would varnish it over anew with a special varnish, which no one else can make; it will then last another 100 years longer than it would before. But don't let anybody else varnish it, for all other varnishes are yellow, and the picture would be ruined for you. And if a thing, on which I have spent more than a year's work, were ruined it would be grief to me. And when you unpack it, be present yourself lest it be damaged. Deal carefully with it, for you will hear from your own and from foreign painters how it is done.

Give my greeting to your painter Martin Hess. My wife asks you for a *Trinkgeld*, but that is as you please, I screw you no higher. And now I hold myself commended to you. Read by the sense, for I write in haste. Given at Nümberg on Sunday after Bartholomew's 1509.

DOCTORS AND MEDICINE

An individual's experience of sickness during the Middle Ages, like so many things, depended on luck, location and birth. A minority turned to trained physicians whilst most turned to the nearest available source of relief.

Professional physicians obtained their education and elevated status by studying at universities with medical faculties such as Montpelier, Paris and Bologna or at medical schools, the most famous being Salerno. At the end of the twelfth century Gerard of Cremona translated the writings of Hippocrates and Galen as well as many Arabic medical texts, into Latin, and these remained the standard sources for students. Emphasis was placed on theory with very little practical training.

Only the wealthy and influential could afford the services of professional doctors with their superior knowledge, ethics and large fees; the vast majority had to depend on the local clergy or barber-surgeons who performed services such as bloodletting and dental surgery. Surgeons formed guilds since their occupation was considered a craft, and they provided a service for those requiring more complicated treatment than the barbers could offer. In medieval manuscripts gory illustrations can be found depicting these surgeons at work and with the lack of modern anaesthetics (although opium was used) and anatomical knowledge it must have been a desperate soul who placed himself in their hands. Many surgeons, particularly in Italy and France were well acquainted with medical treatises despite their inferior status.

Common sense, superstition, herbal remedies from apothecaries as well as astrology and omens all contributed to the ordinary man or woman's experience of ill-health. Neither professionals nor quacks had much effect in the face of widespread malnutrition and diseases of epidemic proportions such as bubonic plague, tuberculosis, smallpox and sweating sickness. The most effective solution was prevention; royalty, merchants and other mobile sectors of the population avoided areas known to be suffering an outbreak of disease. Quarantine and the isolation of those suffering from communicable diseases developed with the spread of the most outwardly obvious form, leprosy.

Hospitals during the medieval period were multi-functional,

caring for the poor and elderly, lodging travellers and harbouring the destitute, the care of the sick being generally combined with all these activities. Monasteries provided infirmaries for the use of the sick, but as their name implies they were initially built to house elderly monks no longer able to cope with the demands of normal monastic life.

Most infirmaries were isolated from the other buildings and were sometimes totally self-contained. At Fountains Abbey the infirmary had its own chapel, kitchens and cellar.

Most hospitals were in towns and cities. The Hospital of St. Giles in London was founded to house forty lepers, in 1117 by Matilda, Queen of Henry I, who provided an allowance each year for every leper. The hospital grew in importance until the dissolution of the monasteries under Henry VIII.

The Bishop of Winchester, Henry de Blois, founded the hospital of St. Cross in 1133-36, this was sponsored by the Knights Hospitaller whose order had developed near a hospice for sick pilgrims in Jerusalem in the eleventh century, however St. Cross mainly acted as an almshouse.

• • • • •

Siena and Beaune were two important European hospitals, the former established its reputation as a shelter for pilgrims but was enlarged due to generous donations, the latter was founded by a private charity and during the fifteenth century enjoyed the patronage of the Burgundian Court.

The following letters illustrate differing several aspects of sickness and medicine during the Middle Ages and highlight the contrasts examined above.

• • •

From Bernard of Clairvaux to the brethren of St Anastasius.

Before 1153.

Latin.

To his very dear sons in Christ, the brethren of St Anastasius, greetings and prayers from Brother Bernard, styled Abbot of Clairvaux.

Heaven is my witness how greatly I love you all in Jesus Christ, and how great would be my desire to see you were such a thing possible, not only on your own account but also my own. It would be an enormous joy and comfort for me to embrace you, my sons, my joy, and my crown.

This is not yet possible for me, but I firmly trust in God's mercy that the day will come when I shall be able to see you, and then my heart will be glad and my gladness no man shall take from me. In the meantime it is certainly a great joy and consolation for me to hear of you from my dear brother-abbot, Bernard. I congratulate you on the satisfaction you have given him by your discipline and zeal in the matter of obedience and poverty; without doubt your reward for this will be great in heaven. I beg and implore you, dearest brothers, so to act, so to stand firm in the Lord, as to be always careful for the observance of the Order that the Order may always be careful for you. Be eager always to preserve unity in the bonds of peace, having towards each other, but especially towards your superiors, the humble charity 'that is the bond that makes us perfect'. Seek humility before all things and peace above all things for the sake of the indwelling Spirit of God which rests only on the peaceful and humble.

But there is one thing your venerable abbot has asked me about which does not seem to me at all good. And I believe that I have the spirit of God and know the will of God in this matter. I fully realize that you live in an unhealthy region* and that many of you are sick, but remember him who said: 'I delight to boast of the weaknesses that humiliate me, so that the strength of Christ may enshrine itself in me', and 'When I am weakest then I am strongest of all'. I have the very greatest sympathy for bodily sickness, but I consider that sickness of the soul is much more to be feared and avoided. It is not at all in keeping with your profession to seek for bodily medicines, and they are not really conducive to health. The use of common herbs, such as are used by the poor, can sometimes be tolerated, and such is our custom. But to buy special kinds of medicines, to seek out doctors and swallow their nostrums, this does not become religious, is contrary to simplicity, and is especially inconsistent with the decency and simplicity of our Order. We know that 'those who live the life of nature cannot be acceptable to God' and for us who 'have received no spirit of worldly wisdom, but the spirit that comes from God' the proper medicine is humility and the most suitable prayer is 'purge me of my sin, the guilt which I freely acknowledge'. This is the health you must try to obtain, seek out, and preserve, dearest brothers, because 'vain is the help of man.'

• • • • •

* The Monastery of St. Anastasius was situated in the Campagna outside Rome. To within living memory this district had been riddled with malaria. St. Bernard's attitude towards medicine was probably wise in the state of medical knowledge at this time. Less wise was the selection of such an unhealthy region for a monastery.

In the following letter a chief justice of the Common Pleas recommends an army surgeon to the Bishop of Chichester, urging him to present a further recommendation to the king. Such surgeons were generally employed to dress wounds and could win great favour if they successfully cured a valued knight. A century later John Ardene, who had begun his career as an army surgeon, made his reputation in this manner. He became a distinguished physician and his writings on medicine and doctors' conduct convey a vivid picture of his profession during the fourteenth century.*

• • •

From Martin de Pateshull, chief justice of the Common Pleas to the Bishop of Chichester.

1222-30.

Latin.

'To the Reverend Father in Christ Ralph, by the grace of God Bishop of Chichester, his M. de Pateshull, greeting and due reverence.

Since, in the siege of castles, physicians are necessary, and especially they who know how to cure wounds. There comes to the army of our lord the king, by my advice, Master Thomas, the bearer of this, whom I have known to be skilful in such knowledge, and I entreat on his behalf, that if you please, you will be willing to consider him commended, and that you will make known his skill to those who shall need his assistance.

May your paternity fare well and long.

• • • • •

John, son of the Duke and Duchess of Brittany had married Beatrice, the second daughter of King Henry III of England in 1259/60. In this charming letter Beatrice's mother-in-law sends news to the King of his daughter's recovery from a fever and the favourable attributes of their mutual grandchild, Arthur, who was born in 1262 and later became Duke of Brittany after his father's death.

• • •

* See John Ardene, *Treatises of Fistual in Ano, haemorrhoids and Cystes* ed. D'Arcy Power, London, 1910, EETS, orig. ser., CXXXIX.

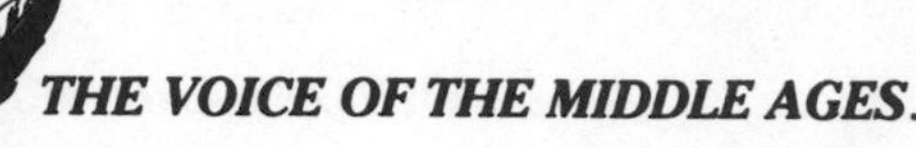

From Blanche, Duchess of Britanny, to Henry III.
1263-70.
Norman French.

To her very lofty and very dear lord Henry, by the grace of God King of England Lord of Ireland, and Duke of Aquitaine, Blanche, Duchess of Britanny, health and reverence, and herself prepared to do his will as to her dear lord.

Sir, I pray you, if you please, to send me word of your state, which our Lord by his grace make always good. For know, my dear lord, that I have very great joy every time that I can hear and know good news of you. Know, sir, that my lady Beatrice, your dear daughter and ours, is still ill with her fever, but she is much better, thank God, and the physicians tell us that her fever cannot last long. And I pray you, my dear lord, that if there is anything in our parts you will send to me for it, and command it as your own; for know, sir, that I have very great pleasure in doing your will to my power.

And know, sir, that Arthur is a very good child, and very pretty, thank God. Our Lord keep you.

• • • • •

Petrarch, the Italian scholar and poet whose ideas formed a basis for humanist thought in the fifteenth century which in turn provided a foundation for the renaissance, was sixty-one years old when he wrote this letter to his very good friend Boccaccio. Sixteen years earlier Petrarch had wounded his leg by tripping over a volume of Cicero's letters which he kept 'standing on my library floor, right next to the door in order to have it always at hand'.* It was of such a size because Petrarch had copied it in his own hand unaided. Petrarch had discovered Cicero's letters to Atticus in Verona in 1343 - they had stimulated his interest in letter collections as a literary genre in their own right and encouraged him to cultivate his own collection.

The damage to his leg this accident caused became infected and despite the efforts of doctors, failed to heal. Petrarch decided to 'banish the doctors and wait the outcome, whatever it might be, to entrust myself to God and nature, rather than to these sawbones trying out their nostrums on my illness.'† In his later years Petrarch had developed decisive views about the practice of medicine and leading

* Bishop, p. 170.
† op. cit. p. 215.

a healthy life, here Boccaccio receives a lengthy discussion on the subject.

A comparison with Ficino's letter is particularly interesting since their divergent opinions of doctors are reconciled by similar views on cures and the importance of nature.

As with law, medicine was a popular course of study during the medieval period since it frequently led to status and wealth, whereas the study of theology and arts usually did not. Aspects of Petrarch's character and wit as well as his love of classical learning are evident in this letter, and like so many which he wrote contain fundamental truths which are as applicable to the lives of men in the twentieth century as those in the fourteenth.

• • •

From Petrarch to Boccaccio.

10 December 1365.

Latin.

I am glad that you approve of my advice, and that you are putting it into practice. Approval is clearly genuine when it is turned into action, while many have learned to exalt in words what they condemn in their hearts. You wrote to me once - I forget when, but I remember the fact - that you had been seriously ill, but that thanks to God and a good doctor you had recovered. I replied (this I do remember) that I was astounded how that vulgar error had lodged in your high intelligence, and that God and your good constitution had done everything. I said that the doctor had done nothing at all, nor could he have done anything beyond the power of a longwinded bore, rich in banalities, poor in remedies. Now you write me that you didn't call in a doctor. I am not surprised that you got well so fast. There is no better way to health than to do without a physician. This may seem shocking to one who has had no experience; but to one who has been through it the words are obvious, tested, and true. Those doctors who profess to be aids to nature often go contrary to nature and fight on the side of disease. The least harmful of them hold to the middle ground and wait to see how the illness will turn out. They are the most truthful and trustworthy of their trade; they are spectators watching for the outcome, ready to jump with fortune. They unfurl their useless banners in honour of the victor, and creep in on the side of glory. Dear God! How many of them are like Metius Sufferius, how few like Tullus Hostilius!*

* Tullus Hostilius was the third legendary king of Rome.

Rome was long free from their monstrous kind, for Tullus Hostilius, in Rome's heyday, foresaw such pests and warned that they should be avoided. Cato, who well deserved the name of the Sage, gave similar counsel, which was disregarded, as is commonly the case. And a great army of doctors descended on our world. Would indeed that they were doctors, and not the army of medicine in the guise of doctors, equipped with their native ignorance under the name of science, and fortified with the folly and credulity of the sick, who are so beguiled by the desire of recovery that they regard one who makes the wildest promises as Apollo in person. Not that these charlatans would ever lack audacity and impudence (that sharp weapon of deceivers) and a look of assurance, being well trained by the art and practice of lying. Add to this their flaunting of costumes to which they have no right, gowns rich with purple, tricked out with various emblems, glittering rings and gilded spurs. Who would not be dazzled by such a sight, even if he were quite well? . . .

Don't you see how they gain control over you by their professional right, how they look for money from your illness, how they learn their trade from your death? They offer you a lethal draught, according to the prescriptions of some authorities of Cos, Pergamum, or Arabia, who may have been learned, but were completely ignorant of our constitutions. Then they sit back and await the result. And you, feeling the ominous poison circulate through your veins and vitals, hope for relief from one who does not recognize your ills, and is meanwhile tortured with his own, for which he can find no cure. One forbids you to eat fruits, another vegetables and greens, without which many, especially of our race, find meals unpalatable, however expensively medicated. It is hard to understand how our study of agriculture, our grafting of trees brought from afar avails if the fruits are to be denied to their planters and cultivators. Of course we have learned that some stocks are noxious, some plants poisonous. But who, I ask you, has ever planted such in his garden, unless perhaps to harm someone else? And who, discovering their invasion, has not in disgust rooted them out? And now this peremptory doctor calls fruits dangerous and abominable because he doesn't like them, or because they did him no particular good. And here is another doctor, perhaps himself bloodless and of low vitality, like so many of his kind, who counsels us never to let our blood but to preserve it as a treasure. But even at my age, if I didn't have an ample bleeding every spring and autumn, I should long since have felt myself oppressed by this Greek treasure. But these 'secretaries of nature,' who know everything, condemn in all what is outside of their own and their friends' experience, and thus they measure everything by themselves. Another doctor, no doubt a drinker of the strong wines of Greece, Crete, and Egypt, therefore uttered the famous condemnation: 'I have found water of no use, except in critical illness.' What a splendid pronouncement! I have made frequent and profitable use of water, and not in critical illnesses, which so far I have not experienced, and I hope I never do. But joking aside, and not to mention the thousands of mighty and healthy men who drink only water and find it healthful and delicious, I can allege my own case. If even in these winter nights I could not drink frequent draughts of cold water I think I should die . . .

Would you like to know how much confidence doctors place in their own devices? (I am speaking of those, few I admit, who retain their innate sense of shame.) I call God and my memory to witness, that I once heard a physician of high standing in his profession say. 'I am aware that I may be called ungrateful for disparaging the art that has brought me wealth and friends. But the truth is more important than one's feelings. Here is my sentiment and my contention. If a hundred men, or a thousand, of the same age and general constitution and accustomed to the same diet should all fall victim to a disease at the same time, and if half of them should follow the prescriptions of our contemporary doctors, and if the other half should be guided by their natural instinct and common sense, with no doctors at all, I have no doubt that the latter group would do better.'

I knew another doctor, rather better known and a man of letters as well. One day in familiar conversation I asked him how it happened that he partook of foods that he forbade to others. He answered placidly, without hesitation: 'If a doctor's life were consistent with his advice, or if his advice were consistent with his life, he would suffer either in his health or in his pocketbook.' This remark is clearly not a confession of ignorance but of untrustworthiness. That is obvious enough.

How may men be saved amid these pestilent creatures? If the well man is in danger, what may the sick man hope for but the end of all his dangers? Certainly no one need wonder if one who harms the hale kills the sickly. It is not easy to pull up a well-rooted tree, but when once it is dislodged one may easily throw it down.

I talked recently with another doctor, a celebrated man, and well versed in many arts besides his own, and a very good friend of mine. I asked him why he did not practice medicine, as do so many who are much inferior to him. He put on a sad and serious look, inspiring sympathy and confidence in his judgement. He said: 'As God watches human affairs, I am afraid of committing an impiety, amounting to a capital sin, by cheating the credulous public. If people knew, as I do, how little, if at all, the doctor helps the patient, how indeed he often does the patient a disservice, the company of physicians would be much smaller and much less bemedaled. Let them act in any way their cynicism and the credulity of their patients may permit; let them abuse the simplicity of the mob; let them promise life, and kill, and make money. But I have no intention of cheating and slaying; I don't want to get richer by doing any man harm. That is why I have shifted to other arts, which can be more innocently practiced.' . . .

I have had many medical friends in the past, but of them all only four remain: one in Venice, one in Milan, and two in Padua. They are all cultivated and courtly men, who talk extremely well, argue with great keenness, harangue either with vehemence or with sweet persuasion; in short, they kill most plausibly, with the most convincing explanations. They have forever on the tip of their tongues Aristotle and Cicero and Seneca, also - this will surprise you - Virgil. Whether it is due to chance or madness or some mental quirk, they know all subjects better than the one trade they profess. But I shall drop this theme. My statement of home truths stirred up too much resentment and hurly-burly in the past. If ever my health is attacked, I shall admit these gentlemen as friends but not as doctors. As one who delights in friendship, I think that for the preservation and restoration of health nothing can match the pleasant faces and pleasant talk of good friends. If they lay any commands on me that fit my own ideas, I obey them and give them the credit; otherwise I just listen, and do what I had intended all along. And I have ordered my attendants that if anything serious should happen to me none at all of the gentlemen's orders shall be executed upon my body, but nature shall be allowed to operate, or rather God who created me and set the term to my life which cannot be overpassed...

• • • • •

From Petrarch to Giovanni Colonna, Minorite Friar and uncle of Cardinal Giovanni and Bishop Giacomo Colonna.

Year uncertain.

Latin.

I am going to tell you an old wives' tale, but fitting the case, as Horace says. A Spider on her travels once happened to meet the Gout. 'Whither away,' she said, 'looking so sad?'

'Well,' said the Gout, 'I had landed on a shaggy peasant. He tortured me with hunger and constant toil. He kept from morning to night out among the clods and boulders. Then we would return wretchedly late at night to his dusty, squalid home, always under a heavy load, never with footgear whole. To the unhappy day succeeded a no happier night. He would treat me to a dismal meal: old hunks of moldy, stony bread, garlic and tough vegetables, washed down with vinegar and muddy water. It was a Saturnalian feast when a bit of Sardinian cheese arrived. After this reception he laid me on a rustic couch harder than his own clods. Rising again at dawn, he returned to the fields and to his hateful tasks. Thus one day followed another with no rest and no hope of it. For on holidays he either washed his master's sheep or cleared out the stream bed or constructed a hedge for the meadowland. Thus, sick of my endless troubles and such an uncomfortable home, I took flight'

The Spider, on hearing this, exclaimed: 'Alas, how different is my situation! My host was effeminate, inert; for him pleasure was not merely the highest good, it was the only good. He rarely set foot outside the house; he prolonged dinner till evening, supper till dawn. The rest of the time he spent wooing sleep on a purple couch. What time remained from his luxurious banquets was given to repose. His life was spent among exquisite foods, peculiar perfumes, imported wines, gold dishes, jeweled goblets silk wall-handings, purple rugs; and withal a solicitous swarm of domestics bustling about. No part of the house was neglected, no corner overlooked. While the floor was swept with brooms and the paneled ceilings were dusted, I was hardly ever able to weave the webs of my craft; and, what is saddest, if I did begin them I found at their first appearance my hopes dashed, my labours mocked. I was harried and thrown out headforemost; I sought for nooks and crannies; there were none. A solid, snowy, marble wall left no hiding place for my despair. So I fled from my persecutor, preferring a quiet exile anywhere to endless domestic labours.'

The other replied: "Alas, how many good things are lost through ignorance or neglect! Ignorance is the mind's blindness, negligence is the spirit's torpor. We should open our eyes, and not fail to seize our opportunities. Look here; according to your words and mine, everything will go well if we exchange our dwellings. Your host will suit me perfectly, as mine will you.' This seemed a good idea, and they changed their quarters. Thus is came about that the Gout dwells amid luxuries and in the palaces of the rich, and the Spider in the slovenly hovels of the poor.

I hear, my friend, that the gout has inveigled herself into your home, and I am surprised. I did not thing there was a place for her in so sober a household. I am afraid she may have found something there to her liking. If that is so, I shudder not so much at the evil as at the cause of the evil. I would rather that your had the spider as your guest. You must resist gout's beginnings' the best way is by vigils, toil, and fasting. When I was a boy I knew a youth with the gout; I saw him in maturity free from it. I asked the reason; he replied only that he had entirely abstained from wine. Cicero reports, and others after him, that certain rich men, crippled by gout, regained their health when they fell into poverty. I don't dare order you to be poor; thought, if you are sensible, you don't need any orders. I hear that you have deliberately taken the vow of poverty, I fear that you may be treasuring up not gold but, in the Apostle's words 'wrath against the day of wrath'. Think about this, for you well remember the pact you made with Christ. If you have forgotten, reread the words written on your bond; you will find what you promised to him, what he to you. I say that I don't order you to be poor, not because good advice is improper for me as giver, for you as hearer, but because I dislike pouring forth vain words. For I see that the very name of poverty is horrid and repulsive to you; but now, since you have embraced it, you can't lightly lay it aside. I give you at least this advice, to live as if you were poor; that is what philosophers call frugality, or voluntary poverty. Let me persuade you of this and point out the one way to bodily health. I am another Hippocrates to you; I offer you a perhaps bitter but health-giving medicine. If you want to be healthy, live as if you were poor. Gold hidden in your strongbox harms only your soul; dainty foods harm both soul and body. So if you want to repel the gout, repel all delicacies; and if you want to repel all evils, repel riches. And so farewell.

•••••

Professional doctors were particularly fortunate if they were employed by the court, in return for their skill they enjoyed many privileges. In the following letter King Henry V requests that the next vacant benefice be given to the Queen's physician. Catherine of Valois was pregnant with the future King Henry VI at this time. She died at the early age of thirty-five.

•••

From King Henry V to the Bishop of Durham.

29 October 1421.

English.

By the King to the honoured in God our most trusty and well-beloved the Bishop of Durham, our Chancellor of England.

Honoured father in God, and our most trusty and well-beloved.

As we understand from the letters you have sent us that our wife the Queen has spoken to you, and would like her physician to be granted a sinecure in our giving, of which matter you wish to know our pleasure, we confirm to you that it is our intention that when any such benefice in our giving becomes vacant, you make it over to him, and then notify us what he has been given.

Given under our signet with our army at Meaulx the twenty-ninth day of October.

Chivyngham.

• • • • •

There were several hospitals and houses attached to churches, outside the walls of the city of London, which cared for lepers, and their names can be found in contemporary wills bequeathing gifts to the lepers and those who tended them. The porters of the City gates were ordered to refuse entry to anybody with the disease, hence the establishment of leper-houses in the outskirts.

The fate of this seventeen-year-old chorister who had succumbed to leprosy was probably better than many others afflicted with the disease. The Queen's letter almost certainly assured him of a home at St Giles where he would not have to resort to begging or suffer constant rejection.

• • •

From Queen Margaret of Anjou to the Master* of St Giles in the Fields beside the City of London.

Before 1447.

French.

By the Queen to the Master of St Giles-in-the-Field near the city of London.

Trusty etc.

Because we have been informed that one Thomas Uphome, aged seventeen, formerly chorister to the most reverend father in God our blessed uncle the Cardinal (whom God pardon) in his College at Winchester, has now by the visitation of God become a leper, we therefore wish and ask of you, seeing it is said that he has no other income or livelyhood to live by, but only the alms of Christian people, that, in reverence to our blessed Creator, you will accept and receive him into your hospital of St Giles, with such maintenance and livelyhood

* Probably Cardinal Beaufort, Bishop of Winchester 1404-47.

as is usual to give the other people there in the same condition, as we trust you. In this you will not only be doing a most meritorious deed, pleasing to God, but will also deserve our most special thanks.

• • • • •

Thomas Betson writes to Elizabeth Stonor, soon to be his mother-in-law (see earlier letters) expressing concern for her husband, Thomas's business partner, who 'had bene verry seeke'. Betson urges Elizabeth to raise her husband's spirits and to stop him worrying since fretting would only cause more harm. His sincerity and the spontaneity of his regards convey the character of the man, 'for honest charm he has no rival save the attractive Margery Brews, who married John Paston the younger, and shows up so pleasantly beside the hard Paston women.'*

• • •

From Thomas Betson to Dame Elizabeth Stonor.

18 June 1478.

English.

Let this be delivered to my sole and most honoured good lady, Dame Elizabeth Stonor, at Stonor.

Most honourable and my only good lady, I send your good ladyship my regards as humbly as I know how, always wishing to hear from you and know that you are doing well, and I pray to Almighty Jesus to preserve you, and please him to give you your heart's desire.

Moreover may your ladyship be pleased to know that I came to London today, and on my return home I was told that my master your husband had been very ill, which I know cannot have been to your pleasure, or to that of your household; and I am truly sorry for it. Nevertheless, I understand from various people that his mastership it fully healed and recovered, for whch I am really glad. And I pray to Almighty Jesus to send him the best of health, as I would like for myself, and for your ladyship also. And I would like you to tell if I can do anything here which will please him and yourself, when it will be done without fail. I certainly take no pleasure in your pain.

Nevertheless your ladyship must make him happy and cheerful,

* Power, p. 117.

and to discard all morbid fancies and unprofitable thoughts, that never bring any good, but only harm. A man can hurt himself by such undisciplined things, and it's best to be careful. Dear lady, I beseech you to be cheerful, and I pray to God to comfort you and send you the best of health. I also ask you to remember Cousin Katherine. I hope she has been doing well, God knows, and I reckon, as you would know, that if I had found her here at home my pleasure would have been all the greater: but I thank God for everything, though my pain is all the more. But I must suffer as I have suffered before, and I will bear it for God's sake and for hers. I send my master a dozen quails to eat. I pray God they may do him good in God's eyes, and all who eat them. I can send no delicacies for your ladyship - I have only just got home. May our blessed lord preserve you good ladyship in virtue forever. Amen.

At London on the eighteenth day of June.

Your servant, T. Betson.

P.S. My lady, Goodard Oxbryge* asks favour of your ladyship, and that you would be kind enough to approach my master your husband for his money. He asked me to write for it, and it would be a good thing if it were paid for various reasons: a cousin of his would have to pay those he owes. And may our blessed lord be with you, ever and forever, Amen.

• • • • •

John Paston, who had been knighted in 1487, asks his wife to send a remedy for the Attorney General's aching knee. Women were expected to have some knowledge of medicines and Margery was probably flattered that her skills had been requested for such an eminent individual.

James Hobart was appointed Attorney General in 1486, and so continued during his life; he was a man of great learning and wisdom, and died full of riches and honour in 1509-10 (F).

• • •

From Sir John Paston to Dame Margaret Paston.

After 1486.

English.

* Betson's assistant

To Dame Margaret Paston, at Oxnead.

Mistress Margery, I recommed me to you, and I pray you in all haste possible to send me, by the next sure messenger that ye can get, a large plaster of your *Flos Unguentorum* for the King's Attorney James Hobart; for all his disease is but an ache in his knee; he is the man that brought you and me together, and I had lever than £40. ye could with your plaster depart him and his pain. But when ye send me the plaster, ye must send me writing, how it should be laid to and taken from his knee; and how long it should abide on his knee unremoved; and how long the plaster will last good; and whether he must lap any more cloths about the plaster to keep it warm or not; and God be with you.

Your John Paston.

• • • • •

Marsilio Ficino embodied the renaissance ideals of a complete man. As well as a philosopher, scholar, musician and priest, he was also a doctor. He had studied medicine at Bologna, a university famous for the study of civil and Canon law, which had formed faculties of medicine and philosophy in about 1200.

Ficino writes of the nobility of medicine arguing that a healthy body is needed to live a good life and that medicine can prolong this as long as it does not interfere in the course of nature, and doctors remember that they are the servants of God, the creator of health. He goes on to discuss Plato's view on the subject, which included the importance of exercise, diet and the dangers of an excessive use of drugs.

Ficino's father had been the Medici family's physician and Ficino inherited this position, never accepting a fee in the tradition of the great Greek physician Hippocrates. He was also an accomplished player of the lyre, and a bust in Florence Cathedral depicts him holding his translation of Plato in the manner of a lyre.

• • •

From Marsilio Ficino to Tommaso Valeri, an outstanding physician.

Before 1499.

Latin.

The nobility, usefulness and practice of medicine.

I have read in Homer that one man of medicine is worth a host of other men, and justly so; for the sacred writing of the Hebrews teach that the power of healing is the gift of God, rather than an invention of men. Let us honour the man of medicine because the Almighty created him of necessity. Furthermore, the Gentiles regard the masters of this art as gods. They bestowed divine honours upon Isis, Apollo and Aesculapius, and also upon outstanding doctors. For they dedicated temples to Chiron, Machaon, Podalirius, Hippocrates and Hermagoras. Hippocrates confirms this in his letter to the Abderites, when he says that medicine is a gift of the gods, that it is free and that he has never accepted a reward for practising it. Also in a letter to Philemon he says that medicine is related to prophecy, because our ancestor Apollo is the father of both arts; he foretells future illness as well as curing those already ill. Hence Pythagoras, Empedocles and Apollonius of Tyana are said to have cured diseases with chants rather than with herbs.

The Magi thought that the mind of the sick should first be cleansed with sacred teachings and prayers before they attended to the body. For clearly such an art as this has been received and is practised through divine grace, because the soul is dependent on God, and the body on the soul. Do not the Hebrews consider that the Archangel Raphael practised this art? Quite apart from other doctors, Christ Himself used to cure all the sick and ailing who were brought to Him, as though He were the doctor of mankind, and He entrusted the power of healing to His disciples. So it is that kings have never scorned to study and practise this most noble art, such as Sapor and Ginges, Kings of the Medes, Sabid, King of the Arabs, Mithridates, King of the Persians, Hermes, King of the Egyptians, and Mesues, nephew of the King of Damascus. Some believe that Avicenna was the Prince of Cordova. Such famous philosophers as Democritus, Timaeus of Locris, Plato, Aristotle and countless others of note have written about this art.

This letter has said almost as much as a letter can about the nobility of medicine. We can see how useful it is, from the fact that the arts which are directed towards the good life seem to be of little benefit without its assistance. We cannot live well if we are not alive! In this short span of life, little can be achieved in any skill without good health; and we cannot easily attain great merit among men or with God unless we live a long and temperate life. The careful application of medicine gives every opportunity to lead such a life. But in the practice of this art there must be the utmost devotion to God, and charity towards men, as Luke the Evangelist and the divine physicians Cosmus and Damian have taught us by their example. For God is the source of all good and so the true doctor is like a god amongst men. He restores them from death to life and so he is worshipped as God, even by kings and wise men when they are ill.

All agree that a doctor needs a keen mind, knowledge and experience. It is clear that his consideration needs to be profound and full of care. But, as Hippocrates says to the Abderites, when a case has been properly considered, delay may be more harmful in this art than in any other. However, in Galen's words to Glaucon, it is even more dangerous to anticipate and interfere with the course of nature. For he says that many lives are lost daily as a result of this error, that is to say, the presumption of doctors who either hinder or hasten nature. The man who does not rely solely on his own skill is less likely to fall into such an error. Hippocrates writes to Democritus that even though he is now very old he has not yet reached the final aim of medicine. Galen also says that it was not until he was ninety that he finally grasped the nature of the pulse. Above all the doctor should remember that the creator of health is God, that nature is God's instrument for establishing or maintaining health, and that the doctor is the servant of both. So he does not provide the strength, but prepares the ground and removes obstacles for the master craftsman. If he rashly wants to change or check the physical condition he often does both badly, and impedes nature which would do both well.

But let us listen to our divine Plato, as he speaks with the authority of the Pythagoreans on this subject in *Timaeus*. In truth the best of all movements is that which arises naturally by itself, as it is most akin to the motion of the mind and of the universe. Movement caused by an outside agency is of a lower order, but the lowest movement of all is when parts of the body are moved by outside agencies, while the body as a whole is at rest. So, of all the ways of cleansing and regulating the body, exercise is the most healthy. Next is the gentle motion of being carried in a ship or some other form of transport. The third sort of movement is only useful under the compulsion of extreme necessity. In no other circumstances should a man of sound mind undertake it, namely the remedy of doctors who are in the habit of using drugs as laxative medicines. Diseases, unless they are very dangerous, should not be irritated by drugs. For the whole constitution of diseases is rather like the nature of living beings. In fact the structure of living beings is bounded from the very beginning of their own generation by a set length of time. The whole genus is subject to this, and each being contains within itself its allotted life span from its birth, unless unavoidable events intervene. For the triangles, that is to say the proportional qualities, from the very beginning hold the life force of every one, and hold together for the purpose of life up to a certain time. Life is not prolonged for any one beyond this fixed time. The same rule of nature applies to diseases. If anyone tries to shorten them by drugs before they have run their allotted course of time, illnesses which were minor or rare usually become serious or widespread.

Therefore diseases should be treated and controlled by attending to diet in so far as each person has leisure for this, lest a difficult and dangerous disease be aggravated by drugs. So says Plato. The Florentine people often commend our Galileo because he observes this rule. For this reason I, too, am full of praise for Lorenzo Martellini, a true doctor, and would also praise Tommaso Valeri - except that I am writing to him!

Farewell, and send my greetings to Antonio Benivieni, the skilled physician. Girolamo Amazzi, our delightful companion in the study of medicine and the lyre, sends his to you.

Once more farewell.

DEATH

Medieval men and women considered life to be a brief interlude in their progress towards eternal life in the kingdom of God. Death was one stage in this inevitable process and life was spent preparing for it; a simultaneous hope of heaven and terror of hell. Death was common, public and generally unpleasant; and opinions as to what happened after this gruelling event were generally unanimous.

Good souls were gently lifted by angels directly into heaven whereas sinful souls were dragged down to hell by demons. Perhaps to medieval people it was their only understanding of equality, the rich and powerful who had enjoyed the material benefits of mortal life were just as likely, if not more so, to suffer hell for their sins of pride and avarice, whereas the humble man's simple good deeds could secure him a place in paradise. Petrarch's letter illustrates this view: Petrarch's steward is at last allowed to rest and to bask in God's favour after his weary lifetime of labour in the fields.

Souls were believed to be weighed, good deeds balancing against bad deeds, but Purgatory, although an indescribably painful experience, offered a hope of eternal salvation for the mass of humanity which was neither perfectly good nor totally bad. Time in Purgatory could be decreased by penance on earth and the acquisition of indulgences which were the rewards for participating in pilgrimages and crusades but which could also be bought. As the concept of Purgatory came to be widely accepted the importance of prayers for the deceased increased. Wills stipulated that prayers were to be said regularly, especially on the anniversary of death, and funds were left for this purpose. The wealthy endowed special chantries for this purpose and we see how Henry III felt that by placing his father's body in the monastery he founded during his lifetime, 'the devotion of the brethren would be more frequently and abundantly aroused to pray for him their common lord, and profit as we believe no less his aforesaid salvation.'

The place of burial was also of great importance as this letter and others make clear, particularly to be on home territory. Sometimes the flesh and bones of a body were buried separately, or certain organs such as the heart, which could be placed in specially designed boxes and moved to a fitting location. The tombs of royalty, members of the nobility and the rich were fashioned with care, reflecting their great and worthy deeds and suitability for heaven. Funeral masses and processions were solemn public events contributing to the medieval love of spectacle as well as acting as yet another reminder of what was coming to all men. The Black Prince who died in 1376 left precise instructions in his will for the performance of his own funeral procession through Canterbury, it was a spectacular display of knightly prowess, featuring heraldic banners and the carrying aloft of the prince's personal armour. The deaths of ordinary people were far from glorious.

• • • • •

The Cistercian abbey of Beaulieu had been founded by King John in 1204.

Since 1200, the king had been using questionable methods in an attempt to impose taxation on the Cistercians in England, and a legend grew up that, shortly before his foundation of Beaulieu, he dreamed that he was being flogged by Cistercian abbots, and as a result repented and decided to found Beaulieu as a penance. *

When King John died in October 1216 at the Bishop of Lincoln's castle at Newark, he was known to have requested that his body be laid to rest within the cathedral church at Worcester and his wish was fulfilled. The following letter, written by his son King Henry III, appears to refute this and makes reference to King John's earlier intention to be buried at Beaulieu. Nonetheless, Pope Honorius III either refused Henry's plea or died before he received it because King John's body remained at Worcester.

• • •

From King Henry III to Pope Honorius III.

1266.

Latin.

Be it known to your holiness that John sometime King of England, our father, of serene memory, founded the house of Beaulieu, as is known to many in England; therefore in the same house he chose his burying place after the common death, and as it is said he solemnly vowed this; but afterwards, in the time of the disturbance of England, a very serious

* Lionel Butler and Chris Given-Wilson, *Medieval Monasteries of Great Britain* pp. 149-151.

strife having arisen between him and his barons, he died in remote parts, so that his body could not be brought to the said house, but the bishop and monks of Worcester, by the grace of hospitality, put the royal clod in their monastery. Since it seems likely, that if in his own house which he founded he could lie buried in his corporal presence, as he also himself disposed in his lifetime, the devotion of the brethren would be more frequently and more abundantly aroused to pray for him their common lord, and profit as we believe no less his aforesaid salvation. It might be very pleasing to you therefore that his vow might be fulfilled on this part, since we are bound to procure his salvation with the Lord in everything that we can. Wherefore also we beg your holiness that you deign to receive the petition of us and the brethren of Beaulieu aforesaid, which by the bearer of these presents they send to the feet of your holiness, for the bringing back of the body of the aforesaid King and our father, if it please you indulgently.

• • • • •

Dante writes to Guido and Oberto, Counts of Romena condoling them on the death of their uncle, Count Alessandro of Romena, chief of the Ghibellines of Arezzo. At this time Dante had been banished from Florence for two years, initially he had been determined to lend his support to other exiles but he became increasingly disillusioned and finally disassociated himself from them continuing to believe in reconciliation rather than force as a means of bringing an end to his exile.

• • •

From Dante Alighieri to the Counts Oberto and Guido da Romena, after the death of their uncle.

1304.

Latin.

Your uncle, the illustrious Count Alessandro, who in these last days returned, after the spirit, to the heavenly fatherland whence he came, was my Lord and his memory will have dominion over me so long as my life shall last in this world; for his nobility of soul, which now is richly recompensed with meet rewards beyond the stars, for long years past, as he willed, made me his servant. And verily this quality, accompanied as it was in him by all the other virtues, caused his name to stand out, as it were in bronze, above the fame of other Italians. And what else did his heroic escutcheon proclaim, but that 'we display the scourge that drives away vice'? for as his outward blazon he bore silver scourges on a purple field, and inwardly a mind repellent of vice in its love of virtue. Lament, therefore, lament, thou noblest of the houses of Tuscany, that shone with the light of so great a man! Lament, all ye his friends and servants whose hope death hath so cruelly stricken; and among the last, woe is me! must I too lament, who, driven from my country, in undeserved exile, was wont, as I brooded over my unhappy fate with unceasing anxiety, to console myself with the hope which I rested in him.

But although the bitterness of grief weigh upon us for the loss of corporeal things, yet, when we consider the intellectual things which remain, surely before the eyes of the mind must arise the light of sweet consolation. For he, by whom virtue was honoured on earth, is now held in honour of the Virtues in heaven; and he who was a Palatine of the Court of Rome in Tuscany now glories as a chosen courtier with the princes of the Blest in the everlasting palace of the Jerusalem which is above. Wherefore, my beloved Lords, with humble exhortation I beseech you to grieve not overmuch, and to put behind you bodily concerns, save in so far as they may serve you for examples; and as he himself, a most just man, appointed you to be the heirs of his possessions, so do you, as those nearest to him, clothe yourselves with his most excellent qualities.

But I must add a word on my own behalf, in appeal to your judgement, to excuse myself, as your servant, for my absence from the mournful ceremony; for it was neither neglect nore ingratitude which kept me away, but the unlooked-for poverty brought about by exile. Poverty, like a vindictive fury, has thrust me, deprived of horses and arms, into her prison den, where she has set herself relentlessly to keep me in durance; and though I struggle with all my strength to get free, she has hitherto prevailed against me.

• • • • •

The Black Death first arrived in Sicily in 1347. During the following years it rapidly spread throughout Europe causing a reduction in the total population of about one third. Many considered the plague to be mankind's punishment from God and Petrarch's letter describes its devastating effects. As T.S.R. Boase has written,

Beyond wars and violence, plague had always been the most dread adversary, but the Black Death of the 14th century had been unprecedented in the scale of mortality and an inescapable warning of how speedily men might be called to their account. *

* T.S.R. Boase, 'Mortality, Judgement and Rememberance' in *The Flowering of the Middle Ages* ed. Joan Evans, 1966. Also see Bishop, *Petrarch and His World* Chapter XXI, 'The Black Death', pp. 269-275.

Petrarch's letter conveys the grief of personal loss which many men and women must have experienced along with the all-embracing economic and social consequences of the plague.

• • •

From Petrarch to 'Socrates'.

May or June 1349.

Latin.

Oh, brother, brother, brother! (That may seem a new way to begin a letter, but in fact it's very ancient; it was used by Cicero nearly fourteen hundred years ago.) Alas, my loving brother, what shall I say? How can I begin? Where shall I turn? Everywhere is woe, terror everywhere. You may see in me what you have read in Virgil of the great city, with 'everywhere tearing pain, everywhere fear and the manifold images of death'. Oh, brother, would that I had never been born or that I had already met my death! And if that is my present wish, what, think you, shall I say if I shall reach extreme old age? How I hope I do not! But if it comes, I fear not a longer life, but a long death . . .

[He continues his lamentations at length.]

I think that my complaints will be excused, if one reflects that I am not mourning some slight distress but that dreadful year 1348, which not merely robbed us of our friends, but robbed the whole world of its peoples. And if that were not enough, now this following year reaps the remainder, and cuts down with its deadly scythe whatever survived that storm. Will posterity credit that there was a time when, with no deluge from heaven, no worldwide conflagration, no wars or other visible devastation, not merely this or that territory but almost the whole earth was depopulated? When was such a disaster ever seen, ever heard of? In what records can we read that houses were emptied, cities abandoned, countrysides untilled, fields heaped with corpses, and a vast, dreadful solitude over all the world? Consult the historians; they are silent. Interrogate the physicists; they are dumfounded. Ask the philosophers; they shrug their shoulders, they wrinkle their brows; finger to lip, they command silence. Posterity, will you believe what we who lived through it can hardly accept? We should think we were dreaming, had we not the testimony of our opened eyes, encountering on our city walks only funerals, and on our return finding our home empty of our dear ones. Thus we learn that our troubles are real and true. Oh how happy will be future times, unacquainted with such miseries, perhaps counting our testimony as fabulous!

I don't deny that we deserve these evils and even worse. But our ancestors deserved them too; may our descendants not deserve them likewise! Why then, most just of judges, should the punishment of thy avenging sword fall particularly on our times? Why, in times when guilt abounded, was punishment withheld? While all sinned alike, now we alone bear the lash. . . .

Can it be that God has no care for the mortal lot?

Surely thou dost care for us and for our affairs, O God; but there is some hidden, unknown reason why, through all the centuries, we have seemed to be the creatures most severely to be punished. Not that justice is the less just because it is concealed; for the depth of thy judgements is inscrutable and inaccessible to human senses. So either we are the worst of all beings, which I should like to deny but dare not; or God is exercising and purging us with present evils for our future good; or there is something at the root which we are totally unable to conceive. Anyway, however hidden the reasons, the results are very evident.

There remained for me here a surivor of the wrecks of last year, a man distinguished above all, and, on my word, great of soul and wise in judgement. This was Paganino da Milano. After several trials of his worth, I found him most congenial. I judged that as my friend he was worthy to be friend to us all. thus I began to regard him as another Socrates. He had your sincerity, your good fellowship; and - the happiest quality in a friend - we shared good fortune and bad, laid bare our inmost feelings, honestly avowed our secrets. . . .

Now he too was suddenly snatched away by the pestilence that ravages the world. He dined in the evening with friends, and afterward he spent some time with me in talk and in friendly discussion of our affairs. That night he was attacked. He bore his sufferings with a stout spirit; and in the morning death came swiftly. And that no evil should be spared him, within three days his children and his whole family followed him to the grave. Oh mortals, strain strive, and sweat, range the earth and sea for riches you will not attain, for glory that will not last! The life we lead is a sleep, and all its businesses resemble those in dreams. Only death shatters the sleep, the dream. Oh, may such an awakening be granted us! But live, meanwhile; and farewell.

But to turn from public griefs to our private ones, hardly a year and a half has gone by since, departing for Italy, I left you in tears by the tearful fountain of the Sorgue. Look no farther back; count these few days, and think what we were and what we are. Where now are those sweet friends, where are the loved faces, where the caressing words, the gay and gentle conversation? What lightning bolt destroyed them, what earthquake overthrew them, what tempest submerged them, what abyss swallowed them? We were a close-knit band; and now we are almost alone. We must make new friendships. Where shall we find them? And to what end, if the human race is almost extinguished, if, as I surmise, the end of the world is at hand? . . .

• • • • •

Petrarch's letters are of great value, not only in what they reveal of the poet's character but in what they tell us about the lives of his friends and acqaintances. The death of Petrarch's steward prompted the following letter which acts as an evocative obituary to a humble medieval man whose 'tough frame' had 'laboured in cold and heat' and whose life and aspirations would probably have passed unrecorded had it not been for his exceptional employer.

• • •

From Petrarch to Cardinals Flie de Talleyrand and Gui de Boulogne.
5 January 1353.
Latin.

When Marcus Attilius Regulus, the first scourge of the Carthaginians, was superintending great and delicate operations of Rome in Africa, he did not blush to ask the Senate, by letter, for a leave, on the grounds that his farmer, who took care of his few suburban acres, had died. Then why should I, who deal with no public business and very little private, blush to beg of you two nobles of the Church a leave of absence for exactly the same reason, to wit that my farmer, whom you knew, who cultivated my few dry acres, died yesterday? Nor do I fear that you will make to me the same reply that the Senate did to Attilius - to get on with his job and leave the care of his lands to the Senate; for his fields were at Rome, and mine at the Fountain of the Sorgue, a place known to you only by its small reputation. There is another and greater reason for my concern. I am not so much worried about my untended lands, but - like that other hammer of Africa, Gnaeus Scipio, who asked leave from his successful campaign in Spain to return and find a dowry for his daughter - I must find a guardian for my library, which is my adopted daughter. Thus I allege the precedents of two illustrious men.

My farmer was a rustic, but more shrewd and comprehending than most city men. I think the earth never bore a creature more faithful than he. By his virtues he compensated for all the iniquities and perfidies of servants, of which I am forever complaining in speech and written words. Thus I entrusted to him my own person and possessions and all the books I have in France. These are of all sorts, with some tiny ones mixed in with great big ones. When I returned after long absences, even of three years, I never discovered any to be missing, or even out of place. Though illiterate, he loved letters; he took particular care of the books he knew to be dearest to me. By long practice he had come to know the classic works by name, and he distinguished them from my own little productions. He was filled with joy whenever I chanced to put a book in his hands; he would strain it to his breast and sigh, and sometimes he would talk in a low voice to the author. Remarkably enough, by merely regarding and touching books he seemed to become wiser and happier.

So then he has left me, this guardian of my possessions, with whom for fifteen years I have shared my domestic cares. I regarded him, in the old phrase, as a priest of Ceres, and his house as the temple of fidelity. Though elderly, he seemed, in Virgil's words, 'green in his latter time, not ripe for plucking'. The day before yesterday I left home, in obedience to your commands; he seemed only slightly ill. But yesterday evening he quitted my service forever, to wait upon a better lord. May God grant him, after all his bodily labors, rest for his soul. One thing he desired of the Lord, one thing he sought after; O Christ, grant that in place of my house, he may dwell in thine all the days of that life following this mortal span, and that he may behold not my will, but God's will, and visit his temple in place in place of my fields, whereon for many years his tough frame has laboured in cold and heat. Wearied in my service, may he rest in thine; released at thy command from this old prison-house, he comes to thee.

One of my servants, who had perhaps seen his passing, brought me the sad news with utmost haste. He arrived late last evening, reporting that in his last moments my steward had my name on his lips, and he invoked the name of Christ with tears. I was deeply distressed, though I should have grieved more if I had not long foreseen the case, on account of his age. I must therefore go to Vaucluse; please give me permission, most glorious Fathers, to leave this city, where I am not needed, for the country, where I must make provision for the care of my little lands and even more of my library.

I wish you both a happy, tranquil life.

• • • • •

In 1403 raiders from Brittany successfully attacked Plymouth and in the following year a similar attempt by 'several hundred' ships occurred at Dartmouth. Dartmouth was an important port, it had developed as a trading centre for wool, iron and particularly wine; in 1190 it had been the point of embarkation for Crusaders destined for the Holy Land.

The raid in 1404 was a failure due to the valiant efforts made by the people of the town to repulse the Bretons. Many Frenchmen were killed including the knight Guillaume, Sieur du Chastel. In the following letter his brother Olivier asks permission to take Guillaume's remains back to Brittany, but the outcome of his request has never been established. The letter was written some time after Guillaume's death, and Olivier appears to have accepted that death is an inevitable consequence of war and writes in a highly reasonable manner rather than in a torrent of sorrow.

The church refered to is that of St Saviour, situated on a hill on the outskirts of Dartmouth.

• • •

Olivier Duchastel, a Breton Knight, to the Mayor and Burgesses of Dartmouth.

c. 1415.

French.

Most dear and good friends, I commend myself to you as much as I can. It is true, as you know, that for those who concern themselves with war, fortunes are sometimes good, and sometimes the contrary, and none knows the outcome but Our Lord; and as it has happened before now to many others, so it happened to my brother, whom God pardon, who landed at Dartmouth in the company of others, and there died As you know everyone could rightly wish to have near him the remains of his close relatives, so as to be reminded to pray, and have prayers said for them. I have already asked the King of England, whom God pardon, to be pleased to give me leave to cross over to his country and bring back the remains of my said brother, who was buried in the church of the said place of Dartmouth (for which my thanks are due to all who did this), and of his grace he granted this to me. To this end he gave me letters, which I send you by John Smeth and Joaquin Mery, to inform you of these things. Because the said remains are of no profit or use to anyone over there, I should like you to be pleased to allow me to have them, if possible, and in order that you may do this, please write to me by the first person you can find, and if there is anything which I can do for you over here, I would ask you to tell me of it, and I shall willingly accomplish it. Most dear and good friends, our Lord Jesus grant you His grace.

Written at Treffmasan, 26 December. (signed) Olivier Duchastel.

• • • • •

Marsilio Ficino, the son of a prominent physician, was encouraged by Cosimo de Medici to lead the revival in platonic thinking. Ficino translated all Plato's writings from the original Greek and set about relating the teachings of the ancient philosophers to a true understanding of Christian beliefs. His main achievement was the disassociation of the ancients with paganism, thus encouraging an appreciation of classic culture which no longer conflicted with Christian aspirations.

The following letter was written to Gismondo della Stufa, a man of letters, whose fiancée Albiera delgi Albizzi had died on July 14th, the eve of their wedding. Ficino writes of spiritual love which he considered to be God-given and a higher achievement than physical love which, being connected with matter, inhibited a true affinity with the 'Divine Creator'. Death, Ficino explains, is nothing to be feared since 'the soul is the man himself and the body but his shadow'. It was Ficino's belief in the immortality of the soul which had such a great impact on Christian thought in the next century.

• • •

From Marsilio Ficino to Gismondo della Stufa.

1 August 1473.

Latin.

Consolation on someone's death

Marsilio Ficino gives consolation to Gismondo della Stufa.

If each of us, essentially, is that which is greatest within us, which always remains the same and by which we understand ourselves, then certainly the soul is the man himself and the body but his shadow. Whatever wretch is so deluded as to think that the shadow of man is man, like Narcissus is dissolved in tears. You will only cease to weep, Gismondo, when you cease looking for your Albiera degli Albizzi in her dark shadow and begin to follow her by her own clear light. For the further she is from that misshapen shadow the more beautiful will you find her, past all you have ever known.

Withdraw into your soul, I beg you, where you will possess her soul which is so beautiful and dear to you; or rather, from your soul withdraw to God. There you will contemplate the beautiful idea through which the Divine Creator fashioned your Albiera; and as she is far more lovely in her Creator's form than in her own, so you will embrace her there with far more joy.

Farewell.

1st August, 1473.

Florence.

BIBLIOGRAPHY

Allen, P S and H M eds., *Letters of Richard Fox 1486-1527* (Oxford, 1928)

Bagley, J J, *Historical Interpretations. Volume one: Sources of English Medieval History 1066-1540* (Newton Abbot: David & Charles, 1972)

Barber, Richard, *The Penguin Guide to Medieval Europe* (Penguin Books, 1984)

Barron, Caroline, 'The Lords of the Manor' in *The Making of Britain. The Middle Ages*, Lesley Smith, ed. Chapter 7, pp.101-17

Barton, John and Law, Joy, *The Hollow Crown* (London: Hamish Hamilton Ltd, 1971)

Bennet, H S, *The Pastons and their England* (Cambridge Univ. Press, reprint 1970, first published 1922)

Bingham, Caroline, *The Life and Times of Edward II* (George Weidenfeld and Nicholson Limited and Book Club Associates, 1973)

Bishop, Morris, *Petrarch and His World* (London, 1963)

Bishop, Morris, *Letters from Petrarch* (Bloomington and London: Indiana University Press, 1966)

Bond, G A, Original letters addressed to Henry IV King of England by Elizabeth, Duchess of Bavaria, *Arch.Journal* XII (Arch.Inst. of GB) p.377

Burke, John, *Life in the Castle in Medieval England* (London: Batsford Ltd, 1978)

Butler, Lionel and Given-Wilson, Chris, *Medieval Monasteries of Great Britain* (London: Michael Joseph, 1979)

Cecil, Jane, *The Journal of Christopher Columbus* (London: The Haklyts Society, 1960)

Chancellor, John, *The Life and Times of Edward I* (London: George Weidenfeld and Nicolson Ltd and Book Club Associated, 1981)

Cheney, C R, 'Gervase, Abbot of Prémontré: A Medieval Letter-Writer,' *Bulletin of the John Rylands Library* XXXIII (1950-51) 28

Clanchy, M T, *From Memory to Written Record England 1066-1307* (London, 1979)

Clanchy, M T, *England and its Rulers 1066-1272* (London, 1983)

Comte, Suzanne, *Everyday Life in the Middle Ages* (Geneva: Editions Minverva S.A., 1978)

Constable, Giles, *The Letters of Peter the Venerable* Vols. I, II (Cambridge, Massachussetts, 1967)

Coulton, G C, *Medieval Panorama, The English Scene from Conquest to Reformation* (Cambridge Univ. Press, 1938)

Cumston, C G, *An Introduction to the History of Medicine. From the time of the Pharaohs to the end of the eighteenth century* (London: reprinted 1968, 1921)

Dakmus, Joseph H, *The Prosecution of John Wyclyf* (New Haven: Yale Univ. Press, 1952; London: Geoffrey Cumberlege, Oxford Univ. Press)

Du Boulay, F R H, *An Age of Ambition* (1970)

Duby, Georges, *Medieval Marriage. Two models from Twelfth-Century France*, trans. Elborg Forster (Baltimore and London: The John Hopkins Univ. Press, 1978)

Earle, Peter, *The Life and Times of Henry V* (London: George Weidenfeld and Nicolson

Ltd and Book Club Associates, 1972)

Edward, Second Duke of York, *The Master of the Game*, ed. W A Baillie-Grohman and F Baillie-Grohman (London, 1909)

Ellis, Henry, *Original Letters Illustrative of English History* Vol. I (1846)

Elton, G K, *The Sources of History: England 1200-1640* (London: 1969)

The Letters of Marsilio Ficino. Translated from the Latin by members of the Language Department of the School of Economic Science, London. Preface by Paul Oskor Kristellv. (Columbia Univ. in the City of New York; London: Shepherd-Walwyn, 1975)

Gairdner, J ed. *Paston Letters A.D. 1422-1509* 6 vols. (London: 1904)

Giles, J A, *The Life and Letters of Thomas á Becket* Vols. I, II (London: 1846)

Green, V H H, *Medieval Civilization in Western Europe* (London: 1971)

Greenwood, Alice Drayton, *Selections from the Paston Letters* (London: 1920)

Halliwell, J O, *Letters of the Kings of England* Vol. I (London: 1848)

Hanham, Alison ed., *The Cely Letters 1472-1488* (Early English Text Society, 1975)

Haskins, Charles Homer, *Studies in Mediaeval Culture* (New York: 1929)

Hay, Denis, *The Medieval Centuries* (1953)

Henderson, Ernest F, *Select Historical Documents of the Middle Ages* (London: 1896)

Hill, Rosalind M T, 'A Berkshire Letter-Book,' *Berkshire Archaeological Journal* Vol. 41 (1937)

Hindley, Geoffrey, *England in the Age of Caxton* (1979)

Historical Manuscripts Commission, *14th Report*, Appendix, part VIII

Jackson, A M, *Devon and Cornwall Notes and Queries* XXXI, pp.216-18

James, Bruno Scott, *The Letters of St Bernard of Clairvaux* (London: 1953)

Jones, Michael ed., *Gentry and Lesser Nobility in the Late Middle Ages* (New York: St Martin's Press, 1986)

Kingsford, C L ed., 'The Stonor Letters and Papers,' *Camden 3rd series*, Vols. 29, 30 (PRO 'Ancient Correspondence', 1919)

Knoop, D and Jones, G, *The Medieval Mason* (London: 1933)

Laffan, R G D, *Select Documents of European History* Vol. I (Methuen, 1930) pp.800-1492

Lander, J R, *Conflict and Stability in Fifteenth-Century England* (Hutchinson & Co, 1969)

Latham, R E and Timing, E K, 'Six Letters Concerning the Eyres of 1226-28,' *English Historical Review* Vol. 65 (1950) pp.492-504

Leach, Arthur F, *Educational Chartes and Documents 598 to 1909* (Cambridge: 1911)

Leff, Gordon, *Heresy in the Middle Ages* (Manchester Univ. Press, 1967)

McCall, Andrew, *The Medieval Underworld* (London: Hamish Hamilton, 1979)

Matthew, Donald, *The Medieval European Community* (London: B T Batsford Ltd, 1977)

Miller, J M, Prosser, M H, Benson, T W, eds., *Readings in Medieval Rhetoric* (Bloomington and London: Indiana Univ. Press, 1974)

Monro, Cecil, *Letters of Queen Margaret of Anjou and Bishop Reckington and others. Written in the reigns of Henry V and Henry VI* No. 86 (Camden Society, 1863)

Morely, A and Brooke, C N L, eds., *The Letters and Chartes of Gilburt Foliot* (Cambridge: 1967)

Morison, James Cotter, *The Life and Times of Saint Bernard, Abbot of Clairvaux* (London:

1863)

Murphy, James J, *Three Medieval Rhetorical Arts*, (Berkeley, Los Angeles and London: Univ. of California Press, 1971)

Post, John, 'The King's Peace' in *The Making of Britain. The Middle Ages*, ed. Lesley M Smith (London: 1985) pp.149-62

Power, Eileen, *Medieval English Nunneries c.1275 to 1535* (Cambridge Univ. Press, 1922)

Power, Eileen, *Medieval People* (London: tenth edition 1963, first published 1924)

Power, Eileen, and Postan, M M, *Studies in English Trade in the Fifteenth Century* (1933, reissued 1966)

Powicke, F M, *Handbook of British Chronology* (London: 1939)

Raine, James ed., *Historical Papers and Letters from the Northern Registers* (Roll Series, 1873)

Richter, J P and I A, *The Literary Works of Leonardo Da Vinci* (London: 1939)

Rickert, E, 'Documents and Records: A leaf from a Fourteenth Century Letter Book,' *Modern Philology* XXV (1927-1928) 249.

Rickert, Edith, *Chaucer's World* (London: 1948)

Riley, Henry Thomas ed., *Memorials of London and London Life in the XIIIth, XIVth and XVth Centuries* (London: 1868)

Robbins, Edgar C, *William Paston Justice. Found of the Paston Family 1378-1444* (Norwich: Jarrold and Sons Ltd, 1932)

Salzman, L F, *English Industries in the Middle Ages* (Clarendon Press, 1923)

Saunders, Margaret, *Intimate Letters of England's Kings* (London: Museum Press Ltd, 1939)

Schuster, Lincoln M, *A Treasury of the World's Great Letters* (London: 1941)

Sheppard, J B ed., *Christ Church Letters. A volume of Mediaeval Letters relating to the affairs of the Priory of Christ Church Canterbury* (Camden Society, 1877)

Shirley, W W ed., *Royal and Historical Letters Illustrative of the Reign of Henry III* Roll Series 2 vols. (London: 1862-66)

Smith, Lesley M ed., *The Making of Britain. The Middle Ages* (Macmillan Publishers Ltd, 1985)

Southern, R W ed., *The Life of St Anselm Archbishop of Canterbury, by Eadmer* (1962)

Stapledon, T ed., *Plumpton Correspondence* (Camden 1st Series, 1839)

Steer, F W, *Scriveners Company of Common Paper* (London Record Society, 1968)

Storrs, Richard S, *Bernard of Clairvaux. The Times, The Man, and His Work* (London: 1892)

Strickland, Agnes, *Lives of the Queens of England* Vol. II (Bath: 1972 and London: 1851)

Talbot, C H, *Medicine in Medieval England* (London: 1967)

Toynbee, Paget, *The Letters of Dante* (Oxford: 1920)

Wolffe, Bertram, *Henry VI* (London: Methuen, 1981)

Wood, M A Everett, *Letters of Royal and Illustrious Ladies* Vol. I

Wylie, James Hamilton, *History of England under Henry the Fourth* (London: 1884)

Wylie, James Hamilton and Wough, William Templeton, *The Reign of Henry the Fifth* Vol. 3